MODERNIZATION AS SPECTACLE IN AFRICA

MODERNIZATION AS SPECTACLE IN AFRICA

EDITED BY
Peter J. Bloom, Stephan F. Miescher,
and Takyiwaa Manuh

Indiana University Press

Bloomington and Indianapolis

This book is a publication of

Indiana University Press
Office of Scholarly Publishing
Herman B Wells Library 350
1320 East 10th Street
Bloomington, Indiana 47405 USA

iupress.indiana.edu

Telephone 800-842-6796
Fax 812-855-7931

♾ The paper used in this publication meets the minimum requirements of the American National Standard for Information Sciences—Permanence of Paper for Printed Library Materials, ANSI Z39.48–1992.

Manufactured in the United States of America

Library of Congress Cataloging-in-Publication Data

Modernization as spectacle in Africa / edited by Peter J. Bloom, Stephan F. Miescher, and Takyiwaa Manuh.
pages cm
Includes bibliographical references and index.
ISBN 978-0-253-01229-6 (pbk. : alk. paper) — ISBN 978-0-253-01225-8 (cloth : alk. paper) — ISBN 978-0-253-01233-3 (ebook)
1. Economic development—Social aspects—Africa. 2. Social change—Africa. 3. Africa—Economic conditions—1960- 4. Africa—Social conditions—1960- 5. Africa—Economic policy. I. Bloom, Peter J., editor of compilation. II. Miescher, Stephan F., editor of compilation. III. Manuh, Takyiwaa, editor of compilation. IV. Hintzen, Percy C. After modernization.
HC800.M625 2014
960.32—dc23

2013042002

1 2 3 4 5 19 18 17 16 15 14

Contents

Acknowledgments

THE INITIAL IMPETUS for this volume began with the University of California African Studies Multicampus Research Group, which Peter J. Bloom and Stephan F. Miescher launched in 2007 with faculty from seven UC campuses. In 2008, Takyiwaa Manuh, as director of the Institute of African Studies, University of Ghana, Legon, agreed to host a conference on the theme of Revisiting Modernization, which was held in July 2009. Many of the conference presentations were published in a special issue of *Ghana Studies* 15/16 (2009–2010). The current volume was inspired by this initiative, and consists of original contributions by a wide array of contributors.

We are grateful to several institutions in support of the broader context for this project at the University of California, including the Office of the President and the Humanities Research Institute, as well as the UCLA African Studies Center, the UC Berkeley Center for African Studies, and the UCSB Interdisciplinary Humanities Center. At the University of Ghana, the staff of the Institute of African Studies (IAS), the office of the pro-vice-chancellor, and the chair of the then Research and Conferences Fund provided necessary support and advice.

At UCSB, we would like to acknowledge the encouragement and guidance of David Marshall, Michael Douglas Dean of Humanities and Fine Arts, and Ann Bermingham, former director of the Interdisciplinary Humanities Center. Further, a circle of colleagues in the UC system have supported the project from the beginning. They include Andrew Apter and Edmond Keller (UCLA), Percy Hintzen and Catherine M. Cole (UC Berkeley), Victoria Bernal, Ketu Katrak, and Cecelia Lynch (UC Irvine), Elisabeth Cameron (UC Santa Cruz), Bennetta Jules-Rosette and Ivan Evans (UC San Diego), and Moradewun Adejunmobi (UC Davis).

At the University of Ghana, we would like to acknowledge Professor Kwabena Nketia, emeritus professor of African Studies, and Professor Kwesi Yankah, former pro-vice-chancellor, as well as Brigid Sackey, Esi Sutherland-Addy, Akosua Adomako Ampofo, Kwame Amoah Labi, and Dzodzi Tsikata. In Accra, "Auntie" Emily Asiedu provided hospitality.

Finally, Dee Mortensen, senior editor at Indiana University Press, took an interest in this project and provided extensive feedback and guidance for which we are grateful. We would also like to thank Donald Donham and an anonymous reviewer for their comments, which have greatly improved the manuscript. Lastly, during the production process we have appreciated the contributions of Eric Levy, who served as copyeditor, Angela Burton, who coordinated the publication, and Alex Trotter, who compiled the index.

MODERNIZATION AS SPECTACLE IN AFRICA

Introduction

Stephan F. Miescher, Peter J. Bloom, and Takyiwaa Manuh

In the early years of independence, the discourse of modernization played a central role in imagining a postcolonial African future. Independence as event and spectacle, however, has often overshadowed its emerging context within the paradigm of modernization. It was couched within a preexisting rhetoric of African development proclaiming a new urgency of nation building already set in motion during the 1950s and 1960s. Foregrounding the age of modernization, in contrast to the moment of independence, allows us to propose a more subtle and nuanced understanding of the immediate postwar and early independence period. As less indebted to the quality of independence as historical rupture with the colonial era, an emphasis on the discourse and practices of modernization emphasizes continuities, or an aggregate of events and experiences, on the African continent.

We contend that recent celebrations marking fifty years of independence too easily shift attention away from the colonial legacy. Instead, revisiting modernization as spectacle foregrounds programs of development and citizenship-making claims that have a longer historical trajectory. The notion of "modernization as spectacle" refers to performance, ideology, and public enactment. Spectacle as a process of layering and instances of intersection specifies state-led modernization programs and their effects.[1] By extension, emerging independence-era leaders across the African continent rearticulated the significance and objectives of infrastructure and cultural projects. They re-coded them in the name of nation building and frequently deployed a Pan-Africanist form of expression. In fact, colonial empire was a founding agent of modernization. Since World War I, networks of empire increasingly facilitated contact and movement of bodies and ideas between Africa and its Diaspora in Asia, Europe, and the Americas. This created a powerful dynamic, variously associated with Négritude, Pan-Africanism, and new linguistic communities.

Mass human movements, instantiated by modern forms of air, rail, and road transport, as well as theaters of conflict and educational opportunities, allowed for an emerging context of interaction. The effects of these modern forms of mobility have often been allied with conceptions of modernity. Be it on the battlefield, in the boxing ring, at literary salons, or within the improvisational context of jazz clubs, appropriations of the Other in urban centers, such as Berlin, Paris, and New York, asserted cultural and political prerogative. The discourse of modernity was allied with artistic movements and described by figures allied with the German language critical sociological tradition loosely amalgamated by the Frankfurt School (Jay 1996). It specified how new technologies allied with the urban experience in these world capitals became part of a political and cultural consciousness. "Africa" was a representative concept rather than a lived reality in this initial conception of modernity, which implied a dialectical artistic and political aesthetic. By contrast, African intellectuals adopted modernization as the means of transforming material conditions in order to address historic inequities. We contend that the space of spectacle is where modernity and modernization meet. Moreover, the politics and aesthetics of display so integral to modernity created a desire among Africans to create equivalent conditions and opportunities, well articulated in Edward W. Blyden's early campaign for a West African university in 1872 (Agbodeka 1998). In this sense, spectacle becomes a tool to promote and rally support for modernization programs, but also heralds a new aesthetic and cultural order that seeks to overcome the colonial legacy. In this volume, we seek to address the context for modernization as spectacle in Africa, which becomes fully articulated during the postwar period.

A renewed interest in the historical context of the postwar years has been stimulated by the passing of the generation that shaped this era (Cooper 2008). As a result, excavating these disappearing historical traces has become an ever more urgent task. Notably, the language of modernization has been delegitimized by a profound critique in the social sciences. Yet the need to examine how modernization captivated and informed the imagination of an entire generation of intellectuals and institutional agents has become increasingly significant, particularly in the contemporary era of globalization—a time in which privatization has trumped state-centered initiatives. As infrastructure and rhetoric, modernization projects were initiated in the former European colonial metropoles, along with the centers of postwar institutional power. Postwar technocrats were the genealogical inheritors of colonial bureaucrats (Cooper and Packard 1997; Hodge 2007). These new experts ideologically realigned themselves within the terms of modernization and came to inhabit the rising international organizations of the postwar era in a Cold War context (Mitchell 2002; Gilman 2003).

In brief, this volume sets out to explore the implications and significance of the modernization project as reflected in a series of interconnected "archival objects"—that is, "objects" that may belong to different types and qualities of archives, some recognized as such, others informal and transitory. The contributors draw on a variety of archives to unpack the broad impact and experience of modernization programs in various locations that include Francophone (Gabon, Senegal) and Anglophone Africa (Ghana, Kenya, Malawi, Nigeria, Zambia, and

Zimbabwe). From this perspective, the volume is organized on the basis of various elements implied by the modernization paradigm. Starting with the "package," which was a key metaphor deployed by modernization theorists, we move to a series of contributions focused on film and radio as representational technologies that examine the relationship between modernity and modernization. This is followed by an exploration of modernization as infrastructure with social implications, which is then further elaborated in the context of institutional training of mind and body in Nkrumah's Ghana. The volume's final section addresses the literary imagination as a site for understanding the cultural implications of the modernization project.

Modernization and the Origins of the Package

During the postwar period, development of the global South was imagined in the social scientific literature as a mirror of the European and North American historical experience of industrialization. Postwar social scientists used the vocabulary of the "package" to describe component parts contributing to the implementation of modernization programs. They included a series of socioeconomic, political, and cultural transformations, which meant overcoming a series of oppositions between subsistence and industrialized economies, subject and participant political cultures, extended and nuclear kinship units, as well as religious and secular ideologies (Tipps 1973). There is a significant difference between modernization and modernity. While the latter is most often understood as a condition, modernization implies a process of transformation—from traditional to modern forms of governance, production, and social life. Whereas a number of influential theorists have defined modernization from the perspective of its transformative potential (Apter 1965; Huntington 1968; Tipps 1973), we propose to excavate its twentieth-century cultural and intellectual heritage along with its lived effects on the African continent.

This volume examines the meanings and consequences of the modernization ethos on the African continent. As a shared idiom, it served as a technocratic creed and ideology that unified a heterogeneous array of projects across the continent. While recent work in African studies has explored the African city as a contemporary source of modernity, we seek to specify and historicize this current discussion.[2] Instead of reinforcing the ideological arc of modernization resulting in a multitude of modernities in Africa, or so-called alternative modernities (Gaonkar 2001), this volume proposes to investigate the original context for the conception, implementation, and uneven effects of modernization. In contemporary Africa, modernization is recast as "development," and still resonates as a source of hope in spite of its increasingly avaricious appetite under a neoliberal framework of capital flows and emerging investor nations that include Brazil, China, and India.

In his historical ethnography about the Marxist revolution in Ethiopia, Donald Donham (1999, xv) refers to "vernacular modernisms," or local concepts that can be translated as "modern." He usefully distinguishes between the modern and tradition as narrative signifiers rather than concrete historical frames. A later variation on this approach is Frederick Cooper's (2005) notion of modernity as a claim-making device in the historical imagination. Further, Lynn Thomas's (2011, 739) recent intervention suggests that the modern can be explored "as a discursive tool deployed by historical actors." Our approach to the modern, by extension, is grounded in a lived vocabulary of experience by those engaged in and responding to programs of modernization. We distinguish between the intent and rhetoric of the modernization project by its advocates in relation to those who are subject to its lived effects.

The theme of "African modernities" was celebrated as a successful articulation of difference between the global North and South in spite of economic hardship and the failed promises of independence associated with earlier programs of modernization (Deutsch, Probst, and Schmidt 2002; Geschiere, Meyer, and Pels 2008). Such an approach points to the fragmentary nature of the package of modernization. However, these alternative articulations are most often the outcome of marginalization and simply a deficit of resources (Ferguson 2006). In other words, they are a site of visibility by which African subjects attempt to be seen and heard. Furthermore, we suggest that the scholarship on alternative modernities accentuates inequities in lieu of addressing an ongoing process.

In the opening chapter of this volume, Percy Hintzen presents an intertwining genealogy of modernization and globalization featuring the U2 frontman Bono as poster boy for a dynamic vision of African entrepreneurship. This serves as a starting point for an examination of how modernization, which has since been disavowed by most policymakers, is being reinvented in the name of capital accumulation. The neoliberal turn, Hintzen argues, transformed the category of colonial labor into a conscription of modernity under the sign of modernization. This was a moment of historical transformation that dislodged colonial mercantile interests in favor of U.S. capital accumulation practices predicated on containment, control, and negation. Needless to say, this was presented as a non-ideological strategy. Instead, the effects of modernization reinforced vectors of the colonial paradigm within the terms of underdevelopment (Frank 1972). Here, it is the apparatus of modernization as a technological solution masking a neoliberal reshuffling of managerial elites that further intensified a system of marginalization and proletarianization, or what Loïc Wacqant (2008) has called the *precariat*. Instead of modernization functioning as the financial mechanism that would enable a program of national sovereignty and social rights for all citizens, a globalized system emerged through the fetishization of consumption, production, and accumulation. In the afterglow of modernization, consumer-based development has become the new frontier of humanitarian entrepreneurship. The promise and potential of modernization used to dismantle the colonial paradigm has since become a platform for privatized globalization that supplements an ideology of perpetual consumption.

Hintzen, a former student of David E. Apter who made his mark as a modernization theorist with the publication of *The Politics of Modernization* (1965), is excavating some of the remaining epistemological demons of modernization. Andrew Apter, David Apter's son, and close colleague of Hintzen, approaches the question of modernization from a filial perspective. In his intervention and reflection, modernization appears as a figure of high modernism in the history of U.S. social science, serving as the ultimate refinement of Parsonian functionalism. Apter's genealogical approach evokes the legacy of his father, who passed away in May 2010.

As part of a "working through" of his father's legacy in the history of modernization discourse, Andrew Apter develops a critical sociological context within a Kantian tradition passed on from Max Weber's circle to Talcott Parsons. As he explains, it was the move toward unified conceptual patterns and value relevance that served as a foundation for the construction of ideal types in Parson's oeuvre. This, in turn, was passed on to Marion Levy, David Apter's mentor. This critical legacy, however, is shaded with a series of deconstructive moves in Andrew Apter's text relying on the thematic of "blindness" in Paul de Man's work, Harold Bloom's notion of "misprision," and a Derridean inspired rereading of Rousseau's *Essay on the Origin of Language* (1824). The insistence on "blindness" in Andrew Apter's chapter is especially apt in elucidating a conception of the spectacle that infiltrates consciousness through media representations.

The double articulation of language serves as the basis for a rupture within the genealogy itself such that the critical separation between concept and object in Kant enables an *a priori* approach to language that is taken up by Rousseau. The privileging of speech over the written word, which is often referred to as "phonocentrism" by Jacques Derrida (1976), is a means by which Andrew Apter intervenes in the historical legacy of modernization whose claim to the Weberian machinery of rationalization is a critical point of its unraveling. It is here that we return to David Apter, whose work began to break free of this genealogical grip late in his career. It exhibited a certain generosity of agency demonstrated within his phenomenological studies of political protest, revolution, and a discursive approach to political violence. In the end, however, it is from father to son that the rupture within a reading of modernization is finally completed, and the genealogy becomes rearticulated towards other concepts, objects, and modes of reading.

Andrew Apter's genealogical reflections on modernization theory inadvertently refer to a conjuncture between modernization and modernity. This ongoing relationship is symbolized by the overlapping resonance of critical sociological roots of modernization theory with media and representation most notably in Walter Benjamin's well-known essay "The Work of Art in the Age of Mechanical Reproducibility" (1936), in which he points to the effects of industrial forms of photographic reproduction as an emerging form of aesthetic, social, and political transformation.

Media, Modernity, and Modernization

Media has served as a pliable instrument of modernization in its role as an instructional, aesthetic, and promotional form of address. The historical context for media production and exhibition has been an integral dimension of the modernization project since the interwar period. The representational power of film and radio in particular to reach geographically fragmented audiences extended the very nature of colonial rule and then came to narrate the promise of independence and nationhood.

The relationship between media and modernization has been framed by a critical sociological heritage. Since the interwar period, colonial governments in Africa experimented with new forms of mass education (later renamed community development) to communicate with an emerging conceptualization of the public. Film, radio, and other audiovisual media heralded the emergence of a new international aesthetic of communication and value. It is for this reason that the metaphor and practice of montage is especially pertinent. On the one hand, montage refers to the theoretical register of the apparatus, but it also relates to technique, as in film and sound editing (Agamben 2009). Just as the term "montage" (from *monter* [fr.]) implies the notion of assembly, as on the factory assembly line, its expression as a critical technique of media production is addressed by several authors in this volume.

Montage is a rich metaphor by which to extend the significance of the package of modernization. It also implies a diegetic world, a narrative space specific to the telling of a story with its own vocabulary and techniques of address. As an apparatus of storytelling, montage facilitates an emerging discourse and the imposition of a new political and social order. Media relayed the promise of resources aimed at projecting a better life with electricity, running water, healthcare, and education.

Four chapters on film and radio address the ongoing relationship between media and modernization in Africa. A longstanding issue that has monopolized the attention of most critical writing related to the interwar and postwar history of British-inspired colonial media on the African continent has been the reception of film and radio by African audiences. Framed within the terms of the "African mind," an array of experiments, beginning with the Bantu Experimental Kinema [*sic*] Experiment (BEKE) in the 1930s, were conducted to test African reactions to hygiene, maternity, and farming films in order to determine the best way to promote objectives associated with community development. It was this fixation on the "African mind" as Rorschach test that gave rise to a series of historical and social trajectories that are examined from a variety of perspectives.

Rosaleen Smyth's earlier publications on the history of the British colonial film units of the interwar and immediate postwar periods remain the necessary starting point for a historical examination of this area and related themes.[3] In her contribution here, Smyth repositions the history of British colonial documentary filmmaking within the context of the social message film. She closely examines the interwar period as a point of origin for this genre and traces the history of the social message film as key to understanding the role and function of postwar documentary media.

Media and modernization may be further probed with regard to the question of whether the medium is the message, as Marshall McLuhan (1967) persuasively argued in his examination of television, or merely the channel of communication (Shannon and Weaver 1975). While Smyth emphasizes the role and function of social messages themselves, Aaron Windel's contribution emphasizes film as a channel of transmission through a discussion of *Daybreak in Udi* (dir. Terry Bishop, 1949), which examines the struggle of two local African teachers to establish a rural maternity clinic in south-central Nigeria. Windel's chapter persuasively argues that the early history of educational film experiments was part of a broader context for establishing a series of relevant media pedagogy techniques directly related to cooperative economics. The traveling colonial cine-vans that introduced enthusiastic audiences to films such as *Daybreak in Udi* also presented music, speeches, and commentary by well-known performers on gramophone discs (see Larkin 2008).

Further, with the advent of wired radio in African cities, the cinema-radio liaison became part of an emerging context for mass education and modernization. In this light, Mhoze Chikowero's chapter picks up on the vexed thematic of "radio as modernity" that directly addresses the context for African subjectivity during and after World War II. Although the distribution of radio receivers and licenses was limited throughout Southern Africa prior to the 1960s, there was an extensive array of shortwave broadcasting, and a great interest among colonial officials and Africans alike in the potential for a "wireless-mindedness." Chikowero elaborates on the theme of the "African mind" to demonstrate how a species of innuendo emerged from speech patterning and jokes from African radio announcers, while the inflated egos of colonial experts and expertise were transformed into spectacles.

Peter Bloom's contribution joins this discussion of the "African mind" in his examination of English-language teaching through film and radio with reference to colonial Ghana. He points to an early starting point for spatializing techniques of governmentality associated with the understated power of accent and techniques of English-language training. Drawing on ill-fated interwar efforts in Britain to establish elocutionary norms associated with the British Broadcasting

Corporation's early years, he examines how English-language learning was promoted as standard-bearer of self-government during a period of transition in the late interwar and postwar period. Just as the "African mind" was a site of mediation in arguments about norms of reception for film and radio on the African continent, Bloom argues that the mass education agenda as embodied by English-language learning is rooted in British norms of civility and projective display. In other words, the elocutionary emphasis of spoken word recording and relay served as an index to a developmental ethic of class and cultural difference. Its implications, Bloom surmises, serve as a basis for postcolonial self-government that relies on an emergent transnational spatial restructuring of the nation-state following from indirect rule and administration.

Infrastructure and Its Effects

The question of indirect rule and governmentality is addressed in the register of large-scale infrastructure projects that served as the mainstay of the modernization discourse and its effects during the 1950s and 1960s. Across late colonial Africa, roads, hydroelectric dams, water purification, health facilities, schools, mass education, and agricultural extension programs formed the backdrop of an emerging nationalism in the postwar period. Yet, the arrival of African independence was celebrated as a radical break from the colonial past without taking into account the deeper continuities. We are not claiming that colonial rule was the origin for the modernization ethos per se, but emphasize the impact of the postwar conjuncture. In addition to the effects of returning soldiers, new labor, and education policies, there was a rhetorical shift from a civilizing discourse to that of developmentalism and African self-determination (Cooper 1996). It is the lived effects of these programs within local contexts that is explored in our intervention and critical analysis of modernization.

At issue in contributions by Julia Tischler, Stephan Miescher, and Gabrielle Hecht are the effects and contested construction of meaning associated with large-scale modernization projects. In Tischler's examination of the Kariba Dam, built across the Zambesi River by the Central African Federation in the late 1950s, she examines the role of international technocrats, white settlers, colonial officers, African nationalists, and marginalized rural people. She reconstructs the multiple perspectives on modernization as articulated by these different actors in relation to Kariba. As she explains, the Kariba Dam planners expressed little concern over the fate of the displaced 57,000 Gwembe Tonga people. The white settler Federation government claimed that industrialization would offer employment while also calling for one universal path for human development.

In contrast to the Kariba case, Miescher examines how Ghanaian independence transformed the rhetoric of modernization established under colonial rule in his discussion of the Volta River Project. At first, during the 1950s, dam planners had little to say about those affected by the flooding of the Volta Basin following the construction of the hydroelectric Akosombo Dam. By 1961, when construction of the dam finally began, an emerging generation of technocrats claimed that the displacement of tens of thousands offered a unique opportunity to transform the country's "backward" Volta Basin into a series of 52 townships with modern amenities that would propel the 739 villages into modernity. Miescher explores the diverse knowledge production around resettlement in relation to the construction of the Akosombo Dam as an archival object.

A similar story unfolds in Hecht's examination of the French-owned uranium mine in eastern Gabon. During the 1960s, French technocrats in charge of uranium extraction had to break from their colonial predecessors and become more enlightened, rational, and technologically sophisticated. They no longer considered Africans inferior but rather euphemistically referred to them as "less developed," suggesting that, following a script of modernization, Africans could be transformed through their interaction with technology. By the 1970s, the modernization script had been reshaped when management was nationalized and the Compagnie des Mines d'Uranium de Franceville (COMUF) underwent Gabonization. The Gabonese state and COMUF anticipated that modernization would produce disciplined worker-citizens who would accept the perils of industrialized labor as the price of modernity. Workers, however, did not become compliant industrial citizens; instead they protested against working conditions and industrial accidents.

These examples show how during the late colonial and early independence era, a spectrum of technocratic ideals informed state-led infrastructure projects that were, in turn, supplemented by an emerging popular context for social and ideological reform. Nationalist political leaders sought to expand the role of the state as a means of transforming lived conditions. Ghana served as an important test case for understanding the modernization discourse, in part because of the conditions under which it became independent from Britain in 1957, and Kwame Nkrumah's charismatic leadership as a Pan-Africanist spokesman for a new vision of African developmentalism. Although there are contested legacies regarding Nkrumah's role, the continuities and reformulation of modernization are further crystallized in this volume's several contributions focused on Ghana.

Institutional Training in Nkrumah's Ghana

Under Nkrumah's leadership, the Ghanaian state set up several institutions that sought to instill its citizens with a renewed commitment to Africa, by which to overcome the legacy of colonial education and the colonial mentality. Jean Allman, Nate Plageman, and Takyiwaa Manuh address the creation of cultural policies and institutions during the late 1950s and early 1960s as a recalibration of mind and body under the rubric of Nkrumah's vision of the "African Personality." This cultural policy sought to give "the project of modernization an African soul" (Mkandawire 2005, 6).

Allman contributes a discussion of aviation and the establishment of a national gliding school in Ghana initiated by Nkrumah. She explores how the gliding school founded by the German expatriate flight captain Hanna Reitsch at Afienya, near Accra, became central to Nkrumah's vision and articulation of modernization and nationhood in the final years of his rule. The gliding school not only trained instructors and students, but promoted model building as a subject of secondary school instruction. In fact, Reitsch believed that Ghanaian children were developmentally handicapped, because they did not use their hands and imagination like European children. Model making was intended to overcome this hurdle for the nation's development. In early twentieth-century Europe, aviation had become a marker of modernity and a way to distinguish between Europe and the colonized world. In postcolonial Ghana, conquering the skies—in addition to dams, mechanized agriculture, and factories—became the path to realize the dream of modernization.

In a parallel fashion, Plageman explores the fate of dance band highlife in Ghana during the early years of independence. The supervision and regulation of highlife recreation, once a fluid and inclusive affair, became part of state-sanctioned plans for development that extended beyond industries, infrastructure, and social services. Nkrumah's notion of the African Personality incorporated the merits of "traditional" values and past accomplishments into his efforts to modernize the country and, more broadly, unite Africans under the terms of Pan-Africanism. As elsewhere in Africa, this invented national culture found its expression in the state-sponsored performing arts.[4] The African Personality had gendered components; Ghana's "new" men and women were to dedicate themselves to the process of national development. Efforts to implement these ideas focused on dance band highlife recreation. The Arts Council became the arbiter upholding "Ghanaian" principles not only by training performers but also by setting standards, prescribing modes of dress, promoting specific songs, and scripting the organization of performances. Although these government efforts did not completely remake dance band recreation, they exerted considerable influence on music practitioners and audiences. They indicated the confluence of nationhood, gender, and modernity during Ghana's early independence period.

In Manuh's contribution, she sketches out the history of the Institute of African Studies at the University of Ghana, Legon, where she served as director from 2002 to 2009. The Institute, established with the direct encouragement of Nkrumah, was to serve as bedrock for the promotion of the African Personality, an ideal originally conceived by E. W. Blyden, the nineteenth-century founding figure of Pan-Africanism. The Institute, as part of cultural modernization, was envisioned as a project of recovery and self-assertion that included the study of African history and previously marginalized African languages. It enouraged the pursuit of grounding scientific knowledge within African realities.

At the Institute's formal opening, Nkrumah offered the notion of the "African genius" that should serve as a foundation for re-imagining an African perspective against the grain of colonial scholarship. Nkrumah's (1963, 6) insistence on the African genius is a reaffirmation of what he described as "our traditional statecraft, our highly developed code of morals, our hospitality and purposeful energy." Evoking the African genius was a call to unity and renewed conception of the African continent. This theme developed in Nkrumah's speech remains current in the field of African studies, lest we forget Mahmood Mamdani's insistence on the need for "an African unit of analysis" in *Citizen and Subject* (1996) with regard to deflating various types of South African claims to historical exceptionalism. In addition to developing new research areas focused on the history and languages of the African continent, Nkrumah espoused the need for a generation of Africanist scholars with a new outlook on the project of an African past and present.

After Nkrumah's fall from power in 1966, the Institute's existence was threatened. It only survived by adopting a narrower mandate privileging Ghana, with less purchase on other West African societies or East and Southern Africa. As a result, the prospect for comparative analysis and theory building suffered. Although the Institute's faculty still refers to Nkrumah's "African genius" speech as part of its charter, Manuh argues that the Institute has failed to reassess the changed, neoliberal context (see Olukoshi 2007).

In spite of the shifting context for institution building and the subsequent fall of founding figures from the independence period, an ongoing context for African literary contributions has attempted to reconcile lived experience with rhetorical and event-based theatricalization. African writers reflected upon the history and "traditions" of these new nations. Their work engaged with the modernization paradigm and served as a palimpsest for emerging postcolonial African identity formations.

Modernization and the Literary Imagination

An important effect of interwar literary culture, and part of the context for World War II, was the manner in which Africans studying in Paris and London, as well as colonial soldiers sent to fight on the battlefields of Europe and Asia, came to develop an ethos of shared identity. This might be understood within the paradigm of an emerging postcolonial identity, but one organized around the lived experience of dislocation. Literary works inflected by Pan-Africanism led to a flurry of theatrical productions and poetry that forged a cultural foundation for the independence struggle.

In the postwar period, political claims infused the shaping of an emerging Pan-Africanist cultural agenda. International political gatherings along with the African writers' congresses spawned a series of Pan-African festivals during the

1960s and 1970s (Fabre 1991; Jules-Rosette 1998; Gaines 2006). The historical legacy of the festival genre is most often associated with the international World's Fairs and other colonial exhibitions starting in the mid-nineteenth century, which have been described as part of the "colonial exhibitionary complex" (Mitchell 1991). We argue that the relationship between the postwar political and cultural contexts serves as an immediate source of inspiration for literary creations of the period.

Christina McMahon, Nana Wilson-Tagoe, and Aida Mbowa address the literary imaginary as integral to modernization. Typically, the discourse of modernization has been delegated to the social sciences as a means by which to examine the effects and prospects associated with socioeconomic and political development. Further, an understanding of modernization as process has followed a different trajectory from the condition of modernity and the aesthetics of modernism (Berman 1988; Harvey 1990). However, the contributions here enlarge the context for modernization as conversant with modernity and modernism. A critical literary assessment of the effects of the modernization paradigm relies upon alternate narratives of literary production.

McMahon looks at the connections between Négritude and ideas of development as expressed during the 1966 First World Festival of Negro Arts in Dakar. The literary work of Léopold Sédar Senghor, at once host of the festival and the first president of Senegal, served as a source for the Négritude movement. McMahon examines the staging of Aimé Césaire's play *The Tragedy of King Christophe* (1963) at the Dakar festival. Set in postrevolutionary Haiti, the play features King Christophe assisted by European engineers and other experts in constructing the Citadel fortress, a metaphor for the national patrimony. Whereas Christophe seeks to impose a techno-scientific and culturalist agenda, McMahon argues that Césaire's play comments upon Senghor's pro-development posture as a rift within their jointly elaborated conception of Négritude. A longstanding gestation process that informed the emergence of Négritude and like-minded approaches was coded as a form of literary modernism with a difference.

Wilson-Tagoe begins with a discussion of how nineteenth-century nationalist discourses of early Pan-Africanist Atlantic thinkers, including Alexander Crummell and E. W. Blyden, argued for an African and Diasporic engagement with modernity, but also, crucially, modernization. In J. E. Casely Hayford's autobiographical novel *Ethiopia Unbound* (1969 [1910]), the movement between modernization and a longstanding Pan-Africanist literary imagination reveals a crisis of narrative authority. Wilson-Tagoe examines representative African protagonists in her pairing of *Ethiopia Unbound* with Jomo Kenyatta's *Facing Mount Kenya* (1938). She suggests that modern African literature established nationalist agendas, which distanced the story of modernization from explorations of African identities. Wilson-Tagoe contrasts her interest in modernization and literature with Simon Gikandi's (2008) reflections on African literature and modernity by foregrounding how Africans themselves served as agents of modernization. Crucially, she examines how the construction of modernization in the literary imagination exists in tension with the formation of a gendered postcolonial subjectivity.

While most scholars have focused on Pan-African connections between West Africa and its Diaspora, Mbowa in her contribution examines how East African artists and intellectuals participated in these debates on cultural liberation. The Kenyan playwright Ngũgĩ wa Thiong'o constructed an African aesthetic in conversation with other East African writers, as well as in relation to Diasporic interventions on blackness. An analysis of two plays by Ngũgĩ reveals his understanding of modernization under late colonialism and early independence. In *The Trial of Dedan Kimathi* (1976), Ngũgĩ and his co-author Micere Githae Mugo revisit the contentious Mau Mau period by telling the story of one of its heroes. Challenging the colonial narrative, the play presents Mau Mau as a gendered and racialized class struggle, placing it within the framework of black oppression and liberation. If modernization remains synonymous with capitalism, the suggested Marxist interpretation becomes analogous to an alternative definition of African subjectivity. Ngũgĩ's work, which documents late colonial violence as a form of literary expression, highlights how the technological agency of modernization was grounded in the strategy of counterinsurgency. Finally, *The Trial of Dedan Kimathi* predates a vast body of scholarship that has excavated the history of Mau Mau (Berman and Lonsdale 1992; Anderson 2005).

Conclusion

This volume seeks to revisit modernization as a series of historical and cultural concepts in order to reassess the significance of the "modernization project." We emphasize the manner in which modernization was conceived as projects that materialized as specific events. Just as Live Aid concerts featuring Bono accentuate the urgency of African suffering as a popular event, the ribbon-cutting ceremony for the commissioning of the Akosombo Dam in Ghana may be understood as a theatrical spectacle. The opening of the Institute of African Studies at the University of Ghana heralded an approach to Pan-Africanism that is analogous to the First World Festival of Negro Arts in Senegal. The British colonial film unit's production of *Daybreak in Udi,* which promoted credit cooperatives in Nigeria, won an Academy Award in the United States in 1949. As such, indexical instances of modernization informed relationships between institutions and cultural ideals. As a series of ongoing events, we assert that the event-based nature of the modernization project has been rooted in local meanings that go beyond narrowly construed project mandates. Rather, local adaptations and the lived context in the age of modernization extend our understanding of spectacle during the postwar and early independence period on the African continent.

Notes

1. This is in contrast to Debord's (1994) narrower conception of spectacle as an instance of commodity fetishism, but draws on anthropological approaches to cultural spectacle and locality in different African settings; see Apter (2005); Barber (2000).

2. For a sampling of this work, see Mbembe and Nuttal (2008); DeBoeck and Plissart (2004); Sassen (1991, 2000).

3. Smyth (1979), (1988), (1992); see also Burns (2000).

4. See Askew (2002); Castaldi (2006); Neveu Kringelbach and Skinner (2012).

References

Agamben, Giorgio. 2009. *What is an Apparatus?* Translated by David Kishik and Stefan Pedatella. Stanford, CA: Stanford University Press.

Agbodeka, Francis. 1998. *A History of the University of Ghana*. Accra: Woeli.

Anderson, David. 2005. *Histories of the Hanged: The Dirty War in Kenya and the End of Empire*. New York: W. W. Norton.

Apter, Andrew. 2005. *The Pan-African Nation: Oil and the Spectacle of Culture in Nigeria*. Chicago: University of Chicago Press.

Apter, David E. 1965. *The Politics of Modernization*. Chicago: University of Chicago Press.

Askew, Kelly Michelle. 2002. *Performing the Nation: Swahili Music and Cultural Politics in Tanzania*. Chicago: University of Chicago Press.

Barber, Karin. 2000. *The Generation of Plays: Yoruba Popular Life in Theatre*. Bloomington: Indiana University Press.

Benjamin, Walter. 2008 [1936]. "Work of Art in the Age of Mechanical Reproducibility: Version 2." In *The Work of Art in the Age of Its Technological Reproducibility, and Other Writings on Media*, edited by Michael W. Jennings, Brigid Doherty, and Thomas Y. Levin, 9–55. Cambridge, MA: Belknap Press of Harvard University Press.

Berman, Marshall. 1988. *All That Is Solid Melts into Air: The Experience of Modernity*. New York: Viking Penguin.

Berman, Bruce, and John Lonsdale. 1992. *Unhappy Valley: Conflict in Kenya and Africa*. 2 vols. Athens: Ohio University Press.

Burns, James M. 2002. *Flickering Shadows: Cinema and Identity in Colonial Zimbabwe*. Athens: Ohio University Research in International Studies.

Casely Hayford, J. E. 1969 [1910]. *Ethiopia Unbound: Studies in Race Emancipation*. London: Frank Cass.

Castaldi, Francesca. 2006. *Choreographies of African Identities: Négritude, Dance, and the National Ballet of Senegal*. Urbana: University of Illinois Press.

Césaire, Aimé. 1970 [1963]. *The Tragedy of King Christophe*. Translated by Ralph Manheim. New York: Grove.

Cooper, Frederick. 1996. *Decolonization and African Society: The Labor Question in French and British Africa*. Cambridge: Cambridge University Press.

———. 2005. *Colonialism in Question: Theory, Knowledge, History*. Berkeley: University of California Press.

———. 2008. "Possibility and Constraint: African Independence in Historical Perspective." *Journal of African History* 49, no. 2: 167–96.

Cooper, Frederick, and Randall Packard, eds. 1998. *International Development and the Social Sciences: Essays on the History and Politics of Knowledge*. Berkeley: University of California Press.

DeBoeck, Filip, and Marie-Françoise Plissart. 2004. *Kinshasa: Tales of the Invisible City*. Ghent: Ludion.

Debord, Guy. 1994 [1967]. *The Society of the Spectacle*. Translated by Donald Nicholson-Smith. New York: Zone Books.

Derrida, Jacques. 1976. *Of Grammatology*. Translated by Gayatri Chakravorty Spivak. Baltimore: Johns Hopkins University Press.

Deutsch, Jan-Georg, Peter Probst, and Heike Schmidt, eds. 2002. *African Modernities*. Portsmouth, NH: Heinemann.

Donham, Donald. 1999. *Marxist Modern: An Ethnographic History of the Ethiopian Revolution*. Berkeley: University of California Press.

Fabre, Michel. 1991. *From Harlem to Paris: Black American Writers in France, 1840–1980*. Urbana: University of Illinois Press.

Ferguson, James. 2006. *Global Shadows: Africa in the Neoliberal World Order*. Durham, NC: Duke University Press.

Frank, Andre Gunder. 1972. "The Development of Underdevelopment." In *Dependence and Underdevelopment*, edited by James D. Cockcroft, Andre Gunder Frank, and Dale Johnson, 3–17. Garden City, NY: Anchor Books.

Gaines, Kevin K. 2006. *American Africans in Ghana: Black Expatriates and the Civil Rights Era*. Chapel Hill: University of North Carolina Press.

Gaonkar, Dilip, ed. 2001. *Alternative Modernities*. Durham, NC: Duke University Press.

Geschiere, Peter, Birgit Meyer, and Peter Pels, eds. 2008. *Readings in Modernity in Africa*. Bloomington: Indiana University Press.

Gikandi, Simon. 2008. "African Literature and Modernity." *Matatu: Journal for African Culture and Society* 35, no. 1: 1–18.

Gilman, Nils. 2003. *Mandarins of the Future: Modernization Theory in Cold War America*. Baltimore: Johns Hopkins University Press.

Harvey, David. 1990. *The Condition of Postmodernity: An Inquiry into the Origins of Social Change*. Oxford: Blackwell.

Hodge, Joseph Morgan. 2007. *Triumph of the Expert: Agrarian Doctrines of Development and the Legacies of British Colonialism*. Athens: Ohio University Press.

Huntington, Samuel P. 1965. *Political Order in Changing Societies*. New Haven, CT: Yale University Press.

Jay, Martin. 1996. *The Dialectical Imagination: A History of the Frankfurt School and the Institute for Social Research, 1923–1950*. Berkeley: University of California Press.

Jules-Rosette, Bennetta. 1998. *Black Paris: The African Writers' Landscape*. Urbana: University of Illinois Press.

Kenyatta, Jomo. 1938. *Facing Mount Kenya: Traditional Life of the Gikuyu*. London: Secker and Warburg.

Larkin, Brian. 2008. *Signal and Noise: Media, Infrastructure, and Urban Culture in Nigeria*. Durham, NC: Duke University.

Mamdani, Mahmood. 1996. *Citizen and Subject: Contemporary Africa and the Legacy of Late Colonialism*. Princeton, NJ: Princeton University Press.

Mbembe, Achille, and Sarah Nuttall, eds. 2008. *Johannesburg: The Elusive Metropolis*. Durham, NC: Duke University Press.

McLuhan, Marshall. 1967. *The Medium is the Message.* New York: Random House.
Mitchell, Timothy. 1991. *Colonising Egypt.* Berkeley: University of California Press.
———. 2002. *The Rule of Experts: Egypt, Techno-Politics, and Modernity.* Berkeley: University of California Press.
Mkandawire, Thandika, ed. 2005. *African Intellectuals: Rethinking Politics, Language, Gender and Development.* Dakar: CODESRIA.
Neveu Kringelbach, Hélène, and Jonathan Skinner. 2012. *Dancing Cultures: Globalization, Tourism and Identity in the Anthropology of Dance.* New York: Berghahn.
Ngũgĩ wa Thiong'o, and Micere Githae Mugo. 1976. *The Trial of Dedan Kimathi.* London: Heinemann.
Nkrumah, Kwame. 1963. *"The African Genius": Speech at the Opening of the Institute of African Studies, University of Ghana, Legon, October 25th 1963.* Accra: Ministry of Information and Broadcasting.
Olukoshi, Adebayo. 2007. "African Scholars and African Studies." In *On Africa: Scholars and African Studies,* edited by Henning Melber, 7–31. Uppsala, Sweden: Nordic Africa Institute.
Rousseau, Jean-Jacques. 1824. "Essai sur l'origine des langues." In *Oeuvres completes de J. J. Rousseau,* edited by Victor-Donatien de Musset-Pathay, vol. 2, 415–95. Paris: P. Dupont.
Sassen, Saskia. 1991. *The Global City: London, New York, Tokyo.* Princeton, NJ: Princeton University Press.
———. 2000. *Cities in a World Economy.* Thousand Oaks, CA: Pine Forge Press.
Shannon, Claude E., and Warren Weaver. 1975 [1963]. *The Mathematical Theory of Communication.* 6th ed. Urbana-Champaign: University of Illinois Press.
Smyth, Rosaleen. 1979. "The Development of British Colonial Film Policy, 1927–1939, with Special Reference to East and Central Africa." *Journal of African History* 20, no. 3: 437–50.
———. 1988. "The British Colonial Film Unit and Sub-Saharan Africa, 1939–1945." *Historical Journal of Film, Radio and Television* 8, no. 3: 285–98.
———. 1992. "The Post-War Career of the Colonial Film Unit in Africa: 1946–1955." *Historical Journal of Film, Radio and Television* 12, no. 2: 163–77.
Thomas, Lynn. 2011. "Modernity's Failings, Political Claims, and Intermediate Concepts." *American Historical Review* 116, no. 3: 727–40.
Tipps, Dean C. 1973. "Modernization Theory and the Comparative Study of Societies: A Critical Perspective." *Comparative Studies in Society and History* 15, no. 2: 199–226.
Wacquant, Loïc J. D. 2008. *Urban Outcasts: A Comparative Sociology of Advanced Marginality.* Malden, MA: Polity Press.

PART ONE

Modernization and the Origins of the Package

1 After Modernization

Globalization and the African Dilemma

Percy C. Hintzen

Africa to the Rescue

I recall a meeting that I attended at a time when media reports were circulating raising concerns about South Asia as a cheap location for computer programming and software development. The value of the U.S. dollar was falling on international currency markets, which was having a negative effect on industry profits in South Asia. Increasingly the region was being rendered less competitive relative to the United States. In response, high-tech companies began shifting their operations back to the United States, generating increasing demand for programmers and computer engineers. With increasing U.S. demand came rising salaries and compensation packages driving costs in an upward spiral. The solution, discussed and proposed, was to shift computer programming and software engineering functions to Africa—the last bastion of cheap production in an increasingly competitive globalized economy. This is a particular case of a general trend where foreign direct investments in Africa are seen as a solution to a current crisis of global capitalism that demands reallocation in global production to areas where remuneration and transaction costs are cheapest and where there is rising consumer demand for global products and services.

The shift to Africa is facilitated by the sundering of the relationship between profit accumulation and nationalist agendas for economic development. Such agendas, at one point, had begun to threaten and disrupt a colonial and postcolonial order of "dependency" where economic surpluses generated in the colonies and former colonies are transferred to the developed global north. The goal of retaining economic surpluses in the colonies and former colonies, motivated by reversing relationships of dependency, was at the critical center of narratives of "modernization." In a new development ethic, modernization was to be accomplished through the implementation of policies that would result in dramatic increases in macroeconomic performance (national income, output, savings, consumption, and investment) at the national level. Such policies, it was assumed, would guarantee the accumulation of profits in the former colonies. The "turn to Africa" was being proposed in the wake of declining performance of these very macroeconomic indicators in the "developed," industrialized, "mature" economies. Old patterns of "dependency" had to be turned upside down to accommodate the new reality of dependence on growth in incomes, consumption, and investment opportunities in the former colonies of Europe located in the global south.

In an editorial written for a special edition of *Vanity Fair* on Africa dedicated to a global "Product Red" campaign that he heads, Bono, the lead singer of the Irish band U2, explained that the campaign's purpose was to raise money for a Global Fund, organized as a unique global public/private partnership among government, civil society, the private sector, and affected communities to fight AIDS, tuberculosis, and malaria.[1] The money comes from an allocated percentage of profits earned by participating companies from the sale of targeted "Product Red" goods. In making his appeal, Bono made reference to the health crisis in Africa, and particularly to the prevalence of the three diseases targeted by the fund as an example of factors that constrain, restrain, and prevent the modernization of the continent: "We needed help in describing the continent of Africa as an opportunity, as an adventure, not a burden. Our habit—and we have to kick it—is to reduce this mesmerizing, entrepreneurial, dynamic continent of 53 diverse countries to a hopeless deathbed of war, disease, and corruption" (Bono 2007, 36).

Without knowing it, Bono entered into the fraught field of historicist discourse. His assertion of Africa's dynamic entrepreneurship turns on its head the very foundations of European thought that assigned the continent and its progeny to the constitutive outside of civilization. Entrepreneurship is an exclusive practice of "civilized," "enlightened" subjects located in "modern" spaces. A narrative logic of Africa as the natural home of the "unenlightened" engaged in "traditional" practice placed entrepreneurship outside its realm of possibility. Bono challenges this narrative, proposing instead an alternative explanation—that rational will, as the motive force of entrepreneurship, was snuffed out by the very logic and practices of European colonialism. This came with devastating consequences for Africa, where, according to Bono, we modern Enlightened subjects have rendered the continent "a hopeless deathbed of war, disease, and corruption." Now, the "mesmerizing, entrepreneurial" dynamism of the African continent is on display "where every street corner boasts an entrepreneur" (Bono 2007, 32).

Entrepreneurial dynamism is, singly, the most important marker of the modern enlightened subject. It is the product of reason and rationality. In the narrative of the Enlightenment and its offshoot in German and European idealism, the African is understood to be devoid of rational capacity, trapped in the stasis of a "pre-history" of non-reason. This forecloses participation in enlightened civilization and precludes African entrepreneurship.[2] The idea is founded on the notion that European enlightened rationality and reason have produced, through "rational will," the conditions for human perfection.[3] A "Three Worlds" global division confines Africa to the geocultural space of the "Aboriginal" for whom reason and its provenance in consciousness are foreclosed. The Asian "Oriental" fares little better in this narrative, constrained by an irrational consciousness that misallocates reason to the supernatural in which all conscious action is directed in adoration and worship. The European, as the "universal subject," is distinguished from the African by capacities for cognition, and from the Oriental by self-consciousness. This geopolitically differentiated discourse of difference is at the foundation of Kantian, Hegelian, and Marxist philosophy.[4] In its early formulations, rooted in German Idealism, such difference was cast as the unchanging nature of "natural law."

Changes in the social and technical conditions of industrial capitalism rendered these naturalist assertions untenable as explanations for the division of the world. The need for significant increases in capital investments (including investments in human capital) and in infrastructural development and utilities in European colonies populated by "natives" and "Orientals" demanded a reformulation of naturalist thought. In new discourses of "development," the possibility of the "conscription" of the colonized into the "modern" colonial project was acknowledged along with a full transition from "tradition" to "modernity" in an undefined future. This new discursive pedagogy was foreshadowed by and predicated upon "historicist" representations of geopolitical differentiation that began with Hegel and were subsequently elaborated by Marx. These new representations are critical to any attempt at understanding the discursive preconditions for eventual challenges to European colonialism organized around developmental agendas for capital accumulation. They opened up new horizons of thought and consciousness, allowing for the possibility that the colonized had the potential for civilized enlightenment, and they provided justification and support for the idea of political independence and national self-determination. But any assertions of civilized enlightenment had to be contained if the new historicist representations were to serve the interests of the colonial project. So, in their application to the colonies, the European colonizer was cast as the agent of civilization and betterment. Development became a "universal necessity" and colonialism its instrument (see McMichael 2008, 25). Europe became the prototype of progress to human betterment and the promised future for the colonies. The colonized were inscribed into the new world of development as "*almost the same, but not quite*" as the Enlightened modern self (Bhabha 1994, 86). As such, colonialism received its new legitimation and justification as the historical route of transition to modernity. At some point, however, the inevitable and fraught issues of readiness and timing had to be raised—issues that eventually fueled the anticolonial struggle for independence.

Once development entered into the arena of colonial discourse, the colonial project could be justified only as a form of tutelage. The problem of conceding rational will to the colonized while preserving the global structure of dependency has been at the center of the issue of modernization and development and their derivative practices. The recent "turn to Africa" poses new problems for the preservation of capitalist interests.

The Shift to Modernization and Development

With colonialism under attack, new subdisciplines of political modernization and economic development began to inform understandings of progress. In one influential version of the economic argument (to be discussed later) the world came to be understood as divided into "developed" and "underdeveloped" countries based on location along a range of indicators of material progress. This replaced the colonial traditional/modern binary tied to Manichean notions of cultural difference. The field of development economics informed a critical aspect of this reformulation. In the process it challenged the tutelary claim that the European colonizer was the agent of modernization. Colonialism came to be cast as an impediment to growth, and rational technical application became the motive force of modernization. While acknowledging differences in material outcomes and forms of accumulation across the geographic, racial, cultural, and socioeconomic (class) divisions set in motion by colonialism, the idea of "transformation" was replaced by an argument for "uneven development."[5] At its inception, development economics set out to explain the relative absence of forms of accumulation and of the material conditions of modernity in the colonies and former colonies. Economic growth unleashed by the energies of the formerly colonized, freed from colonial constraints, came to replace the idea of cultural change. The argument for colonial tutelage that rested on cultural transformation was thereby rejected.

The shift to economics was particularly well suited to fundamental changes occurring in the global order after World War II. It was accompanied by the emergence of the United States as the new center of metropolitan capital. The new economics and American global interests combined to support arguments for national self-determination in Europe's colonies as the prerequisite for national development. European mercantilist practices were attacked as impediments to progress because they foreclosed opportunities for the introduction and implementation of the techniques and technologies of modernization. For the United States, access provided to U.S. capital by the European colonies became imperative if the conditions for development were to be satisfied. This argument served as justification for U.S. active, even though ambivalent, involvement in supporting anticolonial aspirations in the colonies (Fraser 1994).

On 20 January 1949, President Harry Truman, in his inaugural speech before Congress, used the term "underdeveloped areas." It was the first time the term was used as a designation for the former colonies of Europe (including Latin America). Countries of the world were now positioned along a new development divide (that nonetheless mirrored the old) according to their gross national product (GNP)—a new measure of productive output designed during World War II to quantify the degree to which the U.S. economy was meeting its goals of war production (Sachs 1996, 239–40). New international institutions were organized to ensure and manage the transition to economic development in a postcolonial and postwar global economy. In July 1949, the International Bank for Reconstruction and Development (the World Bank) made its first foray into the "developing areas" through a program for "multitude improvements and reforms" designed for the economy of Colombia. The program emphasized the need for "careful planning, organization, and allocation of resources" through a "detailed set of prescriptions, including goals, quantifiable targets, investment needs, design criteria, methodologies, and time sequences" (Escobar 1995, 24–26). Even though they retained all of the discursive features of the old historicism, these new understandings of underdevelopment became tied to the narrow economic rationalities of production, consumption, and investment as fundamental conditions of modernization. Economic rationality became the motive force for development against the irrationality of colonial forms of mercantilism. The idea of a cultural transition from the "traditional" to the "modern" was replaced by the notion of progress in a process of modernization directed by policies of rational investments in industrialization, denied by colonial commandment.

West Indian economist and Nobel laureate W. Arthur Lewis was at the center of these new developments (see Tignor 2006). He considered colonialism to be an impediment to modernization and argued that the colonizing project rested upon the maintenance of a strict division of labor necessary to guarantee a supply of cheap raw agricultural and mineral primary commodities needed as inputs to capitalist industry in the colonial centers of Europe. Lewis, as an unmitigated nationalist, challenged British colonial policy on these very grounds. The industrialization of the West Indies (and therefore its modernization), he felt, was stymied by the inevitability of colonial opposition because of the threat it posed to British industry.[6]

Lewis proposed a program of economic development predicated upon national self-determination and independence from Europe. He advocated a proactive role for the postcolonial state and called for the development of international organizations controlled and directed by "development scholars." Capital investments that were denied to the colonies under the colonial project were to be secured through fiscal and other incentives designed to attract foreign industries and foreign investors. He argued for this form of "industrialization by invitation" as the necessary precondition for modernization (Lewis 1950, 1954).

For Lewis, colonialism was the main impediment to modernization because the colonial economy was organized around the export of surpluses. This prevented the accumulation of savings needed for investment. Under such conditions, development transition could not occur. Colonialism denied the colonies an opportunity to embark on the path that led to the industrial revolution in Europe (Lewis 1979, 4). In Africa, the problem of transition was complicated by the presence of a large "subsistence" sector. Independence would provide postcolonial elites with the opportunity to apply their "rational will" to the task of modernization. With the importation of capital, technology, and skills, the "surplus labor" engaged in inefficient production for subsistence would become absorbed into the industrial sector. This would provide the former colonies with a comparative advantage in global trade.

Notwithstanding this new turn, development and modernization continued to be overdetermined by its historicist roots.[7] The historicist assumptions of a natural historical progress were retained in the new developmentalist thinking. This was especially evident in the version of development theory proposed by Walter Rostow, the American economist and advisor to the administrations of Presidents Kennedy and Johnson, which became instrumental in the policies and practices of development economics. As a universal proposition, according to Rostow, countries went through five historical stages of economic growth. History began with "traditional society." Implementation of appropriate policies for accumulation of savings and investments were needed in these societies to create the "precondition for takeoff." The threshold to modernization was crossed during the "takeoff" stage. Once accomplished, it led to a "drive to maturity" that set the stage for an "age of high mass consumption." Rostow's teleological version of history ended in a utopia that was "beyond consumption." Like Lewis, he saw a "centralized nation state" fashioned out of new nationalist coalitions as one of the critical "preconditions for takeoff." With it, the impediments to modernization thrown up by both traditional and colonial interests would be swept aside (Rostow 1953).

Thus, in the new ideology of economic development, the Rubicon of modernization was to be crossed with the accumulation of savings that became available for investments in industrial production. Such investments were foreclosed under colonialism because of the threats they posed to colonial and traditional interests. The success of the anticolonial movement effectively created the space for economic transformation with the removal of the colonizer.

Theorists of political modernization were not as convinced as development economists that the transition from tradition to modernity rested solely on the application of rational economic will. Traditional interests were hard to dislodge, and their continued presence came with resistance to efforts at modernization. Independence had left traditional interests intact to be dealt with as a *political* problem, and so the path to economic rationality was paved by "political order." For them, the imposition and maintenance of order became *the* paramount political virtue. Disorder was the fundamental impediment to progress. Traditional interests (including the peasant and the poor) came to be identified as sources of disorder. They needed to be controlled and contained for eventual conscription into modernization.

The retention of historicist thought based on the Manichean cultural division of tradition and modernity was at the critical center of the political version of "modernization theory" that developed in the 1960s. What differentiated it from colonial understandings was the concession it made to a domestic group of elite "modernizers," already possessed of rational will. This did away with the need for colonial agents of transformation. Modernization theory thus managed to accommodate the new developmentalist thinking while retaining notions of native inferiority. It was proposed that the institutionalization of authority be led by elite "modernizers" if the political order was to be guaranteed as a condition of economic development. Democracy was to be held in check until the forces of tradition were swept away. For Samuel P. Huntington, one of its key advocates, "the problem is not to hold elections but to create organizations . . . to provide an assurance of political order" in the face of the "mobilization of new social forces into politics" (Huntington 1968, 7–9, vii). There is, in his formulation, a "gap" between economic development and political development. The imposition of the absolute authority of a modernizing elite became an "organizational imperative" if disorder stemming from this "gap" is to be prevented (7–8). The process of transition begins with "modernizing monarchs" willing to transform their systems into "modern constitutional monarchies." This sets the stage for assumption of power by "radical praetorians [in] middle class break-through coups"—the latter, in turn and at the appropriate time, to be replaced by modern leaders in a one-party system. There is little room for democratic practice during this transition. Democracy, as it turns out, must wait for the appropriate moment in the process of modernization. This is because democracy requires

> strong, adaptable, coherent political institutions: effective bureaucracies, well organized political parties, a high degree of popular participation in public affairs, working systems of civilian control over the military, extensive activity by the government in the economy, and reasonably effective procedures for regulating succession and controlling political conflict. (1)

In this formulation, the postponing of democracy in postcolonial political organization became, at one and the same time, a necessary condition of progress as well as confirmation that the former colonies were "*almost the same but not quite*" civilized. This, in essence, became the "meaning" of modernization and reflected the way its narrative was overdetermined by traditional historicism. In effect, it was just a different version of colonial reason and practice, with the colonizer replaced by a national elite subservient to the interests of the new bloc of global capitalists centered in the United States.

The retention of historicist discourse in the "American" versions of economic development and modernization theory resolved a fundamental contradiction in the new developmentalism. The goal for the former colonies had less to do with progress and development transition and more with dislodging colonial mercantilist interests who stood in the way of American capital. Development economics and political modernization were handmaidens of a new global hegemony of ruling interests centered in the United States. The twin ideas of progress and development were merely legitimizing rationales for the incorporation of the "modernizing elite" in the global south into a new coalition of interests that replaced the global elite class of colonizers. As petty bourgeoisie, members of this modernizing elite were particularly well suited to the service of American interests in the new global transformations. They employed their newly achieved "legal-rational authority" derived from control of newly independent states to transform their state bureaucracies and their bureaucratized political parties, trade unions, and voluntary organizations into "power instruments of the first order"—an outcome anticipated by nineteenth-century historicist scholar Max Weber (1958, 228).

The goal of "modernization" was not merely the destruction of the institutions of colonial order and demobilization, but control of traditional interests. Proletarianization had produced new "social forces" that challenged the hegemony of American-centered global capital, organized around anticapitalist ideology. Economic development and political modernization were predicated on the containment, control, and negation of these challenges. Modernization was presented as "non-ideological."[8] Ideology, on the other hand, became exclusively tied to socialism and communism, represented as the new forms of nonrational thought and practice. Like "tradition," socialism and communism were cast in the new narrative of modernization as impediments to progress and as sources of disorder. They were to be contained if not destroyed at all costs. Ideology, according to David Apter, one of the major theorists of modernization, was dangerous because

> rhetoric is confused with reality, tactics with values, meaning with motives. The leaders are erratic, aggressive, and given to creating their own rules of conduct. By claiming the future, they disclaim responsibility for the present. And by manipulating political religion, they endow such conduct with morality. (Apter 1965, 388)

At stake was the challenge posed to the hegemony of global capitalist interests by Euro-Communism and Western European forms of socialism. These had begun to inform, direct, and influence campaigns of mobilization in the postcolonial global south.

The point of those who speak of "hegemony" is that it is not static, neither in its structure nor in the composition of its "ruling group."[9] The new American-centered capitalism, because of its challenges to colonial hegemony, incorporated the modernizing elite of petit bourgeois interests in the former colonies into a new social-democratic alliance of global solidarity comprising, according to Samir Amin (1980), metropolitan capitalist interests, the affluent metropolitan middle class (cut off from unprivileged minorities, women, etc.), the "comprador" national capitalists in the global south, and now the latter's petit bourgeoisie. This set the stage for the eventual abandoning of national goals set as targets by the mantra of modernization.

The consequences were inevitable. Rather than transferring the benefits of material progress to the former colonies, modernization (understood as political modernization and economic development) became the legitimizing and justifying narrative deployed in the service of the interests of American-centered global capital. Modernization, through its reformulation of historicist discourse, became the instrumental idea behind the organization of new practices of global power and created a new social mapping of the world that replaced the previous colonial formation. Overdetermined by historicist thinking, it retained the notion of the developmental inferiority of the "underdeveloped" global south by separating the now-globalized "modernizing elite" from the rest of the "native" population (see Escobar 1995, 10–17). This served to naturalize a new system of power that functioned to regulate the practices of the population of the "undeveloped" world and to impose new disciplinary technologies upon its masses. In the process people came "to recognize themselves as developed or underdeveloped" and infused with a "desire for development" (10–11).

In the international arena, the distinction between developed and underdeveloped countries became central to new understandings in the unfolding system of power relations. New forms of national evaluation were introduced based on measures of "economic development." Domestically and internationally, the technical knowledge of development was deployed as an "efficient apparatus" that "systematically regulated [these] new relations of power" (10). The binary divide between the "developed" and the "underdeveloped" at the international level became replicated in distinctions made between the "modern" and "traditional" in the national arena. In this new developmental thinking, progress became the goal and the sole governing principle in the socioeconomic practices of the "underdeveloped" countries. The global north, and particularly North America, came to be represented teleologically as the inevitable "end of history" and ideologically as the new utopia. It was a new version of colonial tutelage by the United States imposed by new international institutions including the Bretton Woods financial institutions of the World Bank and International Monetary Fund and the various arms of the United Nations, all formed during the closing stages of World War II and becoming operative in the war's immediate aftermath.

The "quest for development" came with its own contradictions because of the promise of betterment it made to the "natives." The rationale for the "development project," as argued and presented, was its guarantee of material progress and the transformation of the postcolonial political economies into clones of the developed industrialized North. This led, inevitably, to popular demands for and expectations of "betterment" as central features of postcolonial preoccupations. But development, as ideology, and its promise of modernization were nothing more than hegemonic ruses. They served, following Gramsci (1971), as a mechanism of political and economic control, the means through which the ruling group of interests was able to project its own way of *seeing the world* so that those subordinated by it accepted their conditions as "common-sense" and "natural." This guaranteed their willing and active consent. The promise of modernization was made to instantiate and conscript the participation of Europe's former colonies and their populations into the architecture of American-centered global capital.

The contradictions between the goal of national development and the demands of this new global system of capital began to become evident in the 1970s. Economic growth stemming from development investments was not "trickling down" to the vast majority of the population.[10] National development was showing itself to be incompatible with the accumulative agendas of the new global capitalist order, now freed from the demands and obligations of colonial metropolitan interests. Because of the failure of its promise, radical nationalist agendas, supported and influenced by the Soviet Bloc and China and their anticapitalist Marxist/Leninist and Maoist ideologies, began to infuse postcolonial nationalist formation. Forms of democratic socialism adopted in Europe in the wake of the shift of capitalism's center to the United States began to inform postcolonial nationalist discourse in the erstwhile colonies.[11]

The Neoconservative Transformation

The goal of political modernization, as ideology and practice, was to consolidate the absolute authority of the "modernizing elite" in postcolonial political economy and statist formation. It was accompanied by a phenomenal expansion of new multilateral agencies, including their Bretton Woods versions, in the former colonies. This expansion inserted a new set of global actors into state decision-making. The hegemonic narrative of development naturalized the power and authority of the national and global elite as agents of modernization. In the process, the domestic postcolonial political economy became unhinged from its colonial and quasi-mercantilist roots and inserted into an ever widening and deepening global system. The putative commitment of the postcolonial elite to national development began to erode. The multilateral agencies charged with developmental transformation became instrumental in imposing a new creed of globalization upon the political economies of the global south. A shift to the global was made imperative by new demands stemming from changes in the structure of international capitalism. These changes were produced out of new developments in information, communication, and transportation technology. They ushered in new "disarticulated" forms of production organized in the interests of newly consolidated forms of global commercial, financial, and manufacturing capital (Gereffi 2007, 128–29). A new mantra of economic "globalization" began to take hold as an authoritative imposition on policy and practice in postcolonial states. What resulted, according to Henry Bienen and John Waterbury, was a "neoconservative transformation" where the national and global elite "set out to fundamentally reorganize social and political" order with the aim of redirecting "the pattern of political and social power" away from the nationalist agenda of development (Bienen and Waterbury 1992, 382).

The model and prototype for this transformation emerged in the mid-1970s in a push by newly industrializing countries (NICS) in Latin America and East Asia to develop export industries (Gereffi 2007, 114–34). The success of these countries' efforts convinced many of the decision-makers in Europe's former colonies to follow their example. The global south began a shift to exclusive production of commodities for export (129–30), which was a necessary condition for successful implementation of new disarticulated forms of global manufacturing. What eventually emerged were "commodity chains" of production organized in "export/marketing networks" spanning "several countries, with each nation performing tasks in which it has a cost advantage" (127–28). Countries in the global south began to be differentially inserted into this new global system based on their "comparative advantage" (i.e., the cost advantages they enjoyed) in labor, utilities, inputs, and all other elements involved in the production process, and on the amount of land, labor, capital, and entrepreneurship available for exploitation in the production and sale of goods and services for the global market. They also had to bear the burden of the costs of infrastructural development to support the new export orientation. Many built special industrial parks and developed export-processing zones (EPZs) that were exempt from national regulation and tax regimes. There was tremendous rearticulation of the system of global production with a proliferation of "world factories . . . producing world rather than national products" (McMichael 2008, 89–90). In the new order, "production steps" became "separated and distributed among geographically dispersed sites in assembly-line fashion, producing, and assembling a completed product. World products emerge from a single site or a global assembly line of multiple sites organizing disparate labor forces of varying skill, cost, and function" (89–90). The new global order led to dramatic declines in domestic production, including domestic agriculture. Production of traditional crops was replaced by agro-commodities for export. Most of the nations' productive resources (including capital and entrepreneurship) became hitched to the global economy (see Frobel, Heinrichs, and Kreye 2007, 160–74).

The neoconservative turn transformed the postcolonial social order and its relations of power. Strategic sectors of the population that became mobilized in support of the anticolonial campaign for independence had to be demobilized, disciplined, and/or coerced. Welfare programs, subsidies, and other types of state transfers were reduced or eliminated altogether. They were now seen as external "diseconomies" because of their negative effect on comparative advantage. The public wage bill had to be drastically reduced and real wages had to be lowered (by, for example, delinking them from inflation). Public employees had to be fired and public sector spending had to be reduced drastically. Public assets had to be divested to the private sector, resulting in the elimination of many public enterprises. Cuts had to be made in consumer subsidies and in state-provided services including health, education, welfare, and social security (Bienen and Waterbury 1992, 382–86). A large segment of the public sector bureaucrats had to be cast aside.

All of this had profound implications for elite social formations. Employment in state bureaucracies and state enterprises, transfer payments, state-supported and state-provided subsidies, prices and income guarantees, and state provided services formed the bases of elite reproduction in the postcolonial political economy. The changes that were implemented contributed, particularly, to a decline in the power and influence of that segment of the national elite located exclusively in formal political organizations, especially political parties and trade unions. Their positions in the hierarchy of power became undermined as an increasingly powerful central executive began exercising almost absolute control over policy implementation. Beginning in the 1980s, these policies became defined and dictated increasingly by international financial institutions (IFIs) charged with implementing programs of stabilization and structural adjustment. As a result, the leaders of politically significant voluntary organizations began to find themselves locked out of the corridors of power, and their access to state resources became severely limited. This drastically curtailed the opportunities available to them for economic and cultural accumulation and for the delivery of patronage. Their authority became undermined as their access to these very forms of accumulation and patronage became significantly curtailed. As the institutions that they led became marginalized, the mass public whose interests were represented through them found their influence over public decision-making weakened and their access to public resources diminished. The local capitalist sector was also affected. Import substitution industries, the fashion of the 1960s, found themselves confronted with escalating costs of foreign and domestic inputs and with competition from relatively cheap imports. These were compounded by declining domestic demand stemming from the ongoing and intensifying effects of recessionary crises that became nearly universal features in the peripheral economies of the South during the 1980s.

This laid the groundwork for the "documentary practices" of the new global political economy to become inscribed in policy and practice as "a system of rational action" (Escobar 1995, 108). The central executive came to rely heavily upon managerial and professional elites to organize and manage the neoconservative transformation. The two were joined by a new grouping of merchants involved in importation, wholesale, and retail activities, as well as by a new group of local industrialists. Local capital moved away from the production of domestic goods to "producing orders on a sub-contracting basis for trading and manufacturing firms based in the industrialized economies" (Crow and Thorpe 1988). Tied to the international system of manufacturing as subcontractors, they began to invest in relatively labor-intensive export-oriented and export processing activity to undertake the relatively labor-intensive aspects of a growingly disaggregated system of international manufacturing through investment in export-oriented and export processing activity. They became directly dependent upon the availability of "surplus labor" in their peripheral political economies, including domestic agro-producers dispossessed of their land, and wage and salaried workers displaced from the state sector, from local domestic manufacturing, from the agro-export industries tied to colonial production, and from import-substitution industries. Important for this process was the recruitment of female workers and the "feminization" of labor.

Workers and peasants displaced by the new global order and unable to find work in the new export sectors had to seek out new sources of income and new means of support. Some became dependent upon remittances transferred from abroad by relatives forced to leave their countries in search of jobs. Others became involved in small scale, semi-legal or illegal activities in the "informal sector," many exploiting opportunities to service the needs of the new domestic and international elite. Others became engaged in nonconventional activities including petty trade, smuggling, gambling, outworking, personal services, and the like. In certain countries some became involved in the local and international drug trade and in male and female prostitution, activities directly associated with a growing tourist industry that was playing a central role in the new global order.

In the formal sector, the demobilization of organized male labor and its displacement from state employment and domestic production resulted in significant declines in wages and salaries. The pool of surplus labor was significantly increased with the addition of women to the employment rolls in export-oriented industries as part of a growing global process of the feminization of labor. This resulted in the weakening of income and employment security for both men and women. To supplement family income, women began to increase their participation in the informal sector.

The lowering of labor costs stemming from the above measures was deemed necessary if a country were to gain comparative advantage in the global economy (Standing 1989; Moghadam 2007). The result was a denationalization of both production and consumption. As factors of production were forced into the service of the global market, domestic production was destroyed. Countries began to experience phenomenal growth in demand for globally produced goods and services. There was a burgeoning "growth in the domestic market" that spurred a "surge in the private consumption of goods and services" provided by overseas suppliers (Minder 2010).

These fundamental transformations in postcolonial economies explain the "mesmerizing, entrepreneurial" dynamism observed by Bono in Africa. They are at the root of the continent's "adventure" into "opportunity." Many are pushed into forms of entrepreneurship linked to the global economy. Households are forced to rely on the tertiary sector of a segmented labor market to supplement incomes and to satisfy needs no longer guaranteed by the state, domestic production, or subsistence agriculture (see contributions in Reich 2008). All these have contributed to the impression of entrepreneurial dynamism lauded by Bono.

The former colonies of Europe enjoy an increasing comparative advantage in the new global system because of their growing competitiveness in three main areas: (1) remuneration costs, or the costs of labor; (2) the costs of inputs; and (3) taxes.[12] This is a direct result of the neoconservative transformation. Notwithstanding these advantages, decisions to move production to the global south are weighed against the costs of moving, or *transaction costs.* These costs have been typically high in the global south because of what Immanuel Wallerstein (2004, 80) identified as (1) higher transportation costs due to increased distances, (2) poorer infrastructure, and (3) negative externalities related to "disavowed remuneration to non-employees." Phenomenal developments in transportation, communication, and information technologies significantly reduced many of these costs. Structural adjustment regimes imposed by the IMF and World Bank had the direct effect of reducing significantly or eliminating altogether "negative externalities," particularly in the form of transfer payments charged to international businesses and their domestic partners imposed and supported by the state. Structural adjustment policies also increased "positive externalities" by demanding state investment in supportive infrastructure and state legislation of fiscal and monetary policies favorable to globally engaged business.

Africa as Solution: Resolving the Current Crisis of Global Capital

This is the context within which Bono's discovery of Africa as a "mesmerizing, entrepreneurial, dynamic continent of 53 diverse countries" must be understood. Notwithstanding the claim made about the "natural" rationality (entrepreneurship) of the African, the entrepreneur on "every street corner" (as an object of Bono's fascination) may well be the product of and a response to forced participation in the state's neoconservative turn to globalization. First, there was the phenomenal dispossession of rural labor of its land. This was accompanied by a significant contraction of employment opportunities in the formal economy. These, together, have fueled dramatic growth in the informal sector of a segmented labor market. Many in this sector are forced into quasi-entrepreneurial activities including petty trading, artisanship, and own-account (i.e., self-employed) providing of services. Second, they become available as a "reserve of cheap labor" in a new regime of labor flexibilization. This involves "labor-only-contracting, subcontracting, hiring of casuals and contractuals, [and] the hiring of apprentices" in pursuit of "superprofits" (Lindio-McGovern 2005). In other words, globalization imposes forms of entrepreneurship to cater to new forms of demand (consumption) inscribed in market relations and of supply (production) as they respond to the needs of the new global system. This system eviscerates the distinction between "tradition" and "modernity" that was at the center of "development" and "modernization" paradigms. Everyone becomes a "conscript" of globalization.[13] The role of the state in producing "betterment" disappears.

Bono sees entrepreneurship—the motive force of modernization—as almost embedded in the African character. It was subdued but not destroyed by a violence that reduced the continent to a "hopeless deathbed of war, disease, and corruption." As modern civilization loses its entrepreneurial dynamism in the global north, Africans are supposed to come to its rescue. Bono is reciting a growing sense of a current crisis of global capital. It is particularly strident in concerns over sustainability and in the deep anxiety engendered by these concerns. According to political economist Phillip McMichael,

> These days we talk of globalization as a matter of fact, and often with approval. . . . While over three-quarters of the world's population can access television images of the global consumer, not much more than a quarter have access to sufficient cash or credit to participate in the consumer economy. We are at a critical threshold: Whether consumer-based development remains a minority activity or becomes a majority activity among the earth's inhabitants, either way is unacceptable for social (divided planet) or environmental (unsustainable planet) reasons, or both. Development as we know it is in question. (McMichael 2008, 1)

This sense of anxiety has filtered into popular consciousness. In one particular instance, it has produced a desperate search for a "new age" of enlightened practice, accompanied by comforting assurances of an inevitable utopia that mirrors modernization's promise. It challenges the relationship between rationality and "entrepreneurial dynamism" because of the association of both to materialism. At the very time that entrepreneurship is being appended to forms of African being, it is under assault as destructive. Utopia is to be ushered in by a "revival of spirit." Its inevitability rests not on human effort and character, but on the natural progress of "planetary cycles." The discovery of entrepreneurship, the motive force of modernization and development, as fundamental to African being is made at the very time when its consequences for the potential destruction of the planet are being posited:

> With all the problems we have, it's hard to believe our future is bright. Inflation and recession, environmental deterioration, diminishing resources, un-

> rest and oppression in developing countries, and apathy, loneliness and lack of direction in developed ones all combine to severely cloud the horizon. . . . It wasn't too long ago that we heard about the dawning of the Age of Aquarius, and about the revival of spirit among the new generation. We can still hear the echoes of John Kennedy's call to action and see the vision of Martin Luther King's dream. Before he and his dream were shot down in 1968, he said we, as a people, "would get to the promised land." The promise seems empty now, yet the planetary cycles support his prophecy. For what we discover when we examine these cycles is compelling evidence that a renaissance and a golden age is right around the corner. This is the era of peace, of unity, of love. (Shakti 2010)

What may be critical to the sudden "discovery" of African entrepreneurship may be the potential for the continent to save global capitalism, or to prolong its viability.

African "entrepreneurship" is fast becoming the "solution" to capitalism's crisis. This is the point conveyed in a July 2010 article by Robert Minder in the business pages of the *New York Times* on the economic crisis facing Portugal and on Angola's role in its resolution. The title of the article, "Portugal Turns to Former Colony for Growth," says it all:

> Portugal, one of Europe's ailing economies, is increasingly placing its hopes of recovery on Angola, a former colony that has established itself as one of the strongest economies in sub-Saharan Africa—thanks largely to oil and diamonds. The shift comes as competition is getting stiffer in Brazil, another booming former colony, and as Portugal's traditional European trading partners, led by Spain, struggle under a mountain of debt and soaring joblessness. (Minder 2010)

The article quotes Ricardo Gorjão, a project manager for CPI (a Portuguese company that produces software for banking and other service industries) in its explanation of the rationale behind the relocation to Africa: "We're going through a huge recession in Portugal, while here, the banking sector is having an amazing development, so it has made a lot of sense to be shifting our business toward Angola" (Minder 2010).

This is not an isolated story. A *Newsweek* article titled "How Africa Is Becoming the New Asia" makes the identical point in even more broad and universal terms:

> China and India get all the headlines for their economic prowess, but there's another global growth story that is easily overlooked: Africa. In 2007 and 2008, southern Africa, the Great Lakes region of Kenya, Tanzania, and Uganda, and even the drought-stricken Horn of Africa had GDP growth rates on par with Asia's two powerhouses. Last year, in the depths of global recession, the continent clocked almost 2 percent growth, roughly equal to the rates in the Middle East, and outperforming everywhere else but India and China. This year and in

> 2011, Africa will grow by 4.8 percent—the highest rate of growth outside Asia, and higher than even the oft-buzzed-about economies of Brazil, Russia, Mexico, and Eastern Europe, according to newly revised IMF estimates. In fact, on a per capita basis, Africans are already richer than Indians, and a dozen African states have higher gross national income per capita than China.
>
> More surprising is that much of this growth is driven not by the sale of raw materials, like oil or diamonds, but by a burgeoning domestic market, the largest outside India and China. In the last four years, the surge in private consumption of goods and services has accounted for two thirds of Africa's GDP growth. (*Newsweek* 2010)

As it turns out, it is not the production of commodity exports that is important but the "emerging African middle class" of over three hundred million (Majahan 2009, cited in Minder 2010). The newly discovered African entrepreneurs of "roadside street vendors" are there to service the consumer demands of "these accountants, teachers, maids, taxi drivers" all driving up demand for goods and services (Minder 2010).

While the architecture of global capital is rapidly changing, global corporations maintain their ascendance, and their major shareholders and investors continue to be the primary beneficiaries of globalization. What has changed is that these shareholders and investors have become globalized as the negative effects of global capitalism have spread to the global north with segments of the latter's population joining the "losers" in the global south. The profit motive is what is driving the turn toward Africa in a global search for new consumers and cheaper costs. The previously cited *Newsweek* article mentions an Oxford University study that reported the annual rates of return on capital of 954 publicly traded African companies to be "on average 65 percent higher than those of similar firms in China, India, Vietnam, or Indonesia." Higher profit margins in Africa are spurring a tremendous growth in foreign direct investments and "even Chinese companies are thinking of outsourcing basic manufacturing to Africa" (*Newsweek* 2010).

What this reveals about "modernization" and "development" is that both were ruses to secure the incorporation of the postcolonial global south into a new and rapidly changing global system of capital. "Effective participation in (this new) world economy" was accomplished by a shift away from "national development" under conditions that produced a "freeing of markets for labor, money, goods, and services" (McMichael 2008, 152–53). The national goal of modernization and development quickly became an impediment to profit accumulation, making imperative a shift in the role of the state toward capitalism's global agenda.

What does this mean for the life conditions of populations of the global south in general and of Africa in particular? Will the promise of acquiring the material conditions of modernity be realized with the unfolding of the rational will to entrepreneurship? Or is the new global system merely a continuation, as is argued by Achille Mbembe (2001, 25), of forms of colonial rationality sedimented in the "globalization project"?[14] In capitalism's current iteration, has the postcolonial state become globalization's handmaiden?

The problem addressed by the "Product Red" campaign goes to the heart of capitalism itself: its dependence on the enrapturing of production, consumption, and material accumulation by the ruses of a desired modernity that never existed and never will. This is at the root of capitalism's governmentality, understood here as constituted by relations of power that enlist subjects in the project of their own rule (Foucault 1979, 5–21). The result is a fetishizing of consumption, production, and accumulation, now exercised through displacement, regulation, and the discipline of globalization.

The "development project" and its goal of modernization was made possible by the necessary rejection of "naturalist" claims of an ineluctable racial division that cast Africa as devoid of the Enlightenment's attributes of reason and rationality. The project of globalization had to go even further. The "will to truth" about the enlightened modern selfhood of the African and her/his "natural" predisposition for entrepreneurship is now becoming stridently asserted under current conditions of chaos and the crisis of sustainability facing global capital.[15]

But the crisis is already upon us. It is productive of an even more profound anxiety among the ruling interest of global capital. These are the interests that stand to lose the most. Africa is capitalism's new salvation because of a legacy of colonial commandment that has kept production costs abysmally low and because of the drastic reductions in transaction costs brought about by new developments in technology. The continent's inhabitants have been forced historically to develop strategies to deal with the material consequences of this legacy. Their conscription into globalization now demands new assertions (both from themselves and from elite global interests) of their "will to truth" as modern subjects. This is leading to a dangerous embrace of capitalism's ruses, even if paradoxically in the form of claims to an original, pristine, and "natural" entrepreneurship. Africans are in the throes of harnessing the "opportunities" and "adventure" offered up by global consumption and production with selfish personal "accumulation" now replacing "development" as their goal. The road of "adventure" is paved with "opportunities" for entrepreneurship. This has become evident "on every street corner." But "entrepreneurship" is inextricably tied to global capital's "imperative of endless accumulation" (Wallerstein 2004, 2, 24). Africa's role in this enterprise has always been tied to a highly discounted "exchange value" for its factors of production. The link to global capital is firmly embedded in guarantees of its continued exploitation, now sustained through the "comparative advantage" it enjoys, particularly in the costs of its labor and of goods supplied by its growing export sector performing its role in the commodity chains of global factories, and in the growth of consumer demand for global goods and services. The recently discovered "entrepreneurship" of the African cannot be viable in the current global system of production and consumption unless the "exchange value" of its goods and services remains so low that poverty continues to be the lot of the majority of its population. At the same time, it is compelled to pay world market prices for the goods and services it consumes.

From this perspective, globalization turns out to be just another phase in the global system of capitalist exploitation, consistent with an international division of labor that has always been at its center. Transition to "modernity" was never the goal in any of its phases. From the first trading companies in the sixteenth century introduced by European colonial powers, accumulation was always to be concentrated in the "firm," its corporate offshoots and its elite investors. Over the centuries, the share of accumulated surpluses shifted from the absolutist sovereign, through the merchant plantocracy of the colonial state, to the capitalist elite and privileged sectors of the "working classes" in the global north, and then to elite beneficiaries in the global south who have become imbricated in the global corporate interests and the global elite formations associated with such interests.[16] Accumulation, as its goal, was always accomplished on the backs of the poor and the peasant who comprise the vast majority in the global south. This cannot be reversed with African entrepreneurship.

The problem, therefore, rests with the capitalist imperative of "endless accumulation."[17] No "rational will," however derived, can meliorate the looming crisis of "sustainability" (environmental, income, social) facing "consumer-based development." The three-quarters of the world's population without "access to sufficient cash or credit to participate in the consumer economy" (McMichael 2008, 1) have been forced to develop strategies to deal with this chaos. Despite their intensified conscription into global capital, these strategies can lead, hopefully, to a rejection of capitalism's ruses. Forms of regulation and disciplining that harness the "opportunities" and "adventure" offered up by Africa for consumption, production, and accumulation are acting to forestall such rejection. The task is to find an alternative to endless accumulation in the "ways of being" developed as foils against the forms of violence that conscripted Africa into the project of global capital in the first place. This may be the "true" meaning of modernization.

Notes

1. The Global Fund, see: http://www.theglobalfund.org/en/whoweare.
2. This representation of German Idealism embodied in the neo-humanism of Kant is taken directly from Spivak (2003) in making the distinction between the European as the universal self and its opposite in the "native informant" for whom Enlightenment is foreclosed.
3. This derives directly from Kant (2010 [1787]).
4. See the argument made by Spivak (2003, 1–5). See also Pletsch (1981).

5. From the historicist perspective, it is the "lack" or "absence" of reason and rationality that locates the colonized in the space of modernity's prehistory and that confined them to "an imaginary 'waiting room' of history" (Chakrabarty 2000, 8).

6. See Lewis (1950) and Farrell (1980, 57).

7. Rostow (1953), see especially chapter 4.

8. Signaled in the very title of Rostow's most influential book, *The Stages of Economic Growth: A Non-Communist Manifesto* (1960).

9. Hall (1996) makes this point against the static notion of a totalizing hegemony that denies a universalized and essentialized working class of agency. Hegemony contains the challenges of interest groups within parameters that can be tolerated by the coalition of ruling groups. The constant and political struggle for "position" opens up spaces of possibility for challenges to the hegemonic ruling group.

10. In 1970, recognition of the failure of the promise of development prompted the United Nations to declare its second "development decade," which focused primarily on poverty alleviation, income redistribution, and narrowing the gap between the developed and the underdeveloped countries. See United Nations A/RES/2526 1970, *International Development Strategy for the Second United Nations Development Decade*, 24 October 1970.

11. The new global capitalist order was also having an impact in the United States as capital sought to reduce its fiscal obligations to the state as a consequence of its new global reach.

12. Wallerstein (2004, 78–81) discusses this point as it applies to these three costs.

13. This usage follows David Scott's (2004) application as it pertains to enslaved Haitians in his examination of the accounting of the Haitian Revolution by C. L. R. James.

14. By "globalization project," I refer to the privileging of the rights of corporations "through an emerging vision of the world and its resources as a globally organized and managed free/trade/free enterprise economy" which has "redefined development as a private undertaking" (McMichael 2008, 21, 338).

15. See Alexander's (2005, 121–25) discussion of Margaret Urban Walker's notion of the "right to truth" as a moral imperative (Walker 2001). The discussion relates to Rae Langston's (1992) schema of will, means, and opportunity.

16. In what Samir Amin (1980) termed a "social-democratic alliance" between the metropolitan bourgeoisie, the affluent, metropolitan working class, and the satellite/comprador bourgeoisie in the global South.

17. This is precisely the point made by Wallerstein (2004, 2, 24).

References

Alexander, M. Jacqui. 2005. *Pedagogies of Crossing*. Durham, NC: Duke University Press.

Amin, Samir. 1980. *Class and Nation*. New York: Monthly Review Press.

Apter, David E. 1965. *The Politics of Modernization*. Chicago: University of Chicago Press.

Bienen, Henry, and John Waterbury. 1992. "The Political Economy of Privatization in Developing Countries." In *The Political Economy of Development and Underdevelopment*, 5th ed., edited by Charles Wilber and Kenneth Jameson, 376–402. New York: McGraw-Hill.

Bhabha, Homi. 1994. *The Location of Culture*. London: Routledge.

Bono. 2007. "Message 2U." *Vanity Fair*, July: 36.

Chakrabarty, Dipesh. 2000. *Provincializing Europe: Postcolonial Thought and Historical Difference*. Princeton, NJ: Princeton University Press.

Crow, Ben, and Mary Thorpe, eds. 1988. *Survival and Change in the Third World.* New York: Oxford University Press.

Escobar, Arturo. 1995. *Encountering Development: The Making and Unmaking of the Third World.* Princeton, NJ: Princeton University Press.

Farrell, Trevor. 1980. "Arthur Lewis and the Case for Caribbean Industrialization." *Social and Economic Studies* 29, no. 4: 52–75.

Foucault, Michel. 1979. "Governmentality." In "Governing the Present," special issue, *Ideology and Consciousness,* Autumn: 5–21.

Fraser, Cary. 1994. *Ambivalent Anti-Colonialism: The United States and the Genesis of West Indian Independence, 1940–1964.* Westport, CT: Greenwood.

Frobel, Folker, Jurgen Heinrichs, and Otto Kreye. 2007 [1980]. "The New International Division of Labor in the World Economy." In *The Globalization and Development Reader: Perspectives on Development and Global Change,* edited by J. Timmons Roberts and Amy Bellone Hite, 160–74. Malden, MA: Blackwell.

Gereffi, Gary. 2007 [1994]. "Rethinking Development Theory: Insights from East Asia and Latin America." In *The Globalization and Development Reader: Perspectives on Development and Global Change,* edited by J. Timmons Roberts and Amy Bellone Hite, 113–34. Malden, MA: Blackwell.

Gramsci, Antonio. 1971. *Selections from the Prison Notebooks.* Edited and translated by Quintin Hoare and Geoffrey Nowell Smith. New York: International Publishers.

Hall, Stuart. 1996. "Gramsci's Relevance for the Study of Race and Ethnicity." In *Stuart Hall: Critical Dialogues in Cultural Studies,* edited by David Morley and Kuan-Hsing Chen, 411–40. London: Routledge.

Huntington, Samuel P. 1968. *Political Order in Changing Societies.* New Haven, CT: Yale University Press.

Kant, Immanuel. 2010 [1787]. *Critique of Pure Reason.* 2nd ed. Translated by John Miller Dow Meiklejohn. London: Henry G. Bohn.

Langston. Rae. 1992. "Speech Acts and Unspeakable Acts." *Philosophy and Public Affairs* 20, no. 2: 293–330.

Lewis, W. Arthur. 1950. "The Industrialization of the British West Indies." *Caribbean Economic Review* 2: 1–53.

———. 1954. "Economic Development with an Unlimited Supply of Labour." *Manchester School* 22, no. 2: 139–91.

———. 1979. "The Dual Economy Revisited." *Manchester School* 47, no. 3: 211–29.

Lindio-McGovern, Ligaya. 2005. "Neo-Liberal Globalization in the Philippines: Its Impact on Filipino Women and Their Forms of Resistance." Paper presented at "Women and Globalization," Center for Global Justice conference, San Miguel de Allende, Mexico, 27 July–3 August.

Majahan, Vijay. 2009. *Africa Rising: How 900 Million African Consumers Offer More Than You Think.* Upper Saddle River, NJ: Pearson Prentice Hall.

Mbembe, Achille. 2001. *On the Postcolony.* Berkeley: University of California Press.

McMichael, Philip. 2008. *Development and Social Change.* 4th ed. Thousand Oaks, CA: Pine Forge.

Minder, Ralph. 2010. "Portugal Turns to Former Colony for Growth." *New York Times,* 14 July: B3 (New York edition).

Moghadam, Valentine, 2007 [1999]. "Gender and the Global Economy." In *The Globalization and Development Reader: Perspectives on Development and Global Change,* edited by J. Timmons Roberts and Amy Bellone Hite, 135–52. Malden, MA: Blackwell.

Newsweek. 19 February 2010. "How Africa is Becoming the New Asia." http://www.newsweek.com/2010/02/18/how-africa-is-becoming-the-new-asia.html/.

Pletsch, Carl. 1981. "The Three Worlds, or the Division of Social Scientific Labor, circa 1950–1975." *Comparative Studies in Society and History* 23, no. 4: 565–90.

Reich, Michael, ed. 2008. *Segmented Labor Markets and Labor Mobility*. Vols. 1 and 2. Cheltenham, UK: Edward Elgar.

Rostow, Walter W. 1953. *The Process of Economic Growth*. Oxford: Oxford University Press.

———. 1960. *The Stages of Economic Growth: A Non-Communist Manifesto*. Cambridge: Cambridge University Press.

Sachs, Wolfgang. 1996. "Neo-Development: 'Global Ecological Management.'" In *The Case against the Global Economy: And for a Turn toward the Local*, edited by Jerry Mander and Edward Goldsmith, 239–52. San Francisco: Sierra Club.

Scott, David. 2004. *Conscripts of Modernity: The Tragedy of Colonial Enlightenment*. Durham, NC: Duke University Press.

Shakti, Shri Adi. 2010. "Shri Adi Shaki: Age of Aquarius: Age of Holy Breath by Shri Adi Shakti." Spirituality in Cyprus: A New Consciousness. http://de-de.facebook.com/notes/spirituality-in-cyprus-a-new-consciousness/age-of-aquarius-age-of-holy-breath-by-shri-adi-shakti/119040541475364.

Spivak, Gayatri Chakravorty. 2003. *A Critique of Postcolonial Reason: Toward a History of the Vanishing Present*. Cambridge, MA: Harvard University Press.

Standing, Guy. 1989. "Global Feminization through Flexible Labor." *World Development* 17, no. 3: 1077–99.

Tignor, Robert. 2006. *W. Arthur Lewis and the Birth of Development Economics*. Princeton, NJ: Princeton University Press.

United Nations. A/RES/2526 1970. 1970. *International Development Strategy for the Second United Nations Development Decade*. 24 October.

Walker, Margaret. 2001. "Rights to Truth." Paper presented at "Women's Rights as Human Rights," South-Eastern Women's Studies Association conference, Boca Raton, FL, March.

Wallerstein, Immanuel. 2004. *World-Systems Analysis: An Introduction*. Durham, NC: Duke University Press.

Weber, Max. 1958. *From Max Weber: Essays in Sociology*. Translated, edited, and with an introduction by H. H. Gerth and C. Wright Mills. New York: Oxford University Press.

2 Modernization Theory and the Figure of Blindness
Filial Reflections

Andrew Apter

For David E. Apter. *In memoriam.*

Every poem is a misinterpretation of a parent poem.
—Harold Bloom

However negative it may sound, deconstruction implies the possibility of rebuilding.
—Paul de Man

How does one read a text, or an oeuvre? How does one reread modernization theory? In my own case the answers to these questions are linked by Freud's family romance and "the anxiety of influence" (Bloom 1973), which together guarantee a radical misreading of an intellectual father-figure who was also my father. David E. Apter (1924–2010), a modernization theorist of the 1960s, worked in the Gold Coast and Uganda in the 1950s before turning to issues of comparative development. His Africanist case studies of institutional transfer (1955) and of bureaucratic nationalism (1961) represent two of the four developmental trajectories that he formalized and systematized in *The Politics of Modernization* (1965). This latter text, translated into several languages (Japanese, Spanish, Indonesian, and Mandarin), represents a period of high modernism in American social science, an expansive moment in U.S. liberal empire associated with the wave of decolonization that swept across the postwar globe, and which was particularly associated with "development" in Africa. Motivated by the optimism of postcolonial possibilities in the 1960s, this moment was also shaped by the polarizing pressures of the Cold War (Bandung notwithstanding) and the predicaments these created for emerging new nations.[1]

Viewed today through the bifocal lenses of historical hindsight and cultural critique, *The Politics of Modernization*—like modernization theory writ large—remains a monument to its time: grand in its vision, hegemonic in its claims, resolutely statist with its faith in expert knowledge and bureaucratic rationality, tragic in its underestimation of the rise of military regimes, and dazzling in its elaboration and refinement of Parsonian functionalism. In returning to this text—one that occupied my early childhood as an unintelligible and all-consuming patriarchal vocation—my goal is not to defend it in any literal-minded sense, or "on its own terms." Such a defense would not be difficult to make. For example, one could commend the text's multilinear modernizing trajectories in the face of prevailing unilinear pathways (e.g., Rostow 1960); its exposition of a dynamic rather than static notion of tradition, including varieties of re-traditionalization; its diagnosis of military regimes as weak and unstable, given their coercion-information curves; its prescient prediction of the presidential monarch (before Bokassa, Mobutu, and Amin declared themselves presidents-for-life); its emphasis on youth culture as a potent mobilizing force; its sensitivity to the mythic dimensions of modernizing ideologies, drawing on Sorel and Freud; and its full recognition of socialist regimes as modernizing agents, unusual within the genre. But such a defense is in fact a diminution of the text, an underestimation of its broader place and significance within the field.

Rather I wish to return to those forms of blindness it shared with the genre at large, not to debunk a style of theory, which, like any strong fashion statement, is easily caricatured in retrospect, but to excavate its epistemological history (back to Kant) and recuperate a radical reversal within its Rousseauian myth of origins. By focusing on the insight buried deeply within its blindness, I invoke two literary critics whose innovative work helped inaugurate the "linguistic turn" in social theory, and who transform my filial perspective from a psychoanalytical liability to an intuitive advantage. First there is Harold Bloom, whose *Anxiety of Influence* (1973) reveals how every major modern poet misreads "his" father-figure according to a hermeneutics of misprision; second there is Paul de Man, whose groundbreaking essay "The Rhetoric of Blindness" (1983 [1971]) exemplifies the method of deconstructive criticism, showing how every philosophical-literary insight requires figural and rhetorical reversals that undermine its claims, as evidenced by Derrida's reading of Rousseau's *Essai sur l'origine des langues.* I will not engage these texts in great depth, save only to frame the related problems of *genealogy* and of *origins* in *The Politics of Modernization* and the genre to which it belongs.

Genealogies of Misprision

As a narrative genre, modernization theory reinscribes the grand discourses of European empire as they developed in the nineteenth century—those of civilizing savages, saving souls, cultivating wilds, or healing the sick, within the ratifying pseudoscience of Victorian evolutionism.[2] The oppositions that structured these heroic discourses are by now well-documented, whether in the explicit ideological negations of not-civilized, not-human, not-rational, not-moral, not-healthy, not-white, and (with Hegel's coup-de-grâce) not even historical, representing the condition of savagery as one of absence or lack, or in the positive redemptive pathways leading toward civilization, affirming Europe's "higher" virtues and values through the holy alliance of missionary and colonizer. It takes no great leap of the imagination to see modernization theory as a secular variation of this grand imperial theme, drawing implicitly on those associated sociological distinctions between *Gemeinschaft* and *Gesellschaft*, mechanical and organic solidarity, status and contract, that reinforced the picture.[3] Nor do we need Harold Bloom at this point to apprehend the larger politics of narrative revision at work: in *disavowing* imperial ideology and its associated forms of colonial overrule, modernization theory reproduced its dominant discourse. In its Parsonian incarnations, modernization theory embraced self-determining nation-states as they moved away from ascribed roles and primordial affiliations toward national integration, industrialization, rational planning, democratic rule, functional differentiation, role specification, innovation, and meritocracy—essentially moving from tradition to modernity.

What Bloom does encourage us to find are the genealogies within this genealogy, in this case a genealogy of social theorists who stood on the shoulders of their predecessors while—if Bloom's theory of misprision is correct—kicking their feet out from under them. As Bloom (1973, 5) explains in a nutshell, "Poetic history, in this book's argument, is held to be indistinguishable from poetic influence, since strong poets make that history by misreading one another, so as to clear imaginative space for themselves." One may question my substitution of social theorists for strong poets, who, for the most part, engage language with radically divergent sensibilities. Unlike the vulgar pretensions of Monsieur Jourdain in Molière's *Le petit gentihomme*, there is no danger of social theorists suddenly learning that they have been "speaking" poetry all of their lives! Yet it is precisely a poetics of social theory and social science that illuminates—through rhetorical analysis—its dominant tropes and displacements, whether of the "material bedrock" of productive relations, the collective "effervescence" of social solidarity, or the hypostatized "actors" and self-professed "robustness" of rational choice theory, the latter of which belies more than a little anxiety about its scientific "potency" within the academy. More concretely, strong theorists, like strong poets, have strong personalities, with ego-driven intellects that seek breakthroughs, shift paradigms, and establish interpretive terrains. The fact that I grew up in such a passionate intellectual home environment, heard Bloom's DeVane lectures as a high school student, and came of professional age at the University of Chicago, where my most senior colleagues routinely called me "David"—nominally merging me with the legendary father who had co-founded the Committee for the Comparative Study of New Nations with Edward Shils in the late 1950s—together provided me with specialized training in the anxiety of influence, in its textual, psychoanalytic, and institutional modalities.

Autobiographical self-indulgence aside, I will not pursue modernization theory's genealogy of misprision with the depth and span that it deserves, but invoke Bloom's central insight to bring one form of blindness (my own misreading) to bear on another—the enduring legacy of Weberian rationalization—and so identify the birth of modernization theory with a critical epistemological rupture and reversal. The genealogy I sketch combines academic mentorship with textual filiation (as Bloom says, all poems only exist in other poems), blending literal and figural relationships that trace back to a founding father-text.

Working backward, we begin with David Apter, son of Marion Levy Jr. The filial relation is somewhat skewed, in that Marion was only five years older than my father in chronological time yet served as his dissertation advisor at Princeton. Moreover, my father and Marion were friends—*compadres* in the language of *compradrazgo* when Marion became my sister's godfather (whatever that meant between secular Jews!). But intellectually, Marion was mentor and teacher. His two-semester seminar on historical sociology used Talcott Parsons' *The Structure of Social Action* (1949 [1937]) as a basic text that deeply influenced my father's thinking. So did Marion's own *The Structure of Society* (1952), a book that sought to refine Parsonian structural-functionalism with a near-viral proliferation of concepts and categories that laid out the logic of requisite analysis and distinguished (usefully) between analytic and concrete structures. That some of this artillery appeared in my father's first monograph (Apter 1955, see esp. 325–34), less in his second (Apter 1961), and more again in *The Politics of Modernization*, hardly captures the complex relations of apprenticeship and intertextuality that developed between them. In what might seem like a routine clerical task, my father typed all 541 pages of *The Structure of Society* in final draft, a book that was curiously published in typescript rather than the metal-cast "foundry" or linotype of the day.[4] In this the book bears the imprint not of my father's thinking but of his manual labor, a labor that no doubt influenced his thinking—a way of "working through" the text and being subjugated by it (as amanuensis) captured by registers of mutual recognition and implication. If in 1952 David Apter was thanked for his assistance in the preface of *The Structure of Society*, a larval "ephebe" emerging from the pool, by 1965 he could dedicate *The Politics of Modernization* "To Marion J. Levy, Jr."[5]

Although Levy would later publish two massive volumes on modernization applying the categories of *The Structure of Society* to international relations (Levy 1966), the former work remained his theoretical centerpiece, characterizing his own vexed relationship as an intellectual "son" of Talcott Parsons, who had served as Levy's dissertation advisor. Like many of the tomes at that time within the genre, this was the product of a seminar (three seminars, actually—two at Princeton in 1951 following one at Harvard in 1947, when Levy was still a graduate student in the Department of Social Relations). This was also during the postwar boom of a new social science, with seminars, committees, and workshops funded by the Carnegie Corporation and Ford Foundation, bringing together the best and the brightest—sociologists, anthropologists, psychologists, political scientists, as well as the odd biologist, mathematician, or epistemologist—to form interdisciplinary research teams collaborating on theoretical systems and conceptual schemes. These seminars formed "circles," typically of young men around a mentor (Parsons at Harvard, Levy at Princeton, Shils at Chicago) producing vanguard texts and dense networks of scholars sustained by charismatic relations of reciprocal recognition.[6] Levy's intellectual identity was clearly forged within the Parsonian crucible at Harvard, as his acknowledgment of the "private seminar held at Harvard in the summer of 1947" implies, for it was there that "the definition of the concept of society and the list of functional requisites that form the bases for the present work were produced" (Levy 1952, xiv). And it is here, in his text, that Levy's relationship to his precursor begins to swerve,[7] clearing the ground for an autonomous vision that paradoxically purports to be more faithful to the father than the father was to himself.

First, there is the ambivalent debt. After locating his text within a theoretical genealogy of Durkheim, Pareto, Weber, and Veblen—virtually recapitulating the major figures explicated in *The Structure of Social Action*—Levy foregrounds his teacher for particular attention:

> A special indebtedness is owed, however, to Talcott Parsons. The work grew out of concerns stimulated and encouraged by him and by his work. This work was not done in consultation with him, and it has taken many turns with which I am sure he would not agree. He is certainly not to blame for its shortcomings. Still its indebtedness to him will be obvious enough to the reader, particularly with regard to the distinction of the uses of concepts and theories, the concern with systems of phenomena, and the interrelationship of different aspects of social phenomena. (Levy 1952, xiv)

In this text, and in the "private" Harvard seminar, Parsons figures as the *absent* father, neither consulted during the writing process nor physically present among his neophytes in the summer of 1947.[8] The text's "many turns" deviate from the master, for which he cannot be "blamed," and in effect revise the master plan with even greater methodological rigor. Levy regarded his "requisite analysis" as a necessary corrective to Parsons' functional imperatives, and "the analytic aspects of relationship structures" as an improvement on Parsons' pattern variables. In fact, Levy felt that Parsons betrayed his own principles by failing to refine their methodological implications, a task that his student assumed for himself. For this hubris, Levy was effectively banished from the Parsonian circle, as evidenced by his conspicuous absence from *Toward a General Theory of Action* (1951)—an important volume co-edited by Talcott Parsons and Edward Shils to assess the current state of sociological theory.[9] Levy acknowledged this volume while effectively negating it in *The Structure of Society*, noting that "the final published version of [*Toward a General Theory of Action*] has been under preparation at the same time as the present one, and hence use of its findings has not been made here" (Levy 1952, 19n16). Thus Levy cleared the ground for his own succession, and for his growing circle of acolytes at Princeton.

It is tempting, following Pierre Bourdieu, to pursue the microsociology of these postwar circles as contestations within an emerging field of intellectual capital, converting ideas, resources, debts, and obligations into centers of "excellence" materialized by texts. But my aim here is more limited, emphasizing relations of textual filiation in the reckoning of an intellectual genealogy. In exploring Parsons' filial relationship to Weber, the textual connections are complicated by Weber's prodigious output and the sheer scope of his ideas, ranging from *Die Protestantische Ethik und der Geist des Kapitalismus* (*The Protestant Ethic and the Spirit of Capitalism*) (1904/5)—which so resonated with Parsons' Calvinist background and New England family history—to the methodological essays and substantive studies in economic, religious, and political sociology. Parsons (1980, 38) recounts how Weber "served, in a very real sense, as my teacher," despite the fact that he died five years before Parsons arrived (in the fall of 1925) to study in Heidelberg. Absent the father figure himself, Parsons studied with Max's brother Alfred Weber, attended the "sociological teas" hosted by Max's widow Marianne Weber, thereby entering the "Weber circle" which "was the main center of Heidelberg academic society at that time"[10] (40), and prepared four examination fields, including a minor in Kant with Karl Jaspers. I mention this Kantian focus because it illuminates the analytical register of Parsons' revisionary relationship to Weber.

There is no question that *The Protestant Ethic* was the catalyst of Parsons' Weberian conversion. It was the first of Weber's works that he read, "straight through . . . as if it were a detective story" (1980, 39), inspiring his dissertation topic on the concept of capitalism in German social science literature. And it was the first of Weber's works that Parsons translated, appearing in 1930 for Anglo-American readers, followed much later, in 1947, by Part I of *Wirtschaft und Gesellschaft* as *The Theory of Social and Economic Organization*.[11] But however much it engaged the young Parsons, *The Protestant Ethic* was a stepping-stone toward more fundamental issues of theory and method raised by its use of the ideal type. Parsons' discussion of this important text and its place within Weber's broader religious typology in chapters 14 and 15 of *The Structure of Social Action* segues into a sustained methodological engagement with the strengths and limitations of the ideal type and its associated forms of causal inference and explanation. In chapters 16 and 17, Parsons revises Weber to prepare the ground for his own more generalized analytical theory.

The depth of Parsons' understanding of Weber is based on his extraordinary training in Heidelberg, where he read Weber extensively, studied with Weber's students and contemporaries, and familiarized himself with those debates and polemics concerning the logic of the cultural sciences that Weber had directly engaged. Parsons (1949, 481) frames the initial problematic in terms of a profound Kantian dualism pervading German methodological thought: on the one hand between the "objective" realm of a rule-governed, causally connected, natural and physical world susceptible to scientific analysis; and "that of freedom, of ideas, of *Geist*" on the other, associated with the human and social world. At issue for Kant was the subjective factor governing these radically separated realms: minimal in the world of pure reason and scientific determination,[12] maximal in the world of practical reason where the subject is free to think itself *qua* noumena, or "thing-in-itself," beyond the world of objective determination and thus free as a moral and social agent. The implication for German methodology was something of an impasse between natural science and historicism, giving rise to varieties of "particularism" and "intuitionism" that banished general laws and explanatory concepts from the sociocultural sciences (*Geisteswissenschaften*). For Weber, the problem concerned the place of subjective motivations, intentions, and valuations in the frames of reference of both analysts (so-called "value relevance") and sociohistorical actors (*Verstehen*). The more hermeneutical or idiographic approaches to history and social action grounded in the interpretation of subjective meanings could never achieve the nomothetic status of the natural sciences and their general laws.

For Parsons, Weber's methodological achievement was to bring the sociocultural sciences, infused by *Verstehen,* within the fold of general explanatory concepts and causal analysis. Working within the human sciences, Weber organized the manifold complexity of historical reality into "unified conceptual patterns" (1949, 603) or ideal types that brought out the order, clarity, and logical relations governing "historical individuals" and their causal pathways. His methodological failure, for Parsons, was that he didn't push this generalizing logic into a unified theoretical system.

Parsons drew heavily on the work of Alexander von Schelting (1934) in developing a critique of the ideal type, a "not altogether satisfactory" analytical device that blends "two quite heterogeneous categories of generalizing and individualizing concepts" that need to be rigorously distinguished. The individualizing concepts of Weber's ideal types refer to those "concrete historical individuals" such as feudal society, bourgeois capitalism, the Indian caste system, or Chinese patrimonial bureaucracy that are abstracted into essential dimensions and characteristic features as objects of causal analysis and historical explanation. Nor are such individualizing typifications limited to corporate structures and institutional complexes; they apply equally to religious ideas such as Calvinistic theology or the Brahmanic philosophy of karma. Such "slippage" between institutional and ideological spheres is in fact methodologically justified by Weber himself within the broader epistemological context of *value-relevance.*

In Parsons' work, by contrast, the problem was that of general theory construction. As an abstraction, the individualizing ideal type remained potentially ad hoc and trapped in analytical amber, frozen, as it were, by its "mosaic atomism" (Parsons 1949, 610), unable to make the leap from morphology to general dynamics (with codependent variables). That the "generalizing" function of the ideal type could lead the way forward is a theme that Parsons draws from von Schelting, with specific reference to rationality and causality. First, the very idea of rational action, derived from neoclassical economics, constitutes a generalizing ideal type in that the maximization of means-ends relations establishes the starting point of meaningful behavior. Such a generalizing dimension thus informs any ideal-typical characterization of a concrete historical individual. Secondly, any causal explanation of an individualized ideal type requires the hypothetical consideration of its necessary conditions—what must have been in place for X to emerge. Thus "a general ideal type" for Parsons (605) is a hypothetical construction of conditions or events that generate "a typical course of action, or form of relationship." That such generalizing functions of the ideal type were lost on Weber, who shifted the burden of causal explanation onto separate considerations of objective possibility and adequate explanation, explains, for Parsons, what Weber himself could never see—that "an ideal type . . . is always a generalized unit of a social system" (619).[13]

Thus would Parsons "complete" the Weberian project, systematizing the general analytics of ideal types and their principles of classification into an action-oriented theory of society sui generis (Parsons and Shils 1951; Parsons 1952)—a direction Weber explicitly disavowed from the standpoint of cultural hermeneutics. For Weber (1949, 105), general concepts are necessary but always subject to revision because "in the cultural sciences concept-construction depends on the setting of the problem, and the latter varies with the content of culture itself." This position involves more than mere scientific sobriety—a judicious appreciation of the complexity of reality and a wariness of premature generalization—but informs a different epistemological understanding of social theory itself. In his critique of the Historical School, which sought "a 'completed' and *hence* deductive science," Weber reframes the very means-ends relationship between theoretical concepts and historical reality. In a revealing Kantian invocation, theory serves history rather than the other way around:

> If one perceives the implications of the fundamental ideas of modern epistemology which ultimately derives from Kant; namely, that concepts are primarily analytical instruments for intellectual mastery of empirical data and can be only that, the fact that precise genetic concepts are necessarily ideal types will not cause him to desist from constructing them. *The relationship between concept and historical research is reversed for those who appreciate this;* the goal of the Historical School appears as logically impossible, the concepts are not ends in themselves but are means to the end of understanding phenomena which are significant from concrete individual viewpoints. (106; emphasis added)

In effect, Parsons' revisionary "completion" of Weber swings back to the position of the Historical School, reversing Weber's prior reversal to endorse a deductive commitment to social theory. Unlike Levy's "completion" of Parsons, which works within the same "scientific" paradigm, Parsons completes Weber through antithesis, reinverting the very means-ends relationship between theory and sociohistorical reality. Here we see Bloom's revisionary ratio of *tessera* at work, whereby "a poet antithetically 'completes' his precursor" by radically revaluing the terms of the parent-poem (Bloom 1973, 14). Here too we see Weber's profound commitment to Kant.

Is it fair to skip generations, as it were, past Weber's neo-Kantian influences (Rudolph Stammler, Wilhelm Windelband, Ernest Troeltsch, and most notably Heinrich Rickert) to the founding father himself? Is it fair to claim Weber's "filial" relationship to Kant? Such genealogical "telescoping" is of course an established anthropological truism—the further back we go, the more generations "collapse"—and in our case we are emphasizing texts and paradigms over persons. Weber's engagement with Kant is beyond dispute in his methodological essays, and, as Brand (1979, 8) points out, by the fact that Weber's first philosophy professor was Kuno Fischer, an established Kantian whom Weber considered "brilliant."[14] Beyond "world view" and general epistemological orientation, however, I would argue that Weber's debt to Kant is more directly connected to the ideal type, with specific reference to causal explanation and historical interpretation. Against the grain of most Weber scholarship that relates his concerns with free will and causality—autonomy and heteronymy—to the moral philosophy of Kant's second *Critique* (of practical reason), I suggest that we return to Kant's *Critique of Pure Reason* (1973 [1781]), and reinterpret Weber's ideal type as a restoration of the subjective deduction—in his case, as "pure concepts" of historical understanding.[15]

Let us recall the Kantian divide between natural and cultural sciences, and Parsons' claim that Weber began to bridge the gap but ultimately fell short of a generalizing synthesis. We can certainly read this in Weber up to a point. In "'Objectivity' in Social Science and Social Policy," Weber's seminal methodological essay inaugurating the *Archiv für Sozialwissenschaft und Socialpolitik's* new editorial philosophy and leadership (of Max Weber, Werner Sombart, and Edgar Jaffé), the problem of objectivity poses something of a paradox. How can the fundamentally *subjective foundations* of cultural and historical understanding give rise to an objective form of knowledge? How is objective knowledge of social reality possible? Like Kant's world of experience, the sociohistorical manifold must be "conditioned" by a prior framework in order to be "synthesized" and apprehended. Causal understanding, in particular, is never simply ascertained from facts, but belongs to the prior segmentation of the infinitely complex sociohistorical continuum:

> How is the *causal explanation* of an *individual* fact possible—since a *description* of even the smallest slice of reality can never be exhaustive? The number and type of causes which have influenced any given event are always infinite and there is nothing in the things themselves to set some of them apart as alone meriting attention. . . . Order is brought into this chaos only on the condition that in every case only a *part* of a concrete reality is interesting and *significant* to us, because only it is related to the *cultural values* with which we approach reality. Only certain sides of the infinitely complex concrete phenomenon, namely those to which we attribute a general *cultural significance*—are therefore worthwhile knowing. They alone are objects of causal explanation. (Weber 1949, 78; emphasis original)

What Weber so clearly establishes here are the conditions of sociohistorical object-construction through operations of logical selection and abstraction that, in revised Kantian terms, are located within a *cultural* a priori.[16] Transcendental because they are necessary, they are nonetheless fluid rather than fixed because of the subjective character of their determination, motivated by (historically specific) cultural values and interests, from "*particular points of view*" (81; emphasis original). "Objectivity" in the social sciences begins, then, with the construction of sociohistorical objects and the imputation of causal relationships. From its subjective points of entry, social science approaches objective knowledge through the development and deployment of ideal types, those analytical constructs that accentuate the distinctive attributes of ideologies, institutions, and developmental sequences to establish their causal conditions and scientific significance. As with Kant's separation of concept and object, Weber rigorously distinguishes between ideal type and historical reality. Ideal types are conceptual "utopias" precisely because they do not actually exist in the world but are used to render the world intelligible. They are fictions, heuristic devices that must not be hypostatized into the naturalizing fallacies of social science dogmas (whether the psychological reductionism of "free market" economics or the metaphysical determinism of historical materialism). And it is precisely to avoid such naturalistic fallacies that Weber remonstrates against those pseudosocial sciences professing general laws and axioms that would assimilate the cultural to the natural sciences.

Let us now shift perspectives and view the problem of objectivity from the other side of the Kantian divide. If for Parsons, Weber's cultural hermeneutics fell short of a fully scientific sociology—a diatribe developed further in his introduction to *The Theory of Social and Economic Organization* (Parsons 1947)—what of the transcendental conditions of natural science as the proper domain of objective knowledge? As we read Weber on Kant and the core epistemology of his first *Critique* (of pure reason), we glimpse a radical assimilation of science itself to the evaluative ideas of cultural interests, one that reframes "the naturalistic viewpoint" in historical and cultural terms. At the end of his "objectivity" essay, Weber (1949, 110; emphasis original) reminds us that "the *objective* validity of all empirical knowledge rests exclusively upon the ordering of the given reality according to categories which are subjective in a specific sense, namely, in that they present the *presuppositions* of our knowledge and are based on the presupposition of the *value* of those *truths* which empirical knowledge alone is able give us. . . . It should be remembered that the belief in the value of scientific truth is the product of certain cultures and is not a product of man's original nature." Presumably Weber is still talking about social science, but the slippage between the cultural and natural sciences, and "the hair-line which separates science from faith," remains ambiguous. We could read this passage as a resurrected subjective deduction of Kant's pure concepts of understanding, relocating the grounds of scientific objectivity within a prior cultural framework of evaluative ideas. From this perspective, transcendental synthesis is always culturally mediated.

Evidence for this more radical assimilation appears in "Science as a Vocation," where Weber (1958) likens Kant's epistemology to a form of rational theology:

> All theology represents an intellectual rationalization of the possession of sacred values. No science is absolutely free from presuppositions, and no science can prove its fundamental value to the man who rejects these presuppositions. Every theology, however, adds a few specific presuppositions for its work and thus for the justification of its existence. Their meaning and scope vary. Every theology, including for instance Hinduist theology, presupposes that the world must have a meaning, and the question is how to interpret this meaning so that it is intellectually conceivable.
>
> It is the same as with Kant's epistemology. He took for his point of departure the presupposition: "Scientific truth exists and it is valid," and then asked: "Under which presuppositions of thought is truth possible and meaningful?" (Weber 1958, 153–54)

As Barker (1980, 226) points out, Kant is here "relativized" as another theology in which "the objectivist component of his categorical system swallows itself up." Indeed, Kant's *Critique of Pure Reason* is positioned *beyond* reason to locate the conditions of its valid employment, and in this sense the transcendental domain retains the whiff of an evaluative theology. To be sure, Weber was not alone in revising Kant, but took his place within an impressive range of neo-Kantians who tampered with the foundations of his architectonic. But what is so striking in

Weber's particular revisionary strategy is how he "absorbs" or assimilates Kant's epistemology to his own more evaluative a priori framework.[17]

Ultimately the case against "science" remains moot because of Weber's unyielding commitment to causality, not in the form of abstract laws but as necessary conditions of concrete cultural phenomena illuminated by ideal types. In this, Weber remains a Kantian, first by locating causal relations within the a priori framework of analytical concepts, and secondly by defining causal relations in the transcendental terms of the following form: what are the conditions necessary for the possibility of X? This latter formulation illuminates the entire tradition of "structural" social science that followed from Weber, whether in Parsons' functional imperatives, Levy's structural requisites, or the more general typologies and trajectories of modernization theory. But it is with the former Kantian characteristic of causality, the critical separation of concept from object—of analytical construct from apprehended "reality"—that I would like to identify the birth of modernization theory, inaugurating a principled critique of positivism and empiricism within a specific tradition of critical sociology. It was the turning point or epistemological rupture that Kant himself called his Copernican revolution in response to David Hume (Kant 1973, 22, 25*a*).

We need go no further back in our genealogical search for the founding father of modernization theory, since Kant's critical awakening from his "dogmatic slumber" (Kant 1976, 8) established a radical reversal of "things" and "representations" to restore causal necessity to objective experience. As Kant showed contra Hume, if all of our knowledge begins with experience, it does not follow that it arises out of experience, but rather that it derives from a priori concepts and judgments that render experience possible. The resurrection of causality from Hume's empiricist critique demoted the empirical world of things to a secondary or derivative epistemological status in relation to prior concepts and laws. And within this reversal of concept and object, I will argue, lies an important insight in modernization theory's blindness, one that faithfully devolved through lines of misprision even as it was deeply buried or overlooked for generations. Before developing this argument further, however, I will try to relate modernization theory's eponymous ancestor to a different yet complementary kind of philosophical origin associated with Rousseau's "Essay on the Origin of Languages."[18]

The Language of Origins

The "birth" of modernization theory as rupture with the given object, a "Copernican" reversal of sign and referent, cause and effect, "language" and "world," mirrors very nicely the reversal of speech and writing developed in Derrida's reading of Rousseau (Derrida 1976, 165–268). The implications of this latter reversal for redressing the blindness of modernization theory concern less the chains of genealogical transmission discussed above than the disruption of that prelapsarian plenitude—what Derrida calls "presence present to itself"—associated with the origin of language in a mythic state of nature that persists like a palimpsest within models of traditional society. We can gloss this as the *mythos* of modernization theory and break it down into three linguistic "stages": signaling, associated with pure expression and subsistence; negation, associated with displacement and alienation; and supplementation, associated with writing and surplus production.

For Rousseau, the first significant expressions, motivated by the passions, were both gestural and vocal, articulating not objects or things but fears and desires in the "signaling" mode of spontaneous outcry.[19] Here, in the state of nature, at the very beginnings of human sociation, we find a "natural" and relatively unmediated form of expression, one limited by the immediacy of space and time to the proximate situations of selves and others. In some ways this natural protolanguage works like poetry and music, connoting feelings and emotions with little or no denotational value, thus "le premier langage dut être figuré" (Rousseau 1824, 424).[20] The referential properties of language will emerge, but in its earliest stages, the world, indeed consciousness, is not yet divided into words and things. Mankind in this natural state inhabits the fullness of the moment within a continuous present tense, a world in which need is satisfied by subsistence, onomatopoeia resonates with nature, and pure expression involves "the unmediated presence of the self to its own voice" (De Man 1983, 114). Clearly such a mythic origin remains a hypothetical baseline of language evolution even for Rousseau, who was only too willing to draw valid conclusions from conjectural assumptions, and thus develop the idea of method in the social sciences. For this very reason, the myth of original symbolic and material plenitude survives within our models of social differentiation and evolution, whether conceived as a counterfactual point of departure or as "the original affluent society" (Sahlins 1972).

Whatever its status as mythic origin, however, the natural condition of protolinguistic plenitude is broken by the emergence of language proper, with its more complex semantic and syntactic functions based on the power of negation. For only through negation can the fateful transition from "natural" signals to "conventional" signs take place, differentiating sounds from the particular things and classes of objects that they "re-present." A sign can only represent a thing which it is not, but for which it stands. A self becomes a grammatical subject in relation to objects, actions, and others whom he or she is not. We need not engage the specific sequences of substantives, particles, and adjectives in Rousseau's theory to appreciate the critical power of negation in setting language and the world apart by the *social* institution of linguistic conventions. As spoken language develops and emerges, the "natural" relation between meaning and expression in the original outcry is displaced by the social relation between words and things, just as the denotatum is severed from the sign. Man is thus "alienated" from the condition of natural plenitude when transformed into a grammatical and social subject, disconnecting from the state of nature while becoming linguistically interpolated as a socially organized and mediated being.

If we shift to the Second Discourse, we see that negation serves as the precondition of civil society, of private property and thus of inequality. In the famous opening of Part 2:

> The first person who, having enclosed a plot of land, took it into his head to say *this is mine* and found people simple enough to believe him, was the true founder of civil society. What crimes, wars, murders, what miseries and horrors would the human race have been spared, had someone pulled up the stakes or filled in the ditch and cried out to his fellow men: "Do not listen to this imposter. You are lost if you forget that the fruits of the earth belong to all and the earth to no one!" (Rousseau 1987, 60)

In this mythic charter of "primitive communism," the alienation of man and land co-occurs through the speech act of physical enclosure, in which "this" plot of land is not "that," in which "mine" is not "yours," and in which the property of negation creates the value of property. From such a logically primitive starting point develops a chain reaction of alienating social forms, from pride, vanity, shame, and envy to violence, cruelty, and the exploitation of labor. Rousseau's critique of civilization, prefiguring Marx's critique of capitalism, is thus intrinsically grounded in a theory of language and its discriminating capabilities.

With writing comes a more "advanced" stage of alienation from natural discourse in Rousseau, one associated with the triumph of reason over passion, but also the "enervation" of spoken language as its emotive base is rationalized. Writing for Rousseau is thus secondary to speech, the written sign of a verbal sign, thus twice removed from pure expression, a graphic doubling of verbal articulation. Such a parasitic notion of writing as that which "feeds" off a prior spoken code valorizes the spoken over the written word, which "is nothing but a *supplement* of speech" (Derrida 1976, 295; emphasis original), fixing it with graphic exactitude while paradoxically transforming it with "an additive substitution" (270). We need not engage Rousseau's discussion of pictorial, ideographic, and phonetic scripts to appreciate the general hierarchy toward "higher" civilizations which the sequence reflects, a movement that refines language as it simultaneously muzzles the popular voice. The excess and surplus of supplementary writing, like the excessive surplus of civilized society, set the stage for a reappropriation of *la volonté générale*, a political project for *The Social Contract* that corresponds linguistically to the recuperation of an original voice. The problem for Derrida—foregrounded by De Man—is that any such return to an original source is always already supplementary, predicated on an infinite chain of displacements and substitutions (*mise en abyme*):

> Whenever Rousseau designates the moment of unity that exists at the beginning of things, when desire coincides with enjoyment, the self and the other are united in the maternal warmth of their common origin, and consciousness speaks with the voice of truth, Derrida's interpretation shows, without leaving the text, that what is thus designated as a moment of presence always has to posit another, prior moment and so implicitly loses its privileged status as a point of origin. Rousseau defines voice as the origin of written language, but his description of oral speech or of music can be shown to possess, from the start, all the elements of distance and negation that prevent written language from ever achieving a condition of unmediated presence. All attempts to trace writing back to a more original form of vocal utterance lead to the repetition of a disruptive process that alienated the written word from experience in the first place. (De Man 1983, 115)

Derrida thus assimilates original speech into the prior framework of *écriture,* of "writing" as semiosis or signification tout court, as the cause rather than the effect of unmediated presence. The birth of *écriture* as a deconstructive philosophical register that relegates speech to a secondary effect of semiotic differentiation, or of writing writ large, signals the rhetoric of blindness operative in all systems of representation. To be brief, Hume's object is to Kant's concept as Rousseau's speech is to Derrida's *écriture:* the thing-in-itself, the myth of full meaning, the primary plenitude which signified meanings "re-present," are effects of the signifying system itself, traces of figurative language.

We have followed two paths to the same destination where different forms of blindness converge. The first genealogical chain of transmission traced the blindness of misprision back to Kant's Copernican revolution, recuperating a critical reversal of concept and object within a "structural" genre of modernization theory. The second traced a chain of rhetorical displacements from writing to the "origin" of linguistic representation, effecting a critical reversal of signifier and signified within Rousseau's protolinguistic state of nature. From this philosophical topos of an absent presence, we can turn modernization theory on its head.

We seem to have traveled far from modernization theory, but we have reached its figural ground, its myth of origin: namely, "traditional society" or in another context what Jonsson (2001) has called "society degree zero." True to the genre, modernization theory posits a global shift from traditional societies through periods of colonization (when modernizing trends are put in place) into independent nation-states, where the stakes of modernization really count. Whatever their specific locations, traditional societies are precapitalist and in a Weberian sense prerational, following "conservative" peasant subsistence strategies, nonproductive logics of surplus extraction, mystifying forms of "traditional" authority, redistributive "extended" families, and nonscientific cultural worldviews, all of which hinder meritocratic mobility and "economic take-off."[21] But like the spoken ground of written language, or the "givenness" of known objects, the original "primitive" or traditional society was never there "in the first place," but was produced by the ideological engines of colonization as part and parcel of the civilizing mission—a trace or effect of modernizing colonies, not preexisting conditions. The "traditional society" of modernization theory is always already mediated by colonial modernity's production of tradition, and here lies its compound blindness: (1) traditional society is misapprehended as a precolonial condition rather than a colonial artifact (objectified by colonial exhibitions and the ratifying science of anthropology),[22] whereby the imprint of colonial culture and hegemony is largely neglected; and (2) colonialism is credited with the making of new elites and professionals by transcending tradition rather than actively producing it.

Nowhere is this logic of transcendence more clearly illustrated than in the treatment of primordial "tribal" affiliations that must be integrated into more rational nation-states. According to the standard modernization model, affective attachments to "tribe" reinforce ascribed roles and hinder the more rational discourse of democratic pluralism that allows achieved roles and equitable interest-articulation to emerge as the hallmark of postcolonial modernity. We now know that so-called "tribalism" is a consequence of colonial governance, and that it emerges when ethnicity becomes politicized as a source of political capital in the postcolonial state, and thus it cannot be said to predate the state as such.[23] And if national integration "solves" the problem of tribalism within the emergent framework of legal-rational authority, the road or pathway from mythic origin to disenchanted destination describes a secondary mythic narrative loaded with ideological baggage, rearticulating "la mission civilisatrice" within the Weberian machinery of rationalization.

This compound blindness in modernization theory, however, touches upon a critical slippage between political institutions and their associated ideologies, and here is where I would like to return to my father's text. I have already noted that the concept of traditional society developed in *The Politics of Modernization* began to break free from its mythic conventions by recasting them in functional terms. In chapter 3, "The Analysis of Tradition," traditional societies are already flexible, innovative, cosmopolitan, stratified, multiethnic, etc., and are furthermore refashioned to provide cognitive closure in rapidly changing situations. Moreover their significance begins to shift, less as a starting point for diachronic trajectories and more as rhetorical material for structuring change in recognizable terms. Modernizing ideologies, whether neotraditional or radically utopian (or as in the Tanzanian case of *ujamaa,* both) operate like political religions, and are basically mythic in structure and function. "Myth is the social equivalent of metaphor," Apter (1965, 278) writes, whether grounded in visions of traditional village harmony or in "the myth of the proletarian general strike"

(279), because it builds solidarity around moral community. The deeper implications of this insight were set into motion but did not yet emerge. Throughout the book, the mythic core of modernizing ideologies still "functions" in relation to a material system, in strategic, affective, legitimating, mobilizing, and solidaristic capacities; that is, in relation to some other bedrock reality—including the state—that in some sense "precedes" ideology even if shaped and transformed by it. If myth becomes central to modernization, it still remains hidden within the theory itself.

It is this slippage between the institutional bases of power and the symbolic foundations of authority, between the system as such and its ideological representation, that provides a dialectical opening into modernization theory's blindness, one that resurrects Kant's Copernican revolution and (following Derrida) reverses Rousseau's natural history of discourse. I am not suggesting a collapse of all political regimes into purely occult forms of mystification, since authority types, systems of political representation, class formation, and social stratification, if abstractions, are also real and variable. But the language with which we engage these abstractions belongs, in part, to the systems in which we operate, and remains—as my father later argued in a hefty book manuscript (Apter n.d.) that he never published—part of the problem. This reflexive and indeed deconstructive dimension was beginning to emerge from *The Politics of Modernization* and eventually led to phenomenological studies of political protest (Apter and Sawa 1984) and revolution (Apter and Saich 1994), and to a discourse theory of political violence (Apter 1997, 2010). But that is another story, another set of texts.

Notes

An earlier version of this paper was presented at the "Revisiting Modernization" conference held at the University of Ghana, Legon, on 30 July 2009. My thanks extend to Edmond Keller and Yao Graham for their conference comments, and to David Apter for his comments on a later draft.

1. For a remarkable study of modernization theory in both institutional and global contexts of American social science, see Gilman (2003).

2. See, e.g., Brantlinger (1986), Comaroff and Comaroff (1991, 86–125), and Stocking (1987).

3. See of course Tönnies (1957 [1887]), Durkheim (1984 [1893]), Maine (1861), and Morgan (1877).

4. Far from resenting what I incorrectly assumed was a passing form of academic domination, or, more dramatically, a developing master-slave dialectic, my father was quite grateful for the three hundred dollars Marion provided for the job—a significant sum in those days. But again, my reading is *necessarily* a misreading. As for the typeset, Levy (1952, vii) explains that "the tentative nature of this volume cannot be emphasized too strongly. It was in the effort to accent this that the decision was made to publish the material in its present format rather than in a letterpress edition."

5. My father's intellectual influences were hardly defined by Levy's mentorship, but also included the behavioralism of Heinz Eulau at Antioch College, the phenomenology of Harold Garfinkel (and the legacy of Alfred Schütz) at Princeton, a lifelong friendship with Clifford Geertz (from their Antioch days), and a formidable command of Marx and Marxist theory.

6. Gilman (2003) develops "microhistories" of Harvard's Department of Social Relations (DSR) under Parsons, the Social Science Research Council's Committee on Comparative Politics (CCP), and the Massachusetts Institute of Technology's Center for International Studies (CIS).

7. In this case Bloom's revisionary ratio of *clinamen* applies with near-perfection: "A poet swerves away from his precursor, by so reading his precursor's poem as to execute a *clinamen* in relation to it. This appears as a corrective movement in his own poem, which implies that the precursor poem went accurately up to a certain point, but then should have swerved, precisely in the direction that the new poem moves" (Bloom 1973, 14).

8. Those listed are David Aberle, Albert Cohen, Arthur Davis, Francis Sutton, and Levy himself (Levy 1952, xiv).

9. This account of Levy's exile from the Parsonian circle at Harvard comes from David Apter, personal communication, 21 August 2009.

10. The circle included Georg Simmel, Ferdinand Tönnies, Werner Somart, and Alexander von Schelting.

11. *Die Protestantische Ethik und der Geist des Kapitalismus* first appeared as two installments in the Archiv für Sozialwissenschaft und Socialpolitik, 1904 bis 1905. (20. Bd., Heft 1, S. 1–54; 21. Bd., Heft 1, S. 1–110). Parsons' translation of *Wirtschaft und Gesellschaft*, however, was highly mediated and intertextual, with the first two of its four chapters based on a prior (but freely revised) translation by A. M. Henderson, and chapters 1–3 reappearing in Weber (1978, 3–301). Parsons (1980, 42) furthermore recalls that his revision of Henderson's chapter 1 was "greatly helped by a mimeographed draft translation which had been worked out by Edward Shils and Alexander von Schelting." Such levels of implication and revision between translators could be developed in a richer discussion of influence and intertextuality, but such concerns lie beyond the scope of the present essay.

12. Witness Kant's attempt to edit out the subjective deduction in the B edition of his *First Critique*.

13. Käsler (1988, 183) distinguishes the individualizing and generalizing ideal types in terms of "historical" and "sociological ideal types," the latter emerging in Weber's last phase of work pursuing a more universal historical sociology.

14. As Brand (1979, 11n7) further notes, "Weber's interest for [*sic*] Kant can also be gauged from his notes and underlinings in his own copy of Windelband's *Geschicte der Philosophie*, of which the first edition appeared in 1889 but of which Weber possessed the fourth edition of 1907."

15. My awareness of Weber's debt to Kant traces back to a dazzling lecture by Seyla Benhabib, which she presented in the 1970s while still a graduate student at Yale, called "The Philosophical Foundations of Weber's Methodology and Theory of Value"—specifically the section on Weber's epistemological foundations and the Kantian tradition. See also Benhabib (1981).

16. A perspective developed earlier by Herder and von Humboldt and later elaborated by Ernst Cassirer. See also Lash (2009) for a remarkably similar discussion of the *social* a priori in relation to Kant, Durkheim, Weber, Simmel, Marx, and even Parsons.

17. Here we witness Bloom's revisionary ratio of *daemonization* at work, whereby "the later poet opens himself to what he believes to be a power in the parent-poem that does not belong to the parent proper, but to a range of being just beyond that precursor. He does this, in

his poem, by so stationing its relation to the parent-poem as to generalize away the uniqueness of the earlier work" (Bloom 1973, 15). For Weber, Kant's epistemology itself becomes an ideal type of a rational theology.

18. My interest in Kant's critical method as the textual genesis of modernization theory stems from my 1978 Yale College honors thesis (philosophy), co-advised by Rulon Wells and Seyla Benhabib, entitled "Is the Subjective Deduction Indispensible to Kant's *First Critique?*" Riding the wave of deconstruction during this exciting time, I answered that it was the only deduction possible, after reducing a priori synthesis, recast as synthetic unity, to self-referring functions of metaphorical substitution. Perhaps the association of Kant's critical philosophy with the metaphysics of modernity/modernization is not so far-fetched?

19. This is not the place to delve into Rousseau's own writings on language with any rigor, including comparison with his linguistic rumination in "Discourse on the Origin of Inequality," (1987 [1755]), but to foreground Derrida's deconstruction of Rousseau's apparent position.

20. On this point De Man develops a meta-critique of Derrida's blindness, in his refusal to see the deconstructive strategy already at work in Rousseau's assertion of a "figural" baseline, but this level of argument lies beyond the scope of my concerns, and in any case appears overly contrived.

21. The notion of "take-off" belongs of course to stage three of Walt Rostow's "non-Communist manifesto" (Rostow 1960), and was rejected by more Parsonian theorists. I would argue, however, that its spirit, if not its letter, pervades the modernization genre more generally. See, e.g., Geertz's application of Rostow in *Peddlers and Princes* (1963).

22. For the colonial production of culture as an anthropological object-domain see Andrew Apter (1999a, 1999b, 2002).

23. The ideology of tribalism is particularly associated with Africa, where racial colorations in the western imagination meet local idioms of ethnic purity and pollution, but it extends implicitly to all figurations of "backwardness."

References

Apter, Andrew. 1999a. "Africa, Empire, and Anthropology: A Philological Exploration of Anthropology's Heart of Darkness." *Annual Review of Anthropology* 28: 577–98.

———. 1999b. "The Subvention of Tradition: A Genealogy of the Nigerian Durbar." In *State/Culture: State-Formation After the Cultural Turn,* edited by George Steinmetz, 213–52. Ithaca, NY: Cornell University Press.

———. 2002. "On Imperial Spectacle: The Dialectics of Seeing in Colonial Nigeria." *Comparative Studies in Society and History* 44, no. 3: 564–96.

Apter, David E. 1955. *The Gold Coast in Transition.* Princeton, NJ: Princeton University Press. Revised and reissued as *Ghana in Transition,* 1962, 1972.

———. 1961. *The Political Kingdom in Uganda: A Study in Bureaucratic Nationalism.* Princeton, NJ: Princeton University Press.

———. 1965. *The Politics of Modernization.* Chicago: University of Chicago Press.

———. 1971. *Choice and the Politics of Allocation.* New Haven, CT: Yale University Press.

———, ed. 1997. *The Legitimization of Violence.* New York: New York University Press.

———. 2010. "Political Violence and Discourse Theory." In *Political and Civic Leadership: A Reference Handbook,* edited by Richard Couto, 128–35. Thousand Oaks, CA: Sage.

———. n.d. “The Mythic Factor in Developmental Ideologies.” Unpublished book manuscript.

Apter, David E., and Nagayo Sawa. 1984. *Against the State: Politics and Social Protest in Japan.* Cambridge, MA: Harvard University Press.

Apter, David E., and Tony Saich. 1994. *Revolutionary Discourse in Mao's Republic.* Cambridge, MA: Harvard University Press.

Barker, Martin. 1980. “Kant as a Problem for Weber.” *British Journal of Sociology* 31 (June): 224–45.

Benhabib, Seyla. 1981. “Rationality and Social Action: Critical Reflections on Weber's Methodological Writings.” *The Philosophical Forum* 12, no. 4: 356–74.

Bloom, Harold. 1973. *The Anxiety of Influence: A Theory of Poetry.* Oxford: Oxford University Press.

Brand, M. A. 1979. “Causality, Objectivity and Freedom: Weber, Kant and the Neo-Kantians.” *Australian and New Zealand Journal of Sociology* 15, no. 1: 6–12.

Brantlinger, Patrick. 1986. “Victorians and Africans: The Genealogy of the Myth of the Dark Continent.” In *“Race,” Writing, and Difference,* edited by Henry Louis Gates Jr., 185–222. Chicago: University of Chicago Press.

Comaroff, Jean, and John L. Comaroff. 1991. *Of Revelation and Revolution.* Vol. 1, *Christianity, Colonialism, and Consciousness in South Africa.* Chicago: University of Chicago Press.

De Man, Paul. 1983 [1971]. “The Rhetoric of Blindness: Jacques Derrida's Reading of Rousseau.” In *Blindness and Insight: Essays in the Rhetoric of Contemporary Criticism,* 102–41. London: Methuen.

Derrida, Jacques. 1976. *Of Grammatology.* Translated by Gayatri Chakravorty Spivak. Baltimore: Johns Hopkins University Press.

Durkheim, Emile. 1984 [1893]. *The Division of Labor in Society.* Translated by W. D. Halls. New York: Free Press.

Geertz, Clifford. 1963. *Peddlers and Princes: Social Change and Economic Modernization in Two Indonesian Towns.* Chicago: University of Chicago Press.

Gilman, Nils. 2003. *Mandarins of the Future: Modernization Theory in Cold War America.* Baltimore: Johns Hopkins University Press.

Jonsson, Stefan. 2001. “Society Degree Zero: Christ, Crowds, and Communism in the Art of James Ensor.” *Representations* 75 (Summer): 1–32.

Kant, Emmanuel. 1973 [1781]. *The Critique of Pure Reason.* Translated by Norman K. Smith. London: MacMillan.

———. 1976. *Prolegomena to Any Future Metaphysics.* Edited by Lewis White Beck. Translated by Paul Carus. Indianapolis: Bobbs-Merrill.

Käsler, Dirk. 1988. *Max Weber: An Introduction to His Life and Work.* Translated by Philippa Hurd. Chicago: University of Chicago Press.

Lash, Scott. 2009. “Afterword. In Praise of the *A Posteriori:* Sociology and the Empirical.” *European Journal of Social Theory* 12, no. 1: 175–87.

Levy Jr., Marion J. 1952. *The Structure of Society.* Princeton, NJ: Princeton University Press.

———. 1966. *Modernization and the Structure of Societies: A Setting for International Affairs.* Princeton, NJ: Princeton University Press.

Maine, Henry J. S. 1861. *Ancient Law.* London: John Murray.

Morgan, Henry Lewis. 1877. *Ancient Society, or Researches in the Lines of Human Progress from Savagery through Barbarism to Civilization.* London: MacMillan.

Parsons, Talcott. 1947. Introduction to *The Theory of Social and Economic Organization,* by Max Weber, 3–86. Edited by Talcott Parsons. Translated by A. M. Henderson and Talcott Parsons. New York: Free Press.

———. 1949 [1937]. *The Structure of Social Action: A Study in Social Theory with Special Reference to a Group of Recent European Writers.* Glencoe, IL: Free Press.

———. 1951. *The Social System.* Glencoe, IL: Free Press.

———. 1980. "The Circumstances of My Encounter with Max Weber." In *Sociological Experiences from Generation to Generation: Glimpses of the American Experience,* edited by Robert K. Merton and Matilda White Riley, 37–43. Norwood, NJ: Ablex.

Parsons, Talcott, and Edward A. Shils. 1962 [1951]. *Toward a General Theory of Action.* Cambridge, MA: Harvard University Press.

Rostow, Walt W. 1960. *The Stages of Economic Growth: A Non-Communist Manifesto.* Cambridge: Cambridge University Press.

Rousseau, Jean-Jacques. 1824. "Essai sur l'origine des langues." In *Oeuvres completes de J. J. Rousseau,* Vol. 2, edited by Victor-Donatien de Musset-Pathay, 415–95. Paris: P. Dupont.

———. "Discourse on the Origin of Inequality." 1987 [1755]. In *Jean-Jacques Rousseau: The Basic Political Writings,* edited and translated by Donald A. Cress, 25–110. Indianapolis: Hackett.

Sahlins, Marshall D. 1972. *Stone Age Economics.* Chicago: Aldine.

Stocking, George. 1987. *Victorian Anthropology.* New York: Free Press.

Tönnies, Ferdinand. 1957 [1887]. *Community and Society (Gemeinschaft und Gesellschaft).* Translated by Charles P. Loomis. East Lansing: Michigan State University Press.

von Schelting, Alexander. 1934. *Max Weber's Wissenschaftslehre.* Tübingen: J. C. B. Mohr.

Weber, Max. 1949 [1904]. "'Objectivity' in Social Science and Social Policy." In *The Methodology of the Social Sciences,* edited and translated by Edward A. Shils and Henry A. Finch, 49–112. New York: Free Press.

———. 1958. "Politics as a Vocation." In *From Max Weber: Essays in Sociology,* edited and translated by C. Wright Mills and H. H. Gerth, 77–128. New York: Oxford University Press.

———. 1978. *Economy and Society: An Outline of Interpretive Sociology.* Vol. 1. Edited by Guenther Roth and Claus Wittich. Berkeley: University of California Press.

PART TWO

Media, Modernity, and Modernization

3 Film as Instrument of Modernization and Social Change in Africa

The Long View

Rosaleen Smyth

Film, Media, and Modernization

In this chapter I will ground the theme of modernization in sub-Saharan Africa in its authentic historical context by demonstrating its colonial roots. The central focus will be the efforts made to use film as an instrument of modernization and development communication. In doing so I will turn the current academic orthodoxy on its head. Development communication did not have "its origins in post-war international aid programs," which were in turn "derived from theories of development and social change that identified the main problems of the post-war world in terms of a lack of development or progress equivalent to Western countries," as stated in a 2001 report to the Rockefeller Foundation (Waisbord 2001). On the contrary, starting in the 1920s ideas about using mass media as a means of changing mindsets from "traditional" to "modern" and encouraging the adoption of new methods of agriculture and healthcare, among other techniques, were being explored and experimented with in Britain's African colonies. This was long before the hatching of modernization and development communication theories in American universities and research institutes were in the heat of postwar reconstruction and enshrined in Daniel Lerner's *The Passing of Traditional Society* (1958), Wilbur Schramm's *Mass Media and National Development* (1964), and David McLelland's *The Achieving Society* (1961). These works were published to great acclaim at the height of the Cold War. And, what is more, it was not just the British colonial administration acting in isolation; even then it was acting in concert with international entities including the aforesaid Rockefeller Foundation.

As early as the 1920s the Colonial State was being influenced by internationally organized modernizing missionaries and American philanthropy. New ideas about imperial trusteeship were floated by the League of Nations, while left-leaning intellectuals in Britain began to consider how the new mass media could be used to help Africans adapt to the new demands of western technological society, and the dislocation taking place in "traditional" societies. A central concern for the

Colonial Office was how the new technologies could be used as a means of socializing Africans into the British Empire and later the Commonwealth. The modernizing media not only included the new media of film and broadcasting, but print-based media, including books, magazines, and government-owned newspapers.

I will link this resetting of the history of development communication, with its focus on the instructional film in its colonial setting, with the other great meta-narrative of the colonial period: the birth of African nationalism. Here it is crucial to establish that the embryonic mass communication efforts were not targeted at the rising intelligentsia but primarily at the vast numbers of illiterate Africans in the villages where this form of political organization was endorsed by the colonial masters with a system of indirect rule. In this system, the chiefs were absorbed like middlemen in a feudal imperial hierarchy, subordinate to colonial administrators, over whom sat the British monarch. While this imperial edifice can be likened to a benevolent autocracy, there was already a restless intelligentsia in 1930s Africa who were absorbing a different political credo of liberal democracy which they saw and many studied firsthand in Britain and the United States. These were the mobile personalities, the inner directed, the early adopters of later postcolonial modernizing theory who founded a critical independent press in West Africa. In the turbulent post–World War II era, they bypassed the traditional chiefs and seized the political kingdom. Kwame Nkrumah started the snowball rolling when the Gold Coast achieved independence as Ghana in 1957.

The Origins of the Development Film in British Africa

The first development films in Britain's African colonies were made by health officials in Kenya and Nigeria, who were confronted with local health problems and seized on the new media of film to get across what they saw as vital health messages to people who were illiterate. In 1926, Dr. A. R. Paterson of the Kenya Department of Medical and Sanitary Service made a 16 mm amateur film to introduce and record a campaign against hookworm on the Kenya coast. In 1926 William Sellers, a health official with the Nigerian government, made a film to combat the outbreak of plague in Lagos and in 1931 introduced a specially designed mobile cinema van. After receiving a grant from the Colonial Development Fund in 1932 he went on to produce fifteen health films on such topics as infant welfare work in Lagos, antimalaria fieldwork, school sanitation, and village improvements. By the mid-1930s he had developed a health propaganda unit within the Nigerian Health Services Department which combined film production, mobile film shows, exhibits, school services, and field days (Sellers 1953).

Meanwhile, in London, development films were on the radar of the Colonial Office. The Advisory Committee on Native Education in Tropical Africa, established in 1923, and the Colonial Films Committee, established in 1929, both showed an interest in the potential of film as an instrument of adult education in the colonies. In 1929, the Advisory Committee sent Julian Huxley, a noted biologist, Fabian Socialist, and member of the London Films Committee, to East Africa to test African reactions to instructional films. In his 1930 report to the Colonial Office, Huxley was enthusiastic about the potential of film in schools and for adult education: "For the latter purpose they will in the present state of tropical Africa be much the most powerful weapon of propaganda which we have at command."[1] Also in 1929, the British Institute of Adult Education and the Association of Scientific Workers set up the Commission on Educational and Cultural Films in order to undertake the first thorough investigation of the film in education, which resulted in the highly influential report *The Film in National Life* (1932), published with the assistance of the Carnegie United Kingdom Trust.

Significantly, American philanthropy has played a seminal role from the start of development communication in Africa. The *Film in National Life* report recommended that a national film institute be established to encourage the development and use of the cinema as a means of entertainment and instruction in both Britain and the empire. The result was the British Film Institute (BFI), founded in 1933. In 1934 the BFI set up a number of advisory panels including the Dominions, India and Colonies Panel, on which the Colonial Office was represented (Dupin 2006). The Panel appointed a subcommittee to investigate the question of providing instructional films for eastern Africa, and Paterson was invited to submit a plan for an experiment which failed to secure financial support.[2]

Members of the emerging international community with an interest in the impact of western capitalism on traditional African society, the International Missionary Council (IMC), and the Carnegie Corporation, kickstarted the first major attempt to use film as an instrument of social change in British Africa. In 1932, J. Merle Davis, director of the Department of Social and Industrial Research of the IMC (later the World Council of Churches), had gone to the Northern Rhodesian Copperbelt to lead an inquiry into the effect of industrialization on African society. The Carnegie Corporation financed the investigation and the results were published in *Modern Industry and the African* (1933). Merle Davis and his team found that the Copperbelt mines had profoundly altered the preindustrial society of Central Africa. He recommended the use of the cinema to help the illiterate African adjust to the coming of western capitalist society, with its alien social and economic standards, and drew up a plan for a film experiment on behalf of the IMC. The experiment would study the use of cinema as an instrument for "educational and cultural adjustment."[3]

The IMC's interest coincided with a plan being put forward by Major L. A. Notcutt and G. C. Latham, which they called the Bantu Educational Kinema [*sic*] Experiment (BEKE). Both men had had African experience: Notcutt was an engineer who, inspired by reading Julian Huxley's *Africa View* (1931), had begun to experiment in making home movies with African actors while he was managing a group of sisal plantations in eastern Africa. Latham had earlier been director of native education in Northern Rhodesia (present-day Zambia).

The BEKE, one of the earliest Western technical aid projects in Africa, was conducted in East and Central Africa between March 1935 and May 1937 under the auspices of the IMC and organized in London under the general direction of Merle Davis. Advice was given by an advisory council representing missionary, educational, mining, and Colonial Office opinion, with Lord Lugard serving as chairman. The BEKE won the endorsement of the IMC, and the Carnegie Corporation came forward to be the principal financial backer. Other financial sponsors were the Roan Antelope, Rhokana, and Mufulira copper mining companies, the Empire Cotton Growing Corporation, and the academically oriented International Institute of African Languages and Culture (now the International African Institute), which itself had been established in 1926 with a grant from the Rockefeller Foundation (Notcutt and Latham 1937, 25). In 1936, additional funds were acquired from the Colonial Development Fund and from the governments of Kenya, Uganda, and Tanganyika, with the proviso that the latter part of the experiment should be devoted to the production and distribution of agricultural instructional films. This was a very modern model of a development project funding mix.

The production side of the experiment started at Vugiri in the Usambara Mountains in Tanganyika (present-day Tanzania), though later films were sometimes made outside the Vugiri studio. Notcutt, the producer, had a staff of five Englishmen and a number of African assistants. The BEKE organizers were emphatic about the "Africanness" of their films. Merle Davis stressed that the BEKE "had not gone into Africa with a predetermined line of films that people in London have decided are 'good for the African.'" Rather they would be guided by African advice and reactions on the spot. African advice was solicited during filming on matters of content and effectiveness, and Africans were trained in all aspects of production and exhibition (Davis 1936, 380–81).

The films, processed locally, were 16 mm and silent, but were shown with gramophone records, which meant that recorded sound could be provided in the languages of many of the areas visited. Where an area's language was not on disk, a narrator was used. The BEKE produced thirty-five films ranging from one to seven reels, and amongst them were nineteen on agriculture and six on health. Latham drove nine thousand miles showing films from the back of a lorry to about eighty thousand people in most venues during ninety-five performances in Tanganyika, Kenya, Northern Rhodesia, Nyasaland, and Uganda (Notcutt and Latham 1937, 98). Subsequent films were influenced by feedback solicited from these audiences. Some films were strictly instructional, such as *Hides* (1935), which demonstrated the correct methods of tanning, and *Tea* (1935), which explained how tea is grown and prepared. Many had story formats, and serve as early examples of the contemporary education-entertainment film. *The Chief* (1935) dramatized the conflict between the old and the new in the village: the protagonists were the sick chief, the witch doctor, and the medical doctor. *Post Office Savings Bank* (1935) was one of the earliest uses of the Mr. Wise and Mr. Foolish theme. Mr. Foolish buries his money in the ground and it gets stolen. Mr. Wise puts his money in the bank. The BEKE's founders had hoped that the experiment would lead to the establishment of a permanent unit with the financial backing of the East and Central African governments. But the only positive response came from Northern Rhodesia, and so the experiment went no further.[4]

The Colonial Office also entertained the idea of a broadcasting equivalent of the BEKE to test the potential of broadcasting in development communication. The BBC launched the Empire Service in 1932 as a means of ensuring that the British voice was heard in the international war of words, and as a means of strengthening imperial ties. It was also the vision of its founder, John Reith, that broadcasting should play an integral role in government administration, on par with defense and social services.[5] With the BBC's encouragement, a committee established by the Colonial Office wrote the Plymouth report (1937), which described colonial broadcasting as an "instrument of advanced administration" to be used particularly "for the enlightenment and education of the more backward sections of the population and for their instruction in public health, agriculture, etc" (Plymouth 1937, 2). The Plymouth report urged colonial governments to help finance experiments concerning the educational potential of broadcasting in adult education comparable to that being conducted by the BEKE. Plans were afoot for such an experiment in the Kiambu Native Reserve near Nairobi in 1936, but when the Carnegie Corporation was only willing to supply half the funds, the Kenyan government lost interest, and remained hesitant because "Mr. Kenyatta would certainly want to have his turn at the microphone."[6] The first steps toward local broadcasting for Africans were taken by colonial Ghana, which had a rediffusion service relaying the Empire Service over telephone wires since 1935;[7] gradually, local programs were added: a local news service, a children's hour, musical programs, and vernacular news.

Not only did the IMC inspire the BEKE but it also played a major role in the promotion of modernizing literature in Africa. It was a literature of the sort designed in postcolonial terms, aimed at creating more modern mindsets. This project started in 1929 when Joseph Oldham, the council's chairman, appointed Margaret Wrong to become secretary of a new subcommittee known as the International Committee on Christian Literature (ICCLA), a position she held until her death in 1948. The ICCLA was financed by grants from American, British, and European missionary societies, religious publishing houses, and some bookshops in Africa. Organizations including the Phelps-Stokes Foundation and the Carnegie Corporation also contributed substantially. The ICCLA acted as a clearinghouse for information on literature projects and publications for different parts of Africa; this was done chiefly through *Books for Africa,* a quarterly bulletin edited by Margaret Wrong which first appeared in 1931. In 1932, she started a simple periodical for village people and school children called *Listen,* which sold for one penny. It was subsidized by an American mission organization and contained simple material on health, African history, and world events; this periodical found its way into schools in the British colonies throughout Africa. By 1939 Wrong had made four major tours of sub-Saharan Africa, two funded by the Carnegie Corporation, in which she consulted not only with colonial officials and missionaries but African pastors, teachers, and journalists, as well as African elites in London, in order to identify relevant literature needs. Her reports emphasized the need for literature in both English and indigenous languages and that African authorship should be encouraged. These principles were exemplified with the establishment in 1937 of the African Literature Committee on the Copperbelt in colonial Zambia (Smyth 1983, 79–86; Compton Brouwer 2002).

Mass Education, Colonial Development, and World War II

We have seen that in the 1930s there was indeed a national as well as international move toward using media as an aid in development communication. It was linked to a concern about the massive disruption taking place in African societies as a result of the colonial takeover and the impact of western capitalism. But a sense of urgency there was not. In the late 1930s, Britain's colonial record was criticized in a number of reports using new social research techniques, foremost of which was Lord Hailey's *African Survey* (1938), funded by the Carnegie Corporation. The survey identified a wide variety of social needs, but with the coming of the war, suddenly the mighty British Empire was on its knees. Its psychological and physical fragility was symbolized by the fall of Singapore and the ideology of imperialism under attack, not only from Nazi Germany but also by the United States, which was not going to be coerced into war to fight for the survival of the British Empire. Suddenly the mass media became vital to secure the loyalty of the colonies, mobilize their support for the British war effort, and convince them that it was only through their membership in the British Empire that they could achieve their moral and material ambitions. The new Ministry of Information, in liaison with the Colonial Office, took charge of war propaganda, with information officers being appointed in the colonies to oversee the dissemination of war propaganda: film, radio, and the press were all utilized to sell the message "This War is Your War Too." The passing of the Colonial Development and Welfare Act in 1940 was cited as evidence that the state was now "a constructive agency" responsible not only for law and order but for the welfare of its citizens.[8] The metropolitan prototype for this social engineering was the groundbreaking Beveridge report (1942), which introduced the welfare state to Britain.

For the first time in its history Britain had to use the media to influence African public opinion and solicit support. African soldiers were needed for the defense forces, and products such as rubber, palm oil, and ground nuts were required particularly when supplies were cut off by the Axis forces. There were explanations of war events, denunciations of the Axis powers, reminders of the dangers that threatened the colonies, appeals for donations to the war effort, and explanations of the shortages of essential commodities. News of the war reached even the remotest villages. Many Africans heard their first radio broadcast or saw their first film as a result of the communications infrastructure set up to transmit war propaganda. The literate could read about the war in government-owned and commercial newspapers, in government leaflets and posters; recruiting vans arrived in villages often showing films to draw the crowds; district officers gave lectures on the war; radio programs explaining the war were broadcast in some colonies; Africans were recruited in the thousands and went off to have their worldview considerably enlarged on the battlefield; and while off duty the army ran adult education programs that included English and literacy classes which, according to the Northern Rhodesia Regiment and East Africa Command, created an insatiable demand for reading material. Sociologist W. C. Little (1947) referred to the army as an "extra-mural university."

The Birth of the Colonial Film Unit (CFU)

The new Ministry of Information established the Colonial Film Unit (CFU) under the direction of William Sellers, the pioneering producer of health films in Nigeria; the Colonial Office had an advisory role. Mobile cinema vans showed films like *This Is an A.R.P. Warden* (1941), *This Is a Barrage Balloon* (1941), *Mr. English at Home* (1940), and *Nurse Ademola* (1943), as did static cinemas in some villages. Sometimes portable projectors and screens were carried on riverboats, trains, or as head loads. In 1941 the CFU introduced what it regarded as its most important war propaganda effort, which included the monthly 16 mm newsreel known as *The British Empire at War,* which ran to twenty-five editions. *Katsina Tank* (1943) and *Soldier Comforts from Uganda* (1942) showed how gifts from the colonies were being used in Britain. *Food from Oil Nuts* (1944) was made to demonstrate to Africans the importance of their raw produce in the manufacture of margarine. *We Want Rubber* (1943) urged Africans to collect wild rubber after the fall of Malaya cut off supplies. In 1942 the Colonial Office included some development films with the aim of "raising the primitive African to a higher standard of culture" (Anon. 1943, 1). To provide footage from Africa, the CFU resorted to using some prewar films as well as providing cameras and film to colonial information officers to make their own films with some guidance from London under the Raw Stock Scheme. One product of the scheme was the Kenya Information Services film *Jonathan Builds a Dam,* later re-edited and retitled *A Kenya Village Builds a*

Dam (1944), in which Jonathan, after obtaining the blessing of the chief and the district commissioner, inspires his village to cooperate to build a dam in order to provide a year-round supply of water, even during the dry season.

While British government propagandists recognized the potential of radio for conveying accurate war news and countering wild rumor, the infrastructure in Africa was extremely limited. Only in West Africa did the BBC provide special programs for Africans, such as "Calling West Africa," hosted by Henry Swanzy. The radio distribution service in Nigeria was very popular, such that in Ibadan alone, there were "over 700 privately hired loudspeakers" and seven "public" street loudspeakers (Clarke 1984). In Nairobi and Lusaka, radio stations transmitted war news, talks, and entertainment programs in English and selected local languages that could sometimes be heard in neighboring countries. Africans listened in on community sets at district headquarters, at mission stations, at listening points in towns, and on farms (Smyth 1983, 216–28). By 1943 there were sixty-five sets at rural stations in Kenya. Public address equipment was also used in a number of towns in the region (Gadsden 1986, 408).

War propaganda undoubtedly met with some success in creating a sense of affiliation with the war effort among Africans. But the war inevitably broadened the horizons and raised expectations not only for returning African soldiers but even among humble villagers and the lumpenproletariat of the towns. In newspapers across the continent and in burgeoning political associations Africans were abuzz with talk about "the New World Order" and the applicability of the Atlantic Charter to Africa. African elites now had a potent political vocabulary which they could use to challenge the legitimacy of the British Empire after the war, leading them to demand self-determination.

Mass Education in African Society

As the fires of African nationalism were being kindled after the war, the Colonial Office was working to a slower time-clock. They turned their attention to mass education programs funded by the Colonial Development and Welfare Act of 1940 and subsequent acts that were guided by the report *Mass Education in African Society* (Colonial Office 1944). The report was the blueprint for state-centered government information services established in Britain's African colonies after the war. The success of the war propaganda initiative had demonstrated the power of the mass media in a targeted, intensive adult education program. The report urged community cooperation in a planned drive for social change in a rapidly changing world, the coordination of welfare plans and mass education, and sociological mapping before programs were devised. A crucial aspect was that the community should be active participants and, if possible, the initiators of improvement schemes.

The recommended mass communication techniques included the press, posters, pamphlets, literacy campaigns, art, music, dancing, and drama, "though the most effective are the cinema and broadcasting," which had demonstrated their efficacy in "propaganda and war information services" and had the potential to bring "a striking new contribution to mass education" (Colonial Office 1944, 29). The report declared that "films would not only be used in areas of health, agriculture, community development, and local government but to promote ideas of citizenship." The acceleration of social and economic change that was happening in Africa (and elsewhere) demanded education for citizenship which would enable people to see themselves as part of larger communities that went beyond "narrow sectionalism." The report went on to recommend films about local government and the production of news films that reported on world, regional, and local interest stories in order to broaden viewer horizons in general and develop a "national" outlook among people of a territory (Colonial Office 1944, 40–42).

Reflected in the report is John Grierson's vision of a government using film as an instrument of government administration to provide public information and education "to bridge the gap between the citizen and the world community." In 1941, Grierson had argued that cinema should be a "deliberate social instrument . . . outside the barricades of social construction" (Grierson 1941, 93).

The Social Message Films of Government Film Units in British Colonial Africa

After the war the fundamental education film went global. International relations were dominated by the Cold War; the UN had been established as the "world's conscience," with UNESCO signaling that it would be the center point and spearhead for an international movement that included fundamental education for the disadvantaged regions of the world. Julian Huxley was appointed the first director general, and Grierson, the founding father of the British documentary movement, became UNESCO's first director of mass communications and public information in 1947. It was also crisis time for the British Empire; in 1948, with the situation heating up on the Gold Coast, a new sense of urgency was injected into postwar developmentalism as the ultimate goal came to be to ensure that as African countries became independent, they remained within the British Commonwealth.

In January 1948 the British Film Institute sponsored an agenda-setting conference called "The Film in Colonial Development." Arthur Creech Jones, the secretary of state for colonies, injected a sense of Cold War urgency as he spoke of the importance for Britain and its international reputation and for Western Europe in general that demonstrable economic and social development should take place in the colonies, and that they should be schooled in the ideals of western civilization and the practice of democratic government. Grierson, then at UNESCO, spoke of the importance of fundamental education in raising living standards in less developed countries, but he stressed that while fundamental education was a world problem, internationalism begins at home. Africa represented an arena for Britain to demonstrate its "modern citizenship," which would benefit not only its economy but also "national morale" through its contribution to technological progress in the colonies (Grierson 1948). A couple of months later Grierson became the controller of the Films Division at the successor to the Ministry of Information, the Central Office of Information (COI), and remained in the post until 1950. The Colonial Film Unit continued to be under the dual control of the COI and the Colonial Office until 1950, when sole responsibility was transferred to the Colonial Office. As Grierson told the Select Committee on Estimates in 1950, "We did not feel familiar enough here in London to be specialists in the fundamental education of peoples. . . . We were horrified at our distance from the problem" (87).

The CFU was reorganized as a development film organization after the war, with crews operating in East and West Africa under the directorship of European filmmakers and the overall leadership of Sellers. In Central Africa, there was a different system of production because white settlers already had legislative control in Southern Rhodesia and campaigned for a federation of Northern Rhodesia, Southern Rhodesia, and Nyasaland to perpetuate the white ascendancy. As a result, the Central African Council, which was a precursor to the Federation established in 1953, set up the Central African Film Unit in 1948 under the leadership of Alan Izod, who had previously been with the Films Division of the Central Office of Information with oversight of the CFU, and who, like Grierson, had been a speaker at the 1948 conference. Development films produced for Africans in Central Africa were paid for out of Colonial Development and Welfare funds until 1956.

The organizations making the films included the Colonial Film Unit's teams in Nigeria and the Gold Coast and their successors beginning in 1950, the Nigerian Film Unit and the Gold Coast Film Unit; the one-year East African foray of Colonial Film Unit teams into Kenya, Uganda, and Tanganyika and the large number of instructional films made by the Central African Film Unit were mostly produced between 1948 and 1953. These social-issue or message films funded under the Colonial Development and Welfare Act contributed to the history of modernization and development communication in Africa in the late colonial period and also made a contribution via UNESCO, as we shall see, to the development of the fundamental education film as a communication strategy to boost development in underdeveloped regions.

Colonial Film Unit in West Africa

The CFU's first health film made in Nigeria was the Sellers production *Fight Tuberculosis in the Home* (1946), which demonstrates the diagnosis and treatment of the disease as well as the precautions that need to be taken against it, using as an example the crowded living conditions and lack of hygiene in the home of a builder and his family in an urban compound.

In *Weaving in Togoland* (1946), students from Achimota College, in cooperation with the chief, demonstrate more advanced methods of weaving to increase productivity and quality using a wider, more modern loom, and persuade the villagers to adopt the new methods. Spinning and weaving become a full-time industry, and according to the commentary more cotton is grown and there is more work for dyers. Material prosperity follows. Before the introduction of new looms, there were less than one hundred children at the village school, but as the commentary informs us there are now two hundred; in addition, there are more teachers, bigger buildings, and a new infant school. Diet is improved as more varieties of food become available at the local market and better-quality stone houses are built. *Better Pottery* (1948) has a similar theme: factory methods substantially increase the number of pots that can be produced, thus leading to greater prosperity. *Good Business* (1947) promotes the work of the cooperative societies of West Africa, following the stages through which Lawani's cocoa harvest passes from picking to marketing and export.

Village Development (1948) is set in the Udi Division of eastern Nigeria where the district officer, E. R. Chadwick, had introduced a number of social services: a leper colony, roads and bridges, successful campaigns in mass literacy, cooperative shops, dispensaries and maternity homes, and finally water supplies, which were planned and carried out by various villages. *Village Development* was the inspiration for the Crown Film Unit's dramatized documentary, *Daybreak in Udi* (1949), and had several sequels highlighting what had been done in other areas, including *Awgu* (1949), *Ahoada* (1950), *Okigwi* (1951), and *Awka* (1951).

Some progress was made in training African technicians in West Africa. Since 1943, Fela Sowande had been the CFU's musical director, and in 1946, Oxford-educated Joseph Odunton joined the Gold Coast Cinema Branch to assist in filmmaking; the branch had an African camera assistant. In 1949, a film training school conducted in Accra was attended by seven trainees from the Gold Coast and Nigeria. The training scheme was successful to the extent that the Gold Coast Film Unit was organized on a professional basis in 1949 immediately following the course. A Nigerian film unit followed a year later. However, significantly, Europeans remained at the helm of both units in the run-up to independence (Smyth 2011).

Smallpox (1950), the first major production of the new Nigerian Film Unit, utilized an education-entertainment format to get the vaccination message across. In this film, "Foolish Alabi," who refuses to get vaccinated in his own village, visits his friend Tijani in another village where smallpox is rampant and catches the disease. Upon his return he tells the doctor in his own village about the outbreak and after treatment recovers in the hospital. Tijani hides when a vaccination team is sent in, and goes blind. Odunton criticized the simplistic Mr. Wise and Mr. Foolish format of this film, among others, writing that films "must speak not only through the local idiom and traditions, but also reflect the social and cultural aspirations of their audience. Patronising commentaries which do not credit the illiterate African with at least some degree of intelligence or shrewd discernment are not likely to leave any mark" (Odunton 1950, 29–32). When *Smallpox* was screened at the beginning of the plenary session of the UNESCO Seminar on Visual Aids in Fundamental Education, held in Messina, Sicily, in 1953, it was pronounced "a 'classic' in the field of fundamental education for its high emotional value" (UNESCO 1955, 66–67).

Odunton commended the Gold Coast Film Unit (GFCU) production *Amenu's Child* because in its structure attempted to overcome the problem of the patronizing commentaries and simplistic plots of many CFU films. *Amenu's Child* was written and produced by the GFCU director, Sean Graham, a Grierson disciple who aimed to make dramatically and technically more sophisticated social message films and get away from "Mr-Clever-Who-Banks-His Savings and the like" (Dickson 1950, 146). *Amenu's Child* was made for the Medical Department's campaign to reduce infant mortality and formed the centerpiece of a mass education campaign to train village leaders in child welfare. The film uses the traditional Ghanaian idiom of oral storytelling. Before the titles a drummer beats two talking drums as the narrator says, "Listen and gather round."

The most ambitious of all the post-CFU films was the Gold Coast Film Unit's *The Boy Kumasenu* (1952), with "documentary boy" Basil Wright as the assistant producer; it was the first full-length feature film to be made by a government film unit in West Africa. A boy fisherman abandons his village for the excitement of Accra and in economic desperation embarks on a life of petty crime. He is rescued from delinquency by an African medical doctor who arranges for Kumasenu to be apprenticed to a driver of motorboats, and is ultimately reunited with his family. As a fisherman using a motorboat—a heavy piece of symbolism—the character combines the old world and the new. While the film has an amateur African cast, the score by Elizabeth Lutyens and the posh Received Pronunciation (RP) of the British narrator not only enhance the colonial feel of the film but cause it to resemble the British documentaries that have cultivated middle-class voice-overs and scripts when talking about the English working class. The later dramatic social message films, which include *Progress in Kojokrom* (1953), an explanation of what the rates paid to the new local councils were used for, and *Mr. Mensah Builds a House* (1955), a propaganda film for a new rural building loan scheme, were praised by Jean Rouch for being "models of their genre" (2003, 66). *Mr. Mensah Builds a House* is particularly innovative for replacing the narrator with dialogue, and the GFCU's social message docudramas overall are notable for trying to add more complexity and realism into the plots of social message films and for breaking away from the simplistic techniques pioneered by Sellers and more characteristic of the work produced by the CFU.

Colonial Film Unit in East Africa

In East Africa, the Colonial Film Unit had a very short career. It was really only fully operational for a year when it was financed from the Colonial Development and Welfare Fund with the idea that the East African governments would then take over financial responsibility—which, as in the case of the BEKE, they declined to do.

The operation started in 1949 with a 35 mm unit stationed in Nairobi and three film officers making 16 mm films attached to the Public Relations Offices in colonial Uganda, Kenya, Tanganyika, and later Zanzibar. The CFU did some research on the types of films that would be required and were informed that East African audiences were less "advanced" than those in West Africa. As Norman Spurr reported, "In East Africa in general, and Tanganyika in particular, the sophistication and general knowledge of the rural peasant is low" (Spurr 1952b, 42). This was also advanced as the reason why a training school for African technicians along the lines of that conducted in West Africa should not be conducted. The dominant position of the white settler community in East Africa probably had not a little to do with the lack of support for this scheme. When Leonard Doob visited East Africa on a social science research expedition funded by the Carnegie Corporation in 1952, reporting on the information services that had been set up since World War II by the British in Central Africa, he noted that while the official belief was that Uganda would go the way of the Gold Coast, white settlers in Uganda and Kenya, like those in the Rhodesias (colonial Zambia and Zimbabwe), felt "that the white man must retain some form of domination" (Doob 1953, 8).

Films made by Norman Spurr in Uganda included *A Challenge to Ignorance* (1950), *Dysentery* (1950), *Murram Block-Making* (1950), and *Why Not You* (1950). In *A Challenge to Ignorance* (1950), classified by UNESCO as "Social Science as Education,"[9] a demonstration team originally recruited from Mangalo arrives in the Public Relations and Social Welfare Department bus. They set up a tent stage and perform a musical selection to attract a crowd, then perform a sketch using an exaggerated clown character, Kapere, to demonstrate better methods of cotton growing and a comedy skit to show the right and wrong way to ride a bicycle.

Both *Murram Block-Making* and its sequel, *Why Not You?*, attempt to diffuse an innovative idea by demonstrating how to build a hut with murram blocks made from rusty-red, iron-oxide rich laterite soil specific to West Africa. The film opens with a view of a dilapidated hut. A more durable solution is then demonstrated. By mixing murram, dung, and water it is shown that a man can produce a building block equivalent in size to six ordinary bricks and can produce twenty-five murram blocks by working five hours a day. Several men join forces to produce a completed house. *Why Not You?* shows how a family unit can organize to construct such a house. Spurr designed his films to illustrate a lecture; he regarded them as visual aids and urged that for the showing of fundamental education films the commentator should be an expert on the subject, trained in methods of extension work and on hand to see the follow-up (Spurr 1952a). *Cattle Thieves* (1950), directed and narrated by Rollo Gamble, is bursting with social realism as it shows how diligent Anatoly, an inspector in the Tanganyika police force, tracks down some Maasai cattle thieves. It has a murder, as well as scenes of Maasai dances, a market, a cattle auction, and jovial drinking at a beer hall. And *Marengo* (1950) demonstrates the benefits for the people of the Chagga chieftainship of Marangu near Mt. Kilimanjaro (in present-day Tanzania) when they apply themselves to the production and export of coffee through a cooperative marketing association "under the wise guidance of their chief."

In 1950, just over a year after the CFU's optimistic beginnings, and with East Africa's governments unconvinced of the viability of its operations, the decision was made to withdraw the production units from the region. After 1950 in Uganda, Kenya, and Tanganyika, development films and newsreels were made by the respective information and public relations departments. This aborted experiment did nonetheless make a significant contribution to instructional film history.

In 1953 Norman Spurr and Sellers were two of the five experts invited to speak at the UNESCO Seminar in Messina, which addressed the urgent need for information on visual materials suitable for fundamental education "designed to bring new ideas, new knowledge and new and improved skills to the populations of economically underdeveloped areas, and to affect the whole community, particularly the adult population."[10] UNESCO subsequently launched a catalogue of visual aids in fundamental education featuring many of the films funded under the Colonial Development and Welfare Act, which included a film library and traveling exhibition of the visual aids. Spurr himself joined the UNESCO staff as a visual aids expert. His murram block films were favorably reviewed for their clarity when they were screened at the Messina seminar and were later included along with *Cattle Thieves, Smallpox, Daybreak in Udi,* and the Central African Film Unit's *Wives of Nendi* and *The Two Farmers* in the UNESCO traveling library.[11]

The Central African Film Unit

The Central African Film Unit (CAFU) made instructional films in the Central African territories of Northern Rhodesia, Southern Rhodesia, and Nyasaland (present-day Malawi) with Colonial Development and Welfare funding between 1948 and 1956. As this was the time of the push toward and beginning of the white settler–

dominated Federation of Rhodesia and Nyasaland, Africans were not given the same opportunities on the film production side as they were by the Colonial Film Unit in West Africa.

By 1953 the CAFU had produced seventy-one instructional films for Africans.[12] All were in color, which often contributed a vivid sense of realism. The films provide a good overview of key aspects of the postwar mass education/community development programs and campaigns promoted by the Colonial Office but are heavily circumscribed by the subservient position of Africans in a white supremacist society. In *Nyono Gets a Letter* (1950), Nyono's wife Agnes is about to give birth to her first child at a time when Nyono has to leave the village and go to work on road construction for the Northern Rhodesian Public Works Department. A mass literacy instructor arrives in the village and Agnes learns to read *Mutende* (the government newspaper for Africans) to the other patients and to write to her worried husband to announce the birth of their child. *Husbands and Wives* (1950) describes a community development project in the area school at Katete in Northern Rhodesia. At this residential school, among others, students were trained in carpentry and road building and were supervised in mass literacy courses; the wives had classes in beadwork, knitting, and home craft. The very successful *Lusaka Calling* (1949) is a promotional film for the "Saucepan Special," a radio designed to enable the Africans of Northern Rhodesia, Southern Rhodesia, and Nyasaland to listen to Lusaka's Central African Broadcasting Station (CABS), the first radio station in Africa that was specifically addressed to Africans (Fraenkel 1959). Izod reported to UNESCO in 1952 on the success of *Lusaka Calling* in stimulating sales of the Saucepan Special (Izod 1952, 55) while Jean Rouch, in a 1960 report on the cinema in Africa, noted that "from the purely cinematographic point of view," many of the films of the Colonial and Central African Film Units were "extremely disappointing, but the educational value has sometimes been considerable," using *Lusaka Calling* as an example (Rouch 1962, 18).

The CABS staff (both European and African) put together a series of experimental programs designed to encourage African music and drama, as well as to engage in mass education and the promotion of government policy. In 1950, inspired by the greatly enlarged radio audiences, the Northern Rhodesian Information Department used all the media at its disposal, which included newspapers, posters, pamphlets, film, and broadcasting, to launch a five-year mass education campaign. The campaign concentrated on six areas that included improved hygiene, education for girls, and better agriculture.

Another type of CAFU film was the "profile film," in the Africans in Action series. It included real-life success stories about individual Africans—such as farmers, a welfare officer, a midwife, and a home demonstrator—who all managed to bridge "the gap between the commercial and industrial world and the primitive tribal life" (Anon. 1947). In the fifth installment of the series, *Herbert Gondwe—Welfare Officer* (1952), Gondwe, who operates in the Dowa district of Nyasaland, is shown riding around on a motorcycle organizing the building of a welfare hall, the repair of a bridge, the acquisition of a film projector, and the editing of a district newspaper.

By far the largest number of CAFU films were on agriculture; other subjects included health and hygiene, the value of self-help and hard work, welfare services, law and order, the lesson that crime does not pay, and road safety. *The Story of Petale*, a forty-five-minute mini-feature, like the short version of the Gold Coast Film Unit's *The Boy Kumasenu*, is about an adolescent schoolboy being caught up in the vices of town life. Petale's life in the Copperbelt town of Chingola is dominated by beer halls, loose women, and petty theft until the European welfare officer and his African staff manage to divert his energies to sporting activities.

One film that prioritizes the participatory approach is *The Wives of Nendi* (1949), which chronicles the work of Mai Mangwende, wife of Chief Mangwende, in forming women's clubs throughout the Mangwende reserve—in spite of the opposition of the headman. The clubs, it is claimed, were responsible for raising the standards of hygiene, cleanliness, cooking, and general housekeeping. In 1952 when it was shown at the UN in the United Kingdom exhibition of colonial films illustrating community development, the UK delegate on the Social Commission remarked that *The Wives of Nendi* was particularly apposite in reinforcing the thesis that among unsophisticated and primitive villagers local leadership, self-help, and the simplest techniques contribute more to the successful creation of community centers than all the paraphernalia of imported technical assistance experts, fellowships, seminars, and the like.[13]

Most of the CAFU films followed a rudimentary education-entertainment format, believing, as had the BEKE before them, in the efficacy of the dramatic narrative to get a social message across. The most sophisticated example is *Philemon the Footballer* (1952), the first CAFU film to have sound added. Philemon, one of the *African Weekly* newsboys, is the goalkeeper in the Harare Wanderers football team, finalists in a cup competition. He is injured as a result of careless cycling while on his newspaper delivery round and is an unhappy witness to his team's defeat in the cup final. *Philemon* was featured at the Edinburgh Film Festival in 1953, and was singled out at the Rencontres Exhibition in Brussels in 1958, along with Jean Rouch's celebrated film *Jaguar*, as an example of a well-made instructional film in which the action tells the story (Rencontres Internationales 1958, 12–13).

The films had their limitations. Fundamental to Britain's postwar development policy was the encouragement of initiative in African society—with the Colonial Office holding a 1947 conference on this theme in London.[14] The orthodoxy was that development would not "take off" if it was imposed from above. But for this initiative the participation in the development process had only a limited amount of room for movement. CAFU films might show Africans at the community level who are already interested in forming a cooperative, joining a farming scheme, or forming a women's club, but when Europeans appear in the films they are always portrayed as authority figures and experts such as government officials, agricultural advisors, doctors, welfare officers, and cooperative society managers. In particular those films made in colonial Zimbabwe to promote better methods of farming were heavily shackled by the Land Apportionment Act, which confined African farmers to the poorer land in crowded reserves and imposed state controls on the production and marketing of commercial crops, which favored the white farmer.

Adult Literacy

The final strand in the colonial modernization story is the adult literacy movement, which received a great boost during the war and was strongly pushed by Margaret Wrong, one of the subcommittee members responsible for *Mass Education in African Society.* Wrong toured West Africa in 1944–1945, which led to the *Report on Adult Literacy and Education in the Gold Coast.* The African intelligentsia was targeted to produce the materials for the newly literate, with a full-time publication bureau being set up with Colonial Development and Welfare funds in West, East, and Central Africa. The East African Literature Bureau, one of the most important regional publishers in Africa today, is a reflection of these efforts. One of the hopes of the adult literacy movement was that the African intelligentsia who contributed to the production of reading material might be diverted from nationalist-type activities. While this did not happen, on a professional level the relationship between the African intelligentsia and the African Literature Committees and Publication Bureaus was mutually beneficial. Chinua Achebe and Wole Soyinka were among those who won the Margaret Wrong Prize for African Literature, first established in 1948.

Mass Education and the March to Independence

This narrative has demonstrated that modernization projects using mass media were being promoted in Britain's African colonies beginning in the 1920s. The pace accelerated dramatically during World War II as new media technologies were used to win African support and cooperation in the war effort and plans were made for postwar colonial development and welfare programs, including mass education, in what was originally envisaged as a very long march to self-government. Enter the *restless intelligentsia.* The mass media infrastructure along with the postwar adult literacy and development communication programs ultimately helped new men like Kwame Nkrumah to mobilize the support of the masses to achieve "self-government now." Once Ghana fired the starting pistol in 1957, the media carried the news all over Africa and the race to independence began.

The Bridge across the Colonial Divide

In the 1960s, independent African countries were catapulted into the New World Order. The United States was spearheading a Cold War on behalf of western capitalism against the communist Soviet Union and its allies. Aid was used to recruit allies in the developing world. In 1958, the year that the UN General Assembly tasked UNESCO with exploring the role the mass media could play in planned development, Lerner published *The Passing of Traditional Society* (1958). UNESCO went on to co-opt Wilbur Schramm in preparatory work, which led to *Mass Media and National Development* (1964). From this moment, modernization and development communication shed their colonial past as well as their early UNESCO history and were reinvented in postwar American social sciences and public diplomacy outreach in the context of the Cold War (e.g., McAnany 2012; Melkote and Steeves 2001). There have been dissenting voices (such as Smyth 2004), and Larkin (2008) has noted, "In many respects Lerner's theory of modernization is more theoretically sophisticated, but in essence it is the same as the ideas motivating British colonial officials in Northern Nigeria in the 1930s, 1940s, and 1950s" (117). Similarly Cooper argues that "the modernizing discourse of the [colonial] bureaucrats predates the rise in the academy of what came to be known as modernization theory" (Cooper 1997, 81).

The Carnegie-funded social science expedition to East and Central Africa in 1952 to study the colonial information departments and their use of the mass media in the process of "acculturation" lends support to this view. The Doob report also reminds us of the intimate relationship between the promotion of development in the Third World, global capitalism, and indeed American philanthro-capitalism via the ubiquitous foundations, including Ford, Rockefeller, and Carnegie, as he writes of "a monumental boom" in agricultural output and minerals "needed by the West," citing colonial Zimbabwe, Zambia, Uganda, Kenya, Tanzania, and the Congo in particular. "In a real sense, Africa, and Central Africa in particular," he writes, "is becoming the western world's substitute for the mainland of Asia which is now either controlled or threatened by the Communists" (Doob 1953, 7–8).

The Social Message Film Today

By the 1980s, disenchantment had set in with the state-directed approach toward development that began in the British case with postwar colonial developmentalism. However, Lerner, Everett Rogers, Schramm, and their disciples framed the mainstream academic discourse on communication for development and social change, and are credited as the founding fathers (e.g., Waisbord 2001, McPhail

2009, McAnany 2012). The notion that there was a linear path from a traditional society to a modern Western-style liberal democratic state connected seamlessly into the global market economy had also been discredited. But global elites continue to intervene, pushing development projects in Africa and elsewhere to promote political, economic, and social change as defined by western neoliberal values and practices.

In the BEKE we had a fleeting glimpse of the twenty-first century modernization paradigm now enveloping the Third World. Today the huge development interventionist industry is conducted by a consortium of international institutions and state and nonstate actors in a complex web of partnerships and "deep coalitions" with groups in Africa and elsewhere. Development has been privatized. The social message films today continue to primarily reflect the concerns of external sponsors and donors, as was the case with the BEKE and the Colonial Film Units. McGuffie (2010) has pointed out that "the influential presence of Euro-American funds, technical expertise, and creative guidance" makes this industry profoundly transnational (105–06). The external actors funding this "non-profit media industry" include UN agencies, NGOs, academic institutions, the national and transnational corporate sector, and the development wing of governments, such as the U.S. Agency for International Development (USAID) and the UK's Department for International Development (DFID), as well as philanthropic organizations like the Ford, Rockefeller, and Kellogg foundations, whose policies are closely allied with U.S. and other Western government interests.

Film and radio programs promoting modernizing social messages in Africa today reflect the international development agenda framed in such terms as sustainable development and rights-based development, and targeting issues such as community development, the plight of widows and orphans, gender-based violence, HIV/AIDS, the environment, and communal violence. In entertainment-education dramas today the plots strive for greater social realism than was evident in most colonial social message films. Glimpses of the future, however, were seen in the work of Sean Graham at the GCFU and in Stephen Peet's *Philemon the Footballer*, which was the first to tap into the popularity of football to frame a social message film. Football surfaces again in the hugely successful *Yellow Card* (2000), filmed in Zimbabwe by Media for Development Trust (McGuffie 2010). The film's hero Tiyane has to give up a soccer career and loses his "true love" Juliet in order to take responsibility for the baby produced as a result of a one-night stand with a classmate who dumps the infant on Tiyane's doorstep; in a subplot, his best friend dies of AIDS. *Remember Eliphas* (2002) draws the audience into the sad fate of its title character, a soldier in the Namibian Army who is infected with AIDS through having unprotected sex outside his marriage. The audience can't help identifying with the remorse-stricken Eliphas and his heartbroken wife as they deal with the aftermath. *Remember Eliphas* is an example of how far the didactic narrative public health film has come from the days of the anti-venereal disease saga *Mr. Wise and Mr. Foolish Go to Town* (Vaughan 1991, 180–89).[15]

Today's social messages are based on more systematic and extensive formative research—using surveys, interviews, and focus groups—than in the colonial era (McGuffie 2010, 115). Eliphas refuses to wear a condom because he "doesn't eat sweets with the wrapper on." *Yellow Card* and *Remember Eliphas,*[16] like other social message films today, are used in social marketing campaigns using radio and other media to maximize the exposure of the message, a strategy first seen in the Sellers era in Nigeria and recommended in *Mass Education in African Society.*

This chapter has demonstrated how colonial officials and members of the international community started the modernization caravan on its journey in the 1920s. Britain's DFID continues to play a prominent role in the transnational aid industry, which continues to intervene in Africa to accelerate social, economic, and political change reflecting the values and priorities of the neoliberal world order. "Development," says DFID in its 2009 white paper *Building Our Common Future,* "is not just a moral cause, but it is in all of our common interests."[17]

Notes

1. J. S. Huxley, "Report on the Use of Films for Educational Purposes in East Africa" (1930), 4, N[ational] A[rchive] C[olonial] O[ffice] 323/1252/30125/1.

2. Minutes of Dominions, India and Colonies Panel, 19 October 1934, NA CO 323/1252/30125/1.

3. J. E. W. Flood, minute, 8 November 1934, NA CO 323/1253/30141.

4. Director of native education to chief secretary, 21 January 1937, N[ational] A[rchives of] Z[ambia]/SEC 2/1121.

5. "The British Broadcasting Corporation Introductory Memorandum on Broadcasting and the Colonial Empire," Broadcasting House, 25 October 1935, NA CO 323/1338/5301/23.

6. Sir Cecil Bottomley, minute, 1 May 1936, NA CO 323/1390/5301/17.

7. Philip Cunliffe-Lister, 8 May 1935, NA CO 323/1338/5302/1.

8. Vincent Harlow, "The British Colonial Empire and the British Public," April 1943, NA CO 875/15/9102/17.

9. Unesco Film Reference Library Catalogue, 1958, http://unesdoc.unesco.org/images/0018/001800/180007eb.pdf, 29.

10. "1953 Seminar on Visual Aids in Fundamental Education," Paris, 25 November 1952, 2, UNESCO/WG/Doc.12.

11. http://unesdoc.unesco.org/images/0017/001795/179507eb.pdf.

12. NAZ CAFU, *Annual Report for 1954*.

13. "Report on Activities of the Central African Film Unit," 1 April 1952 to 31 March 1953, SEC/CAC/34.

14. Colonial Office Summer School on African Administration, "The Encouragement of Initiative in African Society," African No. 1174 (1948).

15. *Remember Eliphas*, supported by the U.S. Department of Defense, is reported to have become so popular that armies throughout Africa have asked for and received copies of the film, and two sequels have been produced: *Remember Eliphas 2* (2007) and *Remember Eliphas 3* (2009). I-TECH, International Training Center on HIV, "I-TECH Namibia Wraps Up Shooting for HIV Educational Film 'Remember Eliphas 3,'" 22 May 2009. See http://www.go2itech.org/itech-news/i-tech-namibia-wraps-up-shooting-for-hiv-educational-film-remember-eliphas-3.

16. http://www.med.navy.mil/sites/nhrc/dhapp/training/Documents/Eliphas.pdf.

17. Department for International Development, *Building Our Common Future—At a Glance*, 2009. See http://consultation.dfid.gov.uk/whitepaper2009/files/2009/03/white-paper_building_our_common_future_hi-res.pdf.

References

Anon. 1943. "Films for African Audiences." *Colonial Cinema* 1, no. 4 (June): 1–2.

Anon. 1944. "An African Comments on 'Mr. English at Home.'" *Colonial Cinema* 2, no. 4: 3.

Anon. 1947. "Film Fans on the Upper Reaches of the Zambezi." *Bulawayo Chronicle*, December 19.

Clarke, Peter B. 1984. "The Impact of Anti-German Propaganda on the Development of Nationalism in Nigeria during the Second World War." Paper presented at "Africa and the Second World War" conference, SOAS, London, May.

Colonial Office, Advisory Committee on Education in the Colonies. 1944. *Mass Education in African Society*. Colonial No. 186. London: HMSO.

Compton Brouwer, Ruth. 2002. *Modern Women Modernizing Men: The Changing Missions of Three Professional Women in Asia and Africa, 1902–1969*. Vancouver: University of British Columbia Press.

Cooper, Frederick. 1997. "Modernizing Bureaucrats, Backward Africans, and the Development Concept." In *International Development and the Social Sciences: Essays on the History and Politics of Knowledge*, edited by Frederick Cooper and Randall Packard, 64–92. Berkeley: University of California Press.

Davis, J. Merle. 1933. *Modern Industry and the African: An Enquiry into the Effect of the Copper Mines of Central Africa upon Native Society and the Work of the Christian Missions*. London: Macmillan.

———. 1936. "The Cinema and Missions in Africa." *International Review of Missions* 25, no. 99: 380–81.

Dickson, Alec G. 1950. "Mass Education in Togoland." *African Affairs* 49, no. 195: 136–50.

Doob, Leonard. 1953. "Information Services in Central Africa." *Public Opinion Quarterly* 17, no. 1: 7–19.

Dupin, Christophe. 2006. "The Postwar Transformation of the British Film Institute and Its Impact on the Development of a National Film Culture in Britain." *Screen* 47, no. 4: 443–51.

Fraenkel, Peter. 1959. *Wayaleshi*. London: Weidenfeld and Nicolson.

Gadsden, Fay. 1986. "Wartime Propaganda in Kenya." *International Journal of African Historical Studies* 19, no. 3: 36–48.

Grierson, John. 1948. "The Film and Primitive Peoples." In *The Film in Colonial Development: A Report of a Conference*, 9–15. London: British Film Institute.

———. 1998 [1941]. "Education and the New Order." In *The Documentary Film Movement: An Anthology*, edited by Ian Aitken, 93–103. Edinburgh: Edinburgh University Press.

HMSO. *Fifth Report from the Select Committee on Estimates*. 1950. London: HMSO.
Izod, Alan. 1952. "Fundamental Education by Film in Central Africa." In *Visual Aids in Fundamental Education*, 45–58. Paris: UNESCO.
Larkin, Brian. 2008. *Signal and Noise*. Durham, NC: Duke University Press.
Little, W. C. 1947. "An African Library 'In Action.'" *Books for Africa* 18, no. 1: 8.
McAnany, Emile G. 2012. *Saving the World: A Brief History of Communication for Development and Social Change*. Champaign-Urbana: University of Illinois Press.
McGuffie, Allison. 2010. "Educating African Sexuality: Processes of Gendering in Sexual Health Message Films, The Case of *Yellow Card*." *Intersections: Women's and Gender Studies in Review across Disciplines* 8: 103–32.
McPhail, Thomas L., ed. 2009. *Development Communication*. New York: Wiley-Blackwell.
Melkote, Srinivas R., and H. Leslie Steeves. 2001. *Communication for Development in the Third World: Theory and Practice for Empowerment*. Thousand Oaks, CA: Sage.
Notcutt, Leslie A., and Geoffrey C. Latham. 1937. *The African and the Cinema: An Account of the Work of the Bantu Educational Cinema Experiment during the Period March 1935 to May 1937*. London: Edinburgh House Press.
Odunton, G. B. 1950. "One Step Ahead." *Colonial Cinema* 8, no. 2: 29–32.
Plymouth, I. Miles Windsor-Clive. 1937. *Interim Report of a Committee on Broadcasting Services in the Colonies*. Colonial No. 139. London: HMSO.
Rencontres Internationales. 1958. *Le cinema et l'Afrique au sud du Sahara*. General report of the Brussels Exhibition. Brussels: Rencontres Internationales.
Rouch, Jean. 1962. *The Cinema in Africa: Present Position and Current Trends*. Paris: UNESCO. http://unesdoc.unesco.org/images/0018/001842/184262eb.pdf.
———. 2003. *Ciné-ethnography*. Edited and translated by Steven Feld. Minneapolis: University of Minnesota Press.
Sellers, William. 1953. "Making Films in and for the Colonies." *Journal of the Royal Society of the Arts* 101: 829–37.
———. 1958. "The Production and Use of Films for Public Informational and Educational Purposes in British African Territories." In *Le cinema et l'Afrique au sud du Sahara*, 35–43. Brussels: Rencontres Internationales.
Smyth, Rosaleen. 1983. "The Development of Government Propaganda Services in Northern Rhodesia." PhD diss., University of London.
———. 1984. "A Note on the 'Saucepan Special': The People's Radio of Central Africa." *Historical Journal of Film, Radio and Television* 4, no. 2: 195–201.
———. 1988. "The British Colonial Film Unit and Sub-Saharan Africa, 1939–1945." *Historical Journal of Film, Radio and Television* 8, no. 3: 285–98.
———. 2004. "The Roots of Community Development in Colonial Office Policy in Africa." *Social Policy & Administration* 38, no. 4: 418–36.
———. 2011. "Images of Empire on Shifting Sands: The Colonial Film Unit in West Africa in the Post-War Period." In *Film and the End of Empire*, edited by Lee Grieveson and Colin MacCabe, 155–75. London: Palgrave Macmillan.
Spurr, Norman. 1952a. "Some Aspects of the Work of the Colonial Film Unit in West and East Africa." In *Visual Aids in Fundamental Education*, 37–44. Paris: UNESCO
———. 1952b. "Visual Aids: Colour or Monochrome." *Colonial Cinema* 10, no. 2: 41–44.
UNESCO. 1955. *Catalogue of Visual Aids for Fundamental Education: Selected Publications, Films, Filmstrips*. Paris: UNESCO. http://unesdoc.unesco.org/images/0017/001795/179503eb.pdf.
Vaughan, Megan. 1991. *Curing Their Ills*. Cambridge: Polity Press.

Waisbord, Silvio. 2001. *Family Tree of Theories, Methodologies and Strategies in Development Communication: Convergences and Differences*. Report prepared for the Rockefeller Foundation, 30 May. http://www.comminit.com/en/node/1547/36.

Filmography

Amenu's Child (dir. Sean Graham, prod. Gold Coast Film Unit [GFCU], 16 mm, 37 min., sound, 1950).
Awka Division Community Development (prod. Community Development Department, Nigeria, 16 mm, 450 feet, 12 min., 30 sec., silent, 1951).
Better Pottery (prod. Colonial Film Unit, Nigeria, 16 mm, 365 feet, 10 min., 8 sec., silent, 1948).
[The] Boy Kumasenu (dir. Sean Graham, prod. GFCU, 35 mm, 5720 feet, 63 min., sound, 1952).
Cattle Thieves (dir. Rollo Gamble, prod. Colonial Film Unit, Tanganyika, 16 mm, 720 feet, 20 min., sound, 1950).
[A] *Challenge to Ignorance* (dir. Norman Spurr, prod. Colonial Film Unit, Uganda, 16 mm, 340 feet, 9 min., 26 sec., sound, ca. 1950s, exact year unknown).
[The] *Chief* (dir. Leslie A. Notcutt, prod. BEKE no. 6, 16 mm, 400 feet, 11 min., 6 sec., 1935).
Community Development in Ahoada Division (prod. Nigerian Film Unit, 16 mm, 890 feet, 24 min., 43 sec., 1950).
Community Development in Awgu Division (dir. A. A. Fajemisin, prod. Nigerian Film Unit, 16 mm, 951 feet, 26 min., 25 sec., 1949).
Community Development in Okigwi Division (prod. Nigerian Film Unit, 16 mm, 1200 feet, 33 min., 20 sec., 1950).
Daybreak in Udi (dir. Terry Bishop, prod. Max Anderson and John Taylor, Central Office of Information, Crown Film Unit, Nigeria, 16 mm, 3595 feet, 39 min., 51 sec., sound, 1949).
Dysentery (dir. Norman Spurr, prod. Colonial Film Unit, Uganda, 16 mm, 418 feet, 11 min., 36 sec., 1950).
Fight Tuberculosis in the Home (dir. William Sellers, prod. Colonial Film Unit, Nigeria, 16 mm [1080 feet], 35 mm [2700 feet], 30 min., 1946).
Food from Oil Nuts (prod. Colonial Film Unit, 16 mm, 114 feet, 3 min., 10 sec., 1944).
Good Business (prod. Colonial Film Unit, Nigeria, 16 mm [773 feet], 35 mm [1932 feet], 21 min., 28 sec., 1947).
Herbert Gondwe—Welfare Officer (prod. Central African Film Unit, Malawi, 16 mm, 1022 feet, 28 min., 23 sec., color, 1952).
Hides (dir. Leslie A. Notcutt, prod. BEKE no. 4, 16 mm, 200 feet, 5 min., 33 sec., 1935).
Husbands and Wives (dir. Louis Nell, prod. Central African Film Unit, Zambia, 16 mm, 631 feet, 17 min., 31 sec., color, 1950).
Jonathan Builds a Dam (prod. Kenya Information Office, 1944).
Katsina Tank (prod. Colonial Film Unit, Nigeria, 16 mm, 300 feet, 8 min., 20 sec., 1943).
[A] *Kenya Village Builds a Dam* (re-edited from *Jonathan Builds a Dam*) (prod. Colonial Film Unit, color, 16 mm, 435 feet, 12 min., 5 sec., 1944).
Lusaka Calling (dir. Louis Nell, prod. Central African Film Unit, Zambia, 16 mm, 725 feet, 20 min., 8 sec., color, sound, 1949).
Marangu (dir. Rollo Gamble, prod. Colonial Film Unit, Tanganyika, 16 mm, 531 feet, 14 min., 45 sec., sound, 1950).
Mr. English at Home (dir. Gordon Hales, prod. Colonial Film Unit, 16 mm, 1040 feet, 28 min., 53 sec., 1940).

Mr. Mensah Builds a House (dir. Sean Graham, prod. GFCU, 36 min., sound, 1955).
Mr. Wise and Mr. Foolish Go to Town (prod. Colonial Film Unit, South Africa, 16 mm, 825 feet, 22 min., 55 sec., 1944).
Murram Block-Making (dir. Norman Spurr, prod. Colonial Film Unit, Uganda, 16 mm, 329 feet, 9 min., 8 sec., 1950).
Nurse Ademola (prod. Colonial Film Unit, 16 mm, 315 feet, 8 min., 45 sec., 1943).
Nyono Gets a Letter (dir. Louis Nell, prod. Central African Film Unit, Zambia, 16 mm, 347 feet, 9 min., 38 sec., color, 1950).
Philemon the Footballer (dir. Stephen Peet, prod. Central African Film Unit, Southern Rhodesia [Zimbabwe], 16 mm, 567 feet, 15 min., 45 sec., color, sound, 1952).
Post Office Savings Bank (dir. Leslie A. Notcutt, prod. BEKE no. 1, 16 mm, 400 feet, 11 min., 6 sec., 1935).
Progress in Kojokrom (dir. Sean Graham, prod. GFCU, 16 mm, 835 feet, 23 min., 11 sec., sound, 1953).
Remember Eliphas (dir. Simon Wilkie, prod. U.S. Department of Defense HIV/AIDS Prevention Program [DHAPP]/Population Services International [PSI], Namibia, 40 min., 2002).
Smallpox (dir. Lionel Snazelle, prod. Nigerian Film Unit, 35 mm, 2122 feet, 25 min., sound, 1950).
Soldier Comforts from Uganda (prod. Colonial Film Unit, 16 mm, 755 feet, 20 min., 58 sec., 1942).
[*The*] *Story of Petale* (dir. Anker Atkinson, prod. Central African Film Unit, Zambia, 16 mm, 1645 feet, 45 min., 41 sec., color, n.d.).
Tea (dir. Leslie A. Notcutt, prod. BEKE no. 5, 16 mm, 200 feet, 5 min., 33 sec., 1935).
This is an A.R.P. Warden (prod. Colonial Film Unit, 16 mm, 987 feet, 27 min., 25 sec., 1941).
This is a Barrage Balloon (prod. Colonial Film Unit, 16 mm, 672 feet, 18 min., 40 sec., 1941).
Village Development (dir. Lionel Snazelle, prod. Colonial Film Unit, Nigeria, 35 mm, 2130 feet, 23 min., 40 sec., sound, 1948).
Weaving in Togoland (prod. Colonial Film Unit, 16 mm, 772 feet, 21 min., 26 sec., 1946).
We Want Rubber (prod. Colonial Film Unit, 16 mm, 507 feet, 14 min., 5 sec., 1943).
Why Not You? (dir. Norman Spurr, prod. Colonial Film Unit, Uganda, 16 mm, 389 feet, 10 min., 48 sec., 1950).
[*The*] *Wives of Nendi* (dir. Stephen Peet, prod. Alan Izod, Central African Film Unit, Southern Rhodesia [Zimbabwe], 16 mm, 712 feet, 19 min., 46 sec., color, sound, 1949).
Yellow Card (dir. John Riber, prod. Media for Development International [MFDI], Zimbabwe, 90 min., 2000).

4 Mass Education, Cooperation, and the "African Mind"

Aaron Windel

THE HISTORY OF credit and farming cooperatives in Africa bridges its colonial and postcolonial past. In the 1960s, cooperatives were linchpins in government programs of rural modernization in post-independence Central and East Africa. Tanzania's *ujamaa* plan for socialist development, spearheaded by President Julius Nyerere, pinned rural development to the creation of state farm cooperatives. In Zambia, there was a similar embrace of cooperative farming under Kenneth Kaunda's direction (Hyden 1980; Quick 1978). In both cases, the state provided land and even subsidies to farmers for clearing it, and Zambians and Tanzanians were encouraged to view cooperatives as places for the discussion of national politics. Elsewhere, cooperatives were sites of nationalist organization in the last gasp of British colonial rule, as among the Gisu in Uganda. Colonial officials in Uganda sometimes interfered with cooperative organization because they feared these were becoming sites of political agitation, and at least one cooperative society in Uganda was disbanded by the government on this count.[1]

The history of cooperation is multivalent, and at turns we see them as grand governmental modernizing schemes (both under European rule and in the post-independence era) but also as locally grown responses to the challenges of wage labor and survival within the cash nexus developed under colonialism. During the colonial period, a kind of credit cooperative structure was widely used in Yoruba and Ibo areas of West Africa. These organizations, known as *esusu* in the Yoruba language, were not connected to any initiative of the colonial state. They required members to commit regular small amounts, and then on a rotating basis larger sums from the pool would be distributed to individual members. For the small cultivator or laborer, savings would thus be regularly supplemented by much larger amounts, depending on the number of members in the *esusu* (Geertz 1962). Cooperatives also occupied a space in the development of the colonial state and its technologies of inspection and revenue collection in rural Africa. Before the establishment of *ujamaa* in Tanzania, there were significant efforts at organizing cooperative farming, especially among the Chagga in northern Tanzania near Kilimanjaro. In the late 1920s and early 1930s, the colonial governor Donald Cameron, a member of the mass education subcommittee discussed below, attempted to fix a place for the Chagga farmer-traders in his administration of indirect rule by registering them in a massive cooperative union that was registered with the government and would collect fees from farmers and have a monopoly to market coffee. The territory's move was met with protests and sabotage from some Chagga farmers for whom the union's fees and governmental controls were oppressive (Coulson 1982, 62; Iliffe 1979, 274–86; McCarthy 1981, 101–102). There also were cases in which settler cooperatives were used by Europeans in order to hedge African farmers out of competition and to fix low wages for labor. The sisal industry in East Africa provides an example. Large-scale European plantations combined in cooperative marketing ventures that made the survival of the small sisal cultivator next to impossible. Settler-run marketing cooperatives, like the Tanganyika Sisal Growers Association, allowed their members to secure a more favorable position in regional and global markets and to coordinate a 50 percent wage cut for African laborers on all the cooperating sisal estates (Westcott 1984).

Before the wave of nationalist independence movements of the 1950s and 1960s, cooperatives figured prominently in imperial planning. Cooperatives seemed to fit well within the new framework of "trusteeship" recommended by the League of Nations after World War I. Article 22 of the League charter put forward the principle that Europeans must rule in the interest of those "not yet able to stand by themselves under the strenuous conditions of the modern world." Trusteeship implied that social welfare must be a part of the mandate of colonial rule, though minimal funds were offered for the task. In the British Colonial Office, the development of a strong cooperative movement for Africa became a priority. Many in the office believed that cooperation would advance African welfare as a form of self-help, and enthusiasm for cooperatives was shared by several colonial governors, district officers, and administrators in agricultural services. The British colonial government administered trusteeship as a vast program of instruction. It stressed lessons in interdependence between metropole and colony rather than national independence. Social welfare, without state funding, became a project of teaching Africans "improved" agricultural methods, hygienic practice, and forms of economic practice, such as cooperatives, that would adapt African production to the demands of a metropolitan-centered cash economy. Rosaleen Smyth has explained that the slogan of "community development" was only adopted in the 1950s to describe official efforts to build community as bulwark for social welfare. However, the ideas of community development were already being elaborated in the Colonial Office and among its expert advisors between the wars (Smyth 2004, 419). The philosophy of community development was most notably promoted by the Advisory Committee on Education in the Colonies (ACEC). Beginning in 1925, the Committee reorganized African education into a uniform system throughout British Africa, promoting reforms that sought to create community-based centers that could train African children and adults in "character" and modern modes of life. In 1943, the ACEC expanded its mission by calling for mass education, making specific recommendations for the introduction of an administrative structure of public information to more rapidly implement community development with support from the newly created Colonial Development Fund.

This chapter examines the community development idea, especially during the interwar period when reform-minded missionaries and colonial officials began to insist that its principles be the basis of state efforts to modernize rural life and provide social welfare. Interwar reformers were motivated by a concern that rapid social change in Africa would create instability and political challenges that could jeopardize the progress of African development and the cohesion of empire. In pursuing community development, colonial administrators and missionaries were preoccupied with the uniqueness of the "African mind" and with finding appropriate media forms and pedagogical forms of address. Film was key to this project. James Burns has shown how experiments with film in Africa, especially the Central African Film Unit (CAFU), intersected with the aims of colonial administration to elaborate this construct of "the African mind" and to hone cinematographic technique to appeal to it (Burns 2002, 96). Smyth also has demonstrated this concern with the African mind at various points in the history of colonial film policy (Smyth 1979, 450). My aim here is to treat plans for creating a mobile cinema system and schemes to promote cooperatives as two aspects of the community development planning effort: that is, to discover and develop new and permanent sites of public instruction tailored to the African mind.

Cooperatives and cinemas may appear very unlike each other, but they were intended to reinforce each other. In discussions of cooperative economics among promoters of mass education and other iterations of community development since the mid-1920s, the "Native cooperative" was imagined to be important foremost as a pedagogical tool, like film. Cooperatives were sometimes dealt with by the Colonial Office as a matter of adult education, and they formed part of the wider search for an idiom with which to translate the principles of community development to rural people. Like film, cooperatives offered a pedagogy in rural economics that could jump "the literacy hurdle" (Smyth 1973, 419). They offered visual, hands-on instruction in accounting, produce grading for market, seed selection, and other aspects of rural marketing. They also provided physical spaces for people to gather. Within the political geography of community development, the mobile cinema and the cooperative were intended to be spaces of congregation at the center of community life, but reformers wanted to ensure control over the messages exchanged in such gatherings. Under the rubric of community development, the pedagogies of cinema and the cooperative aimed to create a depoliticized, cash-cropping peasantry dependent on government-sanctioned seed and Western markets. Officials and missionary reformers wanted the principles of community development to steer African modernization that ensured the continued cooperation between Africa and the West at a time when movements of national independence and Pan-Africanism were calling this relationship into question.

Community development films often featured cooperatives, especially cooperative marketing schemes—after all, a key promise of community development for administrators was its ability to reinforce multiple interventions. Below I explore the place of cooperatives in two colonial film projects. First, the 1930s Bantu Educational Kinema [*sic*] Experiment (BEKE), whose personnel were deeply involved in pushing community development schemes for Africa, depicted cooperatives in film and reinforced lessons in cooperation that the Colonial Office had sought to deploy through a reformed village education system. Second, I look at how, in the wake of the 1943 mass education report, the Crown Film Unit's *Daybreak in Udi* (dir. Terry Bishop, 1949, 39 min., 51 sec.), which was cosponsored by the Colonial Office and the Central Office of Information, promoted credit cooperatives that supported community development efforts envisioned by the Colonial Office and its educational Advisory Committee.[2]

"Native Education" and the "African Mind"

The BEKE project, which experimented with mobile cinemas for rural areas in the mid-1930s, epitomized the community development idea.[3] Glenn Reynolds has explored the BEKE's history in depth and with particular attention to how African audiences experienced the films. He rightly argues that the film project was part of a colonial struggle for hegemony, which from the British imperial point of view fit with other efforts to use film to "bind its African subjects to the metropole" (Reynolds 2009, 57). The vision of rural modernization proffered in the content and rhetorical style of the films relied on the premise that there was an irrevocable market interdependence between settler and native society on the one hand, and Africa and the West on the other—a vision shared with other community development initiatives, notably the Jeanes Schools for rural teacher training. Further, the community development idea held that education in practical lessons of hygiene, money management, and market-oriented techniques in agriculture was key to improving the welfare of Africans within this interdependent "modern world." These themes are abundant in BEKE films. Community development urged a closer cooperation between the various western stakeholders in Africa and an international approach to development planning. The BEKE illustrates this, as it was run from an international missionary organization, operated with American philanthropic funds, and coordinated its film tours with colonial governments and with the Colonial Office in London. The BEKE was a joint effort of the Geneva-based International Missionary Council and the Carnegie Corporation of New York. The aims of both organizations toward African audiences, though, stemmed from a reform movement begun in the early 1920s that embraced an American model of "Negro education" that sought to "adapt" education to the racial proclivities of black people. The 1921 and 1924 Phelps-Stokes Commissions to Africa paved the way, recommending broad reforms in education throughout Africa and insisting that erstwhile missionary-run education efforts had wrongly tried to teach English language and literacy skills to the detriment of rural communities. The Phelps-Stokes Commission's report called for more uniformity in education policy, a bolder role for government, and the reorientation of education with the central aim of encouraging a strict agricultural life, albeit with modern enhancements. The recommendations were embraced by the Colonial Office, which began an overhaul of "Native education." First it set up an Advisory Committee on Education in Tropical Africa (later expanded to the Advisory Committee on Education in the Colonies, bringing the entire empire under its purview). In 1925 the Advisory Committee recommended the scaling back of English education and sought to remove English entirely from the first four grades. The committee, following the theory of "adapted education," emphasized hygiene lessons, the forging of community connections, and the improvement of agricultural technique at all levels of instruction. Adaptation rested on a view that African mentality was wholly different from that of Europeans.[4] Not only did the aims of education need to be changed, but progressive administrators needed to encounter new pedagogies to reach the "African mind."

From early on, cooperatives and film were seized upon as promising avenues for instruction in agricultural practice. James W. C. Dougall, who led the second Phelps-Stokes Commission in 1924 to Central and East Africa, was put in charge of the new government "Jeanes" teacher training school in Kabete, Kenya, near Nairobi. There he oversaw the construction of a "model village" with a school and a cooperative shop at its center. The purpose of the Jeanes Schools, which were supported by the Carnegie Corporation and developed in most territories in British Africa, was to train African instructors who would take the program of adaptation to the African Reserve areas. Under the British system of indirect rule, some territory was *reserved from* white settlement. On these reserves, African Native Courts and tribal custom were supposed to hold sway, though the British always maintained veto power. As social welfare became a greater concern under the theory of trusteeship in the 1920s, the reserves became the main target of community development planning. It was believed that for the new policies to take hold, African interlopers needed to be convinced in order to make the community development agenda more appealing to Africans. Officials and missionaries held out great hope that the Jeanes teacher training centers could provide the personnel for its campaign in rural instruction.

The Jeanes teacher curriculum included a course in practical cooperative economics in the first year, and when the teachers finished their training they would oversee several village schools and encourage adults in rural communities to start cooperative societies. Dougall's mantra was "teach by doing," and he was convinced that cooperative grocery stores along with savings and loan societies were useful as practical sites for the teaching of contractual obligations, cash management, and bookkeeping. Dougall was a respected voice on African education in missionary circles, and in the Colonial Office he was well known as a leader in the campaign to bring "adapted education" to Africa. He also published articles on African mentality and the kinds of pedagogies he found successful at his school (Dougall 1932). Early on in the BEKE project, the filmmakers met with Dougall to solicit advice on African perception and how to hone a pedagogy for the African mind, a task that had preoccupied Dougall as head of the Jeanes School experiment.

While the Phelps-Stokes Commissions and the Advisory Committee on Education in the Colonies set the new standards for education in Africa, it was the International Missionary Council's Department of Social and Industrial Research that organized the BEKE project, which was the first significant film unit guided by "adapted" principles. The organization had important ties to American philanthropies and the Colonial Office's advisory committee, thanks to the IMC's secretary, Joseph H. Oldham, who advised both the Carnegie Corporation and the Phelps-Stokes Fund on colonial matters (Berman 1971; King 1969). Oldham was a founding member of the colonial education Advisory Committee that first declared "adaptation" to be the policy of the Colonial Office (Bennett 1960, 357).[5]

Under Oldham, and heading up the IMC's Department of Social and Industrial Research, was J. Merle Davis. In 1932, the department undertook a major study of the changing condition of African life near the Copperbelt in colonial Zambia (Davis 1933). The findings of the field team, consisting of missionaries, sociologists, and anthropologists, showed that African culture was rapidly changing as a result of the industrial penetration of Central Africa that threatened to rend the social fabric of African traditional life. Aggressive public instruction programs were recommended as a form of social welfare with the added advantage of defusing the political antagonisms that the study group feared could materialize in the midst of the crisis of culture change. One of the key recommendations of the study commissioned by the Carnegie Corporation was that film should be used to reach the largest audience. But film, as Merle Davis argued, should not be deployed in Africa without first studying its reception among African audiences.[6]

The BEKE project started with the mission to investigate and make recommendations for how a system of "wholesome" cinemas could be deployed in rural areas of British Africa. Merle Davis received measured political support for the project from the Colonial Office along with some individual colonial Government Houses. He was granted some funding for the project by the Carnegie Corporation, which had also sponsored the IMC's original Copperbelt study. Merle Davis put George C. Latham, former director of education for Northern Rhodesia (colonial Zambia), in charge of the educational content of the cinema experiment. While serving in colonial Zambia in the 1920s, Latham had transformed the territory's system of "Native Education" following the Phelps-Stokes recommendations. Among other reforms, he had chartered the Jeanes School at Mazabuka (following Dougall's model in Kenya), and years later he would show his BEKE films to the teachers in training there. Joining Latham in the field as cinematographer and engineer was a former army officer and Kenyan plantation manager, Leslie A. Notcutt.

In 1935, the two filmmakers set up a studio in Vugiri, Tanzania, strategically located between the crisis zones of "culture change"—chief among them the Zambian Copperbelt and the Kenyan "White Highlands." The men constructed mobile cinemas that fused a diesel engine with a projector and a screen. The prototype unit would be loaded on a lorry to tour the countryside. First, though, they recruited African actors and directed them in instructional films that generally depicted the kinds of lessons in hygiene, cooperative economics, and animal husbandry recommended by the "adapted" model. The filmmakers would take careful notes on each screening and interview audience members in order to derive guidelines for effectively framing scenarios that could be proven to both appeal to African audiences and convey the proper lessons to the "African mind."

The filmmakers believed they should show scenes of "African progress," and Martin Kayamba, assistant at the Dar es Salaam Secretariat, is likely the person who pointed them to the Chagga cooperatives at Moshi near Kilimanjaro as an early subject for their work.[7] Before any filming was undertaken, Latham toured colonial Tanzania and met with agricultural officers, missionaries, and the marshall of the Prisons Department to solicit advice on relevant themes and how to present them. A note in Latham's diary written during a stop in Mwanza, Tanzania, on the southern shore of Lake Victoria, illustrates his views on social change at the time of the film project. He explained that there was "a social revolution going on. In town a man's prestige depends more on whether he has a bicycle, a lamp, a white suit, than on the number of his cattle," adding that there was also a growing problem of "English-educated natives" in the town for whom no jobs were available.[8]

The film eventually shot at Moshi was one of the BEKE's first productions, though no copy survives and so descriptions of shots and sequences rely on the filmmakers' archived notes and published account of their "experiment." The film featured the Kilimanjaro Native Cooperative Union, which Latham noted had "put 1400 tons of coffee on [the] London market last year."[9] The film attempted to show the Chagga first trying to imitate European coffee farmers but failing for "lack of knowledge of coffee cultivation and disease control." The filmmakers thought through how they would convey the lesson that the Chagga-produced coffee was inferior in quality for not having been cooperatively farmed and marketed, though it is not clear how they came to this judgment in the first place. In order to convey the message on film, they showed the Chagga coffee being drunk by Europeans who then expressed their displeasure with the taste. Then they edited in shots of a Moshi coffee cooperative, "showing the developed cooperative movement and some idea of its activities and value," followed by shots of the same Europeans now smiling and enjoying their coffee.

Notcutt and Latham sought to demonstrate cause and effect through conventional filmmaking techniques, contrasting indigenous African disorder with the improvements of modern methods (Latham and Notcutt 1937, 40). The sequence involving the happy and unhappy consumers of coffee illustrates this, and we see a similar effort to draw cause and effect connections in the BEKE-produced film *Cattle and Disease* (dir. Leslie A. Notcutt, 1936). The object of the film was to connect the problem of diseased cattle to the "witch doctor" and, by contrast, to associate healthy livestock with modern European methods. The film began with shots of Masai people and then a shot focused on a single cattle owner. Next came a shot of dying cattle followed by the cattle owner walking off to consult the witch doctor. The filmmakers found that such "continuity scenes" were essential for African audiences to follow the "argument" of a film. As they wrote later, "The importance of the continuity scene, in this case, is to connect the dying herd scenes with the witch-doctor, the owner being seen to leave his herd and a shot or two later to join the witch-doctor" (Latham and Notcutt 1937, 156).

Another BEKE film, *Marketing Export Native Maize* (dir. Leslie A. Notcutt, 1937), showed the benefits of government-supervised marketing of maize, which was instituted as part of the 1935 Marketing of Native Crops Ordinance. As Anderson and Throup have shown, the ordinance was intended to help establish better prices for African maize, but in the long term it worked to fix the price of "native maize" at half the price that settler-planters received (Anderson and Throup 1985, 336–38). The BEKE film, however, attempted to portray the ordinance and government "native marketing" schemes in a favorable light. The film opened with shots of maize being sold at Karatina Market near Mount Kenya to "wayside buyers, and the cheating that takes place." The film then moved to shots of an "angry crowd," upset by the market cheats. These shots were put in sequence with the chief turning to ask for assistance from a government agricultural officer. The officer assured the chief that the government would soon start a maize marketing scheme, with the hope that his people would supply their produce.

The lesson of the film emphasized improvement and heralded the sort of contemporary rural development initiatives and commercial efforts led by corporations like Monsanto to license and deploy genetically engineered seed. The villagers featured in the BEKE film would be required to use the government-sanctioned "improved seed," which must not be mixed with "native seed." As with the Moshi cooperatives, the filmmakers tried to find ways to refer to the world of consumers in far-off places, reinforcing a central theme of community development films: that the key to improvement lay in connections to the empire's markets. The film on maize marketing concluded with a sequence illustrating the process of packaging, first on its way to Mombasa (Kenya) and then being shipped by sea (Latham and Notcutt 1937, 73). These shots of departure, of movement from the familiar places toward some distant center, seemed to occur to Latham in abundance. He had an idea, too, to shoot the airmail arriving and the loading of bags of letters for an implied distant destination—following Harry Watt and Basil Wright's *Night Mail* (1936, 25 min.).

Films on seed selection were a specialty of the BEKE filmmakers, and the location of the cooperative was their preferred site for demonstrating the superiority of hybrid seeds produced through government-sponsored agricultural research. The filmmakers used the Chagga cooperatives for a series of three films that they termed the "coffee problem series." One of these films featured the government Coffee Research Station at Lyamungu near Kilimanjaro, where government researchers produced clones of coffee plants while collecting and distributing the resulting seed (Munger 1952, 181–85). Focusing on cooperatives and marketing also gave the filmmakers opportunities to produce films warning against soil erosion, reinforcing work that was already being done at government-operated experimental farms that used demonstration plots to offer visual proof of erosion. Latham and Notcutt filmed two soil erosion films; one was shot at the Moshi cooperatives in northern Tanzania, and another at Machakos, Kenya. The first film, *Soil Erosion* (dir. Leslie A. Notcutt, 1935), shot at Moshi, was a disappointment to the filmmakers, and European audience members at the screening told them they had a difficult time discerning the points of instruction that the film hoped to convey. The film was apparently very popular with African audiences in Kenya, however, where settlers had been using what they regarded as Africans' penchant for eroding soil as an excuse for land use and marketing policies favoring European plantations on the "White Highlands" (Latham and Notcutt 1937, 40). Settlers organizing to keep the Kenya highlands a "white reserve" often turned on deploying the propaganda image of dusty, eroded soil as the effect of African misuse (Anderson and Throup 1985, 330).

In addition to demonstrating the causes of soil erosion and ways of preventing it through crop rotation or the slaughter of cattle, the filmmakers were intent on staging the progress of an African tribe thanks to European instruction. One method of filming they considered, which they termed "the *epic* method," showed how a tribe became incrementally impoverished through soil erosion "and how prosperity was regained by the reclamation of these lands by tribal efforts on a large scale." But the filmmakers experimented with other methods, too, since they relied on a theory of instructional cinema. As they explained, "It is the constant repetition of the subject from different points of view which will ultimately influence the masses" (Latham and Notcutt 1937, 140–41). A second film on the subject, *Soil Erosion at Machakos* (dir. Leslie A. Notcutt, 1936), shot in Kenya, tried to capture the rhetorical technique of the agricultural demonstration plot, shooting a colonial agricultural officer using one such plot to demonstrate soil erosion to a group of Africans. A similar technique of appropriating the visual pedagogy of agricultural demonstration plots can be seen in *African Peasant Farms* (dir. Leslie A. Notcutt, 1936, 9 min.), one of the three surviving BEKE films.[10] The film's sequence on crop rotation uses shots of an African farmer instructing another beside a small plot of cotton. The scene shows the farmer etching a grid in the dirt to model an arrangement of ten single-acre plots, then placing different seeds and pieces of cotton into the individual boxes of the grid, and then rotating the contents of each box to demonstrate crop rotation.

The Bantu cinema experiments were conducted from 1935–1937, and upon the return of Latham and Notcutt to England they published a full report that set out recommendations for a grand instructional film system that would scientifically produce scripts based on the best anthropological research and deployed through a vast network of mobile cinemas. While their recommendations to the Colonial Office were not immediately followed, the experiment was one of the only instances of prior research cited by the 1943 mass education report, which officially endorsed a mobile cinema system and established it with subsidies from the Colonial Development Fund.

Cooperatives and the Trustee State

Before turning to the plans for mass education and the state's efforts to publicize community development and cooperatives in the 1940s through mobile cinemas and films like *Daybreak in Udi,* it is useful point out that concurrent with efforts to publicize cooperatives there was a movement within the colonial state to create a legal infrastructure for the registration and control of cooperatives throughout British Africa. The legal reforms are important for explaining why the cooperatives, which often relied on African initiative, later became key sites of peasant struggle with the structures of indirect rule in places like Nigeria, Tanzania, and Uganda. Until the 1930s, African savings and loan cooperatives, in addition to farming cooperatives, stood outside the state's formal jurisdiction. Savings associations collected and distributed funds with oversight by society members, as with the Nigerian *esusu.* Beginning in 1930, though, the Colonial Office under Sidney Webb (a.k.a. Lord Passfield) began to consult with colonial governors in order to transfer a legal system for the promotion and control of "Native cooperatives" from the Punjab in India, which was perceived as a crisis zone of social change and radical politics during the interwar period. Webb had his own interest in seeing the cooperative movement take hold in Britain and throughout the empire. Webb, a Fabian Socialist, had written a book with his wife, Beatrice, on the coming "Socialist Commonwealth" that envisioned neighborhood cooperatives as better institutions of people's democracy than parliaments could provide (Webb and Webb 1920). In Africa, though, Webb helped promote a system of cooperative peasant organization that saw cooperatives as sites of instruction for participation in the international cash economy. Cooperatives, he believed, would help modernize "backward" Africa while providing urgent debt relief for the small landholder or tenant farmer.

Under Webb's short administration and afterward, the Colonial Office took its philosophy on the development value of cooperation from former Punjab civil servant Claude Francis Strickland, the recognized expert on the subject of "Native cooperation." In a series of research trips to Palestine and then Zanzibar and Tanzania, Strickland studied and reported on the feasibility of developing a cooperative movement in each place.[11] Strickland's official mission was to help colonial administrators draft legislation to "constitute and control" cooperatives. He also advised on establishing cooperative laws in colonial Ghana and wrote the cooperatives law that was eventually adopted, with revisions, in colonial Tanzania, Kenya, and Zanzibar. After World War II, Strickland advised the Fabian Colonial Bureau, largely responsible for shaping imperial policy during the postwar Labour ascendancy in British politics. He also had the ear of some of the most influential imperial policymakers, including Frederick Lugard, who wrote the introduction to Strickland's book on the cooperative movement in Africa (Strickland 1933a). The effects of Strickland's influence can be found in the legislation that continues to license cooperatives in much of Africa today.[12]

Like other advocates of community development, Strickland located the problem of imperial government in the growing gap between demands for social welfare and a limitation in administrative capacity to handle new demands. Strickland cautioned that the level of new demands for welfare and services would overwhelm local authorities if the central state did not move quickly. He concluded that Native Councils and chiefs were simply not up to the task. The solution to the sheer burden of new needs and government responsibility could only be addressed by "the presentation of the cooperative movement as the 'core' of a welfare policy" (Strickland 1933a, 39).

For Strickland, cooperatives could serve as effective instruments of self-help and welfare delivery. They could also provide a means of escape from money lenders and even replace some functions of the Native Courts on the reserves by creating elected bodies that might arbitrate economic disputes. Importantly, for Strickland, cooperatives could serve as a popular and stabilizing force against social change and political turbulence that might threaten the colonial order. As a former agricultural officer in the India Civil Service, Strickland was a practiced hand at political economy. His writing on the "rural problem" in India and Africa mingled population statistics with the vivid firsthand experience of an administrator who witnessed rural unrest at the boiling point. Strickland believed that the movement of Europeans into Africa had forced the "static order of native society" into an interdependent relationship with the rest of the world. In the absence of the old order, "Young Africans" were seduced by the easy money to be made with lucrative commercial crops but lacked the necessary "wisdom in the use of wealth" (Strickland 1933b, 17). Cooperation provided a unique opportunity to graft an entirely new "social fabric" into Africans' relationships with each other, and the benefits of planting such a system were manifold. The problem of the selfish, wealth-seeking peasant would be replaced by the boon of newly found "communal restraints." If so-called "Young Africans" were drawn to subversive ideologies and political movements, cooperation, Strickland opined, could counter their influence and reverse the trend. As he wrote, "Co-operation will be a stabilizing, not a subversive force. Political questions are excluded from its purview" (Strickland 1933b, 18). Strickland recognized, though, that cooperatives could themselves be dangerous sites for the organization of oppositional political movements. The legislation he drafted for the African territories gave the cooperatives registrar the authority to disband any society that became a subversive organization, and the surveillance measures imposed by the new laws ensured that the state would be able to annually audit every society, giving the state better vision on the ground. Cooperatives now had to be registered with the state, pay registration fees, submit to the annual audit, and use standardized record-keeping, including minutes of meetings. Cooperative society meetings could never diverge from the narrow purpose of administering cooperative savings, loans, and purchases.

While Strickland's views on cooperation provide insight into the essence of cooperation as a form of community development, perhaps just as instructive were the minority reports on the issue that he dismissed. In 1934, at a joint meeting in London of the African Society and the Royal Society of the Arts, Strickland proclaimed the value of a strictly controlled cooperative movement for Africa. The benefits were only meaningful against the backdrop of political instability. As he told the audience, which included a number of African students associated with the London's West African Student Union (WASU),

> There is a danger that the African village, while remaining populous and even superficially homogeneous, may lose its community spirit and dissolve into a crowd of selfish individuals for whom tribal customs, traditions and authority have no longer a value, but who have not discovered for themselves the right agency for effecting a change, for transforming the village and the mind of the villager from within. (Strickland 1935, 6)

After his speech, Louis Mbanefo, a nationalist who would eventually go on to serve as a court justice in independent Nigeria, argued with Strickland over the need to introduce cooperation, claiming that similar, though less formal, cooperative efforts had been made in Nigeria through the agency of Nigerians themselves in setting up charitable funds to help the poor.[13] Mbanefo predicted that any attempt by government to introduce cooperatives without working through tribal institutions would fail. Strickland countered that such associations could not stand on their own without the help of expert guidance and legal protections that favored African cooperators. The cooperatives registrar could not be a local man, since his function was not local. He should be a European with a whole staff of African supervisors below him, rooted in their local communities and serving as the intermediaries between government and the societies themselves (Strickland 1935, 17–18).

Mass Education and the Geography of Community

Mbanefo was likely pointing to the thriving *esusu* associations of self-help or similar organizations of rotating credit. It was Strickland's cooperative system, though, that prevailed for at least the duration of colonial rule. And just as the newly empowered cooperatives registrar began to bring Yoruba and Ibo credit associations under state scrutiny and control, the publicity wing of state, now pursuing the aims of mass education, sought to erase the history of indigenous cooperation and replace it with a story of European genius and initiative. The first image seen by African and international audiences of *Daybreak in Udi* was a title about the awakening of the Abaja Ibos of eastern Nigeria to community development: "Together they are teaching themselves to read and write, and are building schools, maternity homes, co-operative shops. And many miles of roads. With few resources but their own strength and spirit, they are starting to bridge the centuries dividing their way of life and ours." The plot centers on a community effort to solve the problem of infant mortality by building a maternity home. After a first scene showing adults and children in an outdoor school learning to read, there are shots of several villagers approaching the district officer to get help. The dialogue takes place in his office. "If we had a maternity home," one of the female community leaders explains to the district officer, "the women could have their babies under a trained midwife, and no superstitious old women would be able to scare the mother." The officer tells the group that "maternity hospitals do not grow on trees" and that all the government money would not help because charity is useless. He continues, "I know your village well. The people want progress but don't know how to go about it." He explains that "community development is a new thing" and that farmers are naturally suspicious of change.

While the idea for the maternity home and a paid nurse comes from community leaders, it is the district officer who solves the problem of financing. The officer instructs the woman who has come for advice, "Your job is easy enough. Try to persuade the women to form a cooperative society to raise the money to pay the midwife." As the film continues, this proves to be the most difficult task, since there is a village elder who stands in the way of the project. He has forbidden his wife from joining the cooperative. She, in turn, has influence over the other women in the community, who will not join the credit society either. In the end, the district officer intervenes in a contentious meeting and addresses the recalcitrant woman directly. The officer's reasonable arguments prevail, the woman concedes, and the maternity ward is built from the thrift of the women's cooperative. Scenes at the end of the film include one with shots of a smiling woman in the maternity ward holding a healthy baby and a final sequence with villagers working together to fell trees to build a road.

In fact, *Daybreak in Udi* chronicled events based on the experience of district officer E. R. Chadwick, whose name appears in the credits as "collaborator." Chadwick had published an account of his efforts to bring mass education to Udi Division in south-central Nigeria, though he claimed that the "only things that are new about mass education in Udi are the title" and a new focus on mass literacy (Chadwick 1948, 31). Otherwise, the work described by Chadwick follows the basic patterns of community development in education promoted by the Colonial Office since 1925 and mirrored in much of the rest of British Africa. Chadwick's account focused on community development efforts by the Owa subclan of the Abaja Ibo, recounting efforts, especially, to add new health dispensaries in order to close the extraordinary distances—roughly fifteen miles—between those existing in 1943 when Chadwick began his work. Additionally, he encouraged the voluntary construction of roads and initiated a mass literacy effort (Chadwick 1948, 34). Chadwick's account of his work in the village of Ogwofia, the specific village depicted in *Daybreak in Udi,* shows the processes of community development synoptically:

> In rapid succession the people cleared the bush to provide a village centre, made a short motor road from the civic centre to the nearby N.A. [Native Administration] road, and built, in the following order: a temporary village hall where mass literacy classes could be held; a village reading room of handsome appearance, which now contains a radio set; a co-operative consumers' shop, the first of its kind in Nigeria; a temporary shed to house hand-worked machinery for processing palm fruit; a sub-dispensary; model latrines; an incinerator; and largest and most costly of all, a brick village maternity home, with a 3,000 gallon water tank and a midwife's quarters attached. (Chadwick 1948, 34–35)

The presence of a radio and vernacular reading material fit the Colonial Office's new mandate for mass education. According to Chadwick, the village hall was sometimes converted into a theater with a borrowed Kodascope 16 mm projector from the Native Administration (Chadwick 1948, 36). It is possible that some of the BEKE films had been shown in Chadwick's district, especially since the BEKE had produced a film illustrating the construction of pit latrines and the dangers of hookworm.[14] Chadwick recounted the community's willingness to undergo a hookworm survey and "mass treatment . . . if desirable" (Chadwick 1948, 35).

It is significant that Chadwick claimed that almost all of the community development projects came from the community itself, but he also sketched his own role in recommending that women of the community form a cooperative credit society to pay the midwife's wages. The registrar of cooperatives, a position that had been in place thanks to Strickland's campaign, had been the moving hand behind the construction of the cooperative shop, and according to Chadwick, a total of ten cooperative shops had been registered in Udi Division by 1948 (Chadwick 1948, 36). Strickland had regarded the role of the registrar as something between teacher, promoter, and overseer.[15] From Chadwick's account, Nigeria's registrar, Major E. H. G. Haig, executed his official duties admirably, though he was unable to convince the village to "farm their palm bush on a communal basis, to provide profit for the village fund." However, it would seem from Chadwick's account that the village decided to buy its "hand-worked" farming equipment cooperatively.

Daybreak in Udi, produced as a joint project of the Central Office of Information and the Colonial Office, used Chadwick's story primarily as a vehicle to publicize the Advisory Committee on Education in the Colonies' new plan for mass education. The 1943 report on mass education prescribed a boilerplate for how alliances between local voluntary groups should be formed to tackle community development projects. Voluntary community organizations would collaborate with colonial government, which held the purse strings to the Colonial Development Fund introduced in 1940, on specific projects of community building. The report on mass education was also noteworthy for its consideration of the place of mass media in development planning. While much of the report echoes the essential tenets of interwar community development practiced at the Jeanes School and in the BEKE project, one sea change in the postwar context was its new insistence on a campaign to eradicate illiteracy. While "Native Education" under the committee's watch since 1925 was not completely devoid of literacy training, the ACEC had nonetheless sought to diminish English-language instruction, and since most texts were then in English, this effectively meant a backing away from literacy training altogether. But with mass education, the committee now urged "adult literacy," arguing that broad literacy was necessary in order to mount public information campaigns on matters of agricultural method, hygiene, and nutrition.[16] It emphasized vernacular languages in the literacy campaigns and called for the production of vernacular texts with a new sense of urgency.

The mass education report gave almost equal weight to film as an official tool of propaganda suited for the "African mind," and the committee deliberated extensively on the perception of film as imagined by Africans. The report cited the work of the BEKE filmmakers directly. While conceding that entertaining films were crucial to balance the dry, didactic offerings of instructional cinema, the committee was concerned that the African mind could not properly interpret them. This analysis echoed that of the BEKE filmmakers in 1936. Africans saw images differently, the committee argued. Surprisingly, they tended to avert their attention from the action framed in the center foreground to the background, and could be "distracted" by images that might be secondary to those intended by a filmmaker. It was also claimed that "fading in" and "fading out" were similarly difficult for the African mind to interpret. This conclusion seems to be drawn straight from the earlier BEKE reports, where Latham and Notcutt wrote that they struggled to convey the passing of time or transitions from place to place through fading techniques. The committee concluded that "for them [African audiences], films should have relatively long sequences, the minimum of rapid, unexplained transitions, and no camera tricks" (ACEC 1943, 42).

Arguments like these pointed to the dangers of allowing the unchecked influence of foreign entertainment films on African audiences. Community development would require the establishment of some form of censorship organization (ACEC 1943, 45–46). But the trustee state could not only function repressively; it should also establish mechanisms for the production of films supporting the educational and political intent of the colonial administration. The report specifically recommended films on "trade unions, cooperative societies and local governments," provided that the films be focused on "the principles that determine their constitution and functioning." The committee argued that trade unions would be useful to encourage in towns, but that cooperatives were important for rural development. The report mostly reiterated Strickland's arguments concerning the importance of cooperatives as a stabilizing force against social change, asserting, "They [cooperatives and trade unions] are creating by such activities strong units which can become a community. . . . In areas where old community ties have broken down or hardly existed, such groupings for a common purpose, with a certain order and discipline in their organization, have an importance out of all proportion to their size" (27). Films on cooperative economics would serve as a counter to films that focused on "large scale economic enterprise." Of course, the large-scale economic enterprise in Africa usually relied on the plantation model. The films approved by the ACEC would, by contrast, focus on cottage industries and efforts at bringing their wares to market (41–42). In vivid prose, the subcommittee on mass education explained the importance of teaching marketing: "Thus improved agricultural techniques must relate to internal as well as external marketing in order to awaken the countryside by a thriving exchange of food and other goods" (15).

The committee was assured by the Colonial Office that the Office was currently conceiving a system of film production and distribution in Africa. This was one of the priorities of the BEKE project, too: Latham and Notcutt had developed a plan whereby a central organization would be set up in London and would manage from a distance an army of European and African filmmakers in the field. It would be constituted "somewhat like the BBC," accountable to government, perhaps funded by government grants initially, but with the goal of being financially self-sustaining (Latham and Notcutt 1937, 196). The BEKE filmmakers argued that the central organization in London should have its own studios and that it should be a clearinghouse for scripts and footage shot by film units throughout the empire. The London studios would solicit film scripts, consult with sociologists and anthropologists on educational content, and then coordinate film production, editing new footage provided by the film units in Africa and other colonial settings along with stock footage. Soundtracks and translations would be provided by roving recording specialists who would travel between colonies gathering voice tracks in all languages required by London for a particular script (Latham and Notcutt 1937, 189–90). The BEKE filmmakers hoped that such an organization would allow for a steady flow of new films, and thus the repetition of shots needed for film to have instructive value as propaganda (Latham and Notcutt 1937, 140–41). Finally, the filmmakers conceived of a system that would circulate finished films with mobile cinema units that fused a diesel engine with projector, gramophone, and screen. The mass education committee saw the future of African film likewise in mobile cinemas—"cinema vans" or even steamships rigged as a mobile cinema (ACEC 1943, 45).

Mass education affirmed other tenets of community development as previously conceived by the ACEC. For instance, one of the main goals of mass education was to involve new community institutions in such a way as to support each other's education work. The village school, then, should also be a place for the community to gather for evenings of radio "listening groups." The mass education report cited experiments in Uganda in the use of radio broadcasting that showed that in order to be effective and popular with listeners, broadcasts needed to be in the vernacular languages and spoken by native speakers of the language. Just as the Jeanes teachers' special qualification was their ability to be embedded in the local community and received as a member, broadcasting for mass education needed personnel with "a clear comprehension of the methods and purposes of mass education; the knowledge of their [African audiences'] history, customs, folklore, music and dancing and of the mental attitudes of the audience which only a common kinship can bestow; ability to use the mother tongue accurately and with all the flexibility and the wealth of idiom it may possess" (ACEC 1943, 39).

The push to cluster African economic and political life around community centers first required their construction. These community building programs became an important part of community development as the ACEC envisioned it throughout the interwar and postwar period. The cooperative was key, and its prescribed role in support of community development was reinforced by the new laws that ensured that cooperative societies would be physical structures at the center of the community. They could no longer simply be cohesive associations through rotating contributions and distributions. The new cooperatives law established throughout British colonial Africa required that each registered society have a physical building with the law posted on its wall. In contrast, *esusu* organizations in Yoruba society kept records by etching them on the walls of the huts of individual members (Geertz 1962, 252). Community development required fixed spaces and organizations that would amalgamate community sentiment for the purpose of forging progressive links outward. The community hall, or center, was imagined to forge inward community bonds, ideally sparking a communal desire to build a road outward. Chadwick's report on the progress in Nigeria focused on the popular desire to commit voluntary man-hours of work toward clearing forests for roads. *Daybreak at Udi* ends with a celebration of the awakening of community life thanks to the project, as the community takes pride in "our road" while engaging in a healthy competition with the neighboring village.[17] The inward dynamics of the cooperative reinforced a community will toward those on the outside. Cooperative farming societies taught farmers how to grade their produce and market it to the tastes of distant consumers. Cooperative credit would bring together the funds for the community to make steps outward to connect to the center of machine production—as with the palm processing equipment purchased by Ogwofia.

Conclusion

Community development for Africa was part of an effort to stem the tide of African social change and to graft into "native life" a set of community institutions that could modernize rural practices. Reformers hoped they could redirect economic life and political affiliations into forms that would provide for a self-supporting African welfare system that favored a future role for Europeans in Africa. If rapidly expanded and expertly managed, these sites of community government also might serve as antidotes to threatening African nationalism and Pan-Africanism. Efforts to build these connective institutions privileged film and radio as effective educational tools for reaching a unique "African mind" that thrived when rooted in agricultural work. It was claimed by the ACEC in its 1925 charter that European norms of behavior, culture, and "mind" should merely be "adapted" for Africans. In particular, it was in the sites of community instruction promoted by the new educational reformers—including Oldham, Dougall, and Latham, among many others—that much of the theorizing and research into the African mind was directed. Latham's field notes for the BEKE were a collection of observations on the idiosyncratic tendencies associated with African perceptions of moving images. Dougall's Jeanes School in Kabete was host to the American psychologist who conducted the first intelligence testing experiments on Africans (Oliver 1934). The ACEC's mass education report emphasized the importance of data being collected for the purposes of perfecting propaganda techniques.

Films were only one among other forms of media deployed. Community development presented an array of new programs to speak to the African mind, including posters, demonstration plots, radio, and vernacular reading material. The image of the cooperative shop or credit society as part of the ideal village was one routinely peddled by reformers who believed that connections between metropole and colony were crucial to the wealth of each. This was the philosophy that informed interwar community development reforms. It was summed up well by Latham shortly before he embarked for East Africa to take charge of the Bantu cinema experiment. He wrote in the journal *Africa* that education in the West tended to foster a spirit of nationalism, but he argued that African education should be organized differently to stress interdependence between Africa and the West. "They have everything to gain," he wrote, "by co-operating with western nations, provided we pursue an enlightened and liberal policy in regard to them. They have everything to lose if they become imbued with a spirit of hatred and non-co-operative nationalism" (Latham 1934, 429).

Latham's analysis was both an endorsement of the political economy supported by community development and a recognition that the community development idea competed for audiences against other powerful versions of modernization, such as African nationalism. Latham thought it was not enough that a film's content be instructive in values of community development; the films must also be popular and potentially profitable (in order to be financially self-sustaining). Notcutt and Latham agreed that in a deeper sense development was the outcome of an education and public information system engineered for persuasive effect and maximum exposure. This meant that community development instruction, whether conveyed by the pedagogies of the cinema or the pedagogies of the cooperative (or of the village school itself), needed to be vernacular and visual. The idea of community development—as the version of modernization endorsed in interwar colonial policy—needed to dominate local African social spaces through repetition, using censorship controls and a complex machinery of film distribution to promote its message while hedging out others.

Fragmentary evidence suggests that the BEKE coordinators were concerned about the negative influence of Hollywood films in Africa and the tremendous propaganda gains of state-directed instructional film campaigns in the Soviet Union.[18] But more importantly, the BEKE coordinators knew they competed with local knowledge, and so they made films that ridiculed the "witch-doctor" and made African methods of cultivation seem backward. Their film *Tax* (dir. Leslie A. Notcutt, 1935) used shots of precolonial warfare and the violent exaction of tribute in a first reel and in a second reel staged a contrasting sequence of shots depicting the improving purpose of colonial taxes in "examples of . . . medical attention, education, help in time of famine, maintenance of order and peace." Such a film could only have been made out of competition with a counternarrative that saw hut taxes and other colonial taxes as unjust. Indeed, according to Latham and Notcutt, it was made to address a problem throughout the African empire that "many Natives are under the impression that their tax goes into the pockets of local administrative officers" (Latham and Notcutt 1937, 35). Such counternarratives to the modernizing promise of colonial administration were made all the more threatening in the context of political movements among Africans that sought to challenge the legitimacy not just of colonial taxes, but of colonial rule itself.

Reformers who believed in community development for Africa placed great hope in the creation of communication technologies and administrative structures to control their message, with radio and film being at the forefront. Plans to teach cooperative economics as a centerpiece of development in Africa from the 1920s onward were premised on the conviction that African economic practice must incorporate forms of exchange that would integrate African agricultural production with Western consumption. Further, it was argued that the rapid social changes brought on by imperial expansion should be addressed by new institutions that could forge community ties from the ruins of disrupted societies. From this perspective, Africans would help themselves in the area of welfare provision through the surpluses assured by efficient cooperative marketing and saving, and European consumers would have products grown, processed, and delivered at their table.[19] Community developers, far from pursuing a project of independent nation building, were attempting to script their own future roles in Africa. They believed that rural development would require the continued presence of European experts—what Chadwick called "the vitally important, long-term personal link between Europe and Africa" (Chadwick 1948, 31).

Notes

1. A 1958 Commission of Inquiry into Bugisu cooperatives warned that "the [Bugisu Co-operative] Union has become a symbol of Bugisu unity. Any proposals to reorganize it are liable to be opposed on emotional grounds, and the authors of any such proposals may find themselves accused of 'divide and rule' motives." The 1958 *Report of the Commission of Inquiry into the Affairs of the Bugisu Co-operative Union Limited* is quoted in Young, Sherman, and Rose (1981, 76–78).

2. *Daybreak in Udi* was not only a film intended to be shown to African audiences but also played abroad as a demonstration of the welfare work being done in the empire; in fact it won an Academy Award in the United States. The film can be viewed at the website Colonial Film: Moving Images of the British Empire, found at http://www.colonialfilm.org.uk.

3. Only three of the thirty-five films produced by the BEKE survive; they are held at the British Film Institute. These are *African Peasant Farms* (dir. Leslie A. Notcutt, 1936, 9 min.);

Tropical Hookworm (dir. Leslie A. Notcutt, 1936, 10 min.); and *The Veterinary Training of African Natives* (dir. Leslie A. Notcutt, 1936, 19 min.). All three films can be viewed along with production notes and analysis at the Colonial Film website, http://www.colonialfilm.org.uk.

4. Thomas Jesse Jones, then president of the Phelps-Stokes Fund, believed in the American theory of the "manifest destiny" of the Anglo-Saxon race and was an unwavering advocate of white settlement in Africa. See Berman (1971, 133).

5. The Command paper asserted that "education should be adapted to the mentality, aptitudes, occupations, and traditions of the various peoples, conserving as far as possible all sound and healthy elements in the fabric of their social life; adapting them where necessary to changed circumstances and progressive ideas, as an agent of natural growth and evolution." Command Paper 2374, London: H. M. S. printers, 1925.

6. That film for Africans should be carefully studied was the first assumption of Merle Davis's application to the Carnegie Corporation to fund the BEKE project. "Study of the Cinema as an Instrument for Education and Cultural Adjustment, Africa," Columbia University Special Collections, Carnegie Corporation Grant Files, box 186/18.

7. George C. Latham, journal entry, 14 June 1935, box 263129, fiche 1, International Missionary Council Records, Yale Divinity Library, New Haven, CT.

8. Latham, journal entry, 24 June 1935, box 263129, fiche 1, International Missionary Council Records, Yale Divinity Library, New Haven, CT.

9. Latham, journal entry, 26 June 1935, box 263129, fiche 1, International Missionary Council Records, Yale Divinity Library, New Haven, CT.

10. *African Peasant Farms* can be viewed at the Colonial Film website, http://www.colonialfilm.org.uk.

11. See "Reports etc. by Mr. C.F. Strickland in Regard to Co-operation and Economic Conditions in Palestine, Malaya, Zanzibar, and T.T.," T[he] N[ational] A[rchive] CO 323/1151/6; "Report on Cooperative Methods by C.F. Strickland," TNA CO 323/1071/14; and, especially for Tanganyika Territory (Tanzania), "Cooperative Marketing," TNA CO 691/118/10. Of course, many Chagga coffee farmers had already been organized cooperatively for at least five years before Strickland's visit to Tanganyika Territory.

12. The requirement of a high degree of state scrutiny of cooperative bookkeeping and membership rolls was typical in the postcolonial context. "Cooperation Societies Legislation," TNA CO 533/499. See also Quick (1978), and DeGraft-Johnson (1958, 61–63).

13. Philip Zachernuk includes Mbanefo among a cadre of West African students whose political ideas grew through their association with the WASU hostel in London (Zachernuck 2000, 95–102; see also Matera 2010).

14. *Tropical Hookworm* (dir. Leslie A. Notcutt, 1936, 10 min.) can be viewed at the Colonial Film website, http://www.colonialfilm.org.uk.

15. Strickland knew that the cooperative movement would prosper or fail depending on how well the message was deployed in mass media. Already in the early 1930s he perceived a need for radio receivers in every village. In this way he anticipated the recommendations of the mass education subcommittee in 1943 (Strickland 1933a, 37).

16. The report averred, "So far in the British Colonies we have acted on the assumption that people would eventually adopt improved methods of agriculture, a more nutritious diet, and hygienic surroundings and western medical ideas without learning to read or write." The ACEC arrived at its new conclusion that a mass literacy drive was necessary through its comparative study of education in the Dutch East Indies, China, and Russia, where rapid literacy programs had been tried (ACEC 1943, 14).

17. The mass education report expressed hope that community development would lead to these intervillage competitions to see who could progress the furthest fastest.

18. "Study of the Cinema as an Instrument for Education and Cultural Adjustment, Africa," Carnegie Corporation Grant Files, box 186/18, Columbia University Special Collections, Columbia University, New York.

19. The subcommittee on mass education wrote about the importance of teaching marketing: "Thus improved agricultural techniques must relate to internal as well as external marketing in order to awaken the countryside by a thriving exchange of foods and other goods" (ACEC 1943, 15).

References

Advisory Committee on Education in the Colonies [ACEC]. 1943. *Mass Education in African Society.* London: H. M. S. Printers.

Anderson, David, and David Throup. 1985. "African and Agricultural Production in Colonial Kenya: The Myth of the War as Watershed." *Journal of African History* 26, no. 4: 327–45.

Bennett, George. 1960. "Paramountcy to Partnership: J. H. Oldham and Africa." *Africa: Journal of the International African Institute* 30, no. 4: 356–61.

Berman, Edward H. 1971. "American Influence on African Education: The Role of the Phelps-Stokes Fund's Education Commissions." *Comparative Education Review* 15, no. 2: 132–45.

Burns, James. 2002. *Flickering Shadows: Cinema and Identity in Colonial Zimbabwe.* Athens: Ohio University Press.

Chadwick, E. R. 1948. "Mass Education in Udi Division." *African Affairs* 47, no. 186: 31–41.

Coulson, Andrew. 1982. *Tanzania: A Political Economy.* New York: Oxford University Press.

DeGraft-Johnson. 1958. *African Experiment: Cooperative Agriculture and Banking in British West Africa.* London: Watts.

Dougall, James W. C. 1932. "Characteristics of African Thought." *Africa* 5, no. 3: 249–65.

Geertz, Clifford. 1962. "Rotating Credit Associations: A 'Middle Rung' in Development." *Economic Development and Cultural Change* 10, no. 3: 241–63.

Hyden, Goran. 1980. *Beyond Ujamaa in Tanzania: Underdevelopment and an Uncaptured Peasantry.* Berkeley: University of California Press.

Iliffe, John. 1979. *A Modern History of Tanganyika.* Cambridge: Cambridge University Press.

King, Kenneth. 1969. "Africa and the Southern States of the U.S.A.: Notes on J. H. Oldham and American Negro." *Journal of African History* 10, no. 4: 659–77.

Latham, George C. 1934. "Indirect Rule and Education in East Africa." *Africa: Journal of the International African Institute* 7, no. 4: 423–30.

Matera, Marc. 2010. "Colonial Subjects: Black Intellectuals and the Development of Colonial Studies in Britain." *Journal of British Studies* 49, no. 2: 388–418.

McCarthy, Dennis Michael Patrick. 1981. *Colonial Bureaucracy and Creating Underdevelopment: Tanganyika, 1919–1940.* Ames: Iowa State University Press.

Munger, Edwin S. 1952. "African Coffee on Kilimanjaro: A Chagga Kihamba." *Economic Geography* 28, no. 2: 181–85.

Notcutt, Leslie A., and Geoffrey C. Latham. 1937. *The African and the Cinema: An Account of the Work of the Bantu Educational Cinema Experiment during the Period March 1935 to May 1937.* London: Edinburgh House Press.

Oliver, Richard A. C. 1934. "Mental Tests in the Study of the African." *Africa: Journal of the International African Institute* 7, no. 1: 40–46.

Quick, Stephen A. 1978. *Humanism or Technocracy?: Zambia's Farming Co-operatives, 1965–1972.* Manchester: Manchester University Press for the Institute for African Studies, University of Zambia.

Reynolds, Glenn. 2009. "The Bantu Educational Kinema Experiment and the Struggle for Hegemony in British East and Central Africa, 1935–1937." *Historical Journal of Film, Radio and Television* 29, no. 1: 57–78.

Smyth, Rosaleen. 1979. "The Development of British Colonial Film Policy, 1927–1939, with Special Reference to East and Central Africa." *Journal of African History* 20, no. 3: 437–50.

———. 2004. "The Roots of Community Development in Colonial Office Policy and Practice in Africa." *Social Policy and Administration* 38, no. 4: 418–36.

Strickland, Claude Francis. 1933a. *Co-Operation for Africa.* London: Oxford University Press.

———. 1933b. "Co-operation for Africa." *Africa: Journal of the International African Institute* 6, no.1: 15–26.

———. 1935. "Supplement: The Co-operative Movement in Africa." *Journal of the Royal African Society* 34, no. 134: 1–18.

Webb, Beatrice, and Sidney Webb. 1920. *A Constitution for the Socialist Commonwealth of Great Britain.* London: Cambridge University Press.

Westcott, Nicholas. 1984. "The East African Sisal Industry, 1929–1949: The Marketing of a Colonial Commodity during Depression and War." *Journal of African History* 25, no. 4: 445–61.

Young, Crawford, Neal Sherman, and Tim Rose. 1981. *Cooperatives and Development.* Madison: University of Wisconsin Press.

Zachernuk, Philip. 2000. *Colonial Subjects: An African Intelligentsia and Atlantic Ideas.* Charlottesville: University of Virginia Press.

5 Is Propaganda Modernity?

Press and Radio for "Africans" in Zambia, Zimbabwe, and Malawi during World War II and Its Aftermath

Mhoze Chikowero

Introduction: Radio in a Colonial Context

Anthropologist Debra Spitulnik (1999, 63) observed that the introduction of electronic media in Zambia went hand in hand with the introduction of cultural practices, orientations, and evaluations related to the ideas of progress, sophistication, consumption, innovation, and Westernization. She bundled this nexus under the cover term "modernity." Spitulnik argues that this cover term does both too much and too little. While she problematizes the concept, she proceeds to utilize African radio listener feedback to Lusaka Radio collected by anthropologist Hortense Powdermaker (1962) and broadcaster Harry Franklin (1950) to reinforce the notion that radio was an instrument and signifier of modernity. Spitulnik teases out a question, which I suggest must be reinforced: whose discourse is this "modernity"?

This chapter uses internal official communication among policymakers and memoirs by former broadcasters from World War II and early postwar colonial Zambia, Zimbabwe, and Malawi, not necessarily to search for modernity in Africa, but to show that the metanarrative constitutes what V. Y. Mudimbe calls a "colonizing structure" (Mudimbe 1988, 4).While clothed in the useful register of modernity, this official archive locates the coming of radio as an instrument of colonial statecrafting. I argue that by celebrating "local uses" and readings of Western technology outside this colonial context, we risk legitimizing the colonial designs of the Western technologies simply because Africans, as agents of history, have often put such technologies to (other) use(s). African uses of these technologies will have to be assessed within the broad context of the colonial philosophies and schemes of domination because radio, like the press and cinema, was a technology of domination first and foremost. This colonial archive confesses to this propaganda design, and available African perspectives similarly name it as such.

Bitter Propaganda Pills

In a speech broadcast from Nairobi in 1941, E. R. St. Davis, director of African broadcasting, puzzled over the failure of British radio propaganda for Africans during World War II. He likened Africans' resistance to colonial propaganda to the common aversion to pills: "Most of us dislike pills, and these require a good coating of sugar before we can be persuaded to swallow them." His job was to make sure Africans swallowed the propaganda pills. Davis articulated the problematic for colonial media in general and radio in particular when he pondered, "How are these educational pills to be sugared?"[1] Davis's introspective broadcast teased out not only the imperialistic mode of British media policy in Africa, but also its crisis. Banking on the aura of the radio set as a prized possession and potential symbol of modernity in the eyes of the colonized, British proponents of radio "broadcasting to Africans" hoped that the radio would be a most effective instrument for assimilating the masses of Africans into useful and loyal subjects of empire (Franklin 1949, 13). As such, I argue, British colonial propaganda broadcasting to Africans was a crucial tool for building the British Empire. The British falteringly initiated radio broadcasting to Africans on the back of the dismal failure of a propaganda press that had targeted Africans prior to and in the early stages of World War II. While efforts to nurture the struggling press and a fledgling cinema continued after the war, radio quickly became the chief propaganda tool for persuading Africans to support the war, in marketing the Federation (1953–1963) of these three territories, and in the struggle against African nationalism, which the state framed within Cold War rhetoric as Communism. This chapter examines the formative years of colonial radio from the shadows of a failing propaganda press.

Colonial policymakers broadly framed radio propaganda as education and envisaged the medium itself as a novel vehicle for "civilizing" Africans. They believed that the power of radio would revolutionize African social life by "educating the natives on the right lines in proper hygiene, agriculture, housing and sanitation" while depoliticizing them so as to prevent the "popular influence of the illiterate masses by their intelligentsia class" (Franklin 1949, 13). Radio was therefore deployed as a tool to construct Africans into a self-contradictory, loyalist colonial subjectivity that flaunted sectarian social evolution and criminalized political consciousness. As such, a study of colonial broadcasting allows us to directly confront the twin mythologies of colonialism as modernity on the one hand, and modernity as loyalism and assimilation on the other. Further, it provides the missing context for the fashionable inquiries into the ways in which the colonized contested, subverted, and appropriated the instruments of the state and put them to their own ends and purposes. The latter is a larger concern that I do not have the scope to address here.

The fact that Africans were, like other people, fascinated by radio and enthusiastically welcomed it as part of the novelty of the times should not lead us into the blind alleys of "modernity" uncritically, because Africans were not oblivious to the politics of broadcasting. They not only decoded media messages; they also recoded and redeployed both the messages and the broadcasting and reception technologies in ways that confounded European "experts," their "expertise," and their physical infrastructures (White 1995, 223). Studying radio within this dialectical framework, then, troubles the notion that the radio set was the colonists' unproblematic gift to Africans, and a straightforward symbol of modernity to them. After Brian Larkin (1999), Roger Silverstone and Eric Hirsch (1992), and Spitulnik (2002), it is crucial to bear in mind that a radio set embodied multiply articulated ideologies of power, modernity, and status. In colonial Africa, it was simultaneously a dubious tool of colonial assault; a new, fascinating communication and recreational technology; a prized, symbolically powerful piece of property; and a weapon that enabled the colonized to engage the colonist.

Both James M. Burns (2002) and James Zaffiro (1984) observe that the colonial state delayed the introduction of radio broadcasting to Africans due to official and settler anxieties that "slow-brained" Africans would not understand radio news because the medium was too complicated for them. Similarly, fears abounded that radio could incite Africans to political revolution. This anxiety and the "prose of counter-insurgency" (Guha 1988) that greeted its eventual introduction reveal not just the troubled history of colonist radio but also, more importantly, the nervous condition of colonial authority. These anxieties were most palpable in Southern Rhodesia (present-day Zimbabwe), the shining beacon of British colonialism. The colony belatedly bought the idea of radio propaganda only after some prodding by its northern counterparts and after the failure of the press.

War Rumors: The Fragile Pots of Colonial Propaganda

African loyalty to the British Empire, which in the context of World War II meant supporting the war morally, financially, materially, and with manpower, was not guaranteed. It had to be aggressively cultivated and perpetually nurtured. The war had to be sold as equally important to Africans as it was to Europeans, with its causes, course, and implications persuasively explained. In this regard, state propaganda sought to convince Africans that losing the war would entail enslavement by the Nazis. This was crucial in the context of African anticolonial sentiment, which, in its scandalizing pitch, hailed perceived British routing by the Germans. Stories also circulated in Lusaka and elsewhere suggesting that African recruits perishing in shipwrecks in the Indian Ocean and other mysterious circumstances in faraway warfronts were part of a calculated effort to check the potential threat of African veterans who might rise up to reclaim their own freedom at home (Fraenkel 1959, 11). Similarly, in colonial Zimbabwe, according to Lawrence Vambe (1976, 128), some African veterans reportedly generated the story that "all badly injured black soldiers returning home were put on separate boats and sent to the bottom of the ocean." Vambe also heard the millennial Watch Tower movement preaching from forest clearings and anthills that Hitler was a hand of the Almighty sent to "make the white races pay in blood and tears for their . . . wrongs, especially in Africa" (125).[2]

Colonial administrators were fully aware of the power of rumor in times of crisis. World War II generated its own particular rumors, which reinforced the salience of preexisting ones in the region revolving around matters such as the Banyama, known as mysterious "vampire men." Claims swirled that these Banyama kidnapped Africans not only to supply an allegedly continuing, clandestine European slave trade, but also for cannibalistic purposes and for body parts purportedly used in European pharmaceutical drugs. Much of the rumor also revolved around the perceived fragility of British authority and German invincibility (Musambachime 1988; White 2000). Musambachime observes that rumors about German military prowess were a throwback to the First World War when so-called "natives" "saw [German forces] marching through [northeastern Northern Rhodesia] unopposed, burning and looting while British officials fled" (Musambachime 1988, 203–204). The potent mix of new and persistent old rumors had the potential to jeopardize the imperial war effort, particularly recruitment for the African regiments. In this context, modern media were therefore charged to communicate "facts" not only to counter pernicious rumor, but also to help reshape rumormongers into "rational," "modern" thinkers.

Ironically, however, the colonial state fingered "educated" Africans as the chief culprits in the propagation of the new rumor wave as part of their anticolonial demagoguery. The allegation reflected the official bias against competing centers of knowledge because Africans generally questioned the democratic ideals that defeating Nazism would purportedly accord them. As Vambe (1976) writes, "[The] cynics were not confined to the educated class. They were to be found in all sections of our society." If such "cynics" cared at all about the war, following Vambe, it was because they hoped the outcome would be the toppling of the white power structure that dominated them (125).

The concoction of World War II propaganda for Africans was brewed first in the fledgling government press projects introduced for Africans in the 1930s. In Northern Rhodesia, the pot was *Mutende*, an English-language fortnightly originally introduced to tackle strike-happy Copperbelt mineworkers who allegedly read millennial Watch Tower writings (Smyth 1984, 247). The newspaper was conceived to counter this "unwholesome" literature. With the outbreak of the war, *Mutende* became the state's "principal means of information for Africans" more generally.[3] Under a two-tier editorship by a district officer overseen by the government information officer, *Mutende* churned out about ten thousand copies per print run and, in official estimation, each copy was passed on to up to ten people and reached perhaps more after the introduction of village reader clubs.[4]

In Southern Rhodesia, the Native Affairs Department (NAD) was charged with this mandate among the Africans while the government information officer handled propaganda for Europeans, Indians, and Coloreds through mainstream press like the *Herald*. In the first two weeks of the war, Charles Bullock, the Chief Native Commissioner (CNC), gave talks on the war to Africans at public meetings in the major towns, explaining its causes, course, and how Africans should contribute to the imperial war effort. He tasked his subordinates—the Native Commissioners (NCs) and compound managers—to replicate the talks to Africans in their charge.[5] Later, he committed the talks to press in a weekly bulletin that covered the progress of the war in Europe and developments at home. He sent five hundred copies of each bulletin to the NCs, large employers of Africans, and post offices where they would be translated from English into local languages with the help of trusted "better-educated Africans" for wider readership.

Settlers enthusiastically supported these papers. Writing in 1941, W. R. Hammond, superintendent of Shabanie Mine Native School, requested about a dozen copies of the CNC's bulletin, "a large night school of workers being a good opportunity for the spread of accurate news to Natives through their Native Teachers."[6] Southern Rhodesia's *Bantu Mirror* also compiled "an exhaustive [weekly] war diary" that, in the view of the information officer, proved "excellent propaganda work" if only for the first few weeks of the war. In Nyasaland, the government issued *Nkhani za Nyasaland* for the same purpose, and it was also imported into Southern Rhodesia together with *Mutende* for the reading of migrant "alien natives" working in the labor-importing colony.

How did Africans read this colonial press? According to Vambe (1976, 126), they were quite aware of the agenda, and they scorned the newspapers:

> Caught in this state of official nervousness, the Chief Native Commissioner . . . Bullock . . . decided early on in the war to publish a special bulletin in English, Shona and Sindebele, which was supposed to contain the facts, and was distributed to Africans throughout the country. . . . It was intended to counteract the rumors that Bullock was aware were being bandied about. And yet this bulletin was so biased that, apart from its entertainment value, it was worthless. According to this little paper, all the British, and later, Allied troops were everywhere superior to the Germans. While Hitler's soldiers suffered heavy losses and were very often utterly punished, our side always managed to win great victories or to retreat in splendid order with few losses to themselves. Most of the news it carried was days, if not weeks old, so that those who depended entirely upon it were often grossly misinformed. We called it the Lying Bulletin.

Africans did not sit impassively waiting to be fed "accurate news." They read with a critical mind beyond what was meant for them and they built crucial knowledge about the war and state policy. Vambe (1976) writes that Africans could not avoid reading the local European and foreign newspapers because there was no reliable African press: "We read and listened almost as much as the settlers did. However hard the Rhodesian government tried to keep us immune from influences, it could not regulate our thinking" (120). African reading beyond the colonial schemes compounded the state's nervousness. This led the state to decry Africans' "wrong" reading habits, which allegedly helped to fan rather than stem the pernicious rumors. This crisis spawned internal official skepticism about the effectiveness of the written word on Africans, with critics faulting the form and style of the propaganda machinery.

British colonial education policies were designed to produce barely literate laborers, not masses of well-educated Africans. The contradictory consequences of these policies haunted the state. As J. Blake Thompson, then Salisbury Municipality Health Department's Inspector of Natives, pointed out, a large proportion of this reading population was self-instructed and taught by their own fellows outside the school system.[7] The state questioned this readership's literacy and working knowledge of English. Moreover, the NAD's critics also doubted the reading styles and comprehension capabilities of even those Africans who could understand the simple English of these newspapers. Thus argued Thompson, who also claimed expertise on "the native mind" by virtue of both his anthropological studies in Paris as well as South Africa and of nineteen years of "personal contact with natives." As he writes,

> Owing to the display [of the newspaper] the native does not know how to differentiate enemy statements and British, often leaving the newspaper with confused and wrong ideas which he passes on to his more illiterate friends. Also due to his own system of education through being taught to read a paragraph here and another there not in consecutive order, he rarely reads an article right through even if he understands the words. As a result, he gets garbled ideas of affairs.[8]

The city's location welfare officer, E. A. Cordell, shared this dim view of the African reader, arguing that the "semi-educated native misses the import of a printed statement like: 'A German communiqué states . . .' and accepts the following statement as being accurate news." Cordell charged that the semiliterate African then peddled the resulting "garbled view," poisoning his more illiterate colleagues who happily trusted everything coming from the newspaper as truth.[9] According to him, Africans fully trusted the newspaper, and their peddling of misinformation was only an outcome of their technical incompetence!

However, the point is clear. The state officials certainly acknowledged, and went on to malign, the power of African independent and communal reading, which they could not control. Thus, only a few months after the outbreak of the war, the propaganda press had been thrown into crisis, forcing Southern Rhodesia's NAD to fall back on the poorly attended public meetings, word of mouth, and posters that were similarly open to interpretation. This crisis in communication raised the premium for radio in spite of persistent opposition to the new medium. For example, retaining faith in the written word, the NAD dismissed radio as "scarcely practicable owing to the large number of installations and loudspeakers . . . required to give anything like adequate coverage" of the country.[10] However, the moment of radio had arrived and the department was relentlessly attacked for its oppositional stance.

For instance, the information officer was exasperated that the Southern Rhodesia CNC still preferred the same discredited modes to radio, planning to import "war news" bulletins from as far afield as Uganda and to send his own newsletter to the two northern territories. These ideas, he argued, meant Africans would be fed "stale news" and, more importantly, they would remain inadequate to keep "the native population as fully informed as possible to prevent unhealthy [rumors] from spreading and to maintain their morale."[11] In his opinion, the Secretary for Native Affairs had failed his mandate to manage information for Africans. As such, he unsuccessfully tried to have the "native propaganda" portfolio transferred to him.[12] To remedy the crisis situation, the information officer also pleaded with the prime minister for the introduction of a battery of measures that included more local newsletters, more periodic meetings with Africans, picture sheets to be shown to Africans under the supervision of Europeans, and interrogations of Africans by high-powered committees to ascertain their attitudes to the war. These measures would be capped by the adoption of regular broadcasts to Africans in their principal languages—Shona, Ndebele, and Nyanja (a lingua franca among workers from the northern territories).[13] The latter suggestion had wide resonance.

Returning from South Africa, one J. E. Hawkey of the Salisbury Magistrate's Court had suggested to the information officer that the country should follow the example of its southern neighbor by starting broadcasts on the war to Africans in their own languages. He claimed to have been unsettled by African views about the war:

> I have heard all sorts of ridiculous stories from natives in this country about the unbeatable might of Nazi Germany, and in one case a native houseboy employed by a friend of mine returned to his kraal and stayed there, because, as he said, "Hitler will be here soon." Would it not be possible to arrange broadcasting on similar lines to those introduced in the Union, and arrange for loudspeakers in all municipal compounds and native locations? [Such] an arrangement would be simple, reasonably cheap, and undoubtedly effective.[14]

Southern Rhodesia could have looked south across the Limpopo as per Hawkey's suggestion. However, it made more sense, politically and for practical reasons, to look north over the Zambezi. Policymakers in Lusaka had already reached out to their counterparts in Southern Rhodesia and Nyasaland to suggest a regional approach to the endeavor. Thus, the Northern Rhodesian information officer had written reassuringly to his southern counterpart praising the magical effect of radio once it overcame its own "nervousness that it could merely exaggerate rumors and result in distorted versions of the news through imperfect understanding." His government claimed to have discovered that "broadcasting was the most potent means of stopping rumors and ensuring correct appreciation of the news."[15] This success, opined the information officer, owed to the idea that "the African's normal method of appreciation is the ear rather than the eye."[16] The suggestion was that the press had failed due to Africans' inability to read, and so radio would succeed by just speaking to these supposed natural but illiterate listeners. In any case, Lusaka had started calling, allowing radio to speak for itself.

Lusaka Calling: The Coming of Transterritorial Radio for Africans

Copperbelt district commissioners had taken the plunge to introduce radio in cooperation with the Radio Society at the beginning of 1940. With funding and oversight from the Colonial Office, the Northern Rhodesian government took over the venture in September to put out sixteen and a half hours of programming a week (Healing 1962, 7). Shortwave broadcasts soon reached Africans in at least five of that country's languages. The only shortcomings—which the information officer hoped were temporary—were "the insufficiently powerful transmitter and the lack of receivers at many mission stations and in the tribal areas."[17] Moreover and in spite of the technical and infrastructural limits, these broadcasts were being received throughout the region with the full support of the Nyasaland government and some miners in South Africa and Southern Rhodesia.

When the station was officially opened, Chief Mwase of Kasungu flew over from Nyasaland to grace the event and to make "special" broadcasts to Africans regarding his visit to England the previous year.[18] The Johannesburg Municipality's NAD also officially received the broadcasts with enthusiasm, as did some big South African mining companies and Southern Rhodesia's mission stations and other large employers of Africans (Franklin 1949, 15). One such employer (whose workforce boasted Africans from Northern Rhodesia and Nyasaland) was a Darwendale farmer whose positive feedback to Lusaka constituted part of the Southern Rhodesia information officer's fat dossier commending the medium for the colony. Wrote the farmer: "I have had on an average of forty boys every Tuesday and Friday to hear your news bulletin, and I can assure you that these broadcasts are very much appreciated by the boys."[19]

Another was a Shabanie school superintendent, who wrote that "the Lusaka broadcasts in native languages are greatly appreciated by some of the foreign natives whose employers allow them to listen in," and advising that "their use to the mass natives is however very limited and parallel broadcasts in Sindebele, Chishona, etc would be of great advantage" as locals were also clamoring for them.[20] The broadcasts started with "one talk and two news bulletins a week with plenty of music and local news . . . in simple English and four principal vernaculars."[21] Harry Franklin, the Northern Rhodesia director of information and part-time broadcaster, triumphantly explained that these broadcasts "apparently helped to keep their labour happy." He saw this convergence of interests as an opportunity to inculcate a radio-listening habit among Africans, suggesting that white domestic employers should go a step further and fit cheap extension speakers to their "boys' quarters."[22]

The Southern Rhodesia information officer applauded these spontaneous developments as a good start. He then proposed that the NAD could write all major employers of Africans to replicate these individual initiatives.[23] The political economy of colonialism had reconfigured human geography such that Africans had become concentrated in urban locations, on mine and farm compounds, in rural reserves and on mission stations. This remapped Africans spatially, and greatly helped the argument for radio since receiving equipment could be easily targeted to these compacted areas. At the same time, these were concentrations of the disenfranchised that represented a potential political powder keg. Thus, in that context, the colonial state sought to deploy radio to diffuse the undesirable possibility of political revolution.

Those who considered themselves experts on "the native mind" set to work. Thus wrote Thompson the anthropologist, "The Natives are amenable to mass suggestion and, if not controlled, to mass hysteria."[24] Radio had already arrived, uninvited from Lusaka and as part of the settler's European cultural accoutrements. And the broadcasts were already having some influence on Africans. Within the intimate realm of domestic labor, Thompson wrote, radio was touching "the houseboy class who hears his employer's wireless" and, if he has a good knowledge of English, "he imbibes broadcasts from Zeesen as part of the British broadcast, then passes it on to his friends in ever widening circles." But the realm of domestic labor also worried Thompson because, he pointed out, "this native picks up scraps of talk from his employers, from casual conversations between Europeans in streets and other places often paying more attention to the talk between others than that directed to himself." To remedy the combined effects of "careless talk by Europeans in the presence of natives" and the latter's alleged unintelligent listening, propensity for acquisitive overhearing, and hysterical dispositions, Thompson prescribed "official correction by mass instruction through loudspeakers or some such similar method [that] reaches large groups out in the open."[25] The combined specter of African crowding, undisciplined mobility, and disorderly socialization could be exploited for positive ends after all!

The question of reception, as may already be clear, was an important challenge for these policymakers. They worried about the lack of infrastructure and equipment for public listening. But equally important, they also agonized over "one obvious difficulty of radio, that of Africans buying ordinary receivers." This was a critical arsenal for opponents of radio broadcasting to Africans, particularly in Southern Rhodesia. However, there was no need for apprehension because, as the Northern Rhodesian pioneers had discovered, "the initial cost was heavy and, even in the future, a safeguard will be the expense of maintenance and the inherited inability of the African to operate any delicate mechanism without breaking it."[26] In any case, the good officer suggested an additional safeguard, that "District Commissioners would discourage any such purchases on financial grounds."[27] More than a "mobile machine" (Spitulnik 2002, 334), colonial officials imagined the radio primarily as a colonial voice that could talk to Africans without the latter controlling it. It was therefore reassuring to them that existing sets were under the direct control of Europeans and therefore safe from the potential "abuse" of Africans, particularly teachers who could tune into "enemy propaganda." Intent on reinforcing these "safeguards" as the program expanded into selected villages, urban locations, and mission schools, the Northern Rhodesian government had further proposed that only preset wireless sets would be used.[28] Fraenkel (1959, 31), however, suggests that Franklin, the director, protested and had this measure dropped in the interests of allowing Africans "free choice." Overprotection was apparently unnecessary at this stage; Europeans superintended available sets so that the government felt confident that it had adequate oversight of African listening habits.

For Southern Rhodesia, the potential "dangers" of mobile sets would be averted initially by the adoption of the street loudspeaker system, which many had long advocated. For example in 1940, the Municipality's welfare officer, the chief architect of African urban social control in Salisbury, had urged both the government and the city council to invest in a broadcasting apparatus in the "Native Location" as a matter of urgency. He had already obtained an estimate "for the installation of a microphone and three loudspeakers" as a start, and he elaborated a plan to strategically install the equipment:

> In the Beer Hall at the Native Location; on the Sports Ground near the Location, where some 3000 Africans gather every Sunday afternoon; at one of the stores or eating houses in the Charter Road; at the Native Commissioner's Office near the Market Square. Additionally, one portable set could do good work on Sunday afternoon at various points on the commonage where Africans gather.[29]

The Federation of African Welfare Societies backed the plan, adding that microphones should be installed in the Municipal Welfare Offices to rediffuse Lusaka broadcasts through a network of street loudspeakers (Ibbotson 1942, 42). The idea was thus conceived but it endured a slow birth due to insufficient capitalization. The laying of the elaborate infrastructure was only completed after the war in Harare [Salisbury] and much later in Rugare and elsewhere in the country.

However, in the meantime, the government resorted to mobile loudspeaker vans as a cheap stopgap measure for "maintaining the morale of the natives . . . through news, talks and propaganda by microphone," delivered live or prerecorded.[30] In addition, it began to use the municipality's loudspeaker system—operated from the superintendent's office—even before it could be connected to the radio. At Shabanie Mine, loudspeakers were installed in early 1941 to receive the Lusaka broadcasts, with the mine inquiring about the possibility for broadcasts in Shona and Ndebele too.[31] By 1941, then, there was some form of broadcasting in operation in all three territories. The radio message, if not the receiver, was conceived as a projection of a colonial voice that targeted the itinerant, gregarious, and unruly African sociality. It was deployed to help discipline the "native location" into a sanctioned, legible, and governable social space. But what was the content of the radio broadcasts? And did they achieve their objectives? The issue of program content dogged official imaginations and spawned the same worries that had led them to doubt Africans' capability to read the newspaper. They worried that "the native" might not be capable of listening "intelligently" after all.[32]

"Can the Native Listen Intelligently?": The Quest to Understand the "Native Mind"

We have seen how African reading styles—the "African eye"—confounded colonial propagandists. General ambivalence also beset their efforts to harness the African ear as an alternative portal for capturing African minds. It was only after CNC Charles Bullock was replaced with H. H. D. Simmonds that these misgivings were brushed aside in Southern Rhodesia. A position was then reached to broadcast "war talks" rather than "hard news" to Africans. Thus reported the Southern Rhodesia information officer to the prime minister:

> I have discussed the form these talks should take with Mr. Simmonds (CNC) and we are agreed that they should be a discreet blend of news and propaganda rather than "hard" news which is apt to lead to confusion and misunderstanding. . . . It was this latter type of talk about which Mr. Bullock was apprehensive.[33]

By 1941, then, Africans in Southern Rhodesia received audio broadcasts both from Lusaka and from the Salisbury superintendent's office in the form of approved "pet talks," that is, simplified and colored official interpretations of events rather than the actual reports of the events. For example, when Germany overran France and was encroaching on Britain, Africans were told that "France had stopped fighting" and that most French citizens felt "betrayed by lots of traitors who prevented the French army from fighting properly," with the necessary reassurance that Britain's massive numbers of strong soldiers, big airplanes, and warships would continue to decimate the Germans. The infantile broadcasts also stressed the arrogated role of Africans as soldiers but also as suppliers of minerals, food, and most pertinently tobacco, "which men at war like to smoke" during their patriotic service toward defeating Hitler.[34] They used fear to compel any reluctant Africans to support the imperial war effort. The Southern Rhodesian information officer asked Africans to forget the yoke of British racial imperialism and join forces against a supposedly more universal evil:

> Some of you may think that this is a white man's war. . . . That is not so. It is everybody's war, because if Hitler wins you as well as us will suffer. In a book which he wrote . . . Hitler said the native people were just like baboons, and should be treated like slaves. If the Germans come here you would not be able to go where you liked, to work for whom you liked; you would have to go and work wherever the Germans said and if you did not do so you would be beaten or killed. . . . You would probably get no wages at all no matter how hard you worked. So this is your war.[35]

While avoiding naming them as such, the broadcasts stressed German and Italian racial supremacist policies as "the bad customs" that the two countries practiced and sought to spread to all countries as much as possible.[36]

The Italians were portrayed as a cruel and evil race for "killing thousands of native men, women and children in Libya and Abyssinia." They would do the same if not prevented from coming to Southern Africa. But they were going to fail, thanks to "lots of our Europeans [who] have gone to fight [them]," and to "natives who are everyday being trained as soldiers."[37] The propagandists were clearly hesitant to explicitly argue that British racial colonialism was a blessing while German and Italian fascism was evil. To Africans, being equated with and treated *as* baboons was the essence of colonialism, and that did not belong to a mere realm of a possible Nazi empire. As Clapperton Mavhunga (2011) argues, British colonialism thrived on the animalization of Africans.

We are told that Africans clamored for these broadcasts. For instance, the Shabanie School superintendent informed the information officer that local mineworkers complained that they also wanted broadcasts in their own languages: "One asked me whether the man who speaks from Lusaka does not know Chishona, and another was clearly of the opinion that it was a slur on Southern Rhodesian natives that they should not get what Northern Rhodesians get."[38] But does this mean propaganda radio had succeeded where the press had failed? There is no definite answer and, in private, the official functionaries claimed no victories either. They could only speculate, as did the Northern Rhodesian information officer:

> Well over 3000 recruits have come forward since September and there are signs everywhere of increasing interest in the war and business on the war effort, though how far all this is the result of our information, or how far the effect of the return of a considerable number of elated askari on leave from the front, we do not know, but at least we can say that no considerable consequences have so far arisen from the expansion of our information service into tribal areas.[39]

Many Africans who could listen "beyond their own tongue" actively sought information and duly formed their own opinions. For instance, as students at Kutama Mission, Vambe and his schoolmates not only read "every newspaper from cover to cover," they also listened beyond Rhodesia: "We . . . used to gather in the evenings outside Father O'Hea's office and listen to the world news from his radio, 'wireless,' as it was called in those days" (Vambe 1978, 125). As the story of African nationalism tells us, whatever effort Africans put toward the war reflected broader politics than the mere workings of the state's propaganda. Vambe captures the complex package of hope, political bargaining, and intrigue at play when he points out that "our efforts in the struggle against Hitler were not entirely a result of the propaganda devised by our Native Commissioners."

In fact, as critics charged of the press, the radio also often helped to fan "injurious rumors" rather than smother them. For instance, Lusaka broadcasters were stung by the charge that the radio was the source of the rumor making the rounds in the town that returning Northern Rhodesian Rifles (the same "askaris" of colonial language) were being deliberately drowned in the Indian Ocean (Fraenkel 1959, 11). And as Michael Kittermaster (whose last name became interchangeable with "broadcaster") told his colleague Fraenkel, broadcasting propaganda to Africans was "not a question of scotching one rumor. It's a long term business; there isn't enough faith in official means of communication" (16). Writing in 1946, Southern Rhodesia's Secretary for Native Affairs bluntly pointed out that "wireless propaganda easily becomes suspect as was amply demonstrated when it was used for this purpose during the war."[40] The social context of colonialism clearly helped to frame Africans' reception of radio, and this fact made the radio message mutable. As such, Africans subjected the radio message to decoding, recoding, and reinterpretation to the extent that it often acquired a life of its own, and, horribly for the colonial state, as rumor! It was because of these failures that broadcasting to Africans almost ended with the war (Zaffiro 1984, 51).

Postwar Broadcasting: Cultivating "Wireless-Mindedness," Fighting Phantom Communism

But the end of the war did not mean the "native" ceased to be a "problem." If anything, the war had opened a new, difficult chapter for the state, with Africans demanding political rights rather than merely appealing for colonial reformation. African experiences in the global conflict and their unrequited sacrifices drove a new political consciousness that shook the colonial project. And official worries over "rumors" now took on a strong anti-Communist tinge. The war to construct loyal African subjectivities was thus far from over, particularly with the emergence of Communism as an alternative global political philosophy. Communism appeared attractive to Africans who were victimized by the rapacious colonial capitalism, and it was in this context that even any kind of opposition or independent thinking by Africans courted them the charge of dabbling in Communist mischief (West 2002). Countering such "mischief" became one of the primary objectives of postwar British broadcasting to Africans.

Franklin framed this agenda in a powerful 1949 broadcast in which he advocated a wider adoption of radio broadcasting to Africans. He fanned the blazing anti-Communism flames with a fine turn of colonialese:

> Whether you like it or not, the African mind is awakening, is thirsty for knowledge. Let us give it the right kind of knowledge; if we don't it will surely pick up the wrong. You know the old saying about idle hands and mischief. Well, the same applies to idle minds, and there are always people, even as far afield as Moscow, looking for idle minds in Africa. (Franklin 1949, 14)

The allegedly idle African mind had to be lured, captured, and taught what to and what not to think before it contemplated mischief. The best tool, reasoned Franklin, was the entertainment value of radio:

> We want a happy and contented African people. Now what can the native do when he has finished his work, his own or yours. He can get drunk if he has the money, or gamble or worse. If there is a full moon he can dance. But most nights he can only go back to his hut, with no light and generally no ability to read even if he had light. There he can talk and think. And one of the things he can talk and think about, not very happily, is how much better off you are than he is, you with so many things he hasn't got, including a radio to entertain you. The African loves music, plays, rhetoric[al] argument—all the things that radio can put across so well. Let him have them. (Franklin 1949, 14–15)

Was this "native mind" knowable? And could it, finally, be captured and placated, as Franklin asserts? This became the major problematic for the success of the "second occupation," that is, postwar "developmental" colonialism. More firmly cast in a modernist crucible than ever before, radio became the central tool in the official quest to know, nay, to colonize the African mind. It therefore had to be established on a more permanent footing.

Following a 1947 study by BBC engineer E. C. Varley, the Colonial Office approved a plan to expand radio in Central Africa to keep a hold on the fast-paced social and political change on the continent. This is how the Central African Broadcasting Services (CABS) was conceived. The decisive move was Britain's granting the two Rhodesias and Nyasaland three million pounds in Colonial

Welfare and Development Fund aid in 1948.[41] In a tripartite agreement, the territories agreed that Southern Rhodesia use its allotment to broadcast to all Europeans from Salisbury, with its partners focusing on Africans from Lusaka. This concluded nine years of Northern Rhodesia's begging her two neighbors to join hands with her and share the costs of the Lusaka broadcasts.[42] The disappearance of the war-induced panics did not so much relieve radio of the propaganda burdens as broaden its scope.

From the beginning, proponents of radio had extolled the virtues of the medium for modern administration and service in "educating" Africans "in the broadest sense of the word." The Salisbury Municipality, for instance, had argued that broadcasting could be usefully employed to issue warnings to Location residents on various regulations, including arrears on rent payments and infractions on trading. It could also be used to notify them of planned recreational activities as well as for instructing them on domestic science.[43] While all these functions were inherently political, the explicit political functions of radio are obvious in their silencing. Postwar broadcasting sought to graft not only the developmentalist codicil but also an entertainment face onto the law-and-order, that is, political, foundation of colonial radio. Entertainment was seen as key in cultivating "wireless-mindedness," that is, the baiting of the still-elusive "African mind" for the grander purpose of constructing the people into loyal colonial subjects. That, as the Secretary for Native Affairs expounded, was "education":

> The African people of this colony have not as yet become "wireless minded" to any extent, so I imagine that the first objective at this stage should be to popularize the broadcasts . . . by the provision of entertainment and popular interest programmes, and when these have "taken on," gradually to extend the use of the medium to cover education.[44]

But who was the African targeted by postwar broadcasting? War propaganda had targeted mainly the urban segment of the African population and those in large areas of employment, hoping that "ignorance" would take care of rural dwellers, those "whose mental horizon was the far side of their maize field," as Davis put it.[45] Until its overemphasis on urban and semi-urban Africans ran into crisis, the state had dismissed rural Africans as irrelevant to the outcome of the war. The same approach was likely to run into similar problems in the postwar era. Thus, using 1944 figures, the Secretary for Native Affairs assumed that if every urban African could be reached, this would result in a potential audience of 308,800, which contrasted unfavorably with the one million Africans in rural areas.[46] Popularizing the radio would thus require bringing entertainment not only to the majority of urban dwellers, but also to the rural, disproportionately female dwellers. Moreover, cultivating "wireless mindedness" meant massive investment in listening facilities.

From its belated lead on urban dwellers, the Salisbury Municipality started "rediffusing" Lusaka broadcasts to residents through its PA system in 1949, as it reported to its mayor:

> With the master receiver and microphones in the Welfare Office the installation is used to broadcast radio programmes, news talks broadcast from Lusaka, public announcements and emergency calls. Already a concert party has broadcast a programme directly from the microphones. Although at present loudspeakers are installed in only half of the township area, it is hoped that during next year the whole native urban area will be covered by the system.[47]

Bulawayo would follow suit in Makokoba and Matshobana in the 1950s. But this receiving technology was already being rendered obsolete by an individualized set, the "Saucepan Special."

The "Saucepan Special," Organic Intellectuals: Africans at the Microphone

While the PA system continued operating up to the 1960s, Northern Rhodesia had led a serious hunt for a specialized, dry battery–powered radio receiver affordable to Africans. The result was the "Saucepan Special," an enamel-encased receiver manufactured in England from "surplus enamel saucepans." The *Chronicle* newspaper hailed it for the enamel encasement that rendered it "rust-proof, rot-proof, white ant-proof and tinker-proof to deter the amateur electrician."[48] Southern Rhodesia would lag behind no more; it purchased the sets with state lottery grants and distributed its first batch to about three hundred specially identified locations that included chiefs' homesteads, village centers, government schools, missions, and larger "kraal" schools.[49] More would be sold on the open market at five pounds per set and an additional pound for the Eveready dry battery. But it was the imagined mischief of the African teacher more than the curious fingers of the amateur electrician or the pesky white ants that really worried the state. Thus, in 1948 the CNC directed his subordinates to help thwart the antics of this demagogue:

> In order to dispel the idea that the school teacher is the only suitable agent for furthering the ends of education, it is desirable that the sets should not, if possible, be placed in the charge of Native Teachers, who would tend to regard them as instruments of didacticism. . . . It is suggested that consideration be given to replacing the sets in the charge of suitable senior pupils when not under direct European supervision.[50]

Why did both the medium and the message have to be hedged against the African teacher, if the state was interested in cultivating modernity? African teachers were (self-arrogated) agents of competing, more sovereign notions of modernity and they were models in the eyes of African commoners. This fact further exposes the political agenda behind the state's modernity charade. The stature of African teachers in the eyes of Africans positioned them as the colonial state's nemesis. By 1950, the state had issued twenty thousand sets, with its officials estimating that each was listened to by one hundred or more Africans.[51] Much more than newspaper reading, radio listening was thus a collective practice among Africans.

To capture the previously neglected rural constituency, officials sought to make the little box mirror, rather than revolutionize, "the African mind." Yet "the African mind" remained rather mysterious to colonial officials. Officials grappled with such questions as, "What does interest the African?" and "What does he talk about over the fireside or at the market place?" They answered their own questions by cataloguing everyday rural matters and imagined peasant preoccupations: crops, cattle, lions, weddings, dances, drunks, murders, gossip.[52] The radio would bring these matters right into the peasant's "hut" to satisfy this imagined mind. In addition, postwar radio also concerned itself with the quintessential colonial concern, the promotion of good race relations, and the fostering of "native" music and literature. Again, this ostensibly "apolitical" and petty rural programming thinly disguised the political objective of radio. Until the Saucepan Special became a common feature of African life, broadcasting policy had sought to marginalize those African opinion-makers who could not be co-opted easily to serve the state. As Healing would reveal in 1962,

> We believed that if broadcasting could reach the masses, it could play a great part in the sensible enlightenment of the masses and help to avoid the tragic consequences produced in some colonies where the native population consists of a handful of formally educated "intelligentsia" and a completely ignorant mass, easily misled by discontented agitators of the intelligentsia class. (Healing 1962)

Thus, the colonizers conceived radio as an instrument to foster a class divide between the miniscule middle class and the supposed "ignorant African masses." Radio therefore functioned as a technology of political engineering, a tool of empire.

By the 1950s, the proliferation of the Saucepan Special, "the poor man's radio," forced some kind of policy flip. In an ironic twist, the state began to promote individual ownership of radios, going as far as making credit facilities available to individual Africans to buy the radios. It is unimaginable that the "demagogues" had started to behave themselves. Instead, the state had conceived the Saucepan Special as a long rope in a context of increased availability of alternative sources of information. As one official, D. S. Richards, explained,

> African civil servants who are confirmed in appointment on the permanent staff are allowed, if they make an initial payment of £1/5 shillings . . . to obtain the balance of £5 as a loan from the government to be repaid at the rate of a pound a month. This system was approved by government on the grounds that

> African civil servants formed a large percentage of the native "intelligentsia," which needs, more than any other class, the guidance of wholesome literature and broadcasting material in order to avoid the pitfalls which might be laid before them in undesirable propaganda from other sources.[53]

Thus, by sleight of hand, the state started promoting, rather than prohibiting, the prized, if now ubiquitous, radio set. This agenda fed into Africans' own readings of the machine. Set up to project the facade of African progress under the Federation, the *African Parade,* a middle-class magazine, touted radio ownership by Africans as a most important status symbol:

> A radio set is increasingly becoming an item of necessity in most African homes, something that a man who has some education and money and some standing . . . must have for his and his family's benefit. To the African, [Lusaka] is a channel of education, entertainment and information, a link between men and women, tribe and tribe, Government and people, and white and black.[54]

As Spitulnik argues, these confessions of the "forward march of modernity" are all in English, "the primary language of colonial domination. . . . It is highly possible that such words and phrases were influenced by British modes of speaking about radio, or even from the very words of radio broadcasts themselves" (Spitulnik 1998/1999, 72, 73). The state could bank on "well known natives" like Northern Rhodesian federal MP Dauti Yamba to trumpet these ideas. Yamba told Parliament in 1954, "The saucepan radio is a very cheap set and many Africans in Northern Rhodesia and Nyasaland are buying them. I have bought two since they came on to the market."[55] Fraenkel writes that, with the increase in industrialization at this time, "wireless ownership was rapidly spreading down the social pyramid. . . . [It] was becoming a must, a coveted symbol of status among a wide range of people." But even more than that, it also became a disguise of status so that even a laborer with a wireless in the house appeared "just like an educated man" (Fraenkel 1959, 137). Thus conceptualized, the very fact of owning a radio set signified a modern lifestyle. Postwar programming sought to nurture this "modernist" class aspiration.

Together with Jonah Mbirimi, Shadreck Bepura, Stella Sondayi, and others, Lawrence Vambe, a *Parade* staffer at this time, staged Shona radio dramas that promoted middle-class urban morality and aspirations, the "dignity of labor," and law and order. One thing is clear: we see an important shift in Federation-era broadcasting as Africans were now included as participants, not just as recipients, of radio broadcasts. This shift emerged out of both the failure of an arrogant top-down policy of "broadcasting to Africans" as well as from the imperatives of marketing the Federation as a mutual partnership between the races. Moreover, officials conceded that broadcasting, "as a feature of modern life, portended both good and ill" and that it "could only increase with rising African economic levels."[56] Talking down to Africans during the war did not work; and the Federation was poised to suffer the same fate. Davis of the Nairobi Station had conceded the crisis of colonial "expertise" very early, and blamed Africans for it:

> What is not so easy is to discover what the African really thinks of the programmes and what he learns from [them]. Europeans know how to express themselves and criticize what they hear. Africans find it much more difficult, and anyhow do not readily say what they really think about Government activities. At present our greatest difficulty is to make contact with African listeners.[57]

It was in this context of a failed unilateral quest to understand "the native mind" that we see postwar Lusaka opening its doors to a larger corps of Africans as news gatherers, translators, and announcers on a more permanent basis. These were meticulously selected "makers of [African] public opinion" whom the state believed it could transform into "fervent advocates of the points of view which it is desired to impress upon the native"—that is, if, instead of being antagonized, "they are given lucid explanation in their own languages or elements of their own cultures sublimated to meet the official view."[58] These were organic intellectuals grounded in the fables, stories, songs, and cultural world of Africans who could speak about, for, and to their own people in their own idioms. The hope was that these intellectuals would provide the missing link between the rulers and the ruled.

Another pitfall of wartime propaganda radio had been its depersonalized nature. Africans did not adequately identify with it in spite of official efforts to cultivate interest principally through the playing of gramophone music between "war talks." It had been detached and lifeless, conceded the administrators: "Gramophone records cut out the personal element and give little scope for humour, and lack of humour is perhaps the most cogent criticism that can be laid at our present broadcasts."[59] The Nairobi Station had been unnerved by the African entertainers—the singers, storytellers, and mimics—who were recruited to infuse humor and the right sort of personal touch into its programs. As Davis discovered, that experiment was a lesson in African performative freedom:

> Although it was not difficult to find a good number of them, all they said had to be carefully rehearsed and censored. New African entertainment is essentially impromptu in character. . . . You may rehearse them as often as you like and find that on the actual occasion of the broadcast they may give quite a different version to what they have rehearsed.[60]

Wartime broadcasting did not have the scope to justify the time and resources necessary to appropriately censor and train Africans for such live programming. Thus, it was not until after the war that the idea could be safely tried again. With a new corps of permanent African entertainers, then, the state hoped to avert continued African "antipathy towards Government propaganda."[61] CABS thus became synonymous with men like Edward Kateka, Isaac Siyakulima, Pepe Zulu (an ex-soldier), Andreya Masiye and Edwin Mlongoti—all from Northern Rhodesia. Mlongoti, reminisced Fraenkel, had an infectious sense of humor:

> He spoke four African languages fluently and could give running commentaries on public events and football matches in one after the other, switching after every few minutes. He knew the folklore and proverbs of many tribes intimately and his conversation was usually rounded off by some story of animals or ancestors from his enormous repertoire. (Fraenkel 1959, 42)

Another African from Northern Rhodesia was "the dreamer of songs," ex-soldier Alick Nkhata, a musician-announcer. Together with Masiye and others, Nkhata traversed the region as part of the CABS recording team that built a wide collection of African songs for the radio over the years. The *African Parade* testified that Nkhata's "voice and music delight[ed] countless men and women in Central Africa."[62] Northern Rhodesia also provided the two women in the 1950s, Jessie Lengalenga and Agnes Morton, who did Bemba and Nyanja broadcasts, respectively (Masiye 1977, 96).

From the south, the NAD transferred Cyrus Ntini, Ephraim Chamba, the teachers Samson Zawe and Mhlanga, and then Charles Muchena, the latter "a highly qualified African . . . fluent in English, Sindebele and Chishona."[63] By the time the federal government took over the service as its mouthpiece, rechristening it the Federal Broadcasting Corporation (FBC) in 1958, the African component of the workforce had grown to about sixty, running 142 hours of programming each week (Healing 1962). In addition to the radio workers, officials invited chiefs and other Africans employed in "prestigious" occupations for occasional propaganda talks. The prevailing wisdom was that "a good deal more credence is given to the broadcasts if the voices of well-known natives are occasionally heard by listeners" so that Africans would be disabused of the "good deal of suspicion" with which they had naturally regarded the radio since the war.[64] This new complexion of radio would affect African perceptions of the medium in new ways. Many would identify with it as an aspect of their everyday life, particularly in the early 1950s. Yet, as both Fraenkel and Masiye point out, the identification of radio with the hated Federation (1953–1963) quickly sounded the death knell for colonial radio, with Africans attacking it as a white man's vampire that brought them death (the Federation) at a time they expected independence. The Federation, then, plunged colonial radio into a crisis from which it could only recover with the independence of Zambia and Malawi in 1964, and Zimbabwe in 1980. I explore this crisis in a larger, ongoing project.[65]

This chapter has argued that radio broadcasting to Africans in colonial Zambia, Zimbabwe, and Malawi was introduced to sell the Second World War to the colonized. The British and the respective territorial governments were compelled to counter what they regarded as pernicious rumors that raged in the region, which threatened not only the imperial war effort but also the certitudes of British colonial authority and the colonial project itself among Africans. Moreover, beyond the immediate imperatives of war propaganda, radio took root as part of a broader media scheme that also included the press, cinema, and, later, television, to engineer Africans into loyal subjects of British colonialism. This agenda sought to exploit the novelty, symbolism, and utility of radio as a mobile communication technology. Internal archives generated by policymakers locate radio as a locus of power and an extension of "the colonial mind." While reception studies that depend on commissioned public reports run the risk of reproducing official outlooks, this internal archive gives us a keen peek into the official, "confidential" mind, wherein we can decipher the nervousness of colonial authorities and the messiness of the inflated egos of colonial "experts" and their "expertise." Thus, this archive allows us to reconceptualize radio as a contested instrument of colonization rather than to reinforce the public, colonializing rhetoric of modernization. The discourse of African consciousness helps us in the interrogation of this narrative.

Notes

1. "Some Problems of Broadcasting to Africans: A Broadcast Given from Nairobi on Friday, 8th August 1941 by E.R. St. Davis, in Charge of the African Section of the Kenya Information Office," NAZ S935/14. All references to NAZ in this chapter are to the National Archives of Zimbabwe.

2. This "seditious" movement was banned until the end of the war.

3. Northern Rhodesia information officer to Southern Rhodesia information officer, "Information for Africans," n.d., NAZ S935/14/14.

4. Ibid.

5. *Sunday News* (Salisbury), 6 October 1939.

6. W. R. Hammond, superintendent of Shabanie Mine Undenominational Native School, to information officer, 12 March 1941, NAZ S395/14.

7. Thompson, Inspector of Natives, Salisbury Municipality Health Department, to Gale, information officer, 28 April 1940, NAZ S395/14.

8. Thompson to Gale, 28 April 1940.

9. Salisbury Location welfare officer to information officer, 25 April 1940, NAZ S395/14.

10. *Sunday News*, 6 October 1939.

11. Ibid.

12. Information officer to prime minister, "Propaganda among Natives," 14 March 1940, NAZ S935/14.

13. Ibid.

14. Ibid.

15. Northern Rhodesia information officer to Southern Rhodesia information officer, n.d., NAZ

16. Ibid.

17. Northern Rhodesia information officer to Southern Rhodesia information officer, n.d. NAZ.

18. Press Communique 100/40, Lusaka Broadcasting Station, 9 September 1940, NAZ S395/14.

19. Information officer to Secretary for Native Affairs, "Radio Broadcasts for Africans, 1939–1945," NAZ S935/14.

20. Hammond to information officer, 12 March 1941, NAZ.

21. Northern Rhodesia information officer to Southern Rhodesia information officer, n.d.

22. Harry Franklin, "Government of Northern Rhodesia: Report on the Development of Broadcasting to Africans in Central Africa," 1949, Lusaka, 6, NAZ S482/12/42.

23. Hammond to information officer, 12 March 1941, NAZ.

24. Thompson to Gale, 28 April 1940, NAZ.

25. Thompson to Gale, 28 April 1940, NAZ.

26. Northern Rhodesia information officer to Southern Rhodesia information officer, n.d., NAZ.

27. Ibid.

28. Ibid.

29. Salisbury Location welfare officer to information officer, 25 April 1940, NAZ.

30. Fane's (Rhodesian) Radio Services to O. G. Gale, information officer, 26 April 1940; information officer to prime minister, 27 April 1940, both NAZ S395/14.

31. Hammond to information officer, 12 March 1941, NAZ.

32. Northern Rhodesia information officer to Southern Rhodesia information officer, n.d., NAZ.

33. Information officer to prime minister, 27 April 1940, NAZ.

34. Information officer to prime minister, "Suggested Form of Propaganda Broadcasts," 5 September 1940, NAZ S395/14.

35. Ibid.

36. Broadcast from Station VQ2HC, Nkana, 2 July 1940, NAZ S935/14.

37. Information officer to prime minister, 5 September 1940, NAZ.

38. Superintendent of Shabanie to information officer, 12 March 1941, NAZ S9395.

39. Northern Rhodesia information officer to Southern Rhodesia information officer, n.d., NAZ.

40. Secretary for Native Affairs, "Memorandum: Broadcasting for Africans," 31 January 1946, NAZ S482/12/42.

41. Information and Public Relations Office, Lusaka, to director of information, Salisbury, 5 June 1947, NAZ S932/69.

42. Northern Rhodesia information officer to Southern Rhodesia information officer, n.d., NAZ.

43. Salisbury Location welfare officer to information officer, 25 April 1940, NAZ.

44. Secretary for Native Affairs, 31 January 1946.

45. "Some Problems of Broadcasting to Africans."

46. Secretary for Native Affairs, 31 January 1946.

47. *Native Administration Annual Reports,* Salisbury, 1 July 1948–30 June 1949, 6.

48. George Vine, "Radio Links the Kraals," *Chronicle,* 10 May 1950.

49. Minister of Native Affairs to Director of Native Education and Public Relations, "Broadcasting Programmes in Chishona and Sindebele," 31 July 1948, NAZ S932/69.

50. "Chief Native Commissioner to All Native Department Stations and Missions Accepting Wireless Receiving Sets for Natives," Circular No. 63, 13 December 1948, NAZ S932/69.

51. Director of public relations, Southern Rhodesia, to secretary, Office of the High Commissioner for Southern Rhodesia, London, 17 May 1950, NAZ S932/69.

52. "Some Problems of Broadcasting to Africans."

53. D. S. Richards, "Broadcasting in Rhodesia," June 1952, NAZ FR-298A/25800/GEN/P/21C.

54. "The Mashona Family," *African Parade*, August 1954, 8.

55. Legco Debates, Hansard, 5 August 1954, NAZ.

56. Secretary for Native Affairs, 31 January 1946, NAZ.

57. "Some Problems of Broadcasting to Africans."

58. Thompson to Gale, 28 April 1940, NAZ.

59. "Some Problems of Broadcasting to Africans."

60. Ibid.

61. Chief Native Commissioner to all Native Department stations in Southern Rhodesia, 1 April 1948, NAZ S932/69.

62. "Alick Nkhata: Bridge Between Old and New African Music," *African Parade*, December 1953, 21.

63. Information and Public Relations Office, Lusaka, to director of information, Salisbury, 5 June 1947; Chief Native Commissioner to broadcasting officer, Shona/Sindebele Announcer for Southern Rhodesia, 27 October 1948, NAZ S932/69.

64. "Some Problems of Broadcasting to Africans."

65. Mhoze Chikowero, *Tool of Empire, Technology of Self-Liberation: Radio and State-Making in Zambia, Zimbabwe and Malawi, 1920s–1970s*.

References

Burns, James M. 2002. *Flickering Shadows: Cinema and Identity in Colonial Zimbabwe*. Athens: Ohio University Press.

Franklin, Harry. 1949. *Report on the Development of Broadcasting to Africans in Central Africa*. Lusaka: Government Printer.

———. 1950. *Report on the "Saucepan Special": The Poor Man's Radio for Rural Populations*. Lusaka, Government Printer.

Fraenkel, Peter. 1959. *Wayaleshi*. London: Weidenfield and Nicholson.

Guha, Ranajit. 1988. "The Prose of Counter-Insurgency." In *Selected Subaltern Studies*, edited by Ranajit Guha and Gayatri Chakrabarty Spivak, 45–88. Oxford: Oxford University Press.

Healing, A. S. 1962. "Africans at the Microphone." *Africa Calls*. Lusaka: Government Printer. March–April: 7.

Ibbotson, P. 1942. "Native Welfare Societies in Southern Rhodesia." *Race Relations* 9: 2, 72.

Larkin, Brian. 1999. "Introduction to Media Technologies and the Design for Modern Living." *Visual Anthropology Review* 14, no. 2: 11–13.

Masiye, Andreya C. 1977. *Singing for Freedom: Zambia's Struggle for African Government*. Lusaka: Oxford University Press.

Mavhunga, Clapperton. 2011. "Vermin Beings: On Pestiferous Animals and Human Game." *Social Text* 29, no. 1: 151–76.

Mudimbe, V. Y. 1988. *The Invention of Africa: Gnosis, Philosophy, and the Order of Knowledge*. Bloomington: Indiana University Press.

Musambachime, Mwelwa C. 1988. "The Impact of Rumor: The Case of the Banyama (Vampire Men) Scare in Northern Rhodesia, 1930–1964." *International Journal of African Historical Studies* 21, no. 2: 201–15.

Powdermaker, Hortense. 1962. *Copper Town: Changing Africa; The Human Situation on the Rhodesian Copperbelt.* New York: Harper and Row.

Silverstone, Roger, and Eric Hirsch. 1992. *Consuming Technologies: Media Cultures and Information in Domestic Spaces.* London: Routledge.

Smyth, Rosaleen. 1984. "War Propaganda During the Second World War in Northern Rhodesia," *African Affairs* 83, no. 332: 345–58.

Spitulnik, Debra. 1998/1999. "Mediated Modernities: Encounters with the Electronic in Zambia," *Visual Anthropology Review* 14, no. 2: 63–84.

———. 2002. "Mobile Machines and Fluid Audiences: Rethinking Reception through Zambian Radio Culture." In *Media Worlds: Anthropology on New Terrain,* edited by Faye D. Ginsburg, Lila Abu-Lughold, and Brian Larkin, 319–36. Berkeley: University of California Press.

Vambe, Lawrence. 1976. *From Rhodesia to Zimbabwe.* London: Heinemann.

White, Luise. 1995. "Tsetse Visions: Narratives of Blood and Bugs in Colonial Northern Rhodesia, 1931–9." *Journal of African History* 36, no. 2: 219–45.

———. 2000. *Speaking with Vampires: Rumor and History in Colonial Africa.* Berkeley: University of California Press.

West, Michael. 2002. "The Seeds Are Sown: The Impact of Garveyism in Zimbabwe in the Interwar years." *International Journal of African Historical Studies* 35, nos. 2/3: 335–62.

Zaffiro, James. 1984. "Broadcasting and Political Change in Zimbabwe, 1931–1984." PhD diss., University of Wisconsin.

6 Elocution, Englishness, and Empire
Film and Radio in Late Colonial Ghana

Peter J. Bloom

In the 1936 British Colonial Office's report on broadcasting services in the colonies, a series of recommendations were made to accelerate radio broadcasting throughout the empire in association with the British Broadcasting Corporation (BBC). More specifically, the report explains that the BBC Empire Service should not only be a form of entertainment for Europeans and others with educational means "but also an instrument of advanced administration . . . for the enlightenment and education of the more backward sections of the population and for their instruction."[1] The emphasis on advanced administration serves as a point of departure for exploring the pedagogically informed English spoken voice of film and radio in this essay. The manipulation and directed projection of the spoken voice in its quality as object that manages to hold bodies, languages, and territory together marked a shifting context for colonial administration in the late interwar and postwar period. Colonial Ghana—known as one of the most "radio-minded" of all the colonies and an important site for film training and production—serves as the primary context in the discussion to follow.[2]

In the report cited above, "advanced administration" refers to colonial instruction in the service of public health, agriculture, and English-language training, among other areas. In other words, radio became an instrument in the service of mass education set on imposing order within the colonial culture of indirect administration that appointed native authorities as self-governing local executives with clearly defined responsibilities (Robinson 1950, 14). Moreover, radio came to function as the extension of a modernization discourse that modulated a developmentalist rhetoric of the late colonial period into the early independence era.

From the perspective of the Colonial Office, the most significant point of reference for experimenting with radio on the African continent was the scope and ambitions of the Bantu Educational Kinema [*sic*] Experiment (BEKE) undertaken between 1935 and 1937.[3] Preoccupations with understanding the so-called "African mind," central to the BEKE project, were also integrated into a form of intelligence reporting organized by the BBC Empire Service during the war. In addition to questionnaires that were sent to listeners literate in English and those with radio licenses on the African continent, the Observer Scheme was established. It consisted of a panel of informants who reported directly to the Empire Intelligence Section on the habits and reactions of listeners, providing information for a series of African audience reaction reports.[4]

It is from this perspective that the emergence of British colonial film and radio in the postwar period may be understood as a means of enacting and administering colonial authority through a shifting form of "state spatiality," as James Ferguson and Akhil Gupta (2002) have termed it. The vocabulary of spatialization, which Ferguson and Gupta have associated with "verticality" and "encompassment," is of great relevance to understanding the effects of the recorded voice in particular. The "voice" of authority is grounded in the ventriloquist's art of governance whose power resides in its ability to transform the relationship between sound, image, and presence (Hill 2010). English as the voice of colonial authority became increasingly channeled through film and radio during the postwar period, fulfilling its role of advanced administration. It was also part of a shifting approach initially associated with indirect rule and indirect administration (Robinson 1950, 12–15). Indirect rule, a policy most closely associated with Frederick Lugard's amalgamation of Nigeria during his return as governor general (1914–1919), and later articulated in *The Dual Mandate in British Tropical Africa* (1922), seemed to recognize the precolonial structures of some African societies by governing through indigenous institutions. However, even among figures like Arthur Creech Jones, a Fabian Socialist and secretary of the state for the colonies in the postwar Labor government, there is the admission that "institutions of native authority had to be artificially created" in certain instances, even though this was only in the early stages of the adoption of indirect rule (Creech Jones 1949, 4). Terence Ranger (1983) is more direct about this point in demonstrating that most of the indigenous institutions were either invented or most often emboldened by the colonial administration itself.

The strategy of late colonial "governmentality" that emerged in the postwar period was a shifting target riddled with contradictions on the ground, and the experience of film and radio reflected a complex cast of characters and agendas often at odds with each other. The vocabulary of "governmentality" that has been introduced here refers to a theme developed in Michel Foucault's broader address to "apparatuses of security" in his Collège de France Lectures, leading to an examination of various models of government (Foucault 2007, 29–86). A particularly relevant articulation refers to governmentality as "the science of ruling the state, which concerns politics" (Burchell, Gordon, and Miller 1991, 91). Foucault further notes, "It is the tactics of government which make possible the continual definition and redefinition of what is within the competence of the state and [that] which is not" (103). As I will explain, film and radio embody a tactics of address in the name of government institutions. A significant institutional context is the role and function of mass education as the bulwark of the late colonial state for English-language literacy and development projects (Skinner 2009). In particular, I would like to examine how literacy was used in the name of a tactics of governmentality, starting with a short industrial film.

Cinematic Governmentality: *I Will Speak English*

A curious example of teaching English to African audiences is demonstrated in a one-reel, fourteen-minute educational film produced by the Gold Coast Film Unit in 1954 and released under the title *I Will Speak English*.[5] The film begins with the address of an African teacher to the Ghanaian learning subject, represented by the class—the "I" in the title. It depicts a closely shaven Anglophone African instructor, dressed in a collared white shirt with colonial khaki shorts, demonstrating a "quick method" of English instruction directed toward "new literates in the vernacular" who want to learn and read English. Beginning with a bugle fanfare that becomes more fully orchestrated as the title of the film is spoken, the words *I Will Speak English* appear on a blackboard as the opening title. The subject positioning of teacher and student is immediately presented. The terms "me" and "you" are introduced, leading to the sentences, "This is me," and "This is you." This is then followed by "him" and "her," gender-specific pronouns that do not exist in most Ghanaian languages.

A technique of picture mnemonics is intermittently incorporated into sequences of the film such that a van, for example, refers to the function and identity of a driver. It also refers to how the film itself might be shown, that is, by cinema vans supplied with a screen and loudspeakers that would organize screenings in towns and villages with local language commentators and entertainers. As in most sequences in the film, the instructor places his hand on the person or identifiable object to help us identity its extension and shape, such as, "This is his head." This film was supplemented by a multivolume primer of the same title, as the instructor demonstrates. The film and primer were associated with an extensive mass education literacy campaign initiated in 1952 (Taylor 1953). As Tom Rice (2010) points out, it was tied to the formation of the local Gold Coast civil service, which required a basic level of literacy. The film itself is addressed directly to "new literates in the vernacular," which meant those who had acquired literacy in Ghanaian languages in order to read the Bible, but who had only limited English-language competency. Their spoken English was adapted to a form of pronunciation particular to the spoken languages in colonial Ghana, referred to as Gold Coast Pronunciation of English (or GCP). This variation of English was, as Peter Strevens (1954) has explained, a local adaptation of English that was due in part to a limited English-language education. This type of English has also been associated with an idiom geared toward cooks and domestic servants. Particularly after the war, GCP became a lingua franca, leading to broader questions about whether university students at a higher level of education should be encouraged to speak in this manner as opposed to a more legible and accepted form of pronunciation, as with Southern British Received Pronunciation (RP).

It becomes clear that the film was shot in an ad hoc outdoor studio setting made to look like a rural town or village area, with the instructor's booming voice giving direct instructions in RP to adult education student listeners, modeling them as potential teachers who might then use this method of English-language teaching for their students. This method might have been partially derived from the "Each One Teach One" method typically associated with the American sociologist Frank C. Laubach, who developed the system of picture mnemonics following his experience teaching literacy in Kentucky and then as a missionary among the Marañao in the Philippines. Even the title of the primer and film, *I Will Speak English,* closely resembles the 1940 publication of Laubach's well-known literacy handbook, *India Shall Be Literate* (1940). The design and implementation of the Laubach technique in village settings relied on one-to-one volunteer tutors, a system previously developed by Cora Wilson Stewart, who, as superintendent of schools in Rowan County, Kentucky, pioneered this approach for adults as part of the Moonlight Schools of Kentucky (Sticht 2005).

In addition to being mentioned in the 1943 *Mass Education in African Society* report, there are oblique references in the film to elements of the Laubach technique, such as the continual reference to the instructor's use of students to demonstrate particular sentences. The various illustrations of the film point to methods of teaching literacy, such as the use of the blackboard, sentence patterning techniques that involve tracing over writing for students to practice at home, and field trips to illustrate vocabulary associated with particular demonstrations. In one part of the film, the instructor points to a schematic drawing of a canoe and fisherman on the blackboard. This becomes a means by which we cut to a new setting in which the class is assembled around an actual canoe and fishermen.

While the need for literacy campaigns was duly noted during the war, particularly in the 1943 mass education report, its reception by colonial governors on the African continent met with mixed reactions. The consensus to act in a more direct manner was, in fact, deferred until returning African soldiers along with West African student leaders and political party figures in Britain began to militate against British rule at home (Adi 1998). In Ghana in particular, the transition to "self-rule" was more rapid than previously anticipated by colonial officials. After Kwame Nkrumah was released from prison in 1951 to become leader of government business, he was appointed prime minister in 1952, and in 1954 a new Constitution was established such that independence was nearly declared inevitable by Charles Arden-Clarke, then governor general of the Gold Coast. The movement toward independence points to an amalgamation of the voice as a manifestation of political will, as in the shifting terms and effects of colonial governmentality.

An insistence on the "I" in *I Will Speak English* allows us to return to the object voice as supplement and foundation for sovereignty. An important theme in the work of Michel Chion, the French *musique concrète* composer and sound theorist, is the defining characteristics of the acousmatic voice. It refers to a voice whose source cannot be seen, whose origin cannot be identified. Following its origin, the acousmatic refers to the Pythagorean sect whose followers would listen to their master speak from behind a curtain, so that the sight of the speaker would not distract them from the message. The acousmatic is thus everywhere and is constructed as an all-seeing panoptic fantasy of omnipotence and omniscience (Chion 1999, 19–24). It is in this sense that the radio-cinema English speaking voice may be understood within the elocutionary register of stratification and developmentalism.

The broader implications for examining the voice as a technique of communication that instilled a context for identification among spectators may be further understood through what Chion has called "a pivot of identification" that resonates within us as if it were our own voice, like the voice of the first person. Here there are two technical criteria that help establish this voice as a site of identification: the close miking of the voice, such that vocal presence and definition are featured in spite of low-fidelity recording quality; and the absence of reverb in the voice, or what Chion calls "dryness," allowing the listener to situate the voice within spatial parameters. Here the voice has a bodily or corporeal implication, such that we internalize it as the listener.

These qualities are demonstrated in *I Will Speak English*, notwithstanding the uncertain conditions for its exhibition on traveling cinema vans. The film features the voice of the instructor as a means of creating a context for identification, but also depicts the response of the students, who speak only in unison, repeating after the instructor. Again, it begins by establishing an identification between the pupil and instructor's address that continues among a group of students. Further, the subject positioning of the speaker and a narrative voice that emerges demonstrates how a classroom environment for instruction may be configured. In other words, it becomes a nodal point for English-language teaching as the expansion of roles within a developmental modernizing paradigm.

The film was shown as part of an extended film program by a fleet of twenty-one cinema vans in colonial Ghana that traveled throughout the country and reached a wide array of villages outside Accra. The film was also made in support of the English Literacy Certificate Program that was awarded to approximately 26,300 Ghanaian students in 1954.[6] Scripted by a visual aids officer associated with the mass education program, it is primarily addressed to English-language instructors themselves from the ranks of the police, prisons, and Department of Social Welfare and Community Development. Crucially, however, it was also addressed to the students themselves. George Noble, the British cameraman who worked closely with the director of the unit, Sean Graham, is credited along with Frank Tamakloe and Sam Aryeetey as the key production team. This film followed a pattern of production that served as an abiding context for the movement toward self-rule, with the indexicality of the voice functioning as a significant instrument in the service and art of governmentality.

The Gold Coast Film Unit (GCFU) was analogous to other British film units that were put in place by the end of World War II. They were primarily organized under the Information Services Department and Public Relations Bureaus at a number of different sites throughout the British Empire. Prior to establishing the postwar colonial film units, the Raw Stock [Footage] Scheme was established in 1941. It was organized to bring back footage from the empire by initially sending a group of cameramen-instructors to train willing officials typically associated with information or education. They were then asked to help provide a steady flow of newsreels that were often anthologized as part of the Colonial Film Magazine newsreel series, which remain part of the country-specific colonial film collections (Colonial Cinema 1945, 76–77; see also Colonial Cinema 1947, 1949). In fact, the journal *Colonial Cinema* (1943–1954) always included information about techniques of filmmaking designed to help amateur filmmakers throughout the empire. The footage received through the Raw Stock Scheme was processed and then edited in London, with a soundtrack and explanatory English voice-over narration added. These compilation films would then be shipped back but were made to serve a number of different sites, such that films circulating in Nigeria and the Gold Coast might also find their way to Jamaica, but were finally considered to be a rather lackluster amalgamation of material, and a poor substitute for professional newsreel footage.

This earlier metropolitan-centered technique of film production and circulation was largely considered inadequate particularly in the postwar period. It was, however, analogous to early radio that served as the primary point of reference for spoken media. Radio programs in particular were broadcast and conceived as part of a centralizing ethos of modern citizenship.

Radio as Instrument of Advanced Colonial Administration

The impact of educational film in colonial Ghana was closely associated with a dense network of cinema vans by the late 1940s, a phenomenon that Brian Larkin has examined in the case of Nigeria with remarkable insight (Larkin 2008; see Bloom and Skinner 2009 for colonial Ghana). In addition to the presentation of films on the cinema van tours, gramophone records were also presented. As I will discuss here, it was early radio that demonstrated certain of these themes of the unseen voice in a direct and seemingly magical manner. As noted in the introductory section of this chapter, radio was understood to be the most pointed instrument of advanced administration by the end of the interwar period.

The Colonial Office considered radio to be of great significance in organizing recruiting efforts related to World War II and addressing what they described as "the large mass of Africans."[7] In addition to hailing soldiers to serve, it came to establish its credibility by reporting on the fate of individual West African soldiers on the front in Europe and throughout Asia. The deployment of African and Asian troops was part of a geopolitical shift whose effects were registered in the aftermath of the war upon their return home. This, in turn, culminated in a string of protests linked to a disavowal of benefits for veterans and a lack of employment opportunities, as evidenced by the Accra "riots" of 1948 that resulted in Kwame Nkrumah's initial arrest (Austin 1964).

Prior to the war, there was an expansive experimental radio culture in Accra beginning in 1935. Initially, 350 homes were linked by overhead wires to a small radio relay station known as station ZOY that became known as Broadcasting House. The Palladium Cinema was wired and outfitted with a hundred speakers to serve as the main mass public listening site or showcase for the event of radio. The number of subscribers increased dramatically after the initiation of radio on 31 July 1935, jumping to 756 subscribers by February 1936, and expanding to Kumasi in 1937 at which time wireless sets began to appear.[8] The overhead wired network organized on the model of telephone wiring suspended on a series of wooden poles with steel conductors was the most widely heard form of broadcasting until the arrival of the transistor in the 1970s. By 1939, with the installation of a more powerful 1.3 kw transmitter, 4,000 subscribers were connected to a network of sixteen stations of different wavelengths relayed by station ZOY based in Accra (Ansah 1985, 7). The new transmitter also managed to extend its broadcasting range to relay stations and wireless sets in Nigeria and Sierra Leone in the service of the war effort.

Station ZOY continued to expand after the war, along with the number of attentive listeners with wired sets of their own, but they continued to be broadcast primarily in English. As P. A. V. Ansah (1985) explains, until 1953 local languages were only given eighteen hours a week of broadcasting time, whereas English-language broadcasts, which included an extensive array of BBC relays, still accounted for fifty-eight hours per week of programming. Station ZOY was initially conceived as a relay station for the BBC Empire Service but its rapid expansion was a result of the direct involvement of Arnold Hodgson, governor of the Gold Coast from 1934 to 1941, and the engineer F. A. W. Byron. In the BBC yearbooks and other material on the history of the Empire Service, an extensive array of radio maps illustrate the transmission of radio waves during certain hours of the day from the control station in Daventry to sites around the world. This organizational context heralded a new spatial geography of empire, nominating an international network of relays that allowed for retransmissions and transcriptions. In addition to wireless radio broadcast received by relay stations that would be retransmitted, the most common form of retransmission was gramophone records. Typically, shipments of records served as the mainstay of radio content, including the news, short jingles, light orchestra music, radio plays, lectures, children's stories, and English-language teaching programs.

Most of the BBC radio programs were either electronically transcribed and then read by local announcers, or rebroadcast in relation to relay and transmission schedules determined by the BBC External Broadcasting Services. In the 1956 survey of their operations, they wrote, "In English and in forty-three other languages, the BBC's External Services are heard throughout the world for about eighty hours every day. . . . It includes the transmission of some 48,000 news bulletins and 50,000 talks in the course of a year . . . for which thirty-nine high-power short-wave transmitters are used."[9] Program schedules of the 1950s demonstrate that a large proportion of the shows included BBC British radio programs. The BBC Empire Service programs in particular were organized as part of a package of programs, and placed in prime-time schedule spots.

It was in this context that an array of English-language programming was introduced that served as the organizational core for the advanced administrative ethos. Although the Empire Service was broadly conceived as a means by which to bring together the disparate parts of the empire, John Reith, the first director general of the BBC, already saw some of its potential effects on amalgamating the imperial idea. As he explained in the first broadcast of the Empire Service on 19 December 1932,

> Good evening, Ladies and Gentlemen; this occasion is as significant as any in the ten years of British broadcasting. It is a significant occasion in the history of the British Empire, how significant, it would be unwise at the moment to forecast—a great deal of experiment is yet to be done. . . .
>
> From today, however, programs will be broadcast regularly from the Empire station. The experimental days of broadcasting, as such, are over. There must be few in any civilized country yet to realize that broadcasting is a development with which the future must reckon, and reckon seriously. The more consideration given to it today, the more experience gained, the more it will be realized that here is an instrument of almost incalculable importance in the social and political life of the community. Its influence will be more and more be felt in the daily life of the individual in almost every sphere of human activity in affairs national and international. Now it becomes a connecting and coordinating link between the scattered parts of the British Empire. Here at home, from the earliest days it has been our resolve that the great possibilities

and influences of the medium should be exploited to the highest human advantage. It matters little in what order one puts its various functions, the service as a whole has been, and is, dedicated to the best interests of mankind.[10]

This rather long excerpt from Reith's speech reveals something of his sense of mission and Victorian ethics in which the power of broadcasting, as he later wrote, "will cast a girdle round the earth with bands that are all the stronger because invisible" (Avery 2006, 24). Within the short address itself, there is a reference to a construct of Britishness overseas. Further, it is addressed to a "you," which is embodied with a set of implied qualities including a calm demeanor and imperturbability. The "you" is being interpolated with an array of symbols that includes, in a later section of the address, Christmas, the king, and understatement with regard to the technical difficulties of transmission, all of which underlie an overall sense of modesty.

Finally, the structuring of the voice may not necessarily be limited to accent, pacing, and symbols within a bounded English phonocentric sphere of belonging, as is the case in Reith's address. However, an emphasis on diction and speech patterning among announcers was part of Reith's broader interest in coordinating a style of speech that became associated with BBC English, precisely because of the power of radio to impose a norm of Received Pronunciation.

BBC Radio Pronunciation and Spoken English

While radio infrastructure has been an important theme in a range of current scholarship (Larkin 2008; Pinkerton and Dodds 2009), it is crucially instantiated by the power of the microphone to transmit the voice of authority hailing to the legibility of the English-speaking voice itself. While British Overseas Radio would also broadcast programs in country-specific languages, English, particularly BBC English, gained an authoritative foothold as a trusted voice of authority capable of commanding an unquestioned power of assertion, suggestion, and judicious judgment. BBC English standards were developed with great attention under the purview of the BBC Advisory Committee on Spoken English (1926–1939), which was an effort spearheaded by Reith. He oversaw the formation of this committee, which commissioned the publication of several pamphlets used to standardize pronunciation for announcers.

Arthur Lloyd James, the well-known British linguist at the School of Oriental and African Studies, was charged with developing the pamphlets following the outcome of the Committee's decisions from 1928 to 1938.[11] The curious pronouncements of the committee, inconsistencies, and George Bernard Shaw's disdain for the project of standardized pronunciation were all the more contradictory given that Shaw served as committee chairman. In spite of this, the very existence of such a committee leads us to see the power of affect associated with pronunciation, accent, and word choice as the continuation of the long history of elocution. Marking seemingly minimal differences in language as symptomatic of social class and rank, the standardization of broadcast English was directly associated with the credibility of the information spoken, surpassing that of the announcer, such that the legibility of the spoken utterance also verified its claim to truth.

Pronunciation was a critical dimension of crafting a legitimate and well-respected public image for the BBC. As Reith explained, "No one would deny the great advantage of a standard pronunciation of the language, not only in theory, but in practice. Our responsibilities in this matter are obvious, since in talking to so vast a multitude, mistakes are likely to be promulgated to a much greater extent than was ever possible before" (Reith 1924, 162). He was committed to standardizing English pronunciation as a normative institution projecting values of upper-middle-class propriety, reinventing, perhaps, an emphasis on elocution so critical to the Victorian sensibility of theatricality and political articulations of democratic speech.

As the sociolinguist Jürg Schwyter has explained, the role of BBC announcers was considered equivalent to that of teachers, and a level of cultural refinement became associated with their educated demeanor. The level of formality of their terms of service required that they wear dinner jackets while on duty in the evening, which was considered an act of courtesy associated with the expectation that they would speak good English without affectation (Schwyter 2008, 222). It was none other than the culture of public schools followed by an Oxbridge university education that was being institutionally ratified at the BBC. In fact, Public School Pronunciation (PSP) was the initial terminology for a style of speech, which was, in turn, later abandoned in favor of Received Pronunciation (RP), as it became modulated by the expanding project of BBC English.[12] The standardizing effects of BBC Spoken English of the period were codified by guidelines for radio announcers in the pamphlets mentioned previously. Be they words with so-called "doubtful" pronunciation, place names, or family names and titles, the unending lists of words became a form of folklore unto itself.[13] It also bespoke a powerful logic of hierarchy that was not only internal to class relations within the United Kingdom, but was projected throughout the empire.

Joy Damousi has written extensively about the impact of accent and elocution in her examination of late-nineteenth- and twentieth-century Australia, where English-language radio later served as a critical conduit for what she described as an enduring strand of conservative RP still audible in contemporary versions of Australian English. It is her exploration of the history of elocution in England that directly connects empire, and territorial consolidation, to what she describes as a "linguistic fever" which, by the beginning of the eighteenth century, functioned as a set of rules that enabled a pursuit of clarity that valued the power of communication (Damousi 2010, 13).

The moral countenance of elocution in articulating social identities as well as asserting a form of bourgeois self-legitimation became a midwife to particular movements in the history of British education, which is a significant forebear of postwar mass education government-sponsored programs. This longer legacy of spoken English as a theatrical form of entertainment, instruction, and governance was closely associated with public performances and a hierarchy of speech that was critical to the Victorian era. Damousi also stresses the manner in which elocution was valued as a critical dimension to colonial citizenship by the late nineteenth century (Damousi 2010, 59). Although she addresses colonial Australia, whose early status as a Dominion with a large English-speaking settler population was very different from that of colonial Ghana, her point about elocution is particularly relevant to the history of English-language spoken radio. In other words, it leads us to see that not only was learning English fundamental to ideas about empire and citizenship, but its pedagogical contours go far beyond the instrumental notion of techniques of teaching and learning toward fundamental questions of location, hierarchy, and identity.

English by Radio, Teaching English, and Self-Governance

For this reason, programs focused on learning English were essential. In the postwar period, the English by Radio BBC Unit, led by S. F. Stevens, was established with intermittent subsidy from the Colonial Office that led to the development of an extensive inventory of programs. A large number of these programs were focused on different levels of English-language competency and were organized around pronunciation and sentence patterning for use in schools and on regional radio stations. The extensive catalogue associated with the English by Radio BBC Unit drew on a tradition of radio dramas featuring the theatrical performance while highlighting the continued resonance of a longstanding fascination with elocution (Mugglestone 2003).

Among the wide array of programs produced, some emphasized speaking exercises, such as the Linguaphone series "Spoken English," C. E. Ekersley's "Essential English Series," and Arthur Lloyd Jones's "The English Sounds."[14] Ekersley's programs were broadcast by the BBC starting in 1948 with mixed results, and in 1949 a subcommittee was established to evaluate an array of language methods for broadcast in the colonies. Whereas the Ekersley series, which included "Essential English" and "Sounds of English," were considered somewhat experimental and less effective, a series of programs developed by A. C. Hornby, "English by Radio," was popular and considered effective even though it was pitched at an advanced level.[15] Consisting of 104 lessons divided into seven self-contained subject groups, with recorded sections lasting four minutes that could be replayed, it was broadcast in West Africa starting in 1948, including colonial Ghana.[16] Surveys concluded that the Hornby "English by Radio" programs were effective for advanced speakers, but there was also a concern that they were too advanced for many listeners. As a result, the BBC began to develop a new series, known as "Listen and Speak," consisting of 165 lessons of fifteen-minute duration per program, which was more elementary.[17] In addition, they developed native language lead-in material and translated the "Listen and Speak" newsletter such that the course could be more widely attended by non-English speakers.

While the rudimentary programs such as "Listen and Speak" were focused on questions of pronunciation and sentence structure, more advanced ones focused on specific role behavior in the English household, such as the longstanding "Meet the Parkers" series and the remarkable "Let's Talk English" series produced by Linguaphone in London.[18] The series features the Brockwell family, who embodies the fictionalized upper-middle-class British household. The mother prepares breakfast starting with her husband, who leaves at a quarter to nine in the morning for work at the renowned public school Harrow, followed by her son Dick, who wakes up late but is off to work with his friend Pat, and then her two daughters, Diana and Judith. The linguistic demonstration is organized around maintaining a certain level of conviviality, manifested in one instance by the younger sibling Diana expressing concern for Judith, who debuted in a theatrical production the evening prior to replace the leading actress who had fallen ill.

There is careful attention to the modulation of Judith's character such that she is not seen as being too careerist in the wake of the leading actress's misfortune. Instead, her behavior is shaped in such a manner that she accepts a certain responsibility to perform and is rewarded for it with excellent reviews. This is then followed by Mrs. Brockwell's concern about Diana overextending herself on behalf of Judith. The scripting of this household drama is as much an illustration of a demeanor as guidance in the gendered duties and responsibilities associated with the upper-middle-class British life at home or abroad. In a later program, Mrs. Brockwell discusses the menu with Ellen, their exceedingly competent chief housekeeper capable of running a large multinational corporation. After drawing up a meticulously detailed shopping list with a familiar English menu, the shopping begins, and Harrod's is one of their stops. This series of programs is one of the many not limited to learning English, but rooted in an aspiration toward Englishness in all of its implied projective power. As Mrs. Brockwell quips, "I've never found an error since I've lived in England," which refers at once to the utter precision of the bank clerk at Lloyd's of London, who exchanges pounds sterling for Canadian dollars, and also to others who serve Mrs. Brockwell. We are led to believe that her helpmates would be equally capable of running the empire in addition to taking her orders at the bank, in the department store, or at the dressmaker.

The "Let's Talk English" series was clearly oriented toward advanced speakers but demonstrates the enormous range of programming that was developed. Some of these programs included "Listen and Write," which was intended for the upper classes of higher primary and middle schools, and which was part of student curricula broadcast in Western Nigeria and colonial Ghana, along with "English for You" and "English Intonation."[19]

Within the context of these English-language learning programs, which were once again shipped on 78 rpm records and played at intervals that were integrated into the primary and secondary school curricula, other official broadcasts were played in time slots allowing an extended family to listen. An official message from the British king might be broadcast that was part of a continuity with English-language learning programs. It was as if these learning programs attempted to construct an auditory position for the listener, as distinct from merely understanding the content of the program itself.

At the opening of the Gold Coast Legislative Assembly on 29 March 1951, Charles Arden-Clarke, then governor of the Gold Coast, spoke as he normally would before the Assembly, but on the radio he was introduced with musical fanfare that might indicate the presence or coming of the king. Here, Arden-Clarke introduced the king's remarks by saying, "I have it in command to deliver to this honorable house a gracious message from His Royal Majesty the King [George VI]." The speech itself congratulates the proceedings as part of an evolutionary ethic. Arden-Clarke begins by claiming, "I am glad on the occasion of the formal opening of the Legislative Assembly under the new Constitution of the Gold Coast to express to my peoples of the Gold Coast my great satisfaction at the further and historic advance in the Constitutional Progress of the territory."[20]

Though I am uncertain of the contingencies for the broadcast of this message, it was recorded on vinyl and seems to mark the manner in which authority was being conferred by the king upon the Gold Coast Legislative Assembly through the person of the governor, Charles Arden-Clarke. The speech asserts that "the problems of government with which the assembly and ministers will now have to deal are difficult and complex. And on them will lie a great burden of responsibility for the advancement of the material prosperity of the Gold Coast and of the happiness and well being of my peoples in the territory."[21] The tone of the speech underlies the grave responsibility associated with governing in wake of the election that brought Kwame Nkrumah to power as leader of government business on 12 February 1951, six years prior to independence. This claim to a sense of confidence in eventual self-rule is reinforced when Arden-Clarke says, "I am confident that those who are now undertaking this responsibility will, with the sympathy and good will of my people throughout the Commonwealth, carry it out with courage and honesty of purpose, and with a full sense of the confidence and trust reposed in my peoples of the Gold Coast by this new Constitution which is so largely of their own making." The last sentence of the speech folds in perhaps an advanced English-language lesson on the art of governance in the genre of listening without speaking back: "It is my earnest hope that the work of the new government and Assembly will win for itself an honored place in the history of constitutional evolution in the Commonwealth."

The final section of this speech seems to open up the question of whether Nkrumah as leader of the Convention People's Party is up to the task of claiming the authority to govern, as communicated as an expanded lesson in English-language teaching as governance. The circle of language lessons as advanced administration, moving from the indirect administration of the late interwar period to the local government of the immediate postwar period, as described by Robinson (1950), culminates in a gesture toward self-rule. Nearly ten years later, the Ghana Broadcasting Corporation (GBC) presented a program that followed the queen's November 1961 royal tour of West Africa, which included a two-day visit to Ghana.

The radio coverage of her visit featured several Ghanaian commentators including Festus Adai, Rowland Agodzo, Charles Asinor, Sam Bannerman, Kweku Budu, Miranda Greenstreet, Paul Ridge, and Yao Simmons. At various points, the recording, which was broadcast live on GBC radio during the time of the queen's visit, is punctuated with shifts to Fante programs, among others, as part of the broadcast. However, what is remarkable about the broadcast is not only their embrace of the queen and her retinue, but the manner in which the ceremony and association of British royalty with the Asantehene, among other important figures, are scrutinized in great detail, as if we were witnessing a sporting event. Whether in the offering of a gold chain with a porcupine locket pendant to Princess Anne as a symbol of the Asante, or Queen Elizabeth's participation in the traditional durbar, the ceremony itself was shown to demonstrate how in the four years since independence great progress had been made.

The events held in her honor as part of the itinerary of her visit to Accra, Tamale, and Kumasi were relayed back to Broadcasting House in Accra. The commentators demonstrate the flair with which they describe relevant details while taking on distinctive narrative roles during the broadcast. The most startling perhaps is the only female commentator, Miranda Greenstreet, who served as the fashion commentator in a likely address to adept English-speaking Ghanaian women. Her commentary always seems to begin with how "lovely" Queen Elizabeth is dressed and the details of her luxurious adornments that changed from one event to another. Even as the queen is readying to leave from the airport we learn that she is wearing a crème-colored dress with three-quarter-length sleeves with pale blue lace, while Greenstreet also makes note of the rather low cut of her neckline. The art of description becomes directly associated with the art of governance, in which radio continues to serve the ends of governmentality as part of its shifting context.[22]

Conclusion

In its detachment from the body, the voice functions as an effect without a cause. As the cultural theorist Mladen Dolar has written, "The red thread of the voice resides in the same position as sovereignty, which means that it can suspend the validity of law and inaugurate a state of emergency" (Dolar 2006, 98, 120). We are led to ask what is to be staged, who is to occupy the position of embodied speech, and whether the technology of transmission is more significant than occupying the soundstage itself. In this examination of the role of spoken English in a series of radio programs and the film *I Will Speak English,* the question of how speech discloses rather than reveals remains open. That is, once the source of recorded or mediated speech is revealed it immediately becomes cloaked in a renewed construct of citizenry and exclusion of others. The relationship of the English speaking voice to citizenship implies a colonial identity formation that continued after independence as engineered on an elocutionary gradient of educational accomplishment that was most often associated with British institutions. If British colonial administrative authority was invested with English-speaking settler culture, access to language and its mastery became a window to cultural identity in a reappraisal and respatialization of the postwar nation-state.

The Indian film historian Ashish Rajadhyaksha has suggested that "cinematic governmentality" is a critical context for understanding the relationship between film spectatorship and citizenship in its reliance on an analysis of specific exhibition practices (Rajadhyaksha 2010). As he explains, "cinematic governmentality" challenges theories that have been focused primarily on the "I" as the psychologized individual citizen, instead of the collective nature of the theatergoing experience. It is for this reason that celluloid in its materiality and medium of modernity informs the nature of its circulation and a relationship to spectatorial practice. This figure of governmentality relies on Foucault's analysis of Machiavelli's *The Prince* along with other works that attempts to foreground the tactics of the projected voice in order to remake the political body toward the thematization of self-rule.

An important theme that I would like to refer to here, in closing, is the manner in which the voice may be understood as a fundamental means of forming the subject as part of an emerging modernization ethos. The manner in which radio and other forms of broadcast media deploy the voice to communicate political authority may be understood in the context of Denis Vasse's (1974) insistence on the pairing of the umbilicus and the voice. The insight that Vasse brings to bear is the manner in which the voice is implicated into the umbilical rupture. That is, in severing the child's body from the mother, the child is assigned to reside in its own body, and, crucially, from then on, bodily contact with the mother evolves into mediation by the voice. The umbilical cord and the voice thus constitute a pair in which the umbilicus means closure but is displaced by the voice itself. Whether it names or calls, the voice traverses closure without breaking it in the process (Chion 1999, 61–62; Rosolato 1974).

The ingenious nature of pairing the voice with the umbilical cord as a primal psychosexual feature is the ultimate modulation of the voice as life-giving force. Clearly, it is not the only element, or the primordial one, but it remains critical to the formation of identity. This is not to imply that England serves as mother or father to the empire in a direct manner, but the mediation of the voice through colonial media creates a transactional model of role behavior analogous to parent and child in the developmental imagination and the history of the modernization project.

Further, the ubiquity of English-language speech through film and radio during the late colonial period was mediated by figures such as Lionel Marson of the BBC, whose voice was often heard in voice-over commentaries in a wide range of colonial film productions (Colonial Cinema 1950, 18). The close relationship between film and radio in the colonial context was a means by which cultural authority was assessed and asserted at a moment when colonial hierarchies could no longer be sustained, but were repositioned as a dialectical play of politics and language.

Notes

1. Colonial Office, "Interim Report of a Committee on Broadcasting Services in the Colonies," Miscellaneous No. 469, July 1936, 5, 14, BBC Written Archive Caversham E2/160.

2. "Broadcasting Organizations in the Empire Overseas," 24 April 1939. See the appendix, "Local Broadcasting and Rediffusion in the Colonial Empire," 2, BBC Written Archive Caversham E2/161.

3. See Burns 2002, 27; Chikowero in this volume; Reynolds 2009, 61; Windel in this volume. The Bantu Educational Kinema Experiment was led by Major Leslie A. Notcutt and Geoffrey C. Latham. It attempted to study the use of cinema as an instrument for "educational and cultural adjustment," and served as a follow-up to an earlier study by J. Merle Davis on the effects of industrialization in African society in the Northern Rhodesian Copperbelt, present-day Zambia. Davis, who was director of the International Missionary Council, managed to obtain funding from the Carnegie Corporation for this cinema experiment during a two-year period, with production facilities in present-day Tanzania, where BEKE produced and processed at least thirty-five short films and organized screenings that reportedly reached eighty thou-

sand people (Kerr 1993). The films included semiprofessional Zanzibari theater performers and were variously formulaic, including instructional films related to correct methods for tanning animal hides, the planting and preparing of tea, and avoiding hookworm, among other themes. Some of the early films included knockabout Hollywood farces, a traditional African story featuring an antiwitchcraft theme, and the frequent deployment of the Mr. Wise and Mr. Foolish format—in which the foolish man might bury his money in the ground and find it soon stolen, whereas the wise man is shown to deposit his money in the savings bank. These initial locally produced films along with imported ones were screened extensively in Tanzania, Kenya, Zambia, Zimbabwe, Malawi, and Uganda. At every screening event Latham endeavored to record audience reactions to the best of his ability, inviting audience members to send in their own reports, such that audience reactions were considered in the making of subsequent films following the circulation of the first twelve films (Rice 2010).

4. Intelligence Memorandum, September–March 1942, BBC Written Archive Caversham E2/171/2.

5. On the remarkable website developed by the Colonial Film: Moving Images of the British Empire project, *I Will Speak English* can be streamed, and important filmographic information is provided by Tom Rice. See http://www.colonialfilm.org.uk/node/1451.

6. Colonial Office, *Report on Department of Social Welfare and Community Development in the Gold Coast for the Year 1954*, cited by Tom Rice. See http://www.colonialfilm.org.uk/node/1451.

7. Colonial Office, "Interim Report of a Committee on Broadcasting Services in the Colonies," Miscellaneous No. 469, July 1936, 6, para. 15, BBC Written Archive Caversham E2/160. See also Lawler (2002).

8. *A New Broadcasting House: The Story of Radio Ghana* (Accra: Government Printer, 1958), Melville J. Herkovits Library, Vertical Files, Ghana: Information Services; Northwestern University, Evanston, IL. Thanks to Stephan Miescher for sharing this pamphlet and other material with me. This pamphlet, among others, is available at the Ghana Broadcasting Corporation Library, Accra, Ghana.

9. *The BBC and Its External Services* (London: BBC, 1956), 9, E1/1815/1, item A2247, BBC Written Archive Caversham.

10. John Reith, "Inauguration of the BBC Empire Service on 19 December 1932," British Library Listening Room, Inventory #1CD-249358-BD9. Courtesy of the BBC Archive.

11. The first edition of this series of pamphlets includes a foreword by John Reith, and the essay "Broadcast English" by Arthur Lloyd James (1935, 6–20).

12. Schwyter, who summarizes the legacy of RP in relation to BBC English in great detail, explains that the BBC accent is known to be one of the most fully described forms of English among phoneticians, following the more recent work by Peter Roach, and, in turn, it is used to teach English to foreign language learners (Roach 2000, vii, 3–4, as cited by Schwyter 2008, 222).

13. See in particular the radio program script by Paul Ferris, "English as She Is Broadcast [History of the Spoken English Advisory Committee, 1926–1938]," Radio One, 2 December 1977, Program No. BTB103X235, BBC Written Archive Caversham R6/197.

14. Nearly complete sets of these programs are available on the British Library Archival Sound Recording website. See the section entitled "Early Spoken Word Recordings" (http://sounds.bl.uk/Browse.aspx?category=Arts-literature-and-performance&collection=Early-spoken-word-recordings).

15. C. E. Eckersley, "Sounds of English," 1956. Sounds of British Library Listening Room, Inventory #1CD-249358-BD9. Courtesy of the BBC Archive.

16. In the Ghana Broadcasting Corporation Gramophone Library, a nearly complete set of the A. C. Hornby "English by Radio" series still existed as of July 2012, but these records were most certainly re-edited and rereleased over an extended period of time. They would also be used for classroom teaching as they were coordinated with middle and upper school curricula. See also Hornby (1952).

17. BBC English by Radio Unit, BBC Written Archives Caversham.

18. "Let's Talk English" Series, Dents, October 1946. Original issue on Linguaphone English 2E1. British Library Listening Room database, ICS0011520–525. See http://sounds.bl.uk/Browse.aspx?category=Arts-literature-and-performance&collection=Early-spoken-word-recordings&browseby=Browse+by+date&choice=1930s; go to 1939 for ten programs from this Linguaphone series. It should be noted that these programs are only available on the internet from a United Kingdom–based portal because of copyright restrictions.

19. English By Radio—West Nigeria, July 1949–December 1954; and file E6/60/1, English By Radio—Nigeria (West), 1955–1959, BBC Written Archive Caversham E6/34. See also http://sounds.bl.uk/Browse.aspx?category=Arts-literature-and-performance&collection=Early-spoken-word-recordings.

20. Charles Arden-Clarke, "Accra: Opening of Gold Coast Legislative Assembly; A Gracious Message from HMS the King," 29 March 1951, British Library, Listening Room Sound Archive. Courtesy of the BBC Archive.

21. Ibid.

22. Miranda Greenstreet, alumna of the London School of Economics, went on to teach at the University of Ghana, Legon, and served as director of the Institute of Adult Education. Thanks to Takyiwaa Manuh for clarifying this point.

References

Adi, Hakim. 1998. *West Africans in Britain, 1900–1960: Nationalism, Pan-Africanism, and Communism.* London: Lawrence and Wishart.

Ansah, P. A. V. 1985. *Golden Jubilee Lectures: From Station ZOY in 1935 to GBC in 1985.* Accra: Ghana Broadcasting Corporation.

Austin, Dennis. 1964. *Politics in Ghana, 1946–1960.* London: Oxford University Press.

Avery, Todd. 2006. *Radio Modernism: Literature, Ethics, and the BBC, 1922–1938.* Aldershot, UK: Ashgate.

Bloom, Peter J., and Kate Skinner. 2009/2010. "Modernity and Danger: The Boy Kumasenu and the Work of the Gold Coast Film Unit." *Ghana Studies* 12/13: 121–53.

Burchell, Graham, Colin Gordon, and Peter Miller, eds. 1991. *The Foucault Effect: Studies in Governmentality with Two Lectures by and an Interview with Michel Foucault.* Chicago: University of Chicago Press.

Burns, J. M. 2002. *Flickering Shadows: Cinema and Identity in Colonial Zimbabwe.* Athens: Ohio University Research in International Studies.

Chion, Michel. 1999. *The Voice in Cinema.* Translated by Claudia Gorbman. New York: Columbia University Press.

Colonial Cinema, ed. 1945. "The Raw Stock Scheme: Retrospect and Prospect." *Colonial Cinema* 3, no. 4: 76–79.

———. 1947. "Raw Stock Scheme." *Colonial Cinema* 5, no. 3: 68–70.

———. 1949. "Raw Stock Scheme, 1948." *Colonial Cinema* 7, no. 1: 6–7.

———. 1950. "Sound Track: Colonial Film Unit Films." *Colonial Cinema* 8, no. 2: 18.

Colonial Office. 1954. *Report on Department of Social Welfare and Community Development in the Gold Coast for the Year 1954*. London: Government Printing Office.

Creech Jones, Arthur. 1949. "The Place of African Local Administration in Colonial Policy." *Journal of African Administration* 1, no. 1: 3–6.

Damousi, Joy. 2010. *Colonial Voices: A Cultural History of English in Australia, 1840–1940*. Cambridge: Cambridge University Press.

Dolar, Mladen. 2006. *A Voice and Nothing More*. Cambridge, MA: MIT Press.

Ferguson, James, and Akhil Gupta. 2002. "Spatializing States: Toward an Ethnography of Neoliberal Governmentality." *American Ethnologist* 29, no. 4: 981–1002.

Foucault, Michel. 2007. *Security, Territory, Population: Lectures at the Collège de France, 1977–78*. Edited by Michel Senellart. Translated by Graham Burchell. Hampshire, UK: Palgrave Macmillan.

GBC Golden Jubilee Publicity and Literature Sub-Committee. 1985. *50 Years of Broadcasting in Ghana, July 1935–1985*. Accra: Arakan Printing Press.

Hill, Andrew. 2010. "The BBC Empire Service: The Voice, the Discourse of the Master and Ventriloquism." *South Asian Diaspora* 2, no. 1: 25–38.

Hornby, A. S. 1952. *English by Radio: Part One*. London: Macmillian and Company in association with the British Broadcasting Corporation.

Kerr, David. 1993. "The Best of Both Worlds? Colonial Film Policy and Practice in Northern Rhodesia and Nyasaland." *Critical Arts* 7, no. 1: 11–43.

Larkin, Brian. 2008. *Signal and Noise: Media, Infrastructure, and Urban Culture in Nigeria*. Durham, NC: Duke University Press.

Laubach, Frank C. 1940. *India Shall Be Literate*. Jubbulpore, India: F. E. Livengood at the Mission Press.

Lawler, Nancy. 2002. *Soldiers, Airmen, Spies, and Whisperers: The Gold Coast in World War II*. Athens, OH: Ohio University Press.

Lloyd James, Arthur. 1935 [1928]. *Broadcast English I: Recommendations to Announcers Regarding Certain Words of Doubtful Pronunciation*. London: British Broadcasting Corporation in association with J. J. Keliher.

Lugard, Frederick D. 1922. *The Dual Mandate in British Tropical Africa*. Edinburgh: Blackwood Press.

Mugglestone, Lynda. 2003. *Talking Proper: The Rise of Accent as Social Symbol*. 2nd ed. Oxford: Oxford University Press.

Notcutt, Leslie A., and Geoffrey C. Latham. 1937. *The African and the Cinema: An Account of the Work of the Bantu Educational Cinema Experiment during the Period March 1935 to May 1937*. London: Edinburgh House Press.

Pinkerton, Alasdair, and Klaus Dodd. 2008. "Radio Geopolitics: Broadcasting, Listening and the Struggle for Acoustic Spaces." *Progress in Human Geography* 33, no. 1: 10–27.

Rajadhyaksha, Ashish. 2010. "Colonial Film Policy after the 1925 Imperial Conference." Keynote address presented at the Colonial Cinema: Moving Images of the British Empire conference, Birbeck College, London, 7–9 July.

Ranger, Terence. 1983. "The Invention of Tradition in Colonial Africa." In *The Invention of Tradition*, edited by Eric Hobsbawm and Terence Ranger, 211–62. Cambridge: Cambridge University Press.

Reith, John C. W. 1924. *Broadcast Over Britain*. London: Hodder and Stoughton.

Reynolds, Glenn. 2009. "The Bantu Educational Kinema Experiment and the Struggle for Hegemony in British East and Central Africa, 1935–1937." *Historical Journal of Film, Radio and Television* 29, no. 1: 57–78.

Rice, Tom. 2010. "Bekefilm." Colonial Film: Moving Images of the British Empire. http://www.colonialfilm.org.uk/production-company/bekefilm.

Roach, Peter. 2000. *English Phonetics and Phonology: A Practical Course.* 3rd ed. Cambridge: Cambridge University Press.

Robinson, R. E. 1950. "Why 'Indirect Rule' Has Been Replaced by 'Local Government' in the Nomenclature of British Native Administration." *Journal of African Administration* 2, no. 3: 12–15.

Rosolato, Guy. 1974. "La voix: Entre corps et langage." *Revue Française de psychanalyse* 38 (January–February): 75–94.

Schwyter, Jürg Rainer. 2008. "Setting a Standard: Early BBC Language Policy and the Advisory Board on Spoken English." *Arbeiten aus Anglistik und Amerikanistik* 33, no. 2: 217–50.

Scott, David. 1995. "Colonial Governmentality." *Social Text* 43 (Autumn): 191–220.

Skinner, Kate. 2009. "'It brought some kind of neatness to mankind': Mass Literacy, Community Development and Democracy in 1950s Asante." *Africa: Journal of the International African Institute* 79, no. 4: 479–99.

Smyth, Rosaleen. 1979. "The Development of British Colonial Film Policy, 1927–1939, with Special Reference to East and Central Africa." *Journal of African History* 20, no. 3: 437–50.

Sticht, Tom. 2005. "Seven Pioneering Adult Literacy Educators in the History of Teaching Reading with Adults in the United States." Paper presented at the Adult Literacy Research Working Group (ALRWG) conference, Washington, DC, 10–11 March.

Strevens, Peter. 1954. "Spoken English in the Gold Coast." *ELT Journal* 8, no. 3: 81–89.

Taylor, Ida Mary. 1953. *I Will Speak English: An English Primer for Adults.* London: Longmans, Green.

Vasse, Denis. 1974. "L'Ombilic et la voix." *Le Champ freudien.* Paris: Éditions du Seuil.

PART THREE

Infrastructure and Effects

7 Negotiating Modernization

The Kariba Dam Project in the Central African Federation, ca. 1954–1960

Julia Tischler

On the border between Zambia and Zimbabwe, about 240 miles downstream from the Victoria Falls, you can see a "gracefully curved mass of concrete," "a colossus" which has tamed the "moods of violence" of the Zambezi River (South African News Agencies 1959, 5).[1] The Kariba Dam was built in the second half of the 1950s to meet the growing energy needs of the Federation of Rhodesia and Nyasaland, creating what was, at the time, the biggest artificial lake in the world. Newspapers around the world did not tire of telling "the romantic and adventurous story of how the dark jungle was opened up to provide light and power for a nation."[2] The Kariba Dam and the massive reservoir are a monument to the great expectations that coincided with the establishment of the Federation in 1953.

The dead trees which still stick out at the fringes of the lake remind us, however, that there is another side to the story. High-tech development came at a cost and Kariba has remained notorious for the catastrophic resettlement which its building entailed, as the rising waters submerged the homes of 57,000 Gwembe Tonga north and south of the Zambezi. Moreover, the hydroelectricity project monopolized the Federation's credits for years, channeling vast resources into infrastructural development, which could have been used elsewhere. Hence, Kariba has been interpreted as the epitome of the Federation, for both its aspirations—of becoming a "powerful," "multiracial" nation—and its flaws, seen in white settlers' racist politics.

Kariba was a microcosm of discourses and politics of development and modernization in the turbulent dynamics of decolonization, at the local, colonial, and international levels. In the following, I seek to draw out some of the different visions of development and modernization as imagined and put into practice by various actors involved in the project, and to contextualize them with respect to the dramatic transformations in Central Africa during the 1950s. Hence I use the terms "modernization" and "development" here not as analytical concepts, that is, as a set of more or less defined indicators against which the subject of research is measured. Rather than asking whether Kariba "modernized" Central Africa, this chapter draws out how the historical actors themselves talked about "modernization" and "development" and by which strategies they sought to shape the future accordingly.[3]

According to the American journalist David Howarth, Kariba was inextricably linked to the aim of staying on top of social change. In his 1961 book, he summarized the rationale behind the power scheme: "A colony of this kind can never stand still, . . . : it must either rush on towards becoming an industrial power, or else fall back towards famine and chaos worse than before it began" (Howarth 1961, 34). At a time when the future seemed very close but also very different from the present, Kariba was essentially about controlling and channeling change, defining what progress was, how it would be achieved, and who was to profit from it. As has been the case with similar large-scale projects across time and around the world, the Federation's hydroelectricity project was not universally beneficial; it produced winners and losers.[4] This, however, was not a one-direction process but was subject to negotiation among the various groups of actors involved.[5]

Looking first at the planning process, this chapter explores the connections between Kariba and "high modernist" developmentalism, drawing out, more specifically, the scheme's significance for the newly established "multiracial" Federation. Moreover, I discuss how dam-building linked up with the controversial politics of white nation-building.[6] The second part focuses on Kariba's reverberations in the Gwembe Valley. By showing how district officers "corrected" these effects, how the Native Authority's leader Hezekiah Habanyama negotiated his own vision of development and modernization, and what the enforced changes meant for the displaced population, I demonstrate that high modernism impacted but never simply supplanted locally ongoing transformations.

Planning Kariba

Central Africa's major dam project in the 1950s needs to be seen in the overall context of the "second colonial occupation," when state intervention, in the name of development, gained unprecedented momentum (Low and Lonsdale 1976, 12). As anti-imperial protest grew both in the colonies and in the industrialized countries, the British government stepped up funds, personnel, and technical assistance in order to "reinvigorate and relegitimize empire" and prepare the grounds for its territories' future (indeed far-future) independence (Cooper and Packard 1997, 7). The "development fever" was fueled by a heightened confidence in humanity's capacity to steer social, political, and economic processes, making big-scale projects appear more attractive than "piecemeal" approaches (Butler 1991, 128; Rist 2006, 34).

As much as Kariba represents a prototype of postwar "development colonialism" or high modernism, the case is quite specific.[7] After a series of failures, from the Tanganyikan groundnut program to the Gambian poultry scheme, there was an increased sensitivity among authorities that even the best plans could go awry. Had there been no Federation, anti-Kariba protests claiming that the scheme was destined to become another "white elephant" would have carried greater weight, especially since the Federal government faced the choice between Kariba and a smaller dam on the Kafue River.[8] If Prime Minister Huggins had opted for a Kafue Dam, he could have reduced both costs and hardship, as "only" about one thousand people were to be removed.[9] This chapter examines the cross-fertilizing connections that unfolded between universalistic concepts of economic modernization, settler nation-building, and the Federation's attempt to establish a middle ground straddling black and white "extremism." A short period of multiracial hopes, white identity politics, and an economic boom opened a window of opportunity that allowed the mega-scheme to proceed. In the end, Kariba devoured approximately 40 percent of the young state's gross national product.[10]

In 1953, the British government created the Federation against fierce African opposition. This uneasy union among three very different territories—the British protectorates of Northern Rhodesia and Nyasaland as opposed to self-governing Southern Rhodesia, with its strong settler community—was an example of Britain's experimenting with multiracial constitutions. Compared to the "black" West African states, the question of controlling change in the light of decolonization posed itself differently in Central Africa. Here, the British not only faced the challenge of "African" resistance but also struggled to keep in check the strong nationalism of "European" settlers and the threat of another apartheid-style society.[11]

The Kariba Dam, as a future provider of cheap electricity to the Northern Rhodesian Copperbelt and urban-industrial centers in Southern Rhodesia, constituted a cornerstone of the Federation's development program. Since social and political solutions were so much harder to find, economic expansion was cast as the way out of the multiracial dilemma. In view of the impressive economic growth rate in the earlier 1950s, among the highest in the world, this seemed like a reasonable undertaking.[12] British officers readily supported the Federal government in planning and financing Kariba, with the declared aim that "the Federation should get off to a good start."[13] Treasury members identified the European leadership and business as the state's major development assets: they would spearhead the self-induced "industrial revolution."[14] Optimistic officials envisaged a process of modernization and nation-building which would create a win-win situation all around. Kariba meant economic expansion, which was expected to transfer directly into social progress. Electricity generation was linked to the vision of racial reconciliation that was part and parcel of the Federal experiment. "Taking a long view," a high commissioner found that "Kariba would be of the greatest possible assistance in promoting the economic advancement of the Africans and partnership generally."[15] Raising the standard of living would lead to the envisioned "middle way" between white and black nationalism. As such, no racial group had to give up their share of the pie; the pie just had to become bigger.

The initial enthusiasm wore off quickly, as the Federation's leadership failed to agree on how this new nation should be built. Turning to the links between Kariba and nation-building, this chapter suggests that identity politics was first of all a project of creating cohesion *within* white society and, second, one of emancipation directed *against* the colonial motherland and the indigenous population. Seen in this light, the electricity project was linked to the complex dynamics of decolonization in the Central African settler society, resulting from the whites' position as both colonized and colonizing subjects. Independent settler states, as previous studies have pointed out, arose from a "dual defeat" that included the indigenous peoples, on the one hand, and the colonial motherland on the other.[16]

Before the dam became a symbol of the settlers' national pride, however, the "Kariba-Kafue debate" was one of many struggles which highlighted the tensions within the Federation's diverse white community—foremost the rifts between the north and the south, as well as between the colonial officials and the European settlers. Many Nyasalanders and Northern Rhodesians felt that the Federal government was dominated by Southern Rhodesian parochialism.[17] The Federation was a nation "in progress," a planned community whose internal coherence and legitimacy had to be constantly negotiated, confirmed, and reenacted. Rather than making it a success, the question of hydroelectric development at first almost caused the new state to collapse. While most Northern Rhodesians preferred a smaller scheme on the Kafue River near the northern capital of Lusaka, their southern neighbors stood firm in advocating Kariba, a much larger project on the Zambezi between both territories. When Prime Minister Huggins announced his decision to proceed with the latter, he caused "immediate furore" among the Northern Rhodesian pro-Kafue faction, which refused to regard Kariba as a collective rather than a Southern Rhodesian enterprise. For several days the issue dominated newspaper headlines, a Northern Rhodesian official resigned from the Federal Hydro-Electric Board, and 1,300 Northern Rhodesians assembled in Lusaka to vent their protest.[18]

Opposition from the north was motivated by hard and fast economic interests as much as by symbolic concerns. Northern businessmen feared that the profits from the dam's construction would go to Salisbury instead of Lusaka.[19] Moreover, the issue had aroused considerable "local emotion" in the three territories, which were, according to Huggins, still "highly individualistic countries."[20] The "first big issue calling for a larger Rhodesian point of view" developed as a platform for those sections of the northern public who had never subscribed to the idea of Federation in the first place.[21]

The heated controversy even raised the specter of secession.[22] Especially when the Federal government admitted early in 1956 that the cost estimates had increased by 45 percent, Rhodesians realized that high-tech modernization came at a cost.[23] Even optimists had to concede that Kariba not only strained the Federal budget but also pooled a large share of the available construction services and materials, restricting development potentials in the northern territories for years to come.[24] The image of Kariba as a monument to white settlers' pride was thus highly contested and had to be perpetually reconstructed. Numerous public speeches, radio broadcasts, and newspaper articles reflected the authorities' desire to make the mega-scheme a "binding factor," tying two rivaling countries together "with economic bonds when bonds of affection had failed to materialize."[25] Common ground was to be found by presenting Kariba as a symbol of the aspiring nation's self-confidence, signaling what the Federation was already capable of achieving and demonstrating high hopes for the future. In addition, modernization formed part of the more general project to attract European immigrants to Central Africa. The prime minister pointed out that "its size . . . makes such a popular appeal, and it will be an excellent advertisement for the whole Federal area."[26] Prospects of hydroelectric development, industrialization, and improved living conditions hence appealed to the long-cherished dream of making Rhodesia a "white man's country."[27]

The Kariba-Kafue debate touched upon another controversial issue concerning collective identity formation. In a Northern Rhodesian Legislative Council debate, the so-called official members—civil servants who formed part of the British Colonial Service—had vented their protest very openly.[28] Huggins's irritation that these men, whom he ultimately viewed as representatives of the British government itself, "should have regarded themselves as entitled to cast doubts publicly on his honesty of purpose,"[29] was symptomatic of the Rhodesian settlers' resentment of the remaining influence of the colonial metropole.[30] Federal politicians welcomed the fact that the International Bank for Reconstruction and Development (IBRD, or World Bank) signaled its willingness to support Kariba with a major loan. As an international agency independent from colonial networks, the bank seemed to be conducive to the settlers' struggle for emancipation.[31] However, after months of investigations and tiring negotiations, Federal leaders moaned "that the Federation's lot is at the hands of the Bank worse than a British Protectorate under Treasury control!"[32] The Kariba controversy reflected the ambivalent identity politics in a heterogeneous settler society, which strove to be British (in terms of culture) and non-British (in terms of political dependency) at the same time (see Shutt and King 2005, 357–65).

These struggles over who would be the winner and who the loser of the Federation's development planning overshadowed the exceedingly more obvious sacrifice

Kariba entailed. At no stage did the prospective removal of an estimated 45,000 Gwembe Tonga impact the decision-making process. On the one hand, the evictions followed the "logic" of settler emancipation. As other scholars have argued, "a settler history is per definition a history of indigenous replacement," meaning that settler independence always entailed indigenous oppression.[33] On the other hand, full self-government would not be granted to the aspiring state before its government had reconciled the black majority with the Central African Federation. The Northern Rhodesian governor rightly warned that the evictions, being "the first evil result of Federation to which any African could point," were bound to reinforce anti-Federation resentment, proving that Britain was unable to protect the indigenous population from land-grabbing settlers.[34] How, then, could this extremely expensive scheme, which had no demonstrable benefit for Africans and instead displaced tens of thousands of the poorest, be allowed to proceed in a state whose very *raison d'être* was racial reconciliation? This paradox can only be explained by the new politics of "partnership" and the particular model of modernization Kariba represented. The forced eviction of the Gwembe Tonga people was recast as a necessary means by which to promote African development. Kariba's cheap electricity, Prime Minister Huggins argued, would boost industrialization, which in turn meant that "we can . . . employ our rapidly increasing African population." Claiming that land was "limited," Huggins cast industrialization and economic expansion as the only way for the Federation to advance.[35] Further, actors more directly concerned with African interests were at pains to explain away Kariba's obvious racial bias. The Colonial Office, which served as the constitutional guardian over indigenous concerns in the Northern Rhodesian protectorate, found itself in an embarrassing situation. Since the flood areas in the north were mainly Native Trust and Reserve land—and thus designated by law to the African population—the colonial secretary had to give his official approval for the alienation of this land and sanction the removal. In internal communication, several members of the Colonial Office expressed serious unease. Others argued, however, that the scheme "was of such great public benefit to the inhabitants of the Federation as a whole that it justified the removal" and that "those inhabitants [the Gwembe Tonga] themselves would benefit," adopting a sense of pragmatic optimism.[36]

In various newspaper reports, political statements, and planning documents, the Kariba resettlement was constructed not only as a necessary sacrifice for the national interest but as a measure of "African advancement" in itself. This interpretation was facilitated thanks to the new emphasis on "partnership," in contrast to the principle of "native paramountcy" that had been the guiding paradigm of native policy in the northern protectorates before 1953. While the latter asserted that indigenous interests had to prevail over those of immigrants in case of conflict, the concept of "partnership" did not envisage such a prioritization but instead expressed a vague commitment to "inter-racial cooperation."[37] Further, international modernization policy had shifted toward an economy-centered approach, giving way to a model of "development" in which poor peasants came last.[38] Especially after World War II, international actors as well as colonial bureaucrats increasingly referred to a universalizing concept of Western-style industrialization as the only successful path to modernity. When Huggins stated in the Federal Parliament that "economic development can do a thousand times more to advance the African than franchise laws or cries for social equality," he certainly echoed the views of many British officers and World Bankers.[39]

The latter in fact hardly inquired into the resettlement question during their intensive negotiations with the Federal and the British government. While bank experts stressed that "Kariba would not be feasible if it did not guide the African population into worth-while participation with Europeans in the production of the community's wealth—and also in the sharing of it,"[40] their final appraisal report expressed confidence that the scheme could be beneficial for both "races." The World Bank argued that Africans could be granted improvements without reducing European standards of living only if productivity rose. There was no other possibility but to push forth the "transition from a static tribal society to an individualistic, modern western society," a process which would be spearheaded by European leaders in politics and business. Echoing central tenets of modernization theory at the time, bank experts found that Rhodesian Africans had to break with tradition in order to become part of the modern order.[41] This rationalization reverberated through government discourse as well as the British and Rhodesian media. Since the Gwembe Tonga were allegedly "primitive in the extreme," their forced eviction constituted an exodus to modernity.[42] The sacrifice they had to make was only temporary, since the Tonga and the African population in general would supposedly be drawn into the European-led process of economic expansion.

Kariba is a prominent example of how "large dams offered a way to build not just irrigation and power systems, but nation-states themselves" (Mitchell 2002, 44). As explained above, creating cohesion within was one of Kariba's expected tributes to white nation-building; the aspects of exclusion and emancipation constituted another. Dam building was part of the struggle to cut loose from the metropole. Moreover, it entailed, through the forced evictions, a recolonization of the indigenous population, which was aided by specific shifts in thinking about race and development. This "modern" form of taming nature, of harnessing the Zambezi River and using it for industrialization, blended in with the "great foundational narrative" of "arrival, hardship, and settlement" in the Rhodesian settler colony (Johnston and Lawson 2000, 361). In order to construct a distinctly Central African self-concept, white Rhodesians not only invented a history, but turned resolutely toward the future. Technological achievements, in Rhodesia as elsewhere, evoked local pride and shifted the "periphery" into the center of modernity.

Local Perspectives

The planning of Kariba was a top-down process; local actors were not consulted. Colonial officers and African administrators in the Zambezi Valley and of course the Gwembe Tonga were left to deal with the enormous consequences of the externally devised plans (Colson 1971, 35–37). All the same, it would be an oversimplification to interpret the Kariba Dam project solely as an act of oppression, by which racist settlers in alliance with the colonial power and a neoimperial international agency wiped a poor peasant community from the stage of modernization. The dividing lines, separating the losers and winners of development, did not always follow racial patterns. As will be shown, the perspective of British officers stationed in the valley had much more in common with that of the local African elite than with the position taken by the Federal government. Further, Kariba had many facets. Not only were there competing claims among the more powerful players; local actors also displayed considerable creativity in trying to negotiate their own story of progress. The following section, focusing on how Kariba impacted on life in Northern Rhodesia's Gwembe Valley, examines high modernism on the ground, handling it in a rather more nuanced way than some of the major studies of modernization that have been rightly criticized.[43]

Contrary to what the Rhodesian media projected, the Tonga did not have to be awakened from primeval slumber with Kariba. In the postwar period, they had already experienced their own "second colonial occupation" when various schemes began to be carried out. Looking back on their engagement in the valley before resettlement, Gwembe's administrators reminisced about the pre-Kariba days, when development had, allegedly, come from within, gradually and peacefully. Devoted officials, a memorandum maintained, developed the valley on a small scale and with modest financial means but nevertheless "made a great difference." Roads were built, the quality of seeds improved, wells constructed, and demonstration gardens laid out. According to the administration's idealized recollections, officers had been guided by the realization that the Tonga were "a profoundly agricultural society," and that modernization needed to come as a "series of small measures."[44]

From the local administration's perspective, the resettlement disturbed ongoing developmental activities.[45] Moreover, their vision of a step-by-step improvement was irreconcilable with the model of an exterior modernization done perforce, which the dam project represented. Numerous reports by colonial officers in charge of the resettlement reflected a sense of uneasiness and nostalgia. An officer commented, "What it all adds up to is that the Mwemba people [one of

Gwembe's chieftaincies] may be primitive and may be backward, but they have still got something. Can we retain that something as we bring them fully and finally into the twentieth century?"[46] Here tradition appeared not as an obstacle but as the very foundation of development. African societies had to develop "along their own lines." Tenets of indirect rule, a declining administrative policy which nevertheless still exerted considerable influence, reverberated in resettlement discourse and practice.[47] Governor Benson and the local administration worried that the Tonga would be forced to adopt new agricultural techniques, take up fishing or wage labor, as there was insufficient alternative land to sustain them on their present mode of living. Anxious comments that the Tonga would be forced into a "completely new and strange existence" speak of the officers' essentializing belief in cultural distinctiveness and the racial prejudice inherent in indirect rule more generally.[48]

However, some officers found that the resettlement opened up new opportunities, giving the Tonga "an almost unprecedented chance to take part" in the revolutionary transformation of their valley.[49] The native secretary even foretold that that "a new and better life is within their grasp."[50] The Kariba evictions thus not only brought to the fore the rift between technocratic high modernism and late colonialism but also highlighted ongoing controversies within colonial policy after World War II. Leading experts rebuked indirect rule for being paternalistic, racially biased, and static. Similarly, many "men on the spot" found gradualistic approaches incompatible with the new colonial commitment to active interventionism. In the course of the resettlement program, district officers struggled to navigate high-speed social change, stumbling over late colonialism's unresolved questions.[51]

The relocation program not only posed intellectual problems. From its inception, the operation was bound to become, in Thayer Scudder's (2007, 311) words, a "poorly conceived, and trauma-ridden, crash program." An inexperienced, ill-equipped, and small staff had to shoulder a massive task in an extremely short time period. Scudder and Elizabeth Colson, two American anthropologists who undertook famous before-and-after studies of the relocation, agreed that officers did their best to alleviate the hardships (Scudder 2005, 30; Colson 1971, 35–37). Their best, however, was not good enough. As problems in the operation accumulated—from land shortage and insufficient personnel to two devastating floods in the years 1957–1958—officers failed to live up to the promises they had originally made to the Tonga. The hopelessly overburdened officers faced a loss of control, especially in the two most problematic resettlement areas. Some of Chief Mwemba's people were moved to land unsuitable for cultivation, so they were forced to re-resettle elsewhere. This chaotic operation was beset by extreme hardship—famine, lack of water, loss of cattle and small stock, diseases, and deaths—which also did not escape the press.[52] In Chipepo's chieftaincy, resistance climaxed in a violent clash between police forces and inhabitants of Chisamu Village in 1958, causing eight fatalities and a lasting administrative trauma.[53] These failures not only "made liars of the officers," who were increasingly seen as agents of European interests; they also contradicted the colonial officials' self-image as paternal friends and protectors of the African population. Having to uproot rural Africans for the sake of white industry, especially in such a harmful manner, ran contrary to the "mandate ethos" cultivated in the Colonial Service.[54]

After the officers' role collapsed in the course of the resettlement, they sought to regain authority over the Tonga's supposed transition into modernity through a far-reaching rehabilitation program, which, following Scudder, turned out to have a lasting positive effect.[55] This endeavor to "correct" the disruption "dictated by an outside cause" provoked serious controversy between the Northern Rhodesian administration and the Federal government over the amount of compensation to be paid to the Gwembe Tonga.[56] Pointing out that the resettlers would have to be taught a completely new lifestyle, the administrative team claimed funds exceeding the actual material losses caused by the evictions.[57] What the district staff had in mind amounted to a large-scale social-engineering program by which the Tonga community would be "split up into farmers, fishermen, employees" with considerable governmental assistance.[58] Far from relying on a universalizing calculation, presupposing that rural Africans would automatically be drawn into industrialization, local officers were determined to push through their own program of African development in which they themselves played a central role. The envisaged components of the program, which included education, tsetse eradication, agricultural improvement, and, very importantly, the setting up of an artisan fishery at the new reservoir, were aimed at reducing the pace of social change by keeping intact "existing tribal structures" and by allowing "development" to be generated from within. Under the auspices of the white officers, people would be taught to help themselves.[59]

Gwembe's probably most famous modernizer, however, was not a member of the Colonial Service, but the chief councilor of the Gwembe Tonga Native Authority (GTNA). Hezekiah Habanyama played a leading role in this administrative body consisting of the seven district chiefs and their councilors, who the colonial government considered to be the "traditional" representatives of the Gwembe Tonga population. Colson (1971, 12) noted how the Kariba resettlement "made" local leaders by increasing the importance of the educated elite in the area. At the same time, the evictions undermined the legitimacy of the Native Authority, which had to communicate and enforce the resettlement orders. Habanyama's daughter remembered, "My father said Kariba made him unpopular. He was the one who had to persuade people to move. So that made him unpopular."[60] Judging from officers' praise, Habanyama and the GTNA were perfect *compradors*, government-paid and privileged local mediators, who obediently carried out the centrally devised plans.[61] A closer look, however, reveals that the local authority managed to exploit their position at the operational center of indirect rule and left their own mark upon Gwembe's modernization. Scholars have discussed the ambivalent potential inherent in the indigenous collaborators' role, which defies dualistic conceptualizations of colonial power and clear-cut categorizations such as colonizer/colonized and oppressor/oppressed.[62] Cooperation and resistance, as the example of Habanyama demonstrates, were often not too far apart.

Through a remarkable career, Habanyama had become Gwembe's most sought-after local expert.[63] He was born in the district and received his primary education at a mission school in the Gwembe Valley, and his further education, which included secondary schooling, a certificate of education at Bristol University, and a colonial summer school course in Cambridge, as well as his professional experience in the Native Authority and other administrative committees, qualified him as a local mediator in British eyes, able to navigate between "Western" modernity and "traditional" village life.[64] Having gone through considerable trouble with "nationalist subversion" and Congress-inspired resistance in the valley in the earlier 1950s, European administrators feared that the resettlement would revive opposition. They were hence keen to keep up the GTNA's loyalty and not lose touch with the general population.[65] The members of the Native Authority, being the ones to implement but not to decide on the removal, were reduced to acting as government's scapegoats. At the same time, the GTNA and Habanyama in particular did their best to make most of the limited power at their disposal, which I illustrate in the following by looking at some of the chief councilor's interventions during the resettlement.

Soon after they learned about the Federal government's decision, the chiefs and councilors drew up a list of concessions in return for their cooperation. These "24 Points" they asked to be signed by the governor.[66] In hindsight, this was a crucial step with long-term consequences for the benefit of the northern Tonga (Scudder 2005, 32). Some of the requests were aimed at securing better conditions for the actual removal, while others can be read as an attempt to limit the disruption which the evacuees were bound to face, insisting for instance that the people would not be overburdened with additional "development" schemes. It was especially those points concerning the resettlement's aftermath which had a longstanding impact on the situation of the Northern Rhodesian Tonga. Most crucially, they were consequently allowed to move back to the shore once the reservoir filled up, make use of the fertile drawdown area, and install fisheries—options denied to their southern counterparts, who were permanently barred from the lakeshore and its economic potential.[67] Although it took the Northern Rhodesian government seven months to reply and not all demands were confirmed, the "24 Points" became a frequent point of reference by which the GTNA reminded European officers of the promises they had once made.[68]

Habanyama found various ways to impact on the resettlement and its aftermath. During meetings with the European district team, the Native Authority criticized the course of the operation and made suggestions for improvement.[69] Undertaking his own tours through Gwembe, the chief councilor obtained a first-hand impression about the hardships inflicted on the people.[70] In his annual reports, which the district administration passed on to the governor and the Colonial Office, Habanyama graphically described how the Tonga felt about the resettlement, their "hopelessness and frustration," thus ensuring that their perspective was not entirely overlooked.[71] Largely on the GTNA's initiative, the government considerably improved the educational infrastructure in the district (Scudder 2005, 34; 2007, 312).

One of the Native Authority's most striking successes was its intervention against the formation of a joint company comprising Northern Rhodesia, Southern Rhodesia, and the Federal government to regulate business activities centered on the new Kariba Lake. Here, the chiefs and councilors managed to assert themselves against the two settler-dominated governments.[72] In order to ensure that the Tonga profited as much as possible from the new asset, the Native Authority made it very clear:

> We shall not allow a Southern Rhodesian Government to have a say in our district. We are fully aware of how our brothers and sisters are being treated across the Zambezi. . . . We have no faith in the Federal Government. . . . Southern Rhodesia and Federal Governments are both foreign powers in our Native Reserve and are completely unacceptable to us.[73]

This controversy reflected the Native Authority's growing frustration, after years of disappointment, broken promises, and hardship. While Habanyama had been at pains to navigate between demonstrating his loyalty to the British government on the one hand and finding ways to express his criticism and make demands on the other, his tone appears less diplomatic in later documents.[74]

Indeed, prior to his rising disillusionment, Habanyama adopted a rather pragmatic take on the Kariba affair. Although he admitted later that he personally "did not appreciate the benefits of the scheme,"[75] he never openly protested against Kariba or the resettlement, and instead tried to negotiate the best terms for the Tonga within the existing framework. Through his cooperativeness, he tried to bolster his alliance with the colonial officers against the Federal government which the Native Authority deeply mistrusted.[76] Moreover, Habanyama also saw opportunities arising from the fact that Gwembe District now received governmental assistance to a degree the valley had never known before. The once neglected Tonga "have gained a lot," he noted once the resettlement program was in full swing. They profited from better medical services and additional schools, were taught to fish, were advised on improved agricultural techniques, and found paid employment with the various contractors in the area. Even more importantly, "their voice is heard not only in Northern Rhodesia but also in Britain."[77] Like the colonial officers, Habanyama concentrated his efforts on seizing these chances to realize his own vision of development. This vision had nothing to do with electricity, industrialization, or universal economic rules, but was about schools, boreholes, medical facilities, agriculture, and fishing. Modernization to him was a determined yet gradual process, under the auspices of the colonial government that provided the necessary funds and expertise.[78] As much as this can count as proof that Habanyama was compromised by the colonial power whose salaried servant he was, he did not hesitate to remind officers of their responsibility: "The Northern Rhodesia Government has a duty to develop us. It has an obligation to spend money on our benefit."[79]

Habanyama's statements about the process of modernization in the valley were highly ambivalent. He perceived his community to stand at a turning point of their history, at which every effort had to be undertaken to control the "rapid changes."[80] Modernity not only promised roads, schools, and prosperity but also posed a threat of chaos, crime, and racial strife. The councilor worried about the valley's "gradual awakening to Territorial and even world politics," about "extreme nationalists" taking advantage of the Tonga's frustration, and about the "loose men and women" in the new Kariba township.[81] His hopes and his skepticism are best captured in the conclusion to one of his reports:

> May I end this report by saying that there are people coming into Gwembe from many parts of Africa and from abroad. They bring with them good and bad habits. Roads are getting excellent which will mean easy travelling and easy transport. Cash economy is gaining its way at a terrific speed. All those suggest changes in our social pattern and changes which will come very quickly. Social changes will be made more complicated by the change of old homes into new. Social changes have proved to be very difficult to direct in some countries of the world for they were left too long to get out of hand. Is it not time for us to start now and do something about it?[82]

As much as Habanyama—a son of the Gwembe Valley who played the drums, married a Tonga wife, and shunned the cosmopolitan life that would have been open to a man of his qualification—had an insight into the grievances of the Gwembe Tonga population, his position as their representative was never undisputed.[83] Long before the news of Kariba Dam arrived in the valley, unpopular development measures had alienated the people from their Native Authority.[84] Habanyama painfully noticed how he met increasing resentment during his tours, when village members cold-shouldered him or came to meetings armed with sticks and spears.[85] While this mistrust was clearly one of the prevailing reactions to the resettlement, the scarcity of documents in which the Gwembe Tonga speak for themselves limits the degree to which the historian can reconstruct their perspective. In public discourse, they were cast as primitive tribesmen who lived on unhealthy, barren land and had nothing to lose.[86] Colson and Scudder's anthropological research in connection with the archival documents in the Zambian archives paint a more nuanced picture.[87]

Speaking of "the Tonga perspective" is misleading, since experiences differed from village to village and changed over time. In the Sinazongwe area, which held sufficient arable land to allow resettlers to stay within the chieftaincy, officers found that evacuees quickly recovered from the upheaval, making "rapid progress."[88] Conditions were much less favorable in Chipepo and Mwemba, where communities were split apart and forced to shift to great distances. Here in particular, reports speak of chaos and great hardship during and after the resettlement. Evacuees were moved under great time pressure and—in the case of the Chipepo resisters under physical force—to areas which were unacceptable to them, only to find that their new lands were ill-prepared and unsuitable. Dozens of women and children from Chipepo died from measles, dysentery, and a "mysterious" disease whose cause could not be found. Mwemba's people counted diseases and deaths among their sufferings, as well as famine, lack of water, and material losses.[89]

According to Habanyama's reports, the Tonga's immediate reaction to the resettlement news was disbelief: "People never believed that their mighty Zambezi could ever be dammed."[90] When more and more people realized that Kariba was a reality, at least some were willing to make use of government aid to open up new areas. Colson (1971, 26–29) makes a point of stressing that the affected people were not principally opposed to change, but that it was the way this change was forced upon them which caused bitterness and despair. Attitudes hardened when one promise after another was broken. Not only were the Tonga barred from selecting new lands themselves, officers also withdrew their earlier assurances that evacuees would be allowed to wait and move only once the rising waters proved that their resettlement was necessary. Hardship experienced during and after the actual removal, failed harvests, and two devastating floods added to the despair, so that by the dry season of 1958 most resettlers felt entirely disempowered.[91]

All this did not happen in a vacuum. As Habanyama warned the district administration, "The matter is a bit complicated by the fact that those who are responsible for resettling people are Europeans and those who are being resettled are Africans."[92] Given the history of grossly unfair land politics under the British South Africa Company and the colonial government, land was a highly sensitive issue in Gwembe. Federation had only increased existing anxieties, since most Africans feared it would open the door for even greater settler influence. Many Gwembe Tonga believed that the resettlement was a bluff by which Europeans sought to steal their gardens, a crime that the colonial administration was unable or unwilling to prevent.[93] In a tour report, a colonial officer recounted how he had been reproached by an old headman: "You tax us, you make us pay all sorts of licences, you take our sons for road work, you put up the price of licences and now you evict us although you are our advocate. Why not help us stay where we are?"[94]

The European officers, however, failed to appreciate this political dimension, even when they were directly confronted with it. Facing villagers' stubborn refusal to move out of the Chipepo chieftaincy, officers agreed that "evil men" from the Northern Rhodesian African National Congress had "misguided" the "naïve" tribesmen.[95] Governor Benson, speaking to the resisters personally, did not consider the possibility that the Tonga might be acting on behalf of their own grievances and might possess a form of political awareness. His *indaba* (meeting) at Chisamu can be read as a prime example of colonial miscommunication: a patronizing governor explaining in baby talk that the "Queen loves all her subjects" and had to be obeyed, while the assembled headmen tried to put across that they felt discriminated against.[96] Not only did Congress leaders Harry Nkumbula and Kenneth Kaunda later deny that they had been in involved in the incident, but some of the resisters themselves stated, "Congress is not the thing that told us not to move. It is obvious that this is our land [and] it doesn't need any Congress man to teach one."[97]

This was the most visible incident of popular resistance, which after the "war's" gory conclusion seemed to give way to fear, even deeper distrust, and resignation.[98] Colson elaborated on the process of "rehabilitation" after the disruption, during which resettlers built homes, "learned" their new environment, and reordered social structures.[99] While they had no choice but to deal with the outwardly induced changes, the Gwembe Tonga were selective in what they accepted as suitable improvements and what they didn't. Numerous reports describe the fisheries' success, as the people eagerly seized training opportunities in fishing and boat building, hired equipment, and marketed their catch.[100] However, agricultural projects often did not get the expected positive response.[101] Some touring officers also noticed with disapproval that resettlers outright confronted them with requests for schools, wells, or food. What the former denounced as a "regrettable absence of the concept of self-help" can also be read as a sign of the Tonga's full awareness that the government had a debt to repay.[102]

Conclusion

These local-level interventions show that the Kariba Dam project is not the simple story of how high modernism obliterated a rural community, or of global planners' misunderstanding of local truths. Modernization was, essentially, a practice of inclusion and exclusion, defining winners and losers, costs and benefits, but it was not one that planners completely controlled. Kariba confirms the "basic lesson" that development was and is an oscillating, dynamic process, shaped by diverse actors and forces (Crehan and von Oppen 1994, 10). However, the historian has to be careful not to obscure the vastly asymmetrical power relations which constricted the possibilities for those at the grassroots to impact on the situation. While a few Tonga might have managed to squeeze some development out of the scheme, at least temporarily, and while Kariba might have indirectly created industrial jobs for Africans, the overall picture is extremely imbalanced. Kariba—European settlers' glue for the Federation—separated families and friends along and across the Zambezi River for good, and the Tonga were forced to sacrifice a way of life for "the long-term good of a larger national community" with whom they did not identify (Colson 1971, 3).

The Kariba project bypassed the rural poor, who all happened to be black, and favored white industry. Paradoxically, this example of "racist development" was promoted while a universalistic, "a-racial" notion of modernization came to the fore. Compared with the emphasis on cultural distinctiveness at the heart of trusteeship and indirect rule, the idea that *all* human societies had access to the *same* modernity was a "liberating possibility," as Frederick Cooper and Randall Packard (1997, 9) have rightly highlighted. Here, however, the new language of partnership and economic development legitimized white privilege and obscured the sacrifice enforced upon the Tonga. It was rather the old colonial paternalism that helped to spare the Northern Rhodesian Tonga from experiencing the same complete exclusion from Kariba's modernization as did their southern counterparts.

When the Queen Mother arrived in the Federation for the inauguration of Kariba in May 1960, violent riots in all three territories showed that the experimental state was disintegrating.[103] Little had become of the broad scope of possibilities of 1953, and those who had always claimed that "partnership" was nothing but white supremacy in disguise seemed to be proven right. Presenting the successful dam project as the "symbol of a new and wider understanding through this mighty continent of Africa," the Queen Mother's speech was an obituary of shattered hopes rather than an adequate description of the present.[104]

Notes

1. I thank Mary Davies, African Studies Centre, Leiden, Netherlands, and the editors for their helpful comments on an earlier draft of this chapter. Material in this chapter will also appear in Tischler (2013).

2. B. T. Gilmore to D. J. Kirkness, 6 May 1960, National Archives of the United Kingdom, Kew (hereafter NA) DO 35/7719. The Federation of Rhodesia and Nyasaland is also often called "Central African Federation."

3. I follow Lynn Thomas's (2011, 734) appeal "to reconstruct how people in the past have variously defined the modern, how those definitions have shifted over time, and how they have

been part of important struggles" rather than "engaging modernity as a static ideological formation or our own category of analysis." See Cooper (2005, 113, 118–119); Probst, Deutsch, and Schmidt (2002, 10–11). For reasons of readability, I will refrain from using quotation marks each time the terms are employed.

4. See Blackbourn (2006) on dam-building in nineteenth- and twentieth-century Germany; Mitchell (2002) on the Aswan Dam; Billington and Jackson (2006) on dams in the United States during the New Deal era. McCully (2001) provides a critical overview of dams from around the world; Isaacman and Isaacman (2013) examine the history of the Cahora Bassa scheme in Mozambique.

5. The chapter focuses on the Federal government and the settler society, the British colonial government and its administration in Northern Rhodesia, the International Bank for Reconstruction and Development (IBRD), local elites, and the displaced population on the Northern Rhodesian side of the Zambezi. Elsewhere, I have discussed the role of African nationalist politicians (Tischler 2011). Resettlement experiences on the Southern Rhodesian side, which are not considered here, can be found in McGregor (2009); Weinrich (1977); Tremmel (1994).

6. McGregor (2009, 105–10) discusses similar connections.

7. The former term is Eckert's (2008, 6), originally "*Entwicklungskolonialismus*"; the latter is Scott's (1998).

8. Note by Roy Welensky, n.d., ca. end of 1955, MSS Welensky 338/5, 51–52. On the unsuccessful groundnut scheme and the Gambia poultry scheme, see Cowen (1984); Scott (1998, 225–28).

9. Authorities estimated that 45,000 Tonga would have to be removed for Kariba; the final number was about 57,000 (statement by secretary for native affairs in Northern Rhodesia, Hansard No. 84e., 15 March 1944. Official verbatim report of the Debates of the First Session of the Tenth Legislative Council, NA CO 1015/946, 213). By June 1954, the figures for the two schemes compared as follows: Kafue would cost thirty million pounds to generate between 257 and 340 megawatts by 1960. At an estimated fifty million pounds, Kariba would be significantly more expensive but would have a larger capacity of initially 400 megawatts. In the long term, Kariba was expected to produce more power at a cheaper rate (Brief, "Economic Development Programme and the Kariba/Kafue Problem," 24 June 1954, by CRO, NA CO 1015/944, 67).

10. Percentage taken from "World Bank and the Kariba Scheme," New Commonwealth, 9 January 1956, NA DO 35/5699, 132. This figure refers to the costs of the entire Kariba project, including a second stage of the project. On the Federation, as well as on multiracialism and liberalism generally, see Phiri (2006); Blake (1977); Wood (1983).

11. Low and Lonsdale (1976, 8–11). I refer to "Africans," that is, the black and mostly indigenous population, and "Europeans," meaning the white community of settlers (mainly longstanding residents who considered the Rhodesias their home) and colonial administrators following common usage of the 1950s.

12. Between 1954 and 1958, the national income rose by almost 27 percent. "The Kariba Hydro-Electric Scheme," publicity brochure, Central Office of Information, London, November 1959, NA INF 12/878.

13. "Federation of Rhodesia and Nyasaland. Hydro-Electric Schemes. Brief for Discussions to Be Held with Sir G. Huggins," n.d., ca. January 1955, NA CO 1015/952, 2. The British government had a vital self-interest in the smooth production of copper.

14. "Note on a Visit to Federation of Rhodesia and Nyasaland. 29 June–9 July 1954," 12 July 1954, NA CO 1015/944, 76.

15. Office of the UK High Commissioner Salisbury to H. A. F. Rumbold, 16 March 1956, NA DO 35/5700.

16. Elkins and Pedersen (2005, 4). See also Veracini (2010); Veracini (2007).

17. See Murphy (2005, lix–lxvii); Mlambo (2002, 49).

18. Numerous fiercely critical articles appeared in the *Northern News* in the first week of March 1955; National Archives of Zambia, Lusaka (hereafter NAZ), *Northern News* 1955, vol. 1; quotation taken from the issue of 1 March 1955. See also "Lusaka Meeting Asks Queen-in-Council to Intervene on Kariba," *Rhodesia Herald*, 5 March 1955; "Rhodesia Protest," *Daily Telegraph*, 7 March 1955; Reuter message, 4 March 1955, NA CO 1015/945; McGregor (2009, 107–108).

19. Benson to Gorell Barnes, CO (secret and personal), 1 April 1955, NA CO 1015/946, 214.

20. "Prime Minister on Kariba-Kafue Decision," extract from Federal newsletter, 13 January 1955, NA DO 35/4600, 27.

21. "Power Switch," *South Africa*, 12 March 1955, NA DO 35/4600, 46B.

22. Arthur Benson to William Gorell Barnes, 1 April 1955; Roy Welensky to Lord Swinton, CRO secretary, 18 March 1955, NA DO 35/4602, 1.

23. The new figure was now at seventy-eight million pounds, as compared to the previous estimate of fifty-six million (see "Kariba Power Scheme Cost: Much More than Estimated," *Financial Times*, 6 January 1956, NA CO 1015/948, 366).

24. Minute by Wilson, 1 May 1956, NA CO 1015/948, 475.

25. Minute from principal private secretary to prime minister, 19 December 1958, Rhodes House Library, Oxford (hereafter RHL) MSS Welensky 341/1, 5 (first quotation); Thomas Fox-Pitt, memorandum, "The Kariba Evictions," May 1959, RHL MSS Brit. Empire, S 22, Anti-Slavery Society, G 563 (second quotation).

26. Statement by Godfrey Huggins, Hansard, Parliamentary Debates Federal Assembly, 7 March 1955, NA CO 1015/946, 214.

27. Shutt and King (2005, 359). See Mlambo (2002, 70) on governmental efforts to increase the percentage of the white population, which was a very small minority.

28. Northern Rhodesia, Hansard No. 84e, 15 March 1955, NA CO 1015/946, 213; Northern Rhodesia, Hansard No. 84f, 16 March 1955, NA CO 1015/946, 213; Wood (1983, 27–28).

29. High Commissioner Ian Maclennan to R. W. D. Fowler, 19 March 1955, NA CO 1015/945, 201.

30. The Federal constitution had fallen far short of settlers' aspirations for a self-governing Rhodesia. Darwin (1988, 199); Wood (1983, 28).

31. Treasury brief, "History of the Kafue and Kariba Projects," ca. January 1955, NA CO 1015/952.

32. A. H. Reed to B. R. Curson, 10 February 1956, NA CO 1015/948, 386.

33. Attwood (1996, 116), quoted in Veracini (2007, 5). Veracini notes on decolonization in settler societies, "One decolonisation (settler independence) inevitably constitutes an acceleration of colonising practices at the other end [i.e., recolonizing the indigenous population]" (4).

34. Arthur Benson to William Gorell Barnes, 31 December 1954, NA CO 1015/952, 1; Arthur Benson to colonial secretary, 17 February 1955, NA CO 1015/952, 10.

35. Statement by the prime minister, Hansard, Parliamentary Debates, Federal Assembly, No. 53, 1 March 1955, NA DO 35/4600, 52.

36. J. C. Morgan to J. E. Marnham, 26 January 1955, NA CO 1015/944, minute sheet. See also J. C. Morgan to W. J. Coe, 14 January 1955, NA CO 1015/944, 199; minute by J. C. Morgan, 9 March 1955, NA CO 1015/952; Arthur Benson to colonial secretary, 24 January 1955, NA CO 1015/944, 134.

37. Which was not to be mistaken for immediate—or, to many, even future—equality between black and white (Windrich 1975, 43; Rotberg 1971, 228, 253–55; Wood 1983, 386; Hanna 1965, 194–96).

38. See Kapur, Lewis, and Webb (1997, 93, 115). The authors refer to a "pecking order" of modernization, according to which poor peasants were the last to profit from improvements.

39. Extract Federal Hansard, 12 March 1956, NA DO 35/4603, 163A. See Butler (1999, 124–125); Arndt (1984, 52–53).

40. "Enabled to Play Their Part," *Rhodesia Herald,* 16 March 1956, NA CO 1015/948, 432.

41. IBRD: Department of Operations Europe, Africa and Australasia. The Economy of the Federation of Rhodesia and Nyasaland. Annex to Project Appraisal Report, 13 June 1956, NA DO 35/5702, 328.

42. Quotation from "Gwembe Valley Resettlement in Northern Rhodesia," Northern Rhodesia Information Department brochure, n.d., ca. 1958, NA CO 1015/1486, 106. See "Africans' Enforced Migration Begins," *Observer* (London), 22 July 1956, NA CO 1015/953; "Moving a Tribe to Make Way for the Kariba Lake," *Times* (London), 21 October 1955; "How the Batonkas Are Being Moved to Make Way for the White Man's Dam," *Rhodesia Herald,* 20 September 1956, NA DO 35/4605; "Only Political Agitation Can Bedevil Move of Africans from Kariba Site," *Northern News,* 3 November 1955, NAZ *Northern News,* 1955, vol. 4; McGregor (2009, 120–23).

43. Most famously Scott, *Seeing Like a State* (1998), which argues that "high modernist" schemes went wrong because they ignored local knowledge. Scott's powerful but dichotomous argument has been criticized in many publications; see Alexander (2006: 2–3).

44. "Statement of the Grounds on Which the Claim on the Federal Power Board Is Based," Northern Rhodesia Government, n.d., ca. April 1960, National Archives of Malawi, Zomba (hereafter NAM) Federal Files, 51/1/1, 528B.

45. The resettlement came under the responsibility of the territorial governments of Northern and Southern Rhodesia, respectively, not the Federal government. On the Northern Rhodesian side of the Zambezi, the district commissioner for Gwembe was in charge, while the day-to-day implementation of the move was in the hands of several resident district officers in conjunction with the Native Authority. Press Communique No. 252, 25 November 1955, "Resettlement in the Gwembe Valley," Northern Rhodesia Information Department, NA CO 1015/952, 63; Colson (1971, 176–177).

46. Comment by district commissioner, in Gwembe Tour Report No. 5 of 1960, Chief Mwemba area, N. C. G. Boxer, October 1960, NAZ SP 1/3/24.

47. Colson (1971, 21). For indirect rule, see Hyam (1999); Cooper (1997).

48. Arthur Benson to J. C. Morgan, 23 January 1956, NA CO 1015/952, 75. See Cooper (1997, 71).

49. J. H. Rhodes, agricultural officer, "The Gwembe Valley Resettlement Scheme: A Reconnaissance Report on the Agricultural Conditions in the Proposed Resettlement Areas," December 1956, NAZ SP 4/1/65.

50. Comment, I. M. Eldridge, Ministry of Native Affairs, to provincial commissioner, 2 June 1960, in Gwembe Tour Report No. 2 of 1960, Chief Sinadambwe area, by C. M. Chadwick, 26 March 1960, NAZ SP 1/3/24.

51. W. Arthur Lewis's criticism directed at Margery Perham's "Africans and British Rule" (Tignor 2006, 35–36). See Kirk-Greene (1999, 59–60); Butler (1999, 124–125); Cooper (1997, 71–73, 81); Hyam (1999: 274–77).

52. "Resettled Tonga Face Starvation, Say Their Headmen" *Central African Post,* 1 July 1959, NAZ SP 4/4/22; generally about the Mwemba resettlement, see Gwembe Tour Report No. 6 of 1959, Chief Mwemba areas, W. R. Smith, August 1959, NAZ SP 1/3/8.

53. There is a vast amount of newspaper reporting concerning the "Gwembe shootings," as well as the documents of a commission of inquiry set up to investigate into the incident. "Report of the Commission Appointed to Inquire into the Circumstances . . . ," Northern Rhodesian Government, Government Printer, NA CO 1015/1485, E/87. For a summary of the incident, see Colson (1971, 40–42); McGregor (2009, 114–17).

54. Colson (1971. 30). For the Colonial Service's self-perceptions, see Kirk-Greene (2006, 12).

55. Scudder (2007, 312–313) describes the interventions as "well-planned and successful," especially the fisheries scheme.

56. Gwembe Tour Report No. 1 of 1958, Chief Sinazongwe area, J. C. A. Mousley, 2 June 1958, NAZ SP 1/3/20.

57. Memorandum, Ministry of Economic Affairs, 16 May 1960, NAM Federal Files, 51/1/1, 535; memorandum on Gwembe resettlement, relations with the Federal government, Kariba development officer, 22 September 1959, NAZ SP 4/4/20; confidential memorandum, J. C. Morgan, 1 May 1959, "Cost of Kariba Resettlement," NA CO 1015/1486, 122.

58. Comment by L. I. Mitchell, district commissioner, 12 June 1961, in Gwembe Tour Report No. 3 of 1961, Chief Sinazongwe area, K. Swinhoe, 28 May 1961, NAZ SP 1/3/35.

59. Gwembe Tour Report No. 1 of 1958, Chief Sinazongwe area; Gwembe Tour Report No. 8 of 1959, Chief Sinazongwe area, J. C. Stone, December 1958, NAZ SP 1/3/8; comment by provincial commissioner, in Gwembe Tour Report No. 5 of 1960; minutes of District Team meeting, 9 February 1962, Gwembe Boma, NAZ SP 1/4/22; notes of a meeting held in room 32, the Secretariat, Lusaka, 18 July 1957, NAZ SP 4/2/145.

60. Interview with Nancy Habanyama Hanchabila, Northmeads, Lusaka, 29 January 2008. See Colson (1971, 38).

61. "Annual Report on African Affairs," Gwembe District, Southern Province, 1957, NAZ SEC 2/143; W. F. Stubbs, Native Affairs Department, to J. C. Morgan, CO, 10 May 1956, NA CO 1015/953, 122; D. B. Hall, Native Affairs Department, to J. C. Morgan, CO, 24 December 1956, NA CO 1015/1491, 1.

62. See Cooper (1996, 10) on the "subtle and ongoing interplay of cooperation and critique, of appropriation and denial" that challenged colonial authority.

63. Gwembe Tour Report No. 6 of 1956, Chief Sigongo area, L. G. Butler, 9 May 1956, NAZ SP 4/2/125.

64. Stubbs to Morgan, 10 May 1956; Gwembe District Newsletter, No. 5, November 1960, NAZ SP 4/1/65; "Annual Report on African Affairs," Southern Province, 1953 and 1955, by Gervas Clay, provincial commissioner, 27 March 1954, both NAZ SP 4/2/59; Howarth (1961, 44–46).

65. "Southern Province Intelligence Report for the Period Ending 25 July 1953," Gervas Clay, NAZ SP 1/3/3; "Annual Report on African Affairs," Southern Province, 1955, Gervas Clay, NAZ SP 4/2/59; memorandum, W. G. Reeves, for provincial commissioner, to secretary for native affairs, Influence of Congress on Native Authorities, 28 December 1955, NAZ SP 1/14/18; see Colson (1971, 19).

66. Minutes of the 41st Meeting of the Provincial Development Team, Southern Province, 16 August 1955, NAZ SP 4/4/11.

67. The original text of the 24 Points is in Annexure A to the Minutes of the Meeting of the Gwembe Tonga Native Authority held at Simamba area, 26–27 July 1955; questions asked by the Gwembe Tonga Native Authority, NAZ SP 4/1/61.

68. Minutes of District Team Meeting, 9 February 1962; Gwembe Tonga Native Authority, "Second Annual Report," year ending 31 December 1956, by H. G. Habanyama, NAZ SP 4/2/118.

69. Some examples: district commissioner to provincial commissioner, 12 July 1955, NAZ SP 4/4/11; minutes of the 41st meeting of the Provincial Development Team, Southern Province, 16 August 1955, Annexure C: Kariba Re-Settlement, NAZ SP 4/4/11.

70. Tour of Chief Sinazongwe area, report by chief councillor, Gwembe Tonga Native Authority, 12 February 1959, NAZ SP 4/4/27; tour of Chief Simamba area, report by chief councillor, Gwembe Tonga Native Authority, 22–24 July 1958, NAZ SP 4/12/82.

71. Gwembe Tonga Native Authority, "Second Annual Report."

72. Governor Hone to Roy Welensky and Edgar Whitehead, 20 October 1960, NAZ SP 4/7/17.

73. Gwembe Tonga Native Authority to H. A. d'Avray, Ministry of Legal Affairs, 10 March 1960, NAZ SP 4/7/16.

74. Elsewhere, I elaborate on this aspect (Tischler 2011, 63–67, 71–75). Prime examples of his tactics of negotiation are his annual reports and official speeches: Gwembe Tonga Native Authority, "Second Annual Report"; Gwembe Tonga Native Authority, "Third Annual Report," year ending 31 December 1957, by H. G. Habanyama, NAZ SEC 2/143; Gwembe Tonga Native Authority, "Annual Report," year ending 31 December 1959, NAZ SP 4/2/151; welcome address by H. G. Habanyama, for D. B. Hall, secretary for native affairs, when Hall visited the Native Authority Headquarters in October 1956, NA CO 1015/1484, 19C.

75. Evidence of H. G. Habanyama, record of the hearings of the Gwembe Commission of Inquiry, morning session, 31 October 1958, NAZ SP 4/11/15.

76. "Southern Province Intelligence Report for the Period Ending 25 April 1955," Gervas Clay, provincial commissioner, NAZ SP 1/3/14.

77. Gwembe Tonga Native Authority, "Third Annual Report."

78. Gwembe Tonga Native Authority, "Annual Report," year ending 31 December 1959.

79. Record of views expressed at the Gwembe-Tonga Native Authority Meeting, 1 April 1960, NAZ SP 4/7/17.

80. Gwembe Tonga Native Authority, "Third Annual Report."

81. Gwembe Tonga Native Authority, "Annual Report," year ending 31 December 1959.

82. Gwembe Tonga Native Authority, "Second Annual Report."

83. His daughter highlighted that Habanyama was "very close" to the people (interview with Hanchabila). Howarth (1961, 44–45) portrayed Habanyama as a man who preferred "tribal life" to fulfilling his ambitions in a big city. Although he had obtained "a truly European cast of mind," he "lived humbly, with his Tonga wife and family and was still devoted to his parents."

84. In addition, the supposedly traditional council had always been regarded as a European invention and part of the colonial government (Colson 1971, 19, 21–22, 181; Scudder 2005, 31).

85. Kariba Resettlement, monthly report, Simamba Tour, by chief councillor, 22–24 July 1958, NAZ SP 4/12/82.

86. See above, on British and Rhodesian media discourse on the resettlement and the Gwembe Tonga.

87. The Kariba resettlement has become a prominent case in anthropology, influencing research on dam-building and resettlement worldwide. Since the groundbreaking studies by Colson (1960, 1971) and Scudder (1962), both authors, as well as other scholars, have continued research on the Gwembe Tonga; see http://www.uky.edu/~cligget/docs/Tonga%20Bibliography%20Jan%202008.pdf.

88. Gwembe Tour Report No. 2 of 1962, Chief Sinazongwe area, L. R. Carew, 23 July 1962, NAZ SP 1/3/35; Gwembe Tour Report No. 8 of 1959, Chief Sinazongwe area; tour of Sinazongwe area, report by chief councillor, 12 February 1959.

89. There are numerous documents on the disastrous removals: note on the Gwembe Resettlement Scheme, by Kariba development officer, 22 September 1959, NAZ SP 4/4/20; "Report on Work Undertaken in Connection with the Resettlement of Africans in the Gwembe District," L. F. Leversedge, economic secretary, 19 July 1958, NA CO 1015/1491, 24E; "Annual Report on African Affairs," Southern Province, 1958 and 1959, A. St. J. Sugg, provincial commissioner, both NAZ SP 4/2/59; Colson (1971, 29–35, for Chipepo); note from A. Prior to provincial commissioner, Kariba Resettlement: Mwemba area, 9 October 1958, NAZ SP 4/4/23; Gwembe Tour Report No. 6 of 1959, Chief Mwemba area; comments on the report entitled "Resettled Tonga Face Starvation, Say Their Headmen" (see note 52), L. G. Butler, district commissioner, 15 July 1959 (for Mwemba).

90. Gwembe Tonga Native Authority, "Second Annual Report"; see Colson (1971, 22).

91. Colson (1971, 35–39, 70–71). See also, among other examples, "Report on Work Undertaken in Connection with the Resettlement of Africans in the Gwembe District," 1 June–31 October 1957, D. B. Hall, secretary for native affairs, 11 January 1957, NA CO 1015/1491, 20/E; "Report on Visit to the Lusitu Area of the Gwembe District on the 5th and 6th of December, 1958," by H. A. d'Avray, Kariba development officer, NAZ SP 4/2/134.

92. Gwembe Tonga Native Authority, "Second Annual Report."

93. Colson (1971, 185); Herbert (2002, 9). For land issues, see Hanna (1965, 200–202); Dixon-Fyle (2007, 107–12).

94. Gwembe Tour Report No. 4 of 1956, Chief Sinazongwe area, by W. A. J. Forrest, March 1956, NAZ SP 4/2/125.

95. "Southern Province Intelligence Report for the Period Ending 20 November 1958," A. St. J. Sugg, provincial commissioner, NAZ SP 1/3/18.

96. Indaba of Benson with the people of Chisamu, verbatim record, Chisamu's Village, Chief Chipepo, 7 September 1958 and 8 September 1958, NA CO 1015/1484, 49/E1.

97. Statement made by Lice Siamubi of Chisamu's Village, Chief Chipepo, and Langson Mwemba of Moyo's Village, Chief Simamba, "About Gwembe Trouble Caused by the Government of Northern Rhodesia," 13 September 1958, delivered at Congress Headquarters, United National Independence Party Archives, Lusaka, ANC 7/70.

98. "Annual Report on African Affairs," Southern Province, by A. St. J. Sugg, provincial commissioner, 19 March 1959, NAZ SP 4/2/59; Colson (1971, 41).

99. Colson (1971) explores these changes with a focus on kinship patterns, the family, material gains and losses, political changes, and changes regarding ritual, religion, and medicine.

100. Gwembe Tour Report No. 2 of 1962, Chief Sinazongwe area, 23 July 1962; Gwembe Tour Report No. 7 of 1962, Chief Simamba area, A. W. J. Gunn, 6 December 1962, NAZ SP 1/3/35; see Scudder (2007: 314–16).

101. Gwembe Tour Report No. 8 of 1959, Chief Sinazongwe area; Gwembe Tour Report No. 3 of 1960, Chief Sinazongwe area, K. Swinhoe, ca. August 1960, NAZ SP 1/3/24.

102. Gwembe Tour Report No. 8 of 1959, Chief Sinazongwe area.

103. Early in 1959, a state of emergency had been imposed in all three territories. The Federation broke apart in 1963; see Darwin (1993).

104. "Opening of the Kariba Dam, Tuesday, 17th May, 1960" (second draft), Queen Mother's opening address, NA DO 35/7719.

References

Alexander, Jocelyn. 2006. *The Unsettled Land: State-Making and the Politics of Land in Zimbabwe 1893–2003*. Oxford: James Currey.

Arndt, Heinz Wolfgang. 1987. *Economic Development: The History of an Idea*. Chicago: University of Chicago Press.

Attwood, Bain. 1996. "Mabo, Australia and the End of History." In *The Age of Mabo: History, Aborigines and Australia,* edited by Bain Attwood, 100–16. Sydney: Allen and Unwin.

Billington, David, and Donald Jackson. 2006. *Big Dams of the New Deal Era: A Confluence of Engineering and Politics*. Norman: University of Oklahoma Press.

Blackbourn, David. 2006. *The Conquest of Nature: Water, Landscape and the Making of Modern Germany*. London: Jonathan Cape.

Blake, Robert. 1977. *A History of Rhodesia*. London: Eyre Methuen.

Butler, Lawrence. 1991. "The Ambiguities of British Colonial Development Policy, 1938–1948." In *Contemporary British History 1931–1961*, edited by Anthony Gorst, Lewis Johnman, and W. Scott Lucas, 199–40. London: Pinter.

———. 1999. "Industrialisation in Late Colonial Africa: A British Perspective." *Itinerario: European Journal of Overseas History* 23, no. 3–4: 123–35.

Colson, Elizabeth. 1960. *The Social Organization of the Gwembe Tonga*. Manchester: Manchester University Press.

———. 1971. *The Social Consequences of Resettlement: The Impact of Kariba Resettlement upon the Gwembe Tonga*. Manchester: Manchester University Press.

Cooper, Frederick. 1996. *Decolonization and African Society: The Labor Question in French and British Africa*. Cambridge: Cambridge University Press.

———. 1997. "Modernizing Bureaucrats, Backward Africans, and the Development Concept." In *International Development and the Social Sciences*, edited by Frederick Cooper and Randall Packard, 64–92. Berkeley: University of California Press.

———. 2005. *Colonialism in Question: Theory, Knowledge, History*. Berkeley: University of California Press.

Cooper, Frederick, and Randall Packard. 1997. "Introduction." In *International Development and the Social Sciences*, edited by Frederick Cooper and Randall Packard, 1–41. Berkeley: University of California Press.

Cowen, Mike. 1984. "Early Years of the Colonial Development Corporation: British State Enterprise Overseas During Late Colonialism." *African Affairs* 83: 63–75.

Crehan, Kate, and Achim von Oppen. 1994. *Planners and History: Negotiating "Development" in Rural Zambia*. Lusaka: Multimedia Publications.

Darwin, John. 1988. *Britain and Decolonisation: The Retreat from Empire in the Post-war World*. London: Macmillan.

———. 1993. "The Central African Emergency, 1959." *Journal of Imperial and Commonwealth History* 21, no. 3: 217–34.

Dixon-Fyle, Mac. 2007. "The African National Congress' Anti-Federation Struggle in the Southern Province of Northern Rhodesia, 1946–57." In *The Tonga-Speaking Peoples of Zambia and Zimbabwe: Essays in Honor of Elizabeth Colson*, edited by Chet Lancaster and Kenneth Vickery, 107–23. Lanham, MD: University Press of America.

Eckert, Andreas. 2008. "Spätkoloniale Herrschaft, Dekolonisation und internationale Ordnung: Einführende Bemerkungen." *Archiv für Sozialgeschichte* 48: 3–20.

Elkins, Caroline, and Susan Pedersen. 2005. "Introduction: Settler Colonialism; A Concept and Its Uses." In *Settler Colonialism in the Twentieth Century*, edited by Caroline Elkins and Susan Pedersen, 1–20. New York: Routledge.

Hanna, Alexander John. 1965. *The Story of the Rhodesias and Nyasaland*. London: Faber and Faber.

Herbert, Eugenia. 2002. *Twilight on the Zambezi: Late Colonialism in Central Africa*. New York: Macmillan.

Howarth, David. 1961. *The Shadow of the Dam*. New York: Macmillan.

Hyam, Ronald. 1999. "Bureaucracy and 'Trusteeship' in the Colonial Empire." In *The Oxford History of the British Empire: The Twentieth Century*, edited by Judith Brown and William Roger Louis, 255–79. Oxford: Oxford University Press.

Isaacman, Allen, and Barbara Isaacman. 2013. *Dams, Displacement, and the Delusion of Development: Cahora Bassa and Its Legacies in Mozambique, 1965–2007*. Athens: Ohio University Press.

Jeffries, Charles. 1972. *Whitehall and the Colonial Service: An Administrative Memoir, 1939–1956*. London: Athlone.

Johnston, Anna, and Alan Lawson. 2000. "Settler Colonies." In *A Companion to Postcolonial Studies*, edited by Henry Schwarz and Sangeeta Ray, 360–76. Malden, MA: Blackwell.

Kapur, Devesh, John Lewis, and Richard Webb. 1997. *The World Bank: Its First Half Century*. Washington: Brookings Institution Press.

Kirk-Greene, Anthony. 1999. *On Crown Service: A History of HM Colonial and Overseas Civil Services, 1837–1997*. London: Tauris.

———. 2006. *Symbol of Authority: The British District Officer in Africa*. London: Tauris.

Low, David, and John Lonsdale. 1976. "Introduction." In *History of East Africa*. Vol. 3, edited by David Low and Alison Smith, 1–64. Oxford: Oxford University Press.

McCully, Patrick. 2001. *Silenced Rivers: The Ecology and Politics of Large Dams*. London: Zed Books.

McGregor, JoAnn. 2009. *Crossing the Zambezi: The Politics of Landscape on a Central African Frontier*. Oxford: James Currey.

Michell, Timothy. 2002. *Rule of Experts: Egypt, Techno-Politics, Modernity*. Berkeley: University of California Press.

Mlambo, Alois. 2002. *White Immigration into Rhodesia: From Occupation to Federation*. Harare: University of Zimbabwe Publications.

Murphy, Philip. 1995. *Party Politics and Decolonization: The Conservative Party and British Colonial Policy in Tropical Africa 1951–1964*. Oxford: Oxford University Press.

———. 2005. "Introduction." In *British Documents on the End of Empire. Series B, Vol. 9, Central Africa: Part I; Closer Association, 1945–1958*, edited by Philip Murphy, xxvii–cxvi. London: HMSO.

Phiri, Bizeck Jube. 2006. *A Political History of Zambia: From the Colonial Period to the Third Republic, 1890–2001*. Trenton, NJ: Africa World Press.

Probst, Peter, Jan-Georg Deutsch, and Heike Schmidt. 2002. "Introduction: Cherished Visions and Entangled Meanings." In *African Modernities: Entangled Meanings in Current Debate*, edited by Peter Probst, Jan-Georg Deutsch, and Heike Schmidt, 1–17. Portsmouth, NH: Heinemann.

Rist, Gilbert. 2006. *The History of Development: From Western Origins to Global Faith*. London: Zed Books.

Rotberg, Robert. 1971. *The Rise of Nationalism in Central Africa: The Making of Malawi and Zambia 1873–1964*. Cambridge, MA: Harvard University Press.

Scott, James. 1998. *Seeing like the State: How Certain Schemes to Improve the Human Condition Have Failed*. New Haven, CT: Yale University Press.

Scudder, Thayer. 1962. *The Ecology of the Gwembe Tonga*. New York: Humanities Press.

———. 2005. "The Kariba Case Study." California Institute of Technology. Working Papers 1227. Pasadena. http://www.hss.caltech.edu/SSPapers/wp1227.pdf.

———. 2007. "A History of Development and Downturn in Zambia's Gwembe Valley, 1901–2002." In *The Tonga-Speaking Peoples of Zambia and Zimbabwe: Essays in Honor of Elizabeth Colson*, edited by Chet Lancaster and Kenneth Vickery, 307–43. Lanham, MD: University Press of America.

Shutt, Allison, and Tony King. 2005. "Imperial Rhodesians: The 1953 Rhodes Centenary Exhibition in Southern Rhodesia." *Journal of Southern African Studies* 31, no. 2: 357–79.

South African News Agencies. 1959. *Kariba: The Story of the World's Biggest Man-Made Lake*. Bloemfontein: Friend Newspapers.

Tignor, Robert. 2006. *W. Arthur Lewis and the Birth of Development Economics.* Princeton, NJ: Princeton University Press.

Thomas, Lynn. 2011. "Modernity's Failings, Political Claims, and Intermediate Concepts." *American Historical Review* 116, no. 3: 727–40.

Tischler, Julia. 2011. "Resisting Modernisation? Two African Responses to the Kariba Dam Scheme in the Central African Federation." *Comparativ* 21, no. 1: 60–75.

———. 2013. *Light and Power for a Multiracial Nation: The Kariba Dam Scheme in the Central African Federation.* New York: Palgrave Macmillan.

Tremmel, Michael. 1994. *The People of the Great River: The Tonga Hoped the Water Would Follow Them.* Gweru: Mambo Press.

Veracini, Lorenzo. 2007. "Settler Colonialism and Decolonisation." *Borderlands* 6, no. 2. http://www.borderlands.net.au/vo16no2_2007/veracini_settler.htm.

———. 2010. *Settler Colonialism: A Theoretical Overview.* New York: Palgrave Macmillan.

Weinrich, Anna K. 1977. *The Tonga People on the Southern Shore of Lake Kariba.* Gweru: Mambo Press.

Windrich, Elaine. 1975. *The Rhodesian Problem: A Documentary Record, 1923–1973.* London: Routledge.

Wood, Richard J. 1983. *The Welensky Papers: A History of the Federation of Rhodesia and Nyasaland.* Durban: Graham.

8 "No One Should Be Worse Off"

The Akosombo Dam, Modernization, and the Experience of Resettlement in Ghana

Stephan F. Miescher

Ghanaians express pride about Akosombo, the large hydroelectric dam commissioned in 1966. They consider the Akosombo Dam not only the most impressive testimony to the country's development but also a powerful reminder of how the country's first leader, Kwame Nkrumah, envisioned to reach the elusive goal of modernity.[1] People and institutions have produced competing interpretations of the resettlement caused by building Akosombo. They are reflected in what I call "Akosombo stories." Some of these accounts are emphasized in official records, others have entered the genre of social science literature on Africa's failed or uneven development, and yet another grouping is merely narrated locally, unheard by a broader public.[2] These intersecting and often contradictory stories provide insight into the thick meanings of Akosombo in relation to Ghanaian understandings of development, modernity, and nationhood. These accounts reveal the marginalization of those who experienced resettlement, while also documenting the sense of accomplishment of those who participated in the planning and building of the Volta River Project. Moreover, they demonstrate how Akosombo remains crucial to any discussion about the legacy of modernization in Ghana since the 1950s.

In a different context, David William Cohen and E. S. Atieno Odhiambo, interrogating the complexity around the disappearance and murder of Kenya's foreign minister John Robert Ouko in 1990, have presented a social history of knowledge production. Interested in the processes within the constitution of knowledge, they have asked questions relevant for this study: how people came to know about Ouko's death, how they deployed this knowledge, and "how these uses of knowledge and claims to knowledge marked investigations, inquiries, proceedings, and the nation" (Cohen and Odhiambo 2004, 18). Similarly, this chapter seeks to explore the ways in which accounts of Akosombo resettlement were constituted, how they reflect different centers of power and authority, and how they mark the era of modernization and development in Ghana. An analysis of Akosombo stories shows that modernization is about local meanings that come to the fore especially in recollections of promises, contestations, and disappointments around resettlement.

Volta River Project and Resettlement

The Volta River Project was at the center of Kwame Nkrumah's plan for the development and modernization of Ghana. Nkrumah, since becoming leader of government business in 1951, was a strong supporter of the Volta project. In the 1953 Gold Coast Legislative Assembly debate, Nkrumah and other members of the Convention People's Party (CPP) supported the formation of a commission to study its feasibility, in spite of strong opposition that accused the government of selling out to foreign capital.[3] Three years later, the Preparatory Commission (1956) published a detailed report endorsing the scheme that included a fully integrated aluminum industry, a new city, and miles of railway tracks. After Ghana's independence in 1957, the Cold War dialectic of modernization provided a financial basis for the project. As the United States government looked for an opportunity to assert its influence in sub-Saharan Africa, President Dwight Eisenhower agreed to explore U.S. funding. In 1959, Kaiser Engineers of Oakland, California, proposed a more modest version of the project. They suggested the construction of a dam at Akosombo and an aluminum smelter in Tema that was to be fed with imported alumina, produced from crushed bauxite in a chemical process. This was a significant departure from the aluminum industry proposed by the Preparatory Commission. Instead Kaiser Engineers (1959) postponed processing Ghana's bauxite indefinitely. Despite embracing this scaled-down version, the Ghanaian government fostered hopes of the Volta project as a vehicle for the nation's development. Presenting the scheme to parliament, Nkrumah trumpeted "rapid industrialization" as allied with widely accessible electrical power, transportation routes on Volta Lake, new fisheries, and the introduction of mechanized agriculture.[4]

Initially, advocates for the Volta project were less concerned about its environmental and social effects. They considered the Volta Basin to be mostly uninhabited, and grossly underestimated the number of people to be affected. In 1952, a confidential report stated that "the submersion of the area of the reservoir would inundate very little of economic value." Although it was estimated that about 18,000 people would be displaced, the report expected "little other disturbances" in the area north of the dam.[5] The Preparatory Commission suggested that 62,500 people living in the Volta Basin had to be resettled but underestimated the impact on downstream communities. Whereas the commission recommended monetary compensation for the loss of buildings, land, and tree crops, people were "expected to resettle themselves" over a period of four years prior to flooding.[6] Kaiser Engineers (1959), seeking to cut costs, ignored the dam-affected communities.

In 1961, dam construction began before any steps toward resettlement had been taken, such that previous claims about people resettling themselves were abandoned. Instead, the Volta River Authority (VRA), the agency charged with building and operating the Akosombo Dam, took on the responsibility for resettling the people in the Volta Basin.[7]

Volta River Authority

The Volta River Authority faced an enormous challenge in implementing a resettlement program within a period of less than two years. In May 1962, when the economist E. A. K. Kalitsi was appointed VRA resettlement officer, the dam had been under construction for eight months. To cope with such a "national emergency" (Chambers 1970, 24), Kalitsi formed a "Working Party" that consisted of architects, agricultural officers, engineers, social workers, sociologists, and surveyors recruited from government departments and local universities.[8] How did the VRA administer the biggest development project of the era? What kind of knowledge did this state agency produce about resettlement?

The Volta River Authority became Ghana's most successful parastatal, run by an effective administration that was designed by "modernizing bureaucrats" (Cooper 1997) during the waning years of colonial rule.[9] In 1962, the Canadian hydro engineer Frank Dobson was appointed as its first chief executive. Dobson brought a Canadian directness and hands-on approach that were quite different from the hierarchical and racialized structure of the colonial civil service ingrained in Ghana's public administration. Dobson, according to VRA historian A. B. Futa, judged his Ghanaian and expatriate staff "by the same professional standard and criteria" and looked for "accountability, ability to perform and to deliver and above all, valued initiative, entrepreneurship and innovativeness" (Futa 1992, pt. 1, 39). Departing from bureaucratic practice, Dobson appointed non-engineers and junior Ghanaians as principal VRA officers. This caused a "ripple" (35–36). In particular, Kalitsi's appointment was a sensation: just over thirty years old, he became responsible for overseeing the resettlement of eighty thousand people and a budget of £3.5 million.[10]

The creation of the VRA brought together a group of talented young men who enabled the multipurpose Volta project that included the Akosombo Dam, five hundred miles of electrical transmission lines, the resettlement program, and the new model city at Akosombo. They were attracted by the "intellectual challenge" of shaping an organization that would embody Nkrumah's vision of modernization.[11] Louis Casely-Hayford, a graduate of the Engineering School at the University of Manchester, was eager to participate in the realization of the Volta project—first planned by his father's generation of nationalist politicians.[12] John Osei, an Oxford-trained Ghanaian anthropologist, returned from the United Kingdom to work on resettlement and then became the VRA publicity officer at Akosombo.[13]

The press branded these high modernist technocrats as "Volta men," a nomenclature embraced by VRA officers up to the present day.[14] These Volta men as protagonists in the nation-building narrative were determined to create a record of their achievements that would become an archive of modernization in Ghana.

The VRA founded a resource center that holds publications and conference papers on the technical, economic, sociological, and environmental implications of hydroelectric dams (Cochrane 1971). Establishing the VRA library and archive was an attempt to collect information for training and reference. Yet this production of knowledge also had a symbolic aspect that enhanced the VRA's stature as a state-of-the-art public utility company. This site of knowledge was to assist Ghanaians and other Africans in the acquisition of technological and scientific expertise in the spirit of Ghana's larger Pan-African aspirations as envisioned by Nkrumah. The VRA archive, like any collection, has its ideological pedigree. Created by the Ghanaian elite in the service of the nation, the archive privileges the views of male technocrats and other experts, many of them allied with the government power structure. Experiences of ordinary people—especially those whose lives were radically transformed by the flooding—are only reflected in select files.[15]

Still, the VRA has gathered a wealth of material about the Akosombo resettlement. Social scientists and other experts, most of them expatriates, produced knowledge related to the sociological and technical matters that shaped the policies of the VRA resettlement. Based at the University of Ghana, Legon, and the University of Science and Technology, Kumasi, these experts included the expatriate anthropologists David Brokensha, David Butcher, and Rowena Lawson, the Ghanaian sociologists E. A. K. Afriyie and Martha Dodoo, who conducted surveys among dam-affected communities, and the Hungarian architect Laszlo Huszar, who planned eighteen resettlement towns for more than thirty thousand people.[16] Their studies have become an integral part of the VRA library. Historian Jordan Shapiro (2007, 2) relied on the VRA archive to tell the "story of the preparation, execution, and aftermath" of resettlement, and reconstructed the activities of state actors who brokered resettlement policy with people on the ground.

Modernization and Resettlement

Promoting the Akosombo scheme, Nkrumah's government sought to highlight the positive aspects of resettlement. Already in 1953, Nkrumah declared that "if the Project was carried out, the Government would ensure that no one was made worse off as a result of the creation of the lake."[17] This statement became the official mantra of resettlement. In 1962, Minister of Agriculture Krobo Edusei reminded his audience at the groundbreaking for one of the first resettlement towns that "Osagyefo the President had ruled that no person should be homeless or 'worse off for his sacrifice in the implementation of the Volta dam project.'"[18] By the 1960s, however, the point was no longer merely to guarantee the livelihood of those impacted by Akosombo. Rather, the official discourse linked resettlement to the country's development and a grand vision of modernization (Shapiro 2003).

Instead of encouraging resettlement by self-help, as the Preparatory Commission had suggested, the planners developed strategies of how to improve the social and economic lifestyles of the dam affected people. In 1963, Nkrumah speaking about the Volta project in the national assembly not only repeated the mantra that "no one should be worse off," but added that people's relocation would provide them "with new villages with better communal facilities and better farming methods."[19] The Seven-Year Development Plan, the blueprint for the country's modernization, considered resettlement "an exercise in positive economic development on a regional basis designed to transform the areas and the lives of the people involved" (Ghana 1964, 210). Government was to introduce new forms of farming and fishing for the settlers. Summarizing this reinterpretation of resettlement, a VRA booklet noted that the destruction of homes and lands "could be turned to a good account if better living conditions and more efficient farming methods" were provided. Resettlement became for decision-makers not just "a unique opportunity for planning and developing the affected area on a regional basis" but should serve Ghana's anticipated transition from tradition toward modernity (Jopp 1965, 43).

For the planners, this connection between resettlement and modernization became official policy. In his published assessment, Kalitsi summarized the guiding principles adopted by the Working Party:

> First, that resettlement should be used as an opportunity to enhance the social, economic and physical conditions of the people; second, that the agricultural system should be improved to enable the people to move from subsistence to a cash economy; and third, that the settlements should be planned and located in a rational manner, so that the flood victims as well as others in the area of impact could derive maximum benefits from the changes involved. (Kalitsi 1970a, 39)

The welfare officers who counted the people of the Volta Basin persuaded many to accept resettlement by the VRA with the promise of modern facilities, better housing, and higher incomes through improved agriculture. Still, about twelve thousand people—15 percent of those living in the areas to be inundated—decided to relocate themselves and forego state assistance.[20]

The planners, seeking administrative efficiency for the construction of schools, community centers, and the supply of electricity, suggested combining villages into towns. The Volta Basin Development Plan envisioned the transformation of "hundreds of small subsistence villages along the water's edge to larger and fewer townships with regional markets and industries."[21] This shift to a more urban scale was reflected in the resettlement vocabulary, as the planners no longer referred to the new settlements as "villages" but called them "towns," which in local parlance became "quarters." By 1963, the VRA had launched the construction of fifty-two townships designed to propel the "backward" dwellers from 739 villages into modernity. These townships were seen as "bridgeheads of modernisation in a sea of rural backwardness and underdevelopment" (Diaw and Schmidt-Kallert 1990, 12).

In the early 1960s, Ghana's state-owned newspapers carried stories about resettlement. In spite of the looming hardship, the press accentuated the innovative and uplifting aspects of the project, particularly in the extensive coverage about New Ajena and Nkwakubew.[22] Nkwakubew served as a model town where prototypes of different house types were constructed. In the *Ghanaian Times,* P. H. Johnson described Nkwakubew as "a modern township equipped with all the immediate needs for man." Readers learned that each settler family would receive the so-called nuclear or core house, which could be extended. Johnson contrasted the resettlers' "modern homes" with their former "dilapidated thatch houses" and deflated any potential for resistance by admonishing the settlers "to express their appreciation of the Government's effort by co-operating" in the scheme.[23]

Ajena was the first village to be flooded. When its inhabitants had to move, the press celebrated their "true spirit of national rebuilding." The government staged a colorful evacuation ceremony that drew, according to Johnson, "a mass of gaily dressed people." They included ministers, district commissioners, and chiefs who, in Johnson's metaphor, "flooded" to New Ajena to witness "another turning point in the successful implementation" of the Volta project.[24] Even within the modernity of resettlement there was space for tradition. During the Ajena celebration, chiefs, "adorned in [their] best regalia," poured libations and "danced merrily" to the rhythm of their drums. The regional commissioner gave the assurance that "all troubles would be settled at the administrative level" to avoid "any litigations and waste of money."[25] Thus, as Shapiro (2003, 198) commented, the official resettlement imagery focused neither on the hardships experienced by settlers nor on the government's accomplishment in its implementation. Instead, state propaganda suggested that the relocation "signified a journey into the future."

Prior to the flooding, the livelihood of about 90 percent of inhabitants was based on farming or raising livestock. In line with the Seven-Year Development Plan, the Ministry of Agriculture considered the forced movement of eighty thousand people a "unique opportunity to wean an appreciable proportion of Ghana's farmers from their wasteful, fragmented and shifting system of agriculture to a settled and improved pattern of farming." Intense and mechanized cultivation would overcome the shortage of arable land surrounding resettlement towns in the densely populated areas south of the Afram and east of the Volta. In the northern savannah, existing pastoral farming was to be "improved by the introduction of better goats, sheep and cattle, by disease control and by vegetable production" (Nicholas 1970, 205, 208). The planners envisioned full-fledged mechanization that included preparation of the soil, planting, and application of fertilizers. The individual farmer, as Kalitsi mused, would only be left with "weeding, thinning, carting, harvesting and a number of other jobs."[26]

The press reported on the promotion of "scientific" farming methods among resettlers.[27] The *Ghanaian Times* noted how the VRA chief executive Dobson elaborated on the plans for mechanized farming at the New Ajena celebration.[28] The *Evening News* spelled out these objectives by applauding the arrival of tractors, the ultimate symbol of this new type of farming, and informed readers about the introduction of "large-scale production of pigs, poultry, goats and sheep," intended to help feed Ghana's growing population.[29] New Ajena and Nkwakubew served as models for this "rural development." At the former, 132 farmers jointly cultivated an 80-acre tobacco plot, which journalist Eboe Grey-Mills called a "healthy sign" of the arrival of cooperative farming. At the latter, over 320 acres of maize and 21 acres of oil palm were allocated to resettlers who planted pineapple, citrus, and avocado as cash crops. Grey-Mills considered Nkwakubew a "living testimony" of what could be achieved under mechanized agriculture and "improved modern farming techniques."[30]

These technical innovations were highly subsidized and short-lived. Mechanization became a disaster. Farmers failed to participate, since they resented the authority exercised by junior agricultural staff and preferred to focus on their own food crop production. The four hundred Massey Ferguson tractors, acquired by the VRA at great expense, soon suffered from lack of maintenance and inadequate supply of parts. By 1968, one-third of them had become unserviceable (Afriyie and Butcher 1971, 81). There was also a shortage of the promised seeds and fertilizers. The livestock program did not fare any better. The outbreak of disease decimated boiler chicks and hogs; moreover, the increasing cost of animal feed undermined the program. This was triggered by rising demand for local foodstuff as a result of severe import cuts that had been introduced in 1964. Subsequently, the price for corn, a crucial ingredient of feed, climbed by 400 percent (Chambers 1970: 233–36, 249). In contrast to the planners' prediction, resettlement agriculture did not "automatically produce higher standards of living" (Afriyie 1973, 728).

In an interview, Kalitsi and Casely-Hayford reflected on the challenges of resettlement. The planners did not know the exact number of people to be resettled, nor had they identified the location of the villages to be flooded.[31] Within a few months, planners had to decide which places people were moving to, and how many towns to build. Since most settlers were subsistence farmers, as Casely-Hayford noted, the VRA had to "prepare land for farming and help them get started." Kalitsi credited their "remarkable colleague," the late Godfrey Amarteifio, for the successful evacuation with the help of trucks and military boats. Amarteifio was a physically imposing figure. In his youth, he had been a boxer, then a boxing referee, even participating in that capacity at the Olympic Games of Rome, Tokyo, and Mexico City. During World War II, Amarteifio had served in the military, and he then joined the police force before becoming a social worker within the Department of Social Welfare and Community Development. He made his mark by finding a solution to an impasse in the resettlement for the Tema harbor and later transferred to the VRA as principal welfare officer for resettlement. Kalitsi emphasized that Amarteifio was not only a "charming person" but also had excellent organizational and social skills that served him well before and during the evacuation process.[32]

Most experts agreed that the evacuation, planning, and construction of the fifty-two resettlement towns in such a short period was as a tremendous achievement (Chambers 1970, 267–68). Yet in spite of the praise Kalitsi has received over the last forty-five years, he remains ambivalent about the outcome of the program. Regardless of the size of their previous homes, each household received the one-room "core house" that was supposed to be "the beginnings" of a larger compound house situated within "the beginnings of towns." Many settlers, however, were unable to complete the core house. The planners, seeking to modernize agriculture, took "advantage of the opportunity of resettlement to uplift the people." Although these were "good ideas," as Kalitsi commented, such "grandiose planning" did not succeed.[33] The desertion of resettlement towns could not be halted. Already in 1965, Kalitsi warned at the Volta Resettlement Symposium that "the spectre of a ghost town hangs over every settlement we have built." Five years later, in the published version of his talk, he added, "This spectre can be removed only if support is forthcoming to develop the people's farms and also to build the towns into living and orderly communities."[34] To learn whether this goal was achieved in the perception of the settlers, we need to examine the historical knowledge circulating in the resettlement towns.

Amate

The press reports, VRA publicity material, and expert testimony claimed that there was an orderly and well-organized move into resettlement towns (Jopp 1965; Chambers 1970). However, interviews that I conducted in Amate and Kete-Krachi revealed a different experience. Resettlement, especially the evacuation, was traumatic. In October 1964, the 2,063 inhabitants of the cocoa village of Worobong in the Afram Plains were relocated to Amate, which they shared with 1,200 settlers from thirty-eight other villages. The new town of 621 houses was located in a forest whose canopy had provided shade for cocoa farms. The cocoa trees had been cleared by bulldozers.[35]

In the early twentieth century, the Afram Plains was an agricultural frontier that saw an influx of migrant farmers in search of suitable land to cultivate cocoa. These migrants created a corridor of plantations in the forest between the southern bank of the Afram River and Kwawu's northern slopes. The largest cocoa settlement was Worobong, originally a hunters' village founded in the nineteenth century by people from Kwawu.[36] Abena Animwaa narrated how her father James Anim, an interpreter for the colonial government, took his wife to Worobong in the 1920s. When the Akyem town of Begoro claimed the land around Worobong, Anim played a crucial role in settling the conflict. His testimony secured Worobong for Kwawu, for which Anim had to pay dearly. One evening, he was ambushed and killed. Anim left behind his pregnant wife, who gave birth to Animwaa, nicknamed Anto ("the one who did not meet her father").[37] Older residents of resettlement towns have such personal memories about the places now covered by water. Such stories underlie the pain of leaving their former settlements.

In Worobong, most people did not believe that their homes and farms would be flooded, despite government warnings.[38] In 1961, mass education officer A. K. Osei arranged for a visit to the proposed resettlement site at Amate. Seeking support in Worobong, he relied on the Town Development Committee led by Akwamuhene Nana Anim Baree and its secretary Maxwell Osafo, a local CPP official.[39] A few days later, Osei organized a meeting chaired by Worobong headman Nana Kwasi Dankwa, who assembled chiefs and elders representing twenty villages. Osei, displaying maps of the anticipated flooding, explained the Volta project and sought the delegates' approval for the proposed site. Nana Baree of Worobong and Sam Bediako of Asuboni called on the other villages to join the larger township that would receive "modern amenities" from the government. After some debate, the delegates accepted the site but demanded replacement farms and new roads to save them from starvation and isolation.[40] Five months later, Nana Dankwa petitioned the Volta River Secretariat to conduct a survey for the layout of the new town. Dankwa reported that his people had agreed on a site next to a place "known as 'Amate's camp'" for the "New Oworobon Township." Embracing the rhetoric of modern amenities, Dankwa requested improved houses, schools, and a post office.[41]

Although the VRA archive documents a careful process of site selection that incorporated local power brokers, the arrival of the flood brought great confusion. Even Nana Dankwa, who had known about the Volta project since 1958 and was involved in the planning of Amate, refused to leave Worobong. According to his granddaughter Salome Mirekua, Dankwa had been promised a replacement for his spacious palace at Worobong. When he saw the one-room core house, he declared that he would rather drown. In the end, he was rescued as the water flooded his palace.[42] Adwoa Fosuaa recalled the evacuation. By September 1964, the Afram River was rising rapidly. Lorries took the people of Worobong to

Amate where the houses were unfinished with wet cement. On plots of sixty or seventy by one hundred feet, the VRA had built *one* room for each household and a roofed foundation, where settlers were to erect two additional rooms for which the VRA would provide materials in the spirit of "aided self-help" (Kalitsi 1970a, 41). Yet many houses were never completed; the planned extension into full compound houses of eight rooms was not realized. The construction of a kitchen and bathing facilities had been omitted. Since the resettlers had lost their crops, the World Food Program agreed to feed them with strange food like yellow corn, corned beef, and luncheon meat for six months. "It was a sad story," Fosuaa noted. "Some people cried until their eyes turned red." Some men drowned their sorrows in alcohol.[43]

In VRA records there are many silences about the settler experience. "Trekking Notes" by visiting officers report problems including failing water pumps, tensions among settlers, and insufficient acreage of farmland in the years after the flooding.[44] Yet the bureaucratic language does not capture the sense of loss and agony. While there is documentary evidence of a large exodus of settlers from the townships, their personal stories were not recorded. Social scientists Afriyie and Butcher (1971, 116) estimated that by 1968 only about 38.7 percent of the original settlers remained. Of those missing, some died, while others had gone farming or fishing, returned to their hometowns, or migrated elsewhere. People left due to a shortage of farmland and insufficient room in the core house. Afriyie and Butcher expected that with the implementation of the land-clearing scheme, known as Project 356, the departed settlers might return. The scheme emphasized improved subsistence agriculture, with each entitled settler allocated a three-acre plot to be cleared by hand.[45] Afriyie and Butcher's study, though rich in facts, does not provide personal accounts of those who abandoned the resettlement towns.

In a series of interviews, I reconstructed the experiences of a group of men and women who were resettled in Amate but left because they could not make a living. People from the fishing villages of Nketepa and Ekye Amanfrom never took possession of their allocated houses. Instead they rebuilt homes at the edge of the lake. Other settlers moved to farming villages on higher elevations or to their hometowns. They relied on kinship networks to gain access to land or found other means of survival.[46] Yaa Oforiwaa, a young mother at the time of the flooding, recalled that those who had farms in villages on the ridge, among them Nana Dankwa, left Amate right away.[47] Oforiwaa remained in Amate for over a decade. Initially, the government ploughed three acres for each family to sow corn and raise tobacco. The military regime of I. K. Acheampong then launched an irrigation project along the lake in 1973, which allowed settlers to grow tomatoes, onions, and other seasonal crops. For a while, farmers did well and some people returned.[48] But the irrigation system broke down. A change in climate meant less rainfall and more hardship for the resettlers. By 1977, Oforiwaa had left Amate and moved to her parents' hometown of Abetifi. She expressed bitterness that the government failed to offer any compensation.[49]

My interviews in Amate were a chance for elders to narrate a fuller history that starts with the founding of the now-inundated cocoa village of Worobong in the late nineteenth century.[50] These public accounts of the past were addressed not only to me but also to the local youth who gathered to listen to the interviews. The older generation that experienced resettlement is worried that their emotional relationship with the former cocoa-growing village of Worobong will be lost. For them, Amate should be called New Oworobong, to assure a sense of place. Moreover, Amate/New Oworobong, with its large number of abandoned houses and its poverty, is a prominent example of the "ghost town" deplored by Kalitsi at the Resettlement Symposium. In 2008, Kalitsi and Casely-Hayford contrasted Amate with the more successful outcome in Kete-Krachi, the largest resettled town. Kete-Krachi, unlike Amate, "thrived afterwards" because of its harbor, as Casely-Hayford noted.[51] Interviews in Kete-Krachi did not confirm this assessment.

Kete-Krachi

The old town of Kete-Krachi was located along the Volta River at a major crossroads of trading routes that connected southern Ghana with the northern market of Salaga and, to the west, with Atebubu. For two hundred years, Krachi (Krachikrom) had been the center of the influential Dente shrine and the home of the Krachiwura, the paramount chief.[52] The larger and newer part, Kete, had a multiethnic population, including Krachis, Hausa, Yoruba, and Ewe, who had created an important commercial center since the late nineteenth century.[53] In the 1890s, the Germans had taken over Kete-Krachi and made it a district headquarters, a status it kept in World War I, when it came under British rule. In the 1950s, twice a week, the market of Kete was a "thriving place bristling with activity."[54] The town had large houses and featured "plentiful entertainment" that included highlife dance bands, social clubs, and even a tennis club (Barrington 1972, 49). Much of this life was lost due to the Akosombo Dam. Today, the resettled town of Kete-Krachi, though still an administrative center, sits at the tip of a peninsula surrounded by the Volta Lake, cut off from its former economic connections.

In the early 1960s, the planners debated intensively on where to rebuild and how to structure the resettlement of cosmopolitan Kete-Krachi. According to a survey, two-thirds of its population were engaged in "commerce, the professions, crafts or clerical work," and 71 percent of its inhabitants were "non-Krachi" (Kalitsi 1970a, 47). The planners debated whether the specific nature of this town could be maintained and what to do with the renters living in the large compound houses of Kete. They decided to organize the new Kete-Krachi along ethnic lines, as the resettled town would include people from other villages. Anthropological concepts, common at the time, informed their thinking. The VRA, according to Kalitsi, sought "to maintain a stable social structure in the face of resettlement," and thus the objective of learning about who was "inclined to go with whom" became crucial for resettlement.[55] Time pressure and "fear of arousing envy and resentment" led to the decision that the townspeople of Kete-Krachi would receive "the same types and size houses as the villagers elsewhere" (Barrington 1972, 44). In September 1964, Krachikrom, located closer to the river, was flooded. Kete, on higher ground, received a warning in July 1965 about rising waters, which led to a hasty evacuation.[56]

Reflecting on the changes brought by the flooding, J. B. Donkor, the former registrar of the Krachi Traditional Area, deplored how old Kete-Krachi had lost "everything," including its famed German market, a good water system, and excellent roads lined with trees for three miles leading into town. As all these amenities were flooded, Kete-Krachi's commercial activities came to a halt. The substandard resettlement houses, offered as compensation, took people's dignity. Donkor and his successor Alfred Attafoe engaged in a debate about whether they would have been better off had Nkrumah stayed in power. Attafoe believed that Nkrumah had a plan to assist Kete-Krachi, which was not implemented due to the coup. Donkor, however, stressed that Nkrumah had sufficient time to address Kete-Krachi's woes. Although Nkrumah had visited the town prior to flooding, he did not prevent its decline. Donkor exclaimed, "Where was he, when they were planning this thing? You are the president, if you lead a regime, whatever happens it is your responsibility."[57]

A different story was offered by an elder of the Muslim community, Alhaji A. T. Ibrahimah, and by the Sarkin Zongo, the Muslim leader Alhaji Abu Safiano Baba. The latter contacted me in Accra to be interviewed. Baba welcomed me on his veranda surrounded by documentary evidence that included copies of archival reports, letters, two UCLA dissertations, and photographs of Kete-Krachi's most famous Muslim scholar. Muslims had experienced a history of discrimination, as many of them had arrived for economic reasons and settled in Kete. In 1955, Muslims were identified with the Hausa community that constituted about 35 percent of the population. According to sociologist Austin Tetteh, they felt like "strangers" in the town and did not trust the Krachiwura.[58] Ibrahimah and Baba, conveying their understanding of the past, recalled how they both lived in large family houses. As outsiders in the local power structure, Muslims were hard hit by the creation of Volta Lake. Ibrahimah and Baba recalled that their families suffered after abandoning their homes in Kete and then coping with the limited space of the core house. They were disappointed by the VRA's broken promises and remain concerned about the ongoing tensions between Krachis who claim ownership over the town and surrounding lands, and the local Muslim community.[59]

Nana B. K. Mensah, a ninety-year-old elder with ties to the Krachiwura, highlighted the resistance in Kete-Krachi against the Volta project. The VRA record is remarkably silent about any form of resistance. In his assessment, Robert Chambers (1970, 31) wrote that planning and execution of resettlement was "successful, in some respects outstandingly so," and that this "was achieved without any serious opposition." Mensah, however, recalled how he had spoken up against the resettlement scheme. He was appalled by the fact that the people of Kete-Krachi had to provide communal labor for their own resettlement, and argued that the government had been more generous when resettling other communities. In the 1950s, the government had provided the fishing village affected by the construction of Tema harbor with full replacement of their lost houses. Yet in the 1960s, the VRA resettlement plan allocated each household only the infamous core house to be completed by the settlers. Mensah's agitations had consequences. One night in 1964, he was arrested, jailed, and then exiled to Kumasi.[60] That Mensah was a well-known opponent of the CPP government did not help his case. The CPP government was eager to silence an outspoken critic who challenged the resettlement program.[61]

When I asked Kalitsi and Casely-Hayford about resistance, they acknowledged having had "some problems in Kete-Krachi." While Kalitsi elaborated on the difficulties of moving the Dente shrine, he did not mention Mensah's opposition.[62] For my next visit, Mensah had gathered documentary evidence of his continued agitation against the VRA's resettlement program. In 1969 when he became a member of parliament during the Second Republic, Mensah used his national platform to speak on behalf of the forgotten communities:

> I wish to remind the Government that Krachi in the Volta Region suffered most during the formation of the Volta Lake. It has lost not less than a hundred towns and villages. During the evacuation, families who once lived in mighty and comfortable buildings were forced to assemble themselves in single-roomed nuclear houses, poorly built without kitchen and bathroom. Properties were left outside to be cared for by rain and sun. Though this is very serious, the Volta River Authority created an erroneous impression that the settlers were happy and better off than before. . . . Payment of compensation for crops and properties submerged has been suspended with the excuse of there being no money. I therefore call upon the Government, as a matter of urgency, to set up a commission into the affairs of the Volta River Authority and an independent valuation officer should be appointed to revalue the poultry farm structures they call houses.[63]

Although both the government and the VRA responded to such calls, they did not change the plight of the settlers.

In 1970, the VRA produced a memorandum assessing its resettlement program for the new government of Prime Minister K. A. Busia. Upon completion of the resettlement towns in 1966, the VRA had devolved to other government departments its responsibility for health services, completing of core houses, and providing farms to the settlers. Since this transition did not work, the National Liberation Council, the military regime that succeeded Nkrumah, called on the VRA to take charge again of resettlement agriculture and related activities. By 1970, about six thousand of the thirteen thousand core houses had been extended to two- or three-room structures, and the VRA, in cooperation with the World Food Program, had launched a land clearance project for farms. The memorandum detailed problems in the multiethnic resettlement towns, ranging from deteriorating water systems and schools without furniture to contested authority among local chiefs and town development committees. To some degree, the memorandum blamed the settlers themselves for their own misery, as they lacked a "pioneer spirit" to make the program work and depended too much on government. The VRA stated its commitment to offering some compensation and maintaining the central record office on resettlement, its archive, "for information and reference purpose." Evaluating resettlement, the memorandum did not include any moments of resistance, so eloquently evoked by Mensah.[64]

In 1970, Prime Minister Busia appointed a secret committee of enquiry to investigate the activities and finances of the VRA. Its report, however, fully exonerated the VRA. The initial problems of financing the Volta project had imposed delays in the planning of the resettlement program. These delays created a situation that produced "untold hardship on most of the settlers." In its final analysis, the report even commended individual VRA officers for their "sense of duty" and exemplary service, among them Amarteifio and Kalitsi.[65] Ultimately, none of these interventions changed the conditions of the settlers in Kete-Krachi and those in other resettlement towns. As the VRA archive excludes criticism of resettlement formulated in local communities, elders like Mensah and Alhaji Baba remained eager to tell their story.

Conclusion

The resettlement scheme of the Volta River Project was closely associated with the program of modernization in Ghana. Resettlement became "a crusade for social and economic development" (Chambers 1970, 28). From its inception, social scientists and other experts were closely involved in planning and implementation, conducting ethnographic research on behalf of policymakers (Brokensha 1962, 1963) that initially culminated in the Volta Resettlement Symposium in 1965.[66] Social scientists were not the only experts who produced knowledge about resettlement—administrators, agronomists, architects, engineers, and social workers created a record of their participation.[67] Their process of reflection continues not only in print but also in interviews and at informal gatherings. Although many technocrats have forged for themselves an established version of their contribution, Volta men like Kalitsi and Casely-Hayford remain intellectually astute regarding their own place within this history.

Resettlement schemes have become case studies for scholars to track the ambitions of authoritarian states to reshape rural populations as part of modernization programs, whether as a result of compulsory "villagization," such as the one implemented under Julius Nyerere in Tanzania, or as a result of infrastructure projects, particularly large hydroelectric dams, such as Kariba in Central Africa, Akosombo in Ghana, and Cahora Bassa in Mozambique.[68] Further, studies on resettlement have become rural counterparts to a scholarship on urbanization and industrialization that has examined the tensions between high modernist objectives and lived realities (Ferguson 1999). More recently, historians have contributed to the production of knowledge about development projects. This is part of a shift in historical inquiry toward the last years of colonial rule and early independence—an era when so much seemed possible in Africa, especially in Ghana. Exploring the history of modernization, scholars have turned to archival collections of state agencies, such as the VRA, in order to compensate for gaps in the administrative record.[69]

An examination of the Akosombo resettlement program demonstrates that the experience of modernization is about local meanings. The recollections of Adwoa Fosuaa, B. K. Mensah, and others reveal how its implementation was contested and even led to resistance. The agents of modernization—Volta men, the protagonists of nation building—were unable to recognize this local agency as of value in the process of modernization. The published accounts remain remarkably silent about these kinds of challenges, although the VRA archive contains glimpses of this local participation.

Gathering such Akosomobo stories, this chapter suggests, remains a fertile approach to enriching knowledge gained from archival research with other sources beyond the walls of official repositories. This is not a mere reconstruction of the African past based on archival and oral history research, a methodology perfected in the social history of Africa over the last three decades. Rather this is an invitation to engage with different bodies of knowledge and different interpretations of the past as offered in a variety of locations—what Cohen and Odhiambo have called a social history of knowledge production.[70] In resettlement towns, elders spoke on behalf of their communities. As a form of counter-knowledge, they presented their understanding of the past, which conflicted with other versions found in state archives and social science publications. My interview partners used their encounters with me to tell their version of a contested history. For those who were resettled, Akosombo did not become the success story of the nation's development. Rather, they expressed their frustration about state neglect. These recollections qualify the experience of modernization in Ghana in a different way than other, more widespread critiques of Nkrumah's regime.

Notes

1. This chapter is based on over seventy interviews conducted across Ghana from 2005 to 2011. Research was supported by the American Council of Learned Societies; the President's Research Fellowships in the Humanities, University of California; and the Academic Senate of the University of California, Santa Barbara.

2. For published accounts, see the collection by Chambers (1970). For a critical assessment of the overall Volta River Project see Hart (1980); for its celebration see Moxon (1984). Diaw and Schmidt-Kallert (1990), Tsikata (2006), and Yarrow (2011) have explored the experience of dam-affected communities.

3. Gold Coast (1953, 521–627). Cf. discussion in Apter (1970, 234–41).

4. Nkrumah's speech, "The Volta River Project," 21 February 1961 (Obeng 1997, vol. 2, 33); see, more broadly, Miescher and Tsikata (2009/2010).

5. A "strictly confidential" circular about the proposed Volta River Scheme, 25 January 1951, Public Records and Archives Administration Department (PRAAD), Koforidua, ADM/KD 29/6/624.

6. Preparatory Commission (1956, vol. 1, 46; and vol. 2, 71, 124, 131). See Tsikata (2006) on how Akosombo affected downstream communities.

7. Hart (1977); see also Chambers (1970, 10–33) and Kalitsi (1970a).

8. Kalitsi (1970a). See interviews with E. A. K. Kalitsi, Accra, 25 June and 3 July 2008.

9. The responsibilities of the Volta River Authority were first outlined in a white paper prepared by the Colonial Office (Great Britain 1952, app. III). The Preparatory Commission published a draft of the Volta River Authority Bill (Preparatory Commission 1956, vol. 2, app. XVI). In 1961, the national assembly passed the Volta River Development Act, 1961, (Act 46). For the VRA "success story," see Killick (1978, 249) and Chambers (1970, 20).

10. Originally, the Preparatory Commission had allocated £4 million for resettlement; section 30 of the Volta River Development Act stipulated that £3.5 million of the construction funds were earmarked for resettlement, and anything above that had to be covered by the Ghana government. By 1964, nearly £8 million had been spent on resettlement (Kalitsi 1970a, 37, 56).

11. Interview with A. B. Futa, Accra, 15 July 2008; interview with E. A. K. Kalitsi and Louis Casely-Hayford, Accra, 8 July 2008; and interview with Kalitsi, 25 June 2008. For the Akosombo Township, see Miescher (2012).

12. Interview with Louis Casely-Hayford, Tema, 16 June 2008. His father, Archie Casely-Hayford, served as minister with different portfolios in Nkrumah's governments, 1951–1966.

13. Interviews with John Osei, Akosombo, 17–18 July 2006.

14. See E. A. K. Kalitsi's self-introduction during the Revisiting Modernization conference, Institute of African Studies, University of Ghana, 27–31 July 2009. In training and intellectual orientation, Volta men resembled John Robert Ouko (see Cohen and Odhiambo 2004, 173–83).

15. The archive reflects the institutional success of the VRA, which not only offered the highest salaries among Ghana's large companies but also had a stable leadership, with four chief executives during its first thirty-seven years of existence.

16. Afriyie (1973); Afriyie and Butcher (1971); Brokensha (1962, 1963); Brokensha and Scudder (1966); Butcher (1970); Dodoo (1970); Huszar (1965, 1970); Lawson (1968).

17. Cited by Preparatory Commission (1956, vol. 1, 45). R. G. A. Jackson, special commissioner for the Volta project, declared in a press release, "The people affected by this Scheme—*if* it ever came to life—can be assured that *the Prime Minister and the Government of the Gold Coast will ensure that they will not be worse off as a result of the Scheme*" (Information Ser-

vices Department, 8 July 1953, VRA Archive, Tema [VRA-A], VRP/PC/27; emphasis original). Thanks to Marian Antwi and Charlotte Selom Adza-Yawo for facilitating my research.

18. *Ghanaian Times*, 8 October 1962. See also P. H. Johnson's report, *Ghanaian Times*, 20 April 1963.

19. "The Volta River Project," 25 March 1963 in Nkrumah (1997, 21).

20. Kalitsi (1973, 78). For a study of those who opted to resettle themselves, see E. K. Afriyie, "Report on the Preliminary Social Survey of 4 Krachi Area 'G. E.' (Gone Elsewhere) Villages," Volta Lake Research Project, May 1969.

21. Volta Basin Development Plan, cited in Chambers (1970, 28). For a discussion of regional planning, see Shapiro (2003, 152–62).

22. New Ajena is located just beyond the dam site; Nkwakubew is close to the main road toward the Volta Region. For the beginning of construction, see *Ghanaian Times*, 2 October 1962.

23. *Ghanaian Times*, 20 April 1963, 5; see also Johnson (1970).

24. *Ghanaian Times*, 9 September 1963, 5.

25. Ibid.

26. Kalitsi (1970a, 42). In the early 1970s, the planners and implementers of the forced villagization in Tanzania expressed a similar "blind faith in machines and large scale operations," as Scott (1998, 242) noted.

27. *Ghanaian Times*, 20 April 1963.

28. *Ghanaian Times*, 9 September 1963, 5.

29. *Evening News*, 2 June 1964.

30. *Evening News*, 13 August 1965, 15.

31. See A. K. Osei, assistant mass education officer, who reported, "Four new villages have been discovered around the confluence of Afram and Volta Rivers" (April 1963). Three of these villages elected to join the Mem-Chemfe resettlement, while the fourth one moved back to its hometown (VRA-A, RMT/140).

32. Kalitsi and Casely-Hayford, 8 July 2008. See Amarteifio (1970) and Amarteifio, Butcher, and Whitham (1966).

33. Kalitsi and Casely-Hayford, 8 July 2008. For the core house, see Yarrow (2011).

34. See "Volta River Symposium Resettlement Papers," Volta River Authority and Faculty of Architecture, Kwame Nkrumah University of Science and Technology, Kumasi (1965), 105; Kalitsi (1970b, 225).

35. Interviews with Nana Atuobi Yiadom, Amate, 4 September 2005, and with Togbe Kwame Soku and Hayford Ansong, Amate, 3 September 2005. All interviews in Amate were conducted in Twi. Joseph Kwakye, who participated in the interviews, assisted with translations. For the population figures, see "Resettlement Area Group No. 1," n.d. (1963), "List of Resettlement Sites Area 1 (Kwahu)," 14 June 1963, both in VRA-A, RMT/140; Diaw and Schmidt-Kallert (1990, 243–44). Amarteifio (1970, 145) notes that forty-three villages joined at Amate.

36. See Kwabena Ameyaw, "The Tradition of Worobon," 1–3, recorded 5 December 1963, in "Traditions from the Afram Plains," no. 2, Institute of African Studies, University of Ghana. I use the spelling "Kwawu" and not the anglicized "Kwahu," unless used in original quotations.

37. Interview with Abena Animwaa, Amate, 3 September 2005, with the assistance of Joseph Kwakye. See Ameyaw, "Tradition of Worobon," 4–6, and the file "Begoro-Kwahu Land Dispute," PRAAD-Accra, ADM 11/1/1204.

38. Interviews with Adwoa Fosuaa, Amate, 26 July 2006; Salome Mirekua and Beatrice Nyarkoaa, Amate, 27 July 2006; Nana Birifa Dankwah II, 27 July 2006; all in Amate and with the assistance of Joseph Kwakye.

39. "Visit to Proposed New Site near Worobong," 13 November 1961, VAR-A, RMT/130.

40. Minutes of "Representative Delegates Meeting," 17 November 1961, VRA-A, RMT/140.

41. "Oworobong New Town Survey and Layout," 31 March 1962, and the meeting note for a site selection survey at Worobong, 4 May 1962, VRA-A, RMT/140. For site planning and evacuation, cf. Amarteifio (1970).

42. "Visit to Proposed New Site near Worobong," 13 November 1961, VAR-A, RMT/130. For recollections of Nana Dankwa's refusal, see Salome Mirekua and Beatrice Nyarkoa, 27 July 2006, and Abena Animwaa, 3 September 2005.

43. Adwoa Fosuaa, 3 September 2005. Cf. Hart (1980, 79), and the recollections gathered by Diaw and Schmidt-Kallert (1990).

44. For Amate see "Trekking Notes," May 1966; "Trekking Notes," July 1966; and "Trekking Out Notes," March 1967, VRA-A, RMT/33. For tensions, see Dodoo (1970).

45. Afriyie and Butcher (1971, 44); Afriyie (1973, 728). For discussion of Project 356, see Shapiro (2003, 297–314).

46. See interviews with Yaa Oforiwaa, Abetifi, 13 March 2008; Daniel Kwadwo Yeboah and Kwaku Atuobi Yiadom, Abetifi, 14 March 2008; Janet Obenewaa, Abetifi, 17 March 2008; Kwadwo Okyere, Nkwatia, 20 March 2008; and Kwame Annor Brako, Abetifi, 20 March 2008. All interviews were conducted in Twi; Joseph Kwakye assisted with translations.

47. Kwabena Oboye moved to the village of Aboabo where he had access to good land; Kwabena Oboye and Eric Kwabena Ohene, Abetifi, 19 March 2008.

48. Recollections of Kwaku Atuobi Yiadom, 14 March 2008, and Kwame Annor Brako, 20 March 2008.

49. Yaa Oforiwaa, 13 March 2008.

50. Nana Birifa Dankwah II, 27 July 2006, and Abena Animwaa, 3 September 2005.

51. Kalitsi and Casely-Hayford, 8 July 2008.

52. Maier (1983); Haskett (1981); Barrington (1972).

53. In 1962, Krachikrom had about 155 inhabitants; the highly diversified town of Kete had 4,185, including 1,100 Krachis, 900 Hausa, over 300 Yoruba, more than 200 Ewe, and more than 100 each of Kotokoli, Akan, and Gonja. These figures come from a survey conducted by David P. Butcher and students at the University of Science and Technology, Kumasi, on behalf of the Department of Social Welfare, cited in Barrington (1972, 54).

54. P. Austin Tetteh, "Report on a Preliminary Social Survey of Kete Krachi," Town and Country Planning Department (1956), 25, VRA-A, RMT/82.

55. Kalitsi (1970a, 47). For the aim of keeping villages ethnically coherent in the new towns, see Shapiro (2003, 183) and Brokensha (1962, 122); for a discussion of site selection in Kete-Krachi, see Barrington (1970, 50).

56. Barrington (1970, 51–52). See interviews with Nana Annor Boama III, a former soldier stationed at Kete-Krachi, Abetifi, 15 May 2008; and R. D. Salawu, a mass education officer in Kete-Krachi, Akosombo, 7 December 2007 and 31 March 2011.

57. Interview with J. B. Donkor, Alfred Attafoe, and Nana Kwaku Dente, Kete-Krachi, 30 July 2008.

58. See Tetteh, "Preliminary Social Survey," 32.

59. Interviews with Alhaji A. T. Ibrahimah, Kete-Krachi, 29 July 2008; and Sarkin Zongo Alhaji Abu Safiano Baba, Accra, 6 August 2008. For a history of these tensions, see Maier (1983).

60. Interview with Nana B. K. Mensah, Kete-Krachi, 19 August 2009. For the Tema resettlement, see Amarteifio, Butcher, and Whitham (1966).

61. Maier (1983, 187), who had interviewed B. K. Mensah in 1973 and 1977, connected his arrest and exile with "anti-CPP agitation," without mentioning his opposition to the Volta project resettlement policies.

62. Kalitsi and Casely-Hayford, 8 July 2008. For the challenges of moving the Dente shrine, see Moxon (1984, 167–75).

63. Ghana (1969, 227–28). Interview with Nana B. K. Mensah, Kete-Krachi, 20 August 2009.

64. "Memorandum by the Volta River Authority on the Authority's Resettlement Programme," 9, 10, passim, VRA-A, RMT/123, which includes a copy of Chambers (1970). Cf. interview with E. A. K. Kalitsi, Accra, 2 September 2009.

65. "Interim and Final Reports of the Committee of Enquiry into the Affairs of the Volta River Authority," 30 March 1971, 135, 151, 276, PRAAD-Accra, RG /2/413.

66. Its papers appear in print in Chambers (1970). Social scientists have continued to analyze the Volta resettlement scheme: Afriyie and Butcher (1971); Diaw and Schmidt-Kallert (1990); Tsikata (2006); Yarrow (2011).

67. Kalitsi (1970a, 1970b); Nicholas (1970); Huszar (1965, 1970); Johnson (1970); Amarteifio (1970).

68. For Tanzanian villagization, see Scott (1998, 223–61) and the critique by Schneider (2007). For the Kariba Dam, see Tischler, this volume; for Cahora Bassa, see Isaacman and Isaacman (2013).

69. Shapiro (2003). For a history of development, see Cooper (2010) and Hecht, this volume; for the meanings of independence, see Allman (2008) and Cooper (2008).

70. Cohen and Odhiambo (2004, 28) have observed, "Knowledge is given not only its definitive design but also its unmade, unfinished moment, to allow views of knowledge in formation and to permit an understanding—a new attendance to—the indeterminate and unsettled manifestations of histories and meanings as they are fought over in different African contexts."

References

Afriyie, E. K. 1973. "Resettlement Agriculture: An Experiment in Innovation." In *Man-Made Lakes: Their Problems and Environmental Effects*, edited by William C. Ackermann, Gilbert F. White, and E. Barton Worthington, 720–25. Washington, DC: American Geophysical Union.

Afriyie, E. K, and David A. P. Butcher. 1971. "Socio-Economic Survey of the Volta Resettlement: Four Years after Evacuation." Volta Lake Research Project, Accra.

Allman, Jean. 2008. "Nuclear Imperialism and the Pan-African Struggle for Peace and Freedom: Ghana, 1959–1962." *Souls* 10, no. 2: 83–102.

Amarteifio, Godfrey W. 1970. "Social Welfare." In *The Volta Resettlement Experience*, edited by Robert Chambers, 103–47. New York: Praeger.

Amarteifio, Godfrey W., David A. P. Butcher, and David Whitham. 1966. *Tema Manheam: A Study of Resettlement*. Accra: Ghana Universities Press.

Apter, David E. 1970. *Ghana in Transition*. 2nd rev. ed. Princeton, NJ: Princeton University Press.

Barrington, Leo. 1972. "Migration and the Growth of a Resettlement Community: Kete-Krachi Ghana, 1962 and 1969." PhD diss., Boston University.

Brokensha, David, ed. 1962. *Volta Resettlement: Ethnographic Notes on Some of the Southern Areas*. Legon: Department of Sociology, University of Ghana.

———. 1963. "Volta Resettlement and Anthropological Research." *Human Organization* 22, no. 4: 286–90.

Brokensha, David, and Thayer Scudder. 1968. "Resettlement." In *Dams in Africa: An Inter-Disciplinary Study of Man-Made Lakes in Africa*, edited by Neville Rubin and William M. Warren, 20–62. London: Frank Cass.

Butcher, David A. P. 1970. "The Social Survey." In *The Volta Resettlement Experience,* edited by Robert Chambers, 78–102. New York: Praeger.

Chambers, Robert, ed. 1970. *The Volta Resettlement Experience.* New York: Praeger.

Cochrane, T. W. 1971. *Bibliography of the Volta River Project and Related Matters.* Accra: Volta River Authority.

Cohen, David William Cohen, and E. S. Atieno Odhiambo. 2004. *The Risks of Knowledge: Investigations into the Death of the Hon. Minister John Robert Ouko in Kenya, 1990.* Athens: Ohio University Press.

Cooper, Frederick. 1997. "Modernizing Bureaucrats, Backward Africans, and the Development Concept." In *International Development and the Social Sciences,* edited by Frederick Cooper and Randall Packard, 64–92. Berkeley: University of California Press

———. 2008. "Possibility and Constraint: African Independence in Historical Perspective." *Journal of African History* 49, no. 2: 167–96.

———. 2010. "Writing the History of Development." *Journal of Modern European History* 8, no. 1: 5–23.

Diaw, Kofi, and Einhard Schmidt-Kallert. 1990. *Effects of Lake Volta Resettlement in Ghana.* Hamburg: Institut für Afrika-Kunde.

Dodoo, Martha. 1970. "A Case Study of a Resettlement Town: New Mpamu." In *The Volta Resettlement Experience,* edited by Robert Chambers, 193–203. New York: Praeger.

Ferguson, James. 1999. *Expectations of Modernity: Myths and Meanings of Urban Life on the Zambian Copperbelt.* Berkeley: University of California Press.

Futa, A. B. 1992. "The Volta River Authority: A Study in History, Policy, Public Administration." Unpublished manuscript.

Ghana. 1964. *Seven-Year Plan for National Reconstruction and Development: Financial Years, 1963/64–1969/70.* Accra: Office of the Planning Commission.

———. 1969. *Parliamentary Debates: Official Report, Second Series.* Vol. 1. Accra: Government Printer.

Gold Coast. 1953. *Legislative Assembly Debates: Session 1953, Issue No. 1* (Volume 1). Accra: Government Printing Department.

Great Britain. 1952. *The Volta River Aluminium Scheme,* Cmd. 8702. London: HMSO.

Hart, David. 1980. *The Volta River Project: A Case Study in Politics and Technology.* Edinburgh: Edinburgh University Press.

Haskett, Norman Dean. 1981. "Kete-Krachi and the Middle Volta Basin, 1700–1914: Cockpit of African and European Rivalry." PhD diss., University of California, Los Angeles.

Huszar, Laszlo. 1965. "The Volta Resettlement Scheme." *Journal of the Town Planning Institute* 51, no. 7: 279–82.

———. 1970. "Resettlement Planning." In *The Volta Resettlement Experience,* edited by Robert Chambers, 148–63. New York: Praeger.

Isaacman, Allen F., and Barbara S. Isaacman. 2013. *Dams, Displacement and the Delusion of Development: Cahora Bassa and Its Legacies in Mozambique, 1965–2007.* Athens: Ohio University Press.

Johnson, T. S. 1970. "The Engineering Programme and Problems." In *The Volta Resettlement Experience,* edited by Robert Chambers, 179–92. New York: Praeger.

Jopp, Keith. 1965. *The Story of Ghana's Volta River Project.* Accra: Volta River Authority.

Kaiser Engineers. 1959. *Reassessment Report on the Volta River Project for the Government of Ghana.* Oakland, CA: Kaiser Engineers.

Kalitsi, E. A. K. 1970a. "The Organization of Resettlement." In *The Volta Resettlement Experience,* edited by Robert Chambers, 34–57. New York: Praeger.

——. 1970b. "Present and Future Problems of Administering Resettlement Towns." In *The Volta Resettlement Experience,* edited by Robert Chambers, 217–25. New York: Praeger.

——. 1973. "Volta Lake in Relation to the Human Population and Some Issues in Economics and Management." In *Man-Made Lakes: Their Problems and Environmental Effects,* edited by William C. Ackermann, Gilbert F. White, and E. Barton Worthington, 77–85. Washington, DC: American Geophysical Union.

Killick, Tony. 1978. *Development Economics in Action: A Study of Economic Policies in Ghana.* London: Heinemann.

Lawson, Rowena. 1968. "An Interim Economic Appraisal of the Volta Resettlement Scheme." *Nigerian Journal of Economic and Social Studies* 10, no. 1: 95–109.

Maier, Donna J. E. 1983. *The Case of the Dente Shrine in Nineteenth-Century Ghana.* Bloomington: Indiana University Press.

Miescher, Stephan F. 2012. "Building the City of the Future: Visions and Experiences of Modernity in Ghana's Akosombo Township." *Journal of African Studies* 53, no. 3: 367–90.

Miescher, Stephan F., and Dzodzi Tsikata. 2009/2010. "Hydro-Power and the Promise of Modernity and Development in Ghana: Comparing the Akosombo and Bui Dam Projects." *Ghana Studies* 12/13: 15–53.

Moxon, James. 1984. *Volta: Man's Greatest Lake.* Rev. ed. London: Deutsch.

Nicholas, M. S. O. 1970. "Resettlement Agriculure." In *The Volta Resettlement Experience,* edited by Robert Chambers, 204–16. New York: Praeger.

Nkrumah, Kwame. 1997. *Selected Speeches of Kwame Nkrumah.* Vol. 5. Compiled by Samuel Obeng. Accra: Afram.

Preparatory Commission. 1956. *Reports of the Preparatory Commission for the Volta River Project.* 3 vols. London: HMSO.

Scott, James C. 1998. *Seeing like a State: How Certain Schemes to Improve the Human Condition Have Failed.* New Haven, CT: Yale University Press.

Shapiro, Jordan E. 2003. "Settling Refugees, Unsettling the Nation: Ghana's Volta River Project Resettlement Scheme and the Ambiguities of Development Planning, 1952–1970." PhD diss., University of Michigan.

Schneider, Leander. 2007. "High on Modernity? Explaining the Failings of Tanzanian Villagisation." *African Studies* 66, no. 1: 9–38.

Tsikata, Dzodzi. 2006. *Living in the Shadow of the Large Dams: Long Term Responses to Downstream and Lakeside Communities of Ghana's Volta River Project.* Leiden: Brill.

Yarrow, Thomas. 2011. "Kinship and the Core House: Contested Ideas of Family and Place in a Ghanaian Resettlement Township." In *Recasting Anthropological Knowledge: Inspiration and Social Science,* edited by Jeanette Edwards and Maja Petrović-Šteger, 88–105. Cambridge: Cambridge University Press.

9 Radioactive Excess

Modernization as Spectacle and Betrayal in Postcolonial Gabon

Gabrielle Hecht

In 1982, El Hadj Omar Bongo, president of Gabon, officiated a two-day ceremony to celebrate the opening of his nation's first yellowcake plant.[1] The new factory would transform raw uranium ore extracted by French-run mines into yellowcake, a commodity that could be bought and sold on the world market. The plant itself was not particularly spectacular to behold, and was certainly not a paradigmatic example of the technological sublime (Nye 1996; Larkin 2008). In order to become a symbol of modernization, the plant needed a mise en scène: in this case, a scripted spectacle that explicitly heralded Gabon's ascension in the global technopolitical order and proclaimed the nation's transition from colonial supplier of raw material to direct supplier of nuclear fuel.

The carefully choreographed ceremony performed modernization in several registers. The company awarded medals to employees with twenty-one years of service, to indicate that Gabonese workers had finally transcended their childish colonial selves to become (industrial) adults. Speakers gushed about the Gabonization of the personnel, the mine's magnificently modern infrastructures, and the social harmony permeating the company town. The primary protagonist of this marvelous modernization was the president himself: the local party leader praised "Yaya Bongo's . . . policy of progressive and concerted democracy, spearhead of Gabon's economic and social development."[2] Bongo in turn awarded Gabon's "Étoile Équatoriale" to over forty COMUF managers and employees. In this mise en scène, the company figured as the state's servant in Gabon's modernization.

In many respects, the uranium mining company *had* been an engine of modernization in the Haut-Ogooué. It had built thousands of houses for its workers, along with a substantial transportation infrastructure. Its hospital provided medical services for the entire region, not just its employees. The company trained and promoted its employees, and even provided a few opportunities for some Gabonese to educate their children in France. And some of these developments, as we shall see, did come in response to demands made by Bongo's state.

Nevertheless, like all modernization spectacles, the plant-opening ceremony obscured as much as it revealed. As I have written elsewhere, Bongo and his ministers proved unable to market Gabonese uranium independently of France: in this respect, the yellowcake plant did not live up to its promise as an agent of commercial sovereignty (Hecht 2012). As we will see here, the state proved unwilling to regulate working conditions in the company's mines. This regulatory indifference was readily apparent to the workers who toiled in the uranium mine. For them, the more profound message of modernization's mise en scène had to do with the *alliance* between the company and the state. The state was willing to put its police at the service of the company during times of labor strife, but not to police the company when workers protested labor conditions.

This chapter argues that modernization—as script, as spectacle, as political claim, and as a set of material results—was *jointly produced* by the company and the state. Beginning at the moment of decolonization, I outline the modernization script that French employees brought to Gabon. In the 1970s, emerging state imperatives reshaped the meanings and manifestations of this script and turned it into a political mandate: Gabonization.[3] Together, the state and the company sought to produce disciplined worker-citizens who would readily accept the perils of industrialized labor as the price of modernization. An examination of workplace dangers, however, shows how the experience of modernization constantly exceeded the neat boundaries of its script. Workers did not readily become compliant, industrial citizens. Finally, I go beyond the 1970s in order to examine the environmental legacy of the mine. Built from radioactive mine debris, the material achievements of modernization—houses, schools, clinics—became highly toxic over time. These radioactive structures thus offer a new twist on the apprehension of modernization as a "living archival object."

A Jointly Produced Script

In 1957, geologists working for the French state-owned Commissariat à l'Energie Atomique (CEA) discovered a large uranium deposit in eastern Gabon. By this point, the end of empire was palpable. Concerned that any enterprise run directly by the French government might be readily appropriated by the newly independent state, the CEA invited Mokta, a private mining company with considerable African experience, into a commercial partnership. Together, they formed the Compagnie des Mines d'Uranium de Franceville, or COMUF, to run the site.

Gabonese independence meant that the French employees sent to launch uranium operations could no longer imagine themselves as colonial explorers. The technological success of the mission—and the very future of Franco-African relations—rested on the metropolitan man's ability to break from the clichés of colonial expectations and behavior. This, at least, was what the CEA told its employees in a handbook given to French citizens on their way to Mounana for the first time.

The handbook presented an elaborate script for CEA expatriates to follow. It sternly reminded its readers that they were henceforth subject to the laws of their host country. Frenchmen had to shed colonial prejudices that saw "Blacks [as] impulsive, ungrateful, liars, dirty, somewhat thieving, above all lazy, and in the end incapable of perseverance and personal progress." They had to dismiss claims that Africans mistreated mechanical objects and were "incapable of analysis, unable to conceive of both the whole and its parts, and scornful of the laws of causality."[4] Instead, expats had to understand that technology could transcend racial distinctions: what differentiated individuals was not their skin color but their skill set.[5] This required reframing the colonial prerogative as the prerogative of expertise: "Your skills, which constitute your instrument of work, should contribute to the enrichment of Africa; this is your contribution to the work of civilization, not a source of superiority that entitles you to be haughty and brutal."[6]

This expat script may have prescribed a change in attitude, but it left colonial categories themselves undisturbed. The handbook clung to the category of the *évolué,* the colonial subject who had been successfully civilized and uplifted and who now served as the emblem of Modernity, the proof that Tradition could be transcended. Tradition, in this rendition, was the tribe: colonial obsessions with tribalism ran through the expat script, which described Gabonese as belonging to "multiple tribes of different dialects," all "Black Bantus."[7] Such assertions of tribalism were presented as baseline data, alongside information about surface area, agricultural production, latitude, and climate.

The first generation of COMUF expats used these renditions of modernity and tradition as tools of labor management. The site's first director, Frenchman Xavier des Ligneris, had previously managed uranium mines in the metropole. He contrasted the Gabonese évolués trained as prospectors and technicians with the rest of the workforce, whom he saw as "unsuited to real transformation, continuing to follow their ancient customs." He especially deplored that they were "polygamous as soon as they have the opportunity." The COMUF had originally planned to house all its workers in a modern company town, but polygamy made this impossible, as did "racial rivalries: Bendjabis and Batékés are especially ready to come to blows."[8] Instead, des Ligneris proposed grouping Gabonese workers "in villages, according to race."[9] The company would provide building materials and each worker would get a fixed number of days to complete his dwelling. Polygamists could build huts for their additional wives behind the main cabin, but on their own time, with their own materials, and at their own expense. Gabonese workers who followed a script that involved renouncing both polygamy and tribalism were rewarded with concrete houses equipped with running water and electricity. They could thus join the spectacle of modernization.[10]

During the first few years after independence, Gabon's national leaders—preoccupied with consolidating their power and building the state—paid relatively little attention to the COMUF and its modernization schemes. They occasionally pressed the COMUF to uphold its "development" claims by upgrading living quarters, increasing wages, and promoting Africans. For the most part, though, state officials left the company to its own devices.[11]

That began to change in 1967, when Albert-Bernard Bongo succeeded Léon Mba as president. The same year saw the creation of the massive French oil company Elf and the Biafran secession from Nigeria, events which rapidly became linked. Jacques Foccart, President Charles de Gaulle's "Monsieur Afrique," saw the Biafran secession as a chance to weaken the Nigerian state. Elf saw an opportunity to access oil fields in the Gulf of Guinea. Foccart and his clan had been instrumental in bringing Bongo to power. And so Bongo gladly made Gabon the launch pad for French assistance to Biafra. The French did not get the result they had hoped for, but by the end of the Biafran conflict in 1970 oil revenues from Elf were flowing into the coffers of the Gabonese state—and those of its new president (Verschave 1998; Foccart 1997–2001; Obiang 1997; Yates 1996; Ngolet 2000).

Flush with money and ambition, Bongo imagined Gabon as a modern technological nation, a powerhouse of central Africa, and a player in global oil markets. In 1973, supposedly following advice from Libya's Muammar Gaddafi, he converted to Islam and changed his name to El Hadj Omar Bongo, a move intended to facilitate Gabon's admission into OPEC. A former minister of information and propaganda, Bongo adeptly filled state-owned media with his message of *Rénovation,* which promised to convert revenues from Gabonese natural resources into housing, schools, and hospitals. His signature project was the *Transgabonais:* a modern railroad that connected the coast to the interior—specifically, the Haut-Ogooué, Bongo's province of origin (and the location of the COMUF). Bongo thus sought to bring his power base symbolically and materially closer to Gabon's capital, Libreville. As with large-scale technological projects elsewhere in the postcolonial world, building the Transgabonais became a spectacle in its own right, dramatized in the state-run media as the triumphant victory of modernization over Gabon's notoriously recalcitrant nature (Mauger 2003; Yates 1996). Bongo was thus eager to both extend and display Gabonese sovereignty. And it so happened that starting by the early 1970s, the COMUF was facing serious financial difficulties. Nuclear power plant construction had stalled in France, and uranium prices throughout the capitalist world had hit bottom. Slow cash flow severely threatened the COMUF's growth plans, but expansion was necessary if the company was to become commercially viable.[12]

The COMUF needed money. And it had a singular symbolic advantage: it was located in the Haut-Ogooué, the president's province of origin. Bongo's experience with Elf had already taught him that there was much to be gained—personally and nationally—by cooperating with French corporations (rather than expropriating and nationalizing them). In 1974, the Gabonese state provided the COMUF with a large infusion of capital, enough to acquire a 25 percent ownership of the company and to cover a substantial advance on investments (Ndong 2009). Without these funds the company would have faced severe difficulties not only in financing its future expansion, but even in maintaining its production levels.[13] Officially, however, the capital infusion was framed not as a rescue operation, but as a matter of international relations. By acquiring a minority stake in the company, Bongo publicly asserted Gabon's sovereignty over its natural resources. The COMUF, meanwhile, could vaunt its ability to act as a good corporate citizen in a post-independence framework.

Eager to establish its new influence in the company, the state immediately demanded that the COMUF accelerate its training and infrastructural development programs. The new watchword would be "Gabonization," a process which was supposed to turn the COMUF into a company run and (at least partially) owned by Gabonese citizens. The ad hoc training program run by the company had to become formalized into a concrete, measurable project for training and promoting Gabonese employees into management positions. And the company town had to be expanded, upgraded, and made available to all workers—not just those who followed the company's script. The company need not provide family allowances for more than one wife, but polygamy should not be sanctioned.

In at least one respect, the demand for Gabonization suited COMUF corporate headquarters. Expatriates were expensive: they commanded salaries up to ten times those of Africans, and received supplements for servants, trips home, and boarding schools.[14] Promoting Africans to management positions would cut down considerably on operating costs.[15]

As a sociotechnical mandate and a political aspiration, however, Gabonization had many other significant dimensions, both for the state leaders who demanded it and for the workers who experienced it. Professional training focused not just on the technical skills required for particular jobs, but also on the discipline required to be a responsible industrial worker.[16] Technical training was interspersed with lessons on timeliness, tidiness, and teamwork. Gabonization had totalizing ambitions: transforming the psychological outlook of Gabonese also involved transforming domestic sociotechnical practices. Since the earliest years of the mine's operation, a French social worker had been teaching courses on cooking, sewing, and housekeeping especially aimed at the wives and daughters of évolués.[17] The acceleration of Gabonization brought an increase in the number of Gabonese men promoted to the ranks of "cadre." Promotion entitled these men to housing in the "*cité des cadres*," up on the hill where the Europeans lived. French residents could not cope with such a move unless Gabonese wives could keep house European-style: goats in the yard were definitely not on.[18] For company managers, then, Gabonization came to signify carefully controlled modernization.

State-mandated Gabonization was not just a process. In order to succeed as a political mandate, it had to become a *result,* subject to both statistical tabulation and ceremonial display. When a Gabonese employee was promoted to a supervisory post, both he and his position were data points in the accounting of success.[19] The statistics themselves—generated for the state as proof of the company's compliance—in turn produced a nominal deracialization of the COMUF's internal categories: personnel rosters went from listing employees as "Europeans" or "Africans" to referring to them as "expatriates" and "Gabonese."[20] As an object of statistical accounting, Gabonization offered the company a means to display subservience to the state, and gave the state a means to display its authority over the company. As we saw at the beginning of this chapter, displays of subservience and authority were not limited to technical training and promotion. Bongo enjoyed ceremonies, particularly the opportunities they offered to enact links between modernization and sovereignty. The ceremonial inauguration of the mine's new yellowcake plant was one of half a dozen such occasions for performing Gabonese technological nationalism.

Ceremonial displays notwithstanding, however, modernization was anything but a smooth, unidirectional process by which workers became disciplined, industrialized citizens of a nation. Gabonese had different ideas about how they would live their lives from those prescribed by the company and the state. As the company town grew, households accommodated full families, with fifteen or twenty people living in a two-room house. People modified their dwellings, kept livestock, and grew crops. They used communal water taps for washing as well as drinking. All these actions violated rules, incurring fines and occasionally expulsion.[21] Some Gabonese could not stand the regimentation and left of their own accord. A few of them created their own village: a community of houses made from discarded corrugated metal, nestled snugly in thick vegetation, surrounded by chickens and goats, and ironically dubbed "Cité du Silence."[22]

Still, many residents of the Haut-Ogooué appreciated the steady salaries, the running water, the electricity, and the solid houses that kept out torrential rains. At its peak, the company town housed up to seven thousand people in those dwellings. Built out of concrete made from the plentiful waste rock produced by the mines, these gleaming white houses were ready for occupation starting in the early 1970s.

We will return to these houses at the end of the chapter. First, however, we must delve more deeply into modernization's unruly moments. The next two sections focus on the workplace and its dangers. In order to shed light on how COMUF workers experienced, reacted to, and reshaped their own modernization, I examine the circumstances surrounding a fatal accident in 1965, the construction of radiation safety practices, and the response of one worker to these practices.

Death Underground

Many COMUF workers saw the company and the state as allies in the governance of modernization. And most understood full well that—enthusiastic rhetoric about the marvels of modern life notwithstanding—this alliance did not prioritize citizen welfare. The Gabonese state claimed to represent its citizens, but it provided the company with police whenever labor disputes threatened to disrupt production: clearly, being a cooperative industrial worker was synonymous with being a disciplined citizen of the nation.[23] More subtly, as we will see in this section, the state and the company worked together to normalize workplace danger as the price of modernization: an ordinary part of industrialized labor, a risk of modern citizenship.

The story of the mine's first fatal underground accident offers an early example of the tensions engendered by the corporate-state alliance that sought to shape modern industrial citizenship in the Haut-Ogooué. On Friday, 17 December 1965, a team of five Gabonese workers had begun their shift by hacking away at the walls of an underground chamber in the Mounana mine. Without warning, a huge slab of rock crashed down on top of them. One man was killed instantly. Another survived the blow but died in the hospital an hour later from internal hemorrhaging. Two other workers suffered injuries; only one escaped unscathed.[24]

The accident shocked the entire workforce. Many men were already extremely reluctant to work in the dark, narrow tunnels of the mine. Evil spirits lurked underground, and only bad things could come from disturbing them. The accident constituted proof. When the surviving miners returned to the surface, they were met by a large crowd who undressed them and piled their clothes and equipment in the supervisors' office, apparently to signify that the workers would have no more to do with the underground mine. No one showed up for work the next day.[25]

On Saturday afternoon, des Ligneris called the miners to a meeting, and asked whether they expected to resume work on Monday. They did not reply. "It's very upsetting when one of your friends gets hurt," one worker told me while remembering this incident. "But they just expect you to carry on as though nothing had happened. It's not right."[26] At nine o'clock at night, state officials showed up on the site to discuss the situation with des Ligneris, accompanied by police troops "to avoid trouble."[27]

No one reported for work on Monday morning. In an effort to determine the workers' demands, management questioned the personnel delegates. These delegates—évolués one and all—were designated to facilitate communication between management and labor, but they included no underground miners. Unsurprisingly, therefore, underground workers did not trust the personnel delegates. Nor did they trust the labor union, which had close ties to the state and to Bongo's party. The angry workers appointed five men to meet with government representatives and personnel and union delegates. Des Ligneris reported that "after several hours of discussion among Gabonese, the Director of Mines invited us to join the meeting and transmitted to me the workers' demands: work would only resume if the monthly salary for miners was uniformly raised by 60,000 francs."[28] The monthly income for a miner, including premiums, was less than 10,000 francs.

The audacious demand could be interpreted as the joint product of industrial expectations and local custom. Local practices dictated that the perpetrator of an accidental death offer a large payment to the victim's family in compensation.[29] And underground work was already rewarded by a premium in exchange for the dangers it presented. Why not, therefore, expect an even larger premium once that work had proved not just dangerous but fatal?

Des Ligneris refused the raise: he did not want to set a precedent linking accidents to pay raises. Accidents, he insisted, were a normal part of industrial life. But the miners who had walked off the job were not mollified. State officials, backed by the chief of police, could not persuade them to resume work. Sixty-three miners resigned and returned to their villages. Those who remained refused to work.[30]

In the face of this escalation, the COMUF welcomed a proposal from labor representatives to call in the village heads. A long meeting ensued; once again, management was not invited. The next day, the village heads asked permission to visit the site of the accident. Des Ligneris accompanied them down into the shaft. There are no reports on what happened underground. But the action must have appeased some workers: a few days later, twenty-one men were back at work. Still, the mine remained shorthanded.[31] The situation dragged on for another two months. On any given day, only two-thirds of the labor force showed up for work.[32] By mid-February, the slowdowns had seriously affected the production schedule. At the end of February, management finally agreed to an average salary increase of 13 percent.[33]

This was far less than the workers had asked for, however, and at the end of March the COMUF still needed workers. It once again turned to state officials, this time for recruitment assistance. Although the company would have preferred to take back trained employees, it had reached the point where it would hire anyone willing to work. With help from local authorities, it devised a series of radio advertisements, aired over a five-day period in five local languages plus French. The first went as follows:

> Residents of the Haut-Ogooué:
>
> You're looking for work. You want to practice a good trade, in a big Company in the Region. Quickly, go sign up to be an underground Miner at the COMUF. You haven't done so until now, perhaps because you learned that last year we had an accident that caused the death of two workers. This was a workplace accident, such as might happen in any company. Workplace accidents are not more frequent, and you are no more exposed to them than to hunting accidents, road accidents, etc . . . On the contrary, you are protected by safety measures that have been carefully studied and well adapted. In coming to work at Mounana, you will receive direct professional training on the job and you will earn a very good salary. You will therefore learn a very good trade, with a good future in Gabon.[34]

The ad thus sought to portray the accident as a normal part of work—and, indeed, life. Workers were safer at the COMUF than elsewhere, because safety measures had been carefully elaborated for their protection. The mine offered a way to march into the nation's future.

The next three days repeated this message, adding details concerning salary, training, and promotion opportunities. On the fifth day, the ad pulled out all the stops, mixing a cautionary tale of witchcraft with an appeal to citizenship:

> Once upon a time, gold prospectors, helped by porters, arrived in the village of Mekambo in Bandzabi county. In this village, under a hut, stood a basket of meat destined for the chief of the county. The porters immediately ate all the meat. The county chief and the other tribal chiefs were unhappy. They had a meeting and decided to cast a spell and engage in diabolical operations so that the seekers of gold would find nothing. And no gold was found in Mekambo. They had to go to Bakota county to find some. Since then, the chiefs and residents of the Mekambo region lament their poverty. They regret their initial act, their intransigence. They especially regret having rescinded all possibility of wealth in the future.
>
> WORKERS OF THE HAUT OGOOUÉ!
>
> Do not act like them. Let your reason be sufficiently strong, and know when to profit from the high salaries of the Compagnie des Mines d'Uranium of Mounana. It's for the good of the Nation and the future of Gabon.[35]

In this story, prospectors were the harbingers of wealth. It was not the whites who violated local customs, but the greedy porters whom they had hired. Still, local villagers should have forgiven this trespass. By using witchcraft, they only ended up depriving themselves of prosperity. Wealth, the message ran, would come to someone—it was inevitable (like modernity). Witchcraft could not stand up to modernity; it could only stop those who practiced it from benefiting. In the name of reason and patriotism, workers should abandon their traditional ways, shed their anger and intransigence, and come forth to profit from the COMUF's wealth.

Over the course of the next few months, the COMUF managed to recruit the workers it needed—perhaps thanks to these radio announcements, or perhaps simply because people were desperate for work. But the recruitment levels did not remain stable. For at least the next decade, recruitment problems resurged whenever accidents occurred. COMUF management and state officials could insist that industrial accidents were a normal part of modernization, and that protective measures made workplaces less risky than ordinary activities such as hunting or road travel. Workers, however, saw nothing banal about drowning in a mine flood underground, or being crushed by sudden rock fall. These tragedies of industrial labor, whose aftermaths resonated through the region, were dramas that countered the spectacles of modernization.

Radiation and Refusal

Another, much less visible source of danger in the workplace was radiation. This came in two forms. Gamma rays emanated from the rocks, externally exposing workers to radiation. In addition, uranium decayed into radon—an invisible, odorless radioactive gas which miners inhaled, leading to internal exposures that substantially increased their long-term chances of developing lung cancer.

Viewing the masses as irredeemably tribal did not stop Xavier des Ligneris, the COMUF'S first director, from trying to emulate French radiation protection practices in Gabon. He thus treated radiation separately from other health and safety issues, and appointed a technician solely dedicated to radiation protection. Although he left the development of all other health and safety guidelines to his managers, des Ligneris personally wrote and signed those pertaining to gamma rays, radon, and dust, using French guidelines for maximum permissible limits (MPLs) of these contaminants.[36]

Safety guidelines notwithstanding, the dosimetric film badges that workers wore to track their exposure to gamma radiation kept recording exposures in excess of the MPLs. At first, French supervisors attributed these excesses to African ignorance. They issued repeated directives instructing workers in the proper use of films and threatening sanctions for noncompliance.[37] Supervisors sought ways to "tighten surveillance," making approval of timecards dependent on workers' returning dosimetric films correctly.[38] The hierarchies of modern danger mapped neatly onto this (barely) postcolonial situation: paternalism and authority were now sanctioned by dispassionate rationality. The complexity of the technology, and the dangers it involved, conjugated colonial power into modern industrial discipline.

Enforcing correct procedures, however, did not automatically control gamma exposures.[39] Once underground mining started, radon releases added to the danger. The average concentrations of radon in the stopes regularly exceeded the MPLs—sometimes by a factor of twelve.[40] Many employees consistently exceeded their annual exposure limits. Nor could high radon exposures be attributed to African incompetence. For one thing, radon levels were measured with instruments deployed in the shafts rather than on workers' bodies; good results thus did not depend on individuals' wearing instruments correctly. For another, European employees also charted high readings.[41] All the surveillance in the world could not stop the inexorable course of radioactive decay in the stopes.

At first, des Ligneris sought to manage the situation through job rotation, a practice common in other nuclear workplaces. Employees worked in high-level shafts until they reached (or exceeded) their annual limit, then moved to workplaces with lower radiation levels. In one notoriously high-grade French uranium mine, gamma levels were so high that individuals could only work there for four hours every two weeks (Paucard 1996). The Mounana mine ran on a tighter budget, however, and by 1967 production had fallen well behind schedule.[42] As the mine got deeper and radiation levels increased, management feared it would run out of skilled workers. Continually hiring new personnel offered one solution, since new hires were assumed to be radiation virgins. But the time and effort of training new workers canceled out the exposure benefits from labor turnover.[43] Finally, des Ligneris decided to upgrade the ventilation system—a costly solution, but one that worked to decrease radon levels, at least temporarily.

In the meantime, however, corporate headquarters called for a change in leadership at Mounana. Mokta, the CEA's corporate partner in the COMUF, had expressed displeasure with des Ligneris's direction for some time. It wanted someone less concerned with the nuclear dimensions of his work, and better attuned to the bottom line. In mid-1968, Mokta sent one of its own to replace him: Christian Guizol.[44]

Gabonese employees remembered Guizol as a hard, uncompromising man. His "severity" prompted complaints that "it's South Africa at Mounana, blacks at the bottom and whites on top."[45] When gamma exposures climbed back up in late 1968, Guizol—deeming his predecessor soft on discipline—blamed the workers for not wearing films correctly. He tightened disciplinary and surveillance measures around film use, and placed test dosimeters in the shafts to compare with the ones worn by workers. Test results matched worker badges, however, and radon levels climbed back up. In November 1969, seventy-eight workers registered overexposure.[46]

So Guizol reconfigured the calculus of exposure. He had noticed that the ILO's radon guidelines, which used a different formula to calculate total exposure, ended up being less restrictive than the French guidelines used by the COMUF. After a few numerical gymnastics, Guizol wrote a report that justified the equivalent of a threefold increase in radon MPLs and aligned these with ILO guidelines. The new maximum permissible levels, Guizol remarked bluntly, were "more advantageous" to the company.[47] And their effect was immediate. As of March 1970, not a single worker registered exposures over the new MPLs.[48]

The Gabonese state had no independent expertise in the matter. Besides, it had supported the COMUF in quelling strikes and recruiting labor. So who would object to the change in standards?[49] This particular danger of modernization had been normalized to the point of invisibility.

The state may not have questioned the company's practices, but at least one COMUF worker did. Not long before Guizol raised the MPLs, Marcel Lekonaguia began to express unease about his working conditions. Hired shortly after the mine opened, by the mid-1960s Lekonaguia had risen to the post of shift boss in the shafts, where he took charge of blasting. Company guidelines specified that workers should wait fifteen minutes after a blast before returning to the workplace.[50] Lekonaguia probably did not know that French radiation protection guidelines specified a waiting period of at least thirty minutes, to let the dust settle and to give the ventilation system time to evacuate the extra radon released by blasting rocks apart. What he did know, all too well, was that "after the blast, there's a lot of dust. . . . It's the dust that wasted us. . . . You swallow it, you breathe it." Protective gear did not help: "Those little masks, they didn't hold up well. They're made of paper. . . . If it gets a little wet—paf!" The mask would dissolve. That, he insisted, was how he developed the ailments that would plague him for the rest of his life.

Lekonaguia also wondered about the films—especially given the tight discipline that they incarnated. "They said this film here, you must always keep it. At the end of the month, they check them, they send them to see if the men reached [the limit]. The results, they don't give them to [the] people."[51] All he ever learned was whether he had reached some threshold that prompted job rotation. He never found out what the numbers were, how close to the limit he had come, how much he had accumulated over time, or even what the limit meant. What, he wondered, was all the secrecy about?

His brother, Dominique Oyingha, became convinced that the company—and its doctor, Jean-Claude Andrault—were hiding something. And the state was in on it. "Uranium caused many deaths, but the COMUF didn't want to recognize that," Oyingha told me. "Nor did the state, because this was the big company of the territory, whose secrets couldn't come out . . . so as not to scare the workers."[52] Only independent, external expertise could be trusted. Oyingha took his brother to the Congo for tests. He knew there had once been a uranium mine there, and hoped Congolese doctors might help. Apparently the doctors immediately guessed from Lekonaguia's health condition that he worked at the COMUF.

The two men returned to Mounana and confronted Andrault. The mine doctor scoffed: "Are you crazy? . . . Who told you that uranium made people sick?" Oyingha laughed as he remembered this response. He respected the doctor for the hospital he had set up, which offered free medical care to everyone in the region. That was precious beyond measure. But everyone had their limits, and Oyingha did not expect the doctor to acknowledge the possibility of occupational disease. He threatened Andrault:

> I said, "My friend, you are my friend, we have known each other for a good bit of time, but let me tell you that the sickness that my brother suffers from, it comes from uranium. And if you don't want the news to spread . . . [so that] your workers don't become afraid, take proper care of my big brother. If he dies, I'm coming after you."[53]

The COMUF granted Lekonaguia sick leave. But he wanted permanent leave and compensation. The company refused, insisting that Lekonaguia return underground if he wanted to draw his paycheck. In 1970, the two brothers filed a complaint with the state social security office in Libreville. This produced only a perfunctory inquiry, after which the company agreed to move Lekonaguia to a surface job in the open pit.[54]

Undeterred, Lekonaguia asked for his medical file. Andrault refused, citing professional secrecy. No surprise there: "The doctor, he's just a lawyer for the COMUF." The more the COMUF resisted, the more Lekonaguia and his family became convinced that his illnesses were work-related. Over the course of the 1970s and 1980s, more and more people from the region went to France as students—sometimes even on training stints sponsored by the COMUF—where they witnessed anti-nuclear protests. Lekonaguia's nephew, among others, returned with confirmation that "this product that we're mining, it's a toxic product," Oyingha recalled.[55]

Finally, Lekonaguia decided that if COMUF managers kept rejecting his demands, he would rebuff theirs. He began refusing to turn in his film badges. He suspected that his diagnosis—along with the chain of causality that linked work to illness—could be read directly from the films. One day, he explained as he showed me one of the films, he would find someone else to read the results. Lekonaguia probably was not alone in this reasoning, though it is difficult to tell from the available evidence. By the mid-1980s, COMUF quarterly radiation protection reports routinely recorded the numbers of unreturned films—a statistic which had not appeared in earlier reports. Some months, over 25 percent of the films were not returned.[56] But disorder in the archives made it impossible for me to systematically document dust and radiation exposures over a sustained period. Indeed, I could not even determine whether full records still existed; if they did, they were either buried too deeply in the termite-ridden piles of files, or secured someplace where I did not gain access.

As for Marcel Lekonaguia, he eventually received a series of awards for long and loyal service to the company, presented to him at ceremonies such as the one that opened this chapter. At the end of one of our conversations, he changed into a pristine blue uniform adorned with these medals so that I could photograph him. He thus claimed his role in the spectacle of modernization. At the same time, however, he considered these decorations inadequate compensation for the hardship he had endured. The medals proved that he had played a part in the show, but they also highlighted the extent to which the claims made by modernization-as-spectacle remained unfulfilled. Medals did not contribute to livelihood, let alone wealth. A pickup truck, Lekonaguia suggested, might have constituted adequate compensation. Indeed, it is hard to imagine a more powerful material means of modernization than an independent, motorized source of mobility.

Natural Radiation or Radiated Nature?

As we have seen here, and as other chapters in this volume argue, understanding post-independence enthusiasm for modernization requires tracing continuities from the colonial period. Similarly, understanding modernization as a dynamic historical object—a "living archive," to use the phrase invoked by this volume's introduction—requires us to move past the immediate post-independence period. Some dimensions of modernization were slow to reveal themselves.

As time passed, area residents felt increasingly troubled by the mine's impact on themselves and their surroundings. In 1983, for example, villagers contacted the provincial governor to express concern about water pollution. The COMUF distributed drinking water to its company towns but not to other villages, which instead relied on the river for water. Alarming numbers of dead fish began to appear in the backwaters of the river. Residents worried "that their lives [were] in danger, because they often [got] serious intestinal and other diseases." They also complained that the medical care they received had "little value." In response, the state asked the company to redirect mine water further away from residential zones. "Almost a thousand people are struck by radioactivity," the memo concluded, adding that the "local dispensary should reinforce its monitoring" and deliver "more effective care."[57]

The company responded promptly, but it accepted only partial responsibility. Admitting that one of the more recently uranium deposits had been pumping water toward a certain village, the COMUF rechanneled the waste water toward the abandoned Mounana pit (closed in 1975). The company would clear brush away from the new pipes so that residents could see the change for themselves. Massango village, however, presented a more difficult problem. The company maintained that the dead trees were due "not only" to increased acidity in the water (caused by chemicals used in the treatment plant), but also to an overall increase in water level which had resulted from construction projects conducted by the Public Works Department. The state thus shared the blame.

The COMUF agreed to finance a project to bring potable water to Massango, but it categorically denied that radioactivity contributed to any of the problems. Radiation levels, it maintained, had been under "extreme surveillance since 1962, following international norms. All the tests are done in France." Omitting mention of the overexposures we've just examined, the company stated baldly, "There has never been any irradiation of COMUF workers, let alone village inhabitants." It vigorously defended its medical services. No epidemic in the region could be attributed to pollution. Half of the patients treated in the COMUF's hospital did not work for the company; the clinic conducted a huge number of exams and tests every day; and the medical service was committed to the "perpetual improvement" of its methods. Area residents were thus "highly medicalized."[58]

Management felt that the main motivation behind the complaints was to obtain potable running water. Area residents wanted at least some of the benefits of modernization, whether or not they worked for the COMUF. That responsibility belonged to the state, but company leadership realized that if they made "an effort on this point, we will certainly circumvent many of the complaints." They hoped that ongoing "development"—in the form of expanding basic services—would defuse local criticism.[59]

Yet some in top management clearly knew that there was cause for concern. In 1984, the company decided to develop a more technopolitically robust plan for waste disposal. The biggest puzzle concerned the disposal of "sterile" rock from mining (i.e., ore with insufficient uranium content) and liquid effluents from the yellowcake plant. These could be pumped into the depleted quarries, and from there liquid waste would empty out into the Mitembé and Lekedi rivers. But treating the waste before dumping it, as standard international practice dictated, was costly. The engineer sent to investigate the situation recommended that the company proceed in stages, "depending on the pressure exerted on COMUF."[60]

By 1986, some of Mounana's liquid effluents *were* being treated, but the process "was not very effective by normal criteria." This could become "embarrassing if precise questions arose concerning the results." A conventional tailings dam would provide an alternate remedy, but this would be "very expensive and awkward to build given the local topography and rainfall." Furthermore, a tailings dam would leave the COMUF with "heavy maintenance and surveillance obligations if Gabonese regulations eventually came close to those being implemented in Europe."[61] The company did eventually build such a dam in 1990, but without the surveillance apparatus. When I visited the site eight years later, I saw no warning signs around the tailings pond. Both the (French) associate director of the mine and the (Gabonese) operator who toured me around the plant assured me that children "just knew" to stay away.

In the meantime, COMUF headquarters commissioned a study of the "radiological state" of the site and its environs. The report, published in 1987, compared radon levels around the COMUF with those near uranium mines in France, and found that "in general [the COMUF was] well below the limit for the public of 3 pCi/l of additional radioactivity."[62] But the key to this optimistic assessment was the word "additional." French regulations (there were none in Gabon at this stage) limited the public's exposure to no more than three picocuries over background levels in a particular region. This meant that if the "natural level" of radon in an area was three picocuries, the total radon reading near mining activities should not exceed six picocuries. If the "natural level" was higher (say, five picocuries) then the total reading near mines could go up to eight picocuries. The assumption was that people could easily tolerate whatever radon levels they had been living with: regulation should merely limit how much additional exposure they received.

What if the "natural level" of radon was already high? Dominique Oyingha (and others) told me that people had long suffered strange diseases and early deaths in the region around Mounana—even before the arrival of the COMUF. Oyingha attributed this to the presence of uranium: learning about its health effects on miners made him suspect that it had always had a noxious effect on area residents. But anecdotal accounts of illness—whether in the past or in the present—held no scientific sway.

The 1987 radiological study, then, measured "excess" radon levels on COMUF property. In the COMUF offices and the cité des cadres (management housing), these remained relatively low. In Massango village and the cité for specialized technicians, however, levels were triple those at the offices. In cités for manual workers they were four and a half to thirteen times the office levels. But the study expressed no alarm: mill tailings always emitted low levels of radioactivity. Since they were "of natural origin," the study insisted, they were not significantly more harmful than unmined ore. As long as the mine avoided using tailings in "inappropriate" ways—"like for example . . . [in] the construction of dwellings without taking particular precautions"—everything would be fine.[63]

After the mine shut down in 1999, COMUF workers and area residents grew increasingly suspicious about their health status. Steady salaries no longer served to palliate pollution. Like people in other zones of industrial decline, their focus turned to the debris that mining had left on their land and in their bodies.

Inspired by reports of Aghirin'man, an NGO concerned with occupational and environmental illness in (still very active) Nigérien uranium mines, a group of Mounana residents formed the Collectif des anciens travailleurs miniers de Comuf (CATRAM) in 2005. The CATRAM demanded a health and environmental monitoring program and a fund to disburse medical compensation claims from Areva (the French nuclear fuel cycle corporation formed in 2001, which inherited responsibility for the COMUF).[64] Gabonese retained a powerful sense that their plight was not "like in France." Invoking "ethics, equity, and social justice," one member noted that Gabonese workers "did not, during their entire careers at the Mounana uranium mine, benefit from the attentive medical surveillance reserved for their expatriate colleagues. During their leaves in France, the latter systematically underwent hematology examinations and cancer screening."[65] By contrast, the absence of oncological infrastructures in Mounana meant that sick residents frequently did not even know whether they had cancer.[66] In any case, the absence of a tumor registry made it impossible to determine whether the region suffered from a statistical excess of cancer.

As Gabonese workers soon learned, however, screening had not immunized French expatriates from cancer itself. The same year the CATRAM formed in Gabon, former French COMUF workers and their families began to notice high rates of cancer in their midst. Expats were covered not by France's national social security system, but rather by a separate fund which covered everything *except* occupational illnesses. Those were supposed to be covered by Gabon's social security fund. But that fund required employees to file a claim within forty-eight hours of their diagnosis; it was thus way too late for former expatriates whose cancers were only appearing ten or more years after their return to France. Some of these expats formed their own association, and joined forces with the CATRAM, the Association Mounana, Aghirin'man, and two other French NGOs: Sherpa, a group of high-profile legal experts formed in 2001 to investigate human rights and environmental justice violations perpetrated by French companies, and the CRIIRAD, an independent laboratory created after the 1986 Chernobyl accident in order to develop nuclear expertise unbeholden to the French state. Together they sent a small team to Mounana in June 2006. The team took independent environmental readings and surveyed nearly five hundred former COMUF employees about their health and work experience. In 2007, they published the results of their investigations.[67]

Survey responses echoed narratives I heard from Lekonaguia, Oyingha, and other Gabonese in 1998. The vast majority reported no formal training on radiation or radon-related risks; at best, they learned about risks via word of mouth from other workers. Employees were not required to wear protective gear, and all work clothing was washed at home. "We were so unaware of the risks that we smoked and ate at the workplace, and since we never wore protective gloves, we ate and inhaled whatever was on our hands and in the air, [including] after maintenance operation[s] that left yellowcake powder suspended in the air."[68] Employees did not receive reports of their radiation exposures. Everyone agreed that the Gabonese state had done nothing to monitor working conditions or occupational health. One former medical doctor testified that company clinicians had no training in uranium-related occupational health, and that the company's radiation protection division consistently refused to transmit dosimetric readings to the medical division.

The 2007 report also addressed environmental contamination. It estimated that the COMUF had generated around seven and a half million tons of waste. The company had dumped some directly into the river, buried some in the old Mounana pit and some in the ground around the site under a light layer of dirt, and (after 1990) stored the rest in its tailings pond. Gabon had received thirty-five million euros from the European Union to rehabilitate the site in a program scheduled to run from 2004 to 2010. "One wonders about the quality of these efforts," the report noted with dismay, given that remediation plans consisted only of covering contaminated zones with vegetation. According to the CRIIRAD, this constituted a short-term solution at best; only outright removal of contaminated soil would produce "definitive rehabilitation."[69]

Most alarming of all were the radiation readings found in the community. The housing developments, the maternity ward, the Massango school, and other public buildings—touted by the company and the state as motors of modernization—had been built using "sterile" rock from the mine tailings. A fatal flaw of the 1987 study suddenly became clear: that study had only measured levels on the *streets* of the cités. In 2007, it became clear that *inside* the houses, radiation and radon levels could reach eight times the internationally sanctioned maximum. Mounana residents thus learned that the price of modernization extended far beyond the dangers of the workplace.[70]

Conclusion

By the late 1970s, the COMUF and the Gabonese state had jointly produced a script for modernization in the Haut-Ogooué. In this scenario, uranium mining would turn Gabonese workers into modern citizens who lived in concrete houses equipped with electricity and running water. They would travel to obtain medical care along paved roads. Their once-remote province would be linked to the capital by railroad (which would also serve to convey the uranium they produced to the coast for export). They would be disciplined workers who understood the ordinary dangers of industrial labor and who trusted their employers to manage these risks appropriately. The political outcome claimed by the script was Gabonization, and spectacles that put the script on display gave the state, and its president in particular, the starring role of the big man: Yaya Bongo.

Workers may have appreciated some of the material products with which this script was enacted. This did not mean, however, that they passively accepted workplace risks as the price of increased material comfort. Fatal accidents, such as the one in 1965, caused some men to quit mine work altogether. Others responded with spontaneous work stoppages, actions that did not conform to the parameters set by the state-sanctioned labor union and that prompted the use of the state police. These tragic deaths and the dramas that followed them overshadowed modernization's triumphalist spectacle.

The spectacle's most insidious betrayal, however, would not become fully manifest until after the mine had closed down. Throughout the lifetime of the mine, the risk posed by radiation had largely remained invisible to workers. They inferred the presence of danger from film badges, job rotation, and rumors. But radiation exposure was not like falling rocks or floods. Decades passed before the houses and bodies of uranium workers—"living archives" of radiation—could testify to deadly modernization.

Notes

1. The material in this chapter is adapted from Gabrielle Hecht, *Being Nuclear: Africans and the Global Uranium Trade* (MIT Press and Wits University Press, 2012) and used with permission.

2. *COMUF Panorama* (avril-mai-juin 1982), n° 30. All translations are mine.

3. On modernity as a political claim, see Thomas (2011); Ferguson (2006).

4. CEA/DP/DREM, Groupement Afrique-Madagascar, "Notice d'Information destinée aux Européens susceptibles de partir pour l'Afrique ou Madagascar" (1 February 1963), 2, Cogéma archives, Bessines, France. Henceforth cited as "Notice."

5. Ibid., 22. Although technological sophistication had long served Europeans as a measure of civilization and a justification for colonial rule, concrete attempts to use technical education as a form of uplift belonged to the late colonial/decolonizing era; see Adas (1989); Cooper (1996); Cooper and Packard (1997).

6. "Notice," 14.

7. Ibid., 11.

8. Xavier des Ligneris, sm n. 27, 9 January 1961, Directeur des Exploitations à M. le Directeur Général, "Effectifs—logements—budget 1961," 1. Unless otherwise noted, this and all subsequent archival documents were found in the COMUF archives in Mounana, to which I obtained access in 1998. These archives consisted of several rooms of unfiled and uncategorized documents, spanning the company's activities from 1957 to 1998. After the mine shut down in 1999, some of the documents were moved to France, where they were folded into the archives of Areva, the company that took over the nuclear fuel cycle. It appears that these are no longer accessible to researchers.

9. Ibid.

10. Ibid.

11. UF/JC/JF, "Dispositions prises au passage de M. Guizol les 29 et 30 juillet 1969," 1 August 1969. See also CG/mc, n° 0577/70, "Compte-rendu fait par M. de Courlon de nos entretiens du 28 Juillet 1970—Programme quadriennal 1970–1974 du 21.7.70," 20 August 1970.

12. COMUF, "Plan de decennal," 21 June 1971, JC/JL.W/DT; JC/JF, "Conséquences financières d'une réduction d'activité de Mounana," 11 June 1970. COMUF, LC/JM, "Développement du marché de l'uranium," 12 December 1973.

13. This sum was partly pure investment, and partly an advance. COMUF, "Plan quinquennal 1975–1979," 31 May 1974.

14. "Etudes effectifs," 1960–1970.

15. Lucien Gabillat, "Etude," 13 March 1962. See also Bodu (1994).

16. The core of Gabonization was an increasingly formalized "professional training" program, officially beginning in 1964 with a training program for plant workers. In 1965, miners joined the program, and in 1968 a literacy program was added. By 1973, 140 men had passed through the plant program, 468 through the mining program, and 337 through the literacy program.

17. "Rapport du service social," 1962–1963; "Rapport d'activités, service social," 1967.

18. Interview with M. Malhaby, Mounana, 29 July 1998. All interviews by the author.

19. Progress was steady but slow. Gabonese did not fill half of all "cadres" posts until 1982, and even then there were still twice as many expatriates as Gabonese in the "cadre supérieur" category. Christophe Lindzondo, "Une approche du contrat social de la COMUF," rapport de stage, 1984.

20. COMUF, *Budgets* and *Rapports d'Activité*, 1965–1975. M. Harel to M. le secrétaire d'état auprès du premier ministre chargé des participations, des relations avec les établissements publics et sociétés d'état, 26 May 1975.

21. Examples in "Note de service à MM. les responsables du marché," 8 April 1963; "Note d'information à tous les Agents," 19 February 1964; "Note de service n. 49 à MM: les adhérents et invités du Cercle des Employés," 27 May 1964; "Rapport d'activités, Service Social," 1967.

22. Interview with Juste Mambangui, Mounana, 13 and 16 July 1998.

23. Telex correspondence from H. Basset to Peccia-Galletto, 1975; "Grève des 3–4 Janvier 1975, céroulement des faits," 13 January 1975.

24. Xavier des Ligneris to M. le Président, memo, "Accident chambre 5," 18 December 1965.

25. Xavier des Ligneris to M. le Président, memo, "Suites de l'accident du 17 Décembre 1965," 27 December 1965.

26. Interview with Zacharye Bondji and Ignace Bissikou, Mounana, 16 July 1998.

27. des Ligneris, "Suites de l'accident du 17 Décembre 1965."

28. Ibid.

29. Interview with Mambangui. Note that the COMUF did in fact offer a substantial cash settlement to the parents of the two men who had died.

30. des Ligneris, "Suites de l'accident du 17 Décembre 1965."

31. Ibid.

32. Xavier des Ligneris to M. le Président, memo, 12 December 1966, "Situation du personnel ouvrier de la mine."

33. Xavier des Ligneris to M. le Président, memo, 18 February 1966, "Effectif mine"; Jacques Peccia-Galleto to M. le Directeur des Exploitations, 16 February 1966; Xavier des Ligneris to Jacques Peccia-Galleto, 24 Feburary 1966, BG/AP n. 1549.

34. "Avis Radio," March 1966.

35. Ibid.

36. Xavier des Ligneris to Secrétaire Général, 8 July 1961; Xavier des Ligneris, "Consignes relatives à la protection contre les dangers dus à la radioactivité," Mounana, 5 May 1961; approuvé par le Directeur des Mines du Gabon, Libreville, 1 June 1961.

37. Pierre le Fur, Note de Service 072bis, 3 September 1964; Xavier des Ligneris, "Rapport—contrôle des radiations," HR/AP n° 2076, 5 January 1968.

38. Henri Pello, Service Exploitation, Note d'organisation, "Stockage et distribution des film detecteurs de radioactivité," 26 September 1966.

39. des Ligneris, "Rapport—contrôle des radiations."

40. Ibid.; Xavier des Ligneris, "Rapport—sur le contrôle des risques radioactifs: Février 1968," YT/AP n° 2169, 21 March 1968.

41. des Ligneris, "Rapport—sur le contrôle des risques radioactifs: Février 1968"; Xavier des Ligneris, "Rapport sur le contrôle des risques radioactifs. Mois de Mai 1968," YT/LR n° 2275, 20 June 1968.

42. J. de Courlon to X. des Ligneris, 10 March 1967.

43. Ibid.

44. Paucard (1992); interview with Christian Guizol, 26 February 1998, Paris.

45. Interviews with Juste Mambangui and J.-M. Malékou, Mounana, 16 July 1998; François Mambangui, Libreville, 31 July 1998.

46. Ch. Guizol, "Rapport sur le contrôle des risques radioactifs: Mois de Décembre 1969," YT/sc n° 0118/70, 9 February 1970.

47. Ibid.

48. Ibid.

49. I found no archival evidence that Gabonese state officials ever inspected radiation, radon, or dust in the mines, but this absence is necessarily inconclusive.

50. COMUF, "Consigne pour la distribution et l'emploi des explosifs," Exploitation de Mounana, n.d., ca. 1959.

51. Interview with Marcel Lekonaguia, Mounana, 21 July 1998.

52. Interview with Dominique Oyingha, Mounana, 17 July 1998.

53. Ibid.

54. Christian Guizol to Directeur Général de la Caisse Gabonaise de la Prévoyance Sociale, 19 October 1970, Objet: Allocations familiales de M. Lekonaguia Marcel; Christian Guizol to

Directeur Général de la Caisse Gabonaise de la Prévoyance Sociale, 26 October 1970, Objet: Monsieur Lekonaguia; J. C. Andrault to Docteur C. Gantin, 27 October 1970.

55. Interview with Oyingha.

56. COMUF, "Rapport trimestrielle [*sic*] radioprotection," October-November-December 1984, Mounana; "Rapport Trimestriel Radioprotection," April-May-June 1986.

57. Martin Magnana (gouverneur de la province du Haut-Ogooué) to directeur général de la COMUF, 11 April 1983, n. 231 PHO/CAB and note de renseignements n. 15, 7 April 1983.

58. COMUF, Direction Générale Adjointe Technique, PT/MJM, 29 April 1983, "Compte-rendu de la reunion de travail du 25.04.83."

59. Ibid.

60. V. Jug to J. Moine, 29 May 1986. Also V. Jug, "Dispositions prévues en vue de la protection de l'environnement," 25 March 1985; and VJ/MJM, "Traitement des eaux d'exhaure mines" and "Etapes de mise en place du traitement des effluents usine," 25 March 1985.

61. V. Jug to J. Moine, 28 May 1986.

62. UF/DT-n. 29-VJ/JM, V. Jug to H. Basset, 9 March 1987, Objet: COMUF/État radiologique site de Mounana.

63. N. Fourcade and M. C. Robe, "Synthèse des résultats de mesures de concentration en radon 222 sur le site de Mounana, de 1984 à 1985: Comparaison du site de Mounana avec des site français," rapport n. 4, COM/002 (2), 23 Feburary 1987, CEA, IPSN, Laboratoire de Recherche sur la Protection des Mines, 16.

64. Jules Mbombe Samaki, "Memorandum sur la nécessité de la prise en compte de la Veille sanitaire et du dédommagement des anciens travailleurs miniers," Libreville, 25 April 2005 (private communication). See also reports in the Gabonese press: "Le Collectif des anciens travailleurs miniers interpelle la Comuf," *L'union*, 3 February 2006; and "Les anciens travailleurs miniers de la Comuf réunis en collectif," *L'union*, 17 February 2006.

65. Samaki, "Memorandum."

66. For a discussion of cancer in Africa, see Livingston (2012).

67. Samira Daoud and Jean-Pierre Getti, "Areva au Gabon: Rapport d'enquête sur la situation des travailleurs de la COMUF, filiale gabonaise du groupe Areva-Cogéma," Sherpa, 4 April 2007.

68. Ibid., 7.

69. Ibid., 11–12.

70. The aftermath of this discovery, which I lack the space to discuss here, is explored in Hecht (2012).

References

Adas, Michael. 1989. *Machines as the Measure of Men: Science, Technology, and Ideologies of Western Dominance*. Ithaca, NY: Cornell University Press.

Bodu, Robert. 1994. *Les secrets des cuves d'attaque: 40 ans de traitement des minerais d'uranium*. Paris: Cogéma.

Cooper, Frederick. 1996. *Decolonization and African Society: The Labor Question in French and British Africa*. Cambridge: Cambridge University Press.

Cooper, Frederick, and Randall M. Packard, eds. 1997. *International Development and the Social Sciences: Essays on the History and Politics of Knowledge*. Berkeley: University of California Press.

Ferguson, James. 2006. *Global Shadows: Africa in the Neoliberal World Order*. Durham, NC: Duke University Press.

Foccart, Jacques. 1997–2001. *Journal de l'Elysée*. 5 vols. Paris: Fayard & Jeune Afrique.

Hecht, Gabrielle. 2012. *Being Nuclear: Africans and the Global Uranium Trade*. Cambridge, MA: MIT Press and Wits University Press.

Larkin, Brian. 2008. *Signal and Noise: Media, Infrastructure and Urban Culture in Nigeria*. Durham, NC: Duke University Press.

Livingston, Julie. 2012. *Improvising Medicine: An African Oncology Ward in an Emerging Cancer Epidemic*. Durham, NC: Duke University Press.

Mauger, Delphine. 2003. "Building the *Gabon Nouveau*: Technology and the Construction of the Bongo-State, 1973–1986," unpublished seminar paper, University of Michigan.

Ndong, Robert Edgar. 2009. "Les multinationales extractives au Gabon: Le cas de la compagnie des mines d'uranium de Franceville (COMUF), 1961–2003." PhD diss., Université Lumière-Lyon II.

Ngolet, François. 2000. "Ideological Manipulations and Political Longevity: The Power of Omar Bongo in Gabon since 1967." *African Studies Review* 43, no. 2: 55–71.

Nye, David. E. 1996. *American Technological Sublime*. Cambridge, MA: MIT Press

Obiang, Jean-François. 2007. *France-Gabon: Pratiques clientélaires et logiques d'état dans les relations franco-africaines*. Paris: Karthala.

Paucard, Antoine. 1992. *La mine et les mineurs de l'uranium français*. 3 vols. Paris: Editions Thierry Parquet.

Thomas, Lynn M. 2011. "Modernity's Failings, Political Claims, and Intermediate Concepts." *American Historical Review* 116, no. 3: 727–740.

Verschave, François-Xavier. 1998. *La Françafrique: Le plus long scandale de la République*. Paris: Stock.

Yates, Douglas. 1996. *The Rentier State in Africa: Oil-Rent Dependency and Neo-Colonialism in the Republic of Gabon*. Trenton, NJ: Africa World Press.

PART FOUR

Institutional Training in Nkrumah's Ghana

10 Modeling Modernity

The Brief Story of Kwame Nkrumah, a Nazi Pilot Named Hanna, and the Wonders of Motorless Flight

Jean Allman

On 18 May 1963, a ceremony of much international pomp and spectacle took place near the small village of Afienya, about fifteen kilometers from Accra, the capital of Ghana.[1] The ceremony marked the opening of the newly independent nation's first gliding school. In attendance were members of the international press corps, German and Ghanaian dignitaries, ambassadors from most of the foreign missions in Ghana, chiefs and their advisors, and representatives from the Young Pioneers, the ruling Convention People's Party's youth group. The German Ambassador, on behalf of the West German government, presented a glider, christened Akroma [the hawk], to President Kwame Nkrumah, who, in turn, "dedicated the glider to the youth of Ghana and wished all those who would fly in it 'many hours of enjoyment, recreation and spiritual upliftment.'"[2] As a Ghana newsreel reported live, spectators were then treated to a "magnificent aerobatic display" by the woman responsible for the establishment of the school, "that famous German airpilot Flight Captain Hanna Reitsch." After she landed, Reitsch was congratulated by Nkrumah and his wife, Madame Fathia. "With the establishment of a national gliding school," the newsreel continued, "one can be sure that the youth will pick up the challenge and head for the sky."[3]

What the newscaster that day failed to mention, and a subject, in fact, which was never broached in Ghana's media during the entire history of the school, was that its founder and director—Flight Captain Hanna Reitsch—was not simply an extraordinary woman pilot in a profession dominated by men. In the post–World War II era, what Reitsch was most known for were her very close connections to Adolf Hitler. Perhaps most famously, in the last days of the war Reitsch undertook a dramatic flight into Berlin, landing with Colonel-General Ritter von Greim near the Brandenburg Gate under heavy Soviet Army fire. Reitsch spent two days in the Führer's famous bunker and was one of the last to leave alive. Hers was the last German plane to fly out of Berlin in the final days of the war. Shortly thereafter, both she and von Greim were captured by Allied forces. Reitsch was held and interrogated by U.S. military intelligence for eighteen months. Von Greim committed suicide.[4]

As most scholars are aware, the "work" of nation-building and modernization in Nkrumah's newly independent state was often undertaken with the assistance of expatriates with specialized skills from a range of places and political persuasions—African freedom fighters, white South African communists, Irish nationalists, Russian guards, Chinese architects, French peace activists, Caribbean Pan-Africanists. These were people who shared at least some part or parts of Nkrumah's nationalist and Pan-Africanist dream. But how do we fit Hanna Reitsch onto this list? What might it mean that lofty dreams of youth, flight, and modernization in what was known as the "Black Star of Africa" were inextricably tied to someone who is remembered by many to this very day as an unrepentant Nazi, an "apologist for the Third Reich" (Rieger 2008, 383)?

From her initial visit in March of that year until Nkrumah was overthrown in a military coup in February 1966, Hanna Reitsch and the Afienya Flight School featured prominently in the Ghanaian press. In profound and perhaps unexpected ways—given its small size and comparatively limited resources (especially compared to the Akosombo Dam; see Miescher, this volume)—the school became absolutely central to Nkrumah's vision and articulation of modernization in the era of the First Republic (1960–1966). Based upon Reitsch's memoir, her private papers on deposit at the Deutsches Museum in Munich, local newspaper accounts, and the correspondence of many of her contemporaries (including Nkrumah), this chapter explores the role of Reitsch and her Flight School in animating Ghana's nation-building and modernization initiatives during the First Republic. What did Nkrumah see in ace pilot Hanna Reitsch and what promise did the art of motorless flight hold for a newly independent African state?

The Story of Afienya in Brief

Nkrumah first learned of Hanna Reitsch through independent India's first prime minister, Jawaharlal Nehru, under whose patronage Reitsch had set up a gliding school in Delhi in 1959. In a letter dated 8 January 1962, Nkrumah invited Reitsch to Accra to meet with him in order to consider the possibility of establishing a similar flight school in Ghana (Reitsch 1968, 15).[5] There had been a "gliding club" near Afienya since colonial times, but its membership was made up entirely of British officers and other Europeans, who would spend leisurely weekends soaring above the Shai Hills. The club had never trained a single Ghanaian student. Reitsch arrived in Ghana in March to much fanfare, with the daily papers carefully covering the visit. The *Graphic*'s story was headlined, "Hanna Reitsch, the Woman who Dares the Heavens," and included a brief biography that noted her "carrying out [of] dangerous test flights" during the war and the fact that she had been awarded the "highest German decoration." The article then moved quickly on to the reason for her visit to Ghana. "Anyone who has heard of Hanna Reitsch," the reporter assured her readers, "would expect her to be tall and perhaps masculine in build. But she is only a small woman, hardly above five feet and feminine in every way."[6]

During her visit in March, Reitsch met with Nkrumah on several occasions, as well as with members of Parliament, the commander of the Ghanaian Air Force, the head of the Young Pioneers, and members of the Accra Gliding Club, and began planning for the opening of a flight school on the site in Afienya where the club operated. After three weeks, she flew back to Germany, but with the intent of returning to Ghana in a few months when the construction of the school would be complete.

Those months eventually extended to nearly a year, as the English head of the old Gliding Club and others apparently worked to undermine Reitsch's plans in her absence. But by February 1963, Reitsch was back in Ghana and work was proceeding apace at Afienya on buildings for instruction, eating, accommodation, carpentry, and mechanics.[7] Plans were also underway for a new hangar and Reitsch had succeeded in establishing the Ghana National Aero Club, so that Ghana could affiliate with the International Flyer Association.[8] Minister of Defense Kofi Baako became the chair of the club, and the ministers of education and transport became vice-chairs. Also on the club's Executive Committee were the leader of the Young Pioneers and the head of the Air Force (Reitsch 1968, 40–41).

Although she daily supervised the work at Afienya, Reitsch did not stay there. She was accommodated, at government expense, in what was known as "Asante House" in Accra—the rather infamous palatial residence built by Krobo Edusei, the former government minister whose extravagances had led to his dismissal.[9] From there, she made the drive each day to the school site in a red Volkswagen Karmann Ghia lent to her by Nkrumah's wife, Fathia (Reitsch 1968, 41–43). In addition to supervising construction, Reitsch gave lectures throughout the capital, speaking before Parliament, at the university, and before youth groups and women's organizations as part of a recruitment drive. Finally, on 18 May 1963, though construction was not yet complete, the school was officially opened at the ceremony with which this chapter began. As Reitsch (1968, 47) recalled in her memoir, "anyone who was anyone showed up."

Over the next three years, the school's achievements were chronicled in the papers (often on the front page or with a center spread and multiple photos), from construction of the new hangar, to passing-out ceremonies, to the visits of various foreign dignitaries.[10] By the time of the school's first anniversary in May 1964, much had been accomplished. The school was training future flight instructors, as well as flight students, and had established a program with the Ghana Air Force to train officer cadets (Reitsch 1968, 82). In fact, at the first-anniversary celebration, the school coordinated with the Ghana Air Force in presenting a quite elaborate air show that featured gliders, as well as planes and jets, which flew into the program site from the international airport in Accra. Reitsch (1968, 113) described a scene in which "everyone—the president, the fifteen tribal chiefs with their entourages, the ministers and officers, old and young, rich and poor—was enthusiastic and proud of what they saw accomplished in large part by their own pilots."[11] It was at this first anniversary that Nkrumah provided the school with its motto: "To dare, to do, to serve."[12] It was clear to everyone, Reitsch (1968, 113) remembered, that the gliding school was Nkrumah's "pet project." The press, at the time, would certainly have agreed. A *Times* staff reporter wrote shortly after the anniversary celebration that "surely no institution in Ghana today deserves praise for its wonderful achievement and its unparalleled capability to infuse the spirit of adventure more into our youth than the National Gliding school at Afienya near Tema. . . . The credit goes to Osagyefo Dr. Kwame Nkrumah whose foresight gave birth to the school."[13]

Not all of Reitsch's energies were focused on gliding itself. Very early on, she came to the realization that many students were not particularly enamored with the idea or experience of flight. In response, she turned her attention to model building, which became a core component of the school's mission. Initially, model kits were imported from Germany, but by 1965, kits were being made locally and the building of model gliders was fully incorporated into the curriculum (Reitsch 1968, 64–65, 132–35, 159–60, 201). In addition, the school began conducting model-building workshops for other schools, beginning with Achimota and then Tema Secondary, and moving on from there (Reitsch 1968, 61, 132). The idea behind this effort was that eventually students would be able to instruct in model-making themselves and introduce, in turn, "their future student pilots to the theoretical physics of flight as well as to its application in practice by flying models" (Reitsch 1968, 136). By the beginning of 1966, model making was initiated at ten secondary schools, and an additional twenty schools were to be added in March 1966. "As far as I know," Reitsch wrote, "Ghana was unmatched in this respect by any other country in the world. . . . We hoped that in three to four years all secondary schools as well as all middle schools in Ghana would be offering model making" (Reitsch 1968, 201).

In addition to model making, Reitsch sought to make meteorology a central component of the curriculum at Afienya and to establish a meteorological observation station. She arranged for lectures to be provided to students and, through the head of the German Culture Ministry, for a Ghanaian meteorologist to study the meteorology of gliding in Germany. After attending the world gliding championships in England, a Ghanaian meteorologist did proceed to Munich in the spring of 1965 to study at the German Experimental Institute for Aviation and Space Flight. According to Reitsch's plan, once the meteorologist returned to Ghana, he would be responsible for establishing a new weather observation station at Afienya. But even before his return, Reitsch moved forward with her plans, borrowing some basic meteorological instruments from Ghana's head of meteorology and initiating training of the students herself.[14] Reporting on the plans for the Meteorological Observatory in February 1965, the *Ghanaian Times* predicted, "Much more will be done by the Gliding School as the years go by and what [it] . . . has achieved during this comparatively short period of its existence [can] be attributed to F/Capt. Hanna Reitsch, the Principal, an energetic tutor."[15]

Indeed, by 1965, the Afienya Gliding School was very much a public centerpiece of Nkrumah's modernization efforts, second only to the ongoing construction of the Akosombo Dam, with which it vied for headlines in the daily papers. The school increasingly coordinated with the Air Force, not only in model-building, meteorology, and the training of air cadets, but in fairly grand spectacles of flight performed for a "spellbound" public.[16] In October 1964, the school and the Air Force put on a display in honor of Air Force Day.[17] Several months later, in March 1965, Ghana's first air show took place at the International Airport in Accra. It was a massive display, whose aim, according to Reitsch, was to

> familiarise the population with aviation and awaken young people's interest in it. Moreover, it should strengthen the Ghanaians' self-confidence—they all had reason to be proud of what they'd already achieved through hard work in the few years since their independence. Not least of all, it was a welcome opportunity for the Air Force, as well as for the Gliding School, to reinforce and intensify pilot training and thus, too, to enhance their achievements. (Reitsch 1968, 152–53)

The display was widely and extensively covered in the press on the following Monday, with one of the highlights being the "breath-taking aerobatics" of Reitsch in the presidential glider, Akroma.[18] As the *Evening News* reported,

> Except Miss Hannah Reitch [*sic*] of the National Gliding School and Mr. Fritz Bosch, world champion of radio guided modeling, who gave special demonstration in that event, all the participants were Ghanaian youth trained and qualified.
>
> It was in fact a display of dexterity and bravery, mental poise and alertness, balance and mature nerves, and high intelligence and youthful zest and vitality.[19]

But Afienya was not only a part of Nkrumah's nation-building project. By 1965, the Gliding School was increasingly envisioned as part of his Pan-African agenda for African unity, for a United States of Africa. "Since our school had . . . become the 'pride of Ghana,'" Reitsch (1968, 161) recalled, "the President had announced in 1965 that a tour of the school was to be part of every official state visit from then on."[20] In addition, as early as March of 1965, plans were underway to organize a youth camp at Afienya to coincide with the Organization of African Unity Summit in October. Reitsch (1968, 164) explained that her plan was for youth leaders from throughout the continent to have the "opportunity to experience gliding for themselves, as well as to try out model-making." She herself attended the opening of the OAU and in her memoir wrote of the profound impact of that experience:

> Deeply impressed, the words of Dr. DuBois, the great Pan-African fighter who died in Accra in 1963, came to me as I drove home after the ceremony. He once wrote: "There can be no doubt that Kwame Nkrumah is, more than anyone alive at present, the voice of Africa. He expresses the thoughts and ideals of the Dark Continent and makes it clear to everyone that this continent will move into the frontlines of world events."[21]

During the summit, several visiting dignitaries did visit Reitsch's school, and an air display, again combining the efforts of the Afienya school and the Air Force, was performed in connection with the conference on 24 October.[22] As the *Ghanaian Times* reported, however, most of the leaders were unable to attend the air show, "as they were busy at a meeting affecting the bright future of Africa."[23] Participation by youth leaders at the Afienya-based jamboree was also not what Reitsch had hoped; representatives from Egypt, Mali, the Congo, and Sudan attended, but others, she suspected, were deterred by the travel costs. Still, Reitsch (1968, 165) considered the events of October a "start" and plans were put in place for an "African gliding and model making jamboree . . . to take place . . . every year for two to three weeks."

With the close of 1965, the school's achievements continued to be heralded in the press. In November, two Ghanaian glider pilots established a Ghanaian record of four and a half hours of nonstop flight and three teachers-in-training had flown model planes to a height of 1,600 feet.[24] When Nkrumah visited the school in early December, the *Evening News* story pronounced, "Patriotic Able-Bodied Ghanaians: They Set Out with Wings as Eagles." Center-page coverage, with multiple photos, in the 4 December *Daily Graphic* provided shots of a new glider being assembled by students, Air Force pilots completing their training, and models being constructed.[25] In her memoir, Reitsch described the momentum she believed the school had achieved. Plans were well developed for model making to be introduced into all secondary and middle schools, so that all students would "learn to work nimbly with their hands. . . . They would learn endurance, precision, cleanliness and self-discipline" (Reitsch 1968, 201).[26] She had arranged for a physical education expert to visit the school weekly in order to introduce sports. The meteorological observation station was to move into operation. But all of these plans, as she wrote, "came to an end with the coup" on 24 February 1966 (Reitsch 1968, 165). The Afienya Gliding School was one of the first Convention People's

Party projects closed by the new military government—the National Liberation Council—in the wake of Nkrumah's overthrow. Shortly thereafter, Hanna Reitsch and her two German compatriots were deported and the old Accra Gliding Club members reoccupied the Afienya site.[27]

Why Hanna Reitsch and Why the Art of Motorless Flight?

So how does one make sense of this former Nazi aviatrix turned Pan-Africanist, this key player in the grand narrative of Ghanaian nation-building and modernization? Reitsch's memoir provides few clues. Indeed, for the contemporary reader, the memoir is quite unnerving as it moves seamlessly from quoting Du Bois and extolling Nkrumah's virtues, his foresight, and the promises of Pan-African unity to describing the "uncomplicated *joie de vivre* . . . and the simple naturalness of . . . Ghanaians" (Reitsch 1968, 16). Reitsch does write of a profound epiphany in her understanding of race or difference, as a result of her work in India and then Ghana, but it is an epiphany filtered through a modernizing and profoundly racist discourse about what is "natural," what is "lacking," and how "progress" can be achieved. "For me, the blacks had occupied a sphere that lay somewhere much lower than that of white men," she explains. "Earlier in my life, it would have never occurred to me to treat a black person as a friend or partner or to invite him into my parents' home." She describes a "feeling of guilt" seizing her. "Apart from an equivalent level of education and intelligence,"

> I encountered among these people values that we virtually no longer possess: reverence and kindness, humanity and true brotherliness, the capacity for religious experience, and deep faith. If you have the chance to discover this for yourself, your eyes will open with a shock and with humiliation. (Reitsch 1968, 29–30)

In an especially revealing section of her narrative, Reitsch describes her fondness for, and the great success of, one of her first flight students, Kwesi, an African American youth who had spent his first ten years in the United States. For Reitsch, it is Kwesi who "proves" that, given exposure to the forces of modernization and technology, anything is possible. Kwesi became an "instructive" example, in her words, who disproved the "beliefs" Europeans have. "The technology and civilization in the U.S., as well as the exposure to the people and their customs, bestowed upon [Kwesi] . . . qualities that we found lacking in the Ghanaians who came to us for instruction. Especially important are discipline, the ability to react quickly, technical know-how, and a sense of purpose." After only two weeks of instruction, Kwesi was "advanced enough" to venture out on his "first solo flight" (Reitsch 1968, 30–31).

Several times in her memoir Reitsch juxtaposes Ghanaian students' enthusiasm for model building with their profound fear of flying. She concludes that there was nothing in the way that Ghanaians were brought up that made them "consider it a worthwhile task to conquer their fear" (Reitsch 1968, 62). But Reitsch reports that she found hope in the fact that when students set about catching animals on the school grounds—a rabbit or a snake—"an unbelievable ambition awoke in them—it was the primary instinct of the hunter that they all had in them." It was that "instinct" Reitsch sought to cultivate with model building, as well as "stamina, diligence, dependability, and precision, to name only a few" (Reitsch 1968, 62–64). Indeed, model making would become the core component of the school's modernization efforts. Reitsch believed that Ghanaian children did not have adequate toys in their childhood and therefore did not begin to use their hands and their imaginations in their early years the way European children did. Requiring model building at all levels of education, from the primary to the secondary, she argued, "would help us skip over nearly an entire generation as a result of the progress made" (Reitsch 1968, 63–64).[28]

Several scholars have tried to make sense of Reitsch's efforts to model modernity in Ghana, though most of them are far more concerned with her role in German history, especially her flying exploits during the war and her days in Hitler's bunker, than with her four years in Ghana, which usually appear as a footnote to the main narrative of her life.[29] Some, like Dennis Piszkiewicz (1997, 125) in *From Nazi Test Pilot to Hitler's Bunker,* argue that Reitsch was drawn to Nkrumah by the same "pathology that led to her friendship with Hitler," in other words, she was drawn to "charismatic" and "authoritarian men." Others explain the Ghana years in terms of her effort to rebuild a reputation that had been severely damaged by her associations with the Nazis. As she opined in the postscript to her memoir, *The Sky My Kingdom:*

> The most difficult thing for me to bear has been the way my flight with Generaloberst Ritter von Greim . . . to Berlin, then completely encircled by the Russians was so misrepresented. The slurs continue to this day whenever my name appears in a newspaper. I was and still am, again and again, put into a political arena where I never belonged. . . . These so-called eyewitness reports ignore the fact that I had been picked for this mission because I was a pilot and a trusted friend, and instead call me "Hitler's girl-friend." (Reitsch 1958, 219–20)

Judy Lomax, for example, in her sympathetic portrayal, *Hanna Reitsch: Flying for the Fatherland,* describes a patriotic but naive Reitsch who inadvertently got caught up in a political world she didn't understand:

> Her vision of Nkrumah as a rejected and misunderstood saviour reinforced the belief that she was [a] . . . "quite unregenerate Nazi," and had fallen again under the spell of a dictator.
>
> It was, however, unfair to either compare Nkrumah with Hitler, or to suggest that Hanna had the same attitude to both. Her admiration for Nkrumah was perhaps as politically naïve as her acceptance of Hitler, but was based on

> a far closer acquaintance. Unwittingly, and as usual with the most sincere of motives, Hanna had again set herself on a political stage. (Lomax 1988, 180)

The most recent treatment of Reitsch, Bernhard Rieger's insightful 2008 article in *German History*, "Hanna Reitsch (1912–1979): The Global Career of a Nazi Celebrity," sets out to explain precisely how a woman with Reitsch's history in the Third Reich could go on to a successful global career during the height of decolonization and the Cold War. He finds his answers not only in Reitsch's ability to cultivate "an apparently apolitical public persona," but in the "global obsession with human flight," the politics of modernization in the context of the Cold War, and the constitution of a German diaspora of technological experts, which facilitated both the rehabilitation of Nazis and the diffusion of technology after the war (Rieger 2008, 386). In Rieger's view, Reitsch

> turned Ghana into a site of personal atonement as part of a private displacement strategy that diverted attention from her problematic past by underlining her purportedly compassionate character. Moreover, due to Germany's loss of overseas possessions in 1919, she did not have to wrestle with the issue of colonialism. Africa, then, provided an ideal arena for Reitsch's efforts at moral self-reinvention: it allowed her to parade herself as a racially unprejudiced humanitarian, thereby sidestepping the very political questions of responsibility and guilt that marred her biography. (Rieger 2008, 403)

It is also important to underscore the fact that West Germany relied on the expertise of scientists and technological experts like Reitsch to forge diplomatic relationships with the decolonizing world. "Development policy," as Rieger (2008, 393) writes, "became an important tool for forging ties with new states in Africa and Asia." Still, if Ghana was the "ideal arena" for Reitsch's efforts, Ghana was no tabula rasa upon which she could simply write the script for her new rehabilitated life. If Ghana worked for Reitsch, how and why did Reitsch work for Ghana? What did those Afienya dreams mean for Ghana? For Nkrumah's Convention People's Party (CPP)? For Nkrumah himself?

To begin, it is probably safe to assert that Nkrumah, like many former colonial subjects, did not share the same degree of antipathy to Nazism as Ghana's former colonial overlord, Great Britain. Indeed, Rieger (2008, 401) cites a report from the West German ambassador, which suggests that "Nkrumah . . . held an ambiguous attitude to Hitler" and that he "saw in Reitsch a 'great humanist' devoid of 'ideological fixations,' and 'above all politics.'"[30] But a purported ambivalence to Nazism only moves the analysis so far. It is also important to look at the world in which our two central characters came of age. Both Reitsch (b. 1912) and Nkrumah (b. 1909 or 1912) were born to an era when aviation prowess was the real "index of national vitality and thus national destiny" (Fritzsche 1992, 2).[31] By the mid-1930s, when Nkrumah moved to the United States and Reitsch was establishing her career as a pilot in Germany, aviation was "a crucial part of the modernist experience" and "airmindedness" featured centrally in the public consciousness of both countries.[32] As Peter Fritzsche (1992, 3) has written in *A Nation of Fliers,* "airplanes and airships were the measure of nations at the beginning of the twentieth century, distinguishing not only European genius from an African or Asian mean, but also the truly great powers among the European nation-states." That flight would therefore become absolutely central to Ghana's modernization discourse should come as no surprise. It was hardwired into the modernist master plan. Indeed, more than any other technological innovation of the twentieth century, as Fritzsche (1993, 3, 5) has written, aviation clarifies for us the powerful connections between "national dreams and modernist visions."[33]

And how did those connections manifest themselves in Ghana? As Frederick Cooper reminds us, "the language of modernization" was a

> basis for asserting claims. . . . The idea of modernization was attractive and inspiring, evoking an aspiration for a life that could be understood and changed for the better. A younger generation in the two decades after World War II—in Africa, India, or Europe itself—could distinguish itself from the stodgy traditionalism of its ancestors. . . . The possibilities of attaining modernity were most attractive to those who did not have it, and by the 1950s much of the world's colonized population was insisting their aspirations be taken into account. (Cooper 2005, 118, 131)

In the postwar era, Nkrumah and the CPP's "national dreams" were very much entangled with "modernist visions," but visions which, once materialized through rapid modernization (dams, hydroelectric plants, industries, and mechanized farming, but also gliders, flight, and airmindedness), would fast-forward Ghana into the arena of competing nation-states.

Gliding, which was to play such an important role in Ghana, had its own specific history in this process. What Reitsch imbibed as a young pilot in the 1930s resonated profoundly and directly with Nkrumah's own experiences and with his visions for building a modern Ghana with the First Republic. In Germany, gliding had "served as a congenial allegory for nationalist revival in Germany," even before the rise of National Socialism. By the time Reitsch took her first flight in 1932, it was viewed as "preparing young students for the reckonings of the machine age. Observers honored gliding for promoting technical thinking and providing affinities to the 'technological age'" (Fritzsche 1992, 123). To "fly in the sky without motors," as Fritzsche (1992, 125) writes, "was an allegory for the assertion of self-reliance." During the Third Reich, gliding and model making were put into the curriculum of most schools based on the belief that gliding "taught all sorts of virtuous lessons about self-reliance and patriotism" and that model building provided "invaluable lessons in craftsmanship, collaboration, and persistence" (Fritzsche 1992, 201–202).

As Nkrumah moved toward building socialism after the inauguration of the First Republic in 1960, he viewed the mobilization of youth around projects of self-reliance, patriotism, and discipline as being of paramount importance. The founding of the Young Pioneers in 1961 was aimed at facilitating youth mobilization and severing connections with the Boy Scouts and Girl Guides—organizations that were viewed as reinforcing imperialist connections with Britain. In profound ways, the discourse surrounding the Pioneer movement echoed the very same "virtues" Reitsch had been exposed to in Germany.[34] As former Pioneer M. N. Tetteh (1999, 61, 77) has written, the Pioneer Code of Discipline emphasized patriotism, discipline, obedience, honesty and morality, punctuality, respect for state property, reliability, comradeship, love of work, fieldcraft, and self-control.[35] With Hanna Reitsch in place, these codes of conduct could be inculcated into Ghana's youth as they stood at the vanguard of Ghana's modernization, ready—with motors or without—to "take to the sky." As Nkrumah explained in 1963, gliding "is an education in itself. It develops in men and women qualities of self-discipline, a sense of adventure, self-reliance and responsibility. These are qualities so necessary in the building of personal character and in the general development of a new nation like Ghana."[36]

One year before the 1966 coup that overthrew Nkrumah, a long article in the *Ghanaian Times* laid out in detail the necessary connections between youth, flight, and nation-building. The article began by noting that most Ghanaians were probably wondering, "'What is the need for gliding: what benefit does one derive and what are the prospects for those taking to gliding?'" The answers were simple and straightforward and are worth quoting in full:

> Gliding helps to produce men of character who must be needed in Ghana today to implement the policies of the Government. A nation is not judged only by its fortifications, its material resources and skyscrapers. It is also judged by the quality and character of its citizens and that is exactly the aim of the Gliding School. To be a successful glider pilot requires the qualities of self-discipline, reliability, punctuality, courage and humility.
>
> These qualities are vital for nation-building and especially so in a developing country and it is hoped that the Gliding School will be the nursery from which will bloom modest young men of virtue and self-respect.
>
> Secondly, gliding encourages air-mindedness in the youth.
>
> With the establishment of the school, the youth of Ghana will also acquire the skills for the mysteries of "the world above the ground." . . .
>
> The third and most important role of the Gliding School is that it serves a link between the Armed Forces, particularly the Air Force and one could rightly say that it is a pre-initial training wing of the Air Force, that is it gives the first "taste of the air" to the Air Force cadets.[37]

In many ways, then, Reitsch's work at the Gliding School resonated powerfully with Nkrumah's own modernizing agenda not only for building discipline and courage in the nation's youth, but for building a national military, with air capabilities, to replace the colonial army of old. As Rieger (2008, 388) notes, "gliding was . . . by no means merely a romantic form of soaring in the wind. . . . It provided a cost-effective means of training and research that proved integral to civil and military aviation." In the postcolonial world, gliding, as part and parcel of a high modernist vision, was thus critically situated at the core of both nation-building and the consolidation of state power.

In highlighting the connections, in foregrounding the discursive continuities between the roles of gliding and modernization in the nationalist visions of Nkrumah and Reitsch, I am in no way suggesting, as Piszkiewicz and others have, that Nkrumah was a Nazi-in-the-making and that Reitsch's attraction was purely pathological! My aim in this chapter has been to draw our attention, in ways that it simply has not been, to some of the technological, intellectual, and discursive genealogies that connect "nationalist dreams and modernist visions" globally—including in and through Nazi Germany. From a transnational perspective, not only did former Nazis hold particular technological expertise for which many in the world hungered (let's not forget the German aeronautical engineers who populated the U.S. space program after the war!), but that expertise has a long and enduring history of being inextricably linked to the nation and to nationalism—to the construction and maintenance of competing modern nation-states.[38] Viewed in and through this light, Reitsch appears not as some strange anomaly in the story of African nationalism and African liberation. Her presence in Ghana makes absolute sense, but not only and simply because of her own personal quest for refuge and rehabilitation or because of the exigencies of postwar West German diplomacy, but because the message she brought, the baggage she carried, fit quite comfortably (and in some ways predictably) within the borders of modernizing Ghana.

Notes

1. The material in this chapter is adapted from Jean Allman, "Phantoms of the Archive: Kwame Nkrumah, a Nazi Pilot Named Hanna, and the Contingencies of Postcolonial History-Writing," *American Historical Review* 118, no. 1 (2013): 104–29, by permission of Oxford University Press on behalf of the American Historical Association.

2. *Ghanaian Times*, 20 May 1963.

3. "Visit Afienya Gliding School," Ghana Newsreel Side One, box 49, tape 23, Kwame Nkrumah Papers, Moorland-Spingarn Research Center, Howard University, Washington, DC.

4. For biographical information on Reitsch, see Lomax (1988); Piszkiewicz (1997); Reitsch (1958); Rieger (2008). Reitsch's papers, covering the entire span of her career, are on deposit at Deutsches Museum Archiv in Munich (NL 130), though access to some materials is restricted. At the end of the war, Reitsch's father killed her mother, her sister, and her sister's children, and then himself, rather than face the prospect of living under Soviet rule.

5. Correspondence with regard to Reitsch's posting in Ghana is available in Reitsch Papers, NL 130, 28/1.

6. *Daily Graphic*, 7 March 1962.

7. See Reitsch Papers, NL 130/31, for correspondence related to the construction of the school.

8. The correspondence regarding the certification of the Aero Club can be found in Reitsch Papers, NL 130/30.

9. For her account, see Reitsch (1968, 42).

10. See, for example, *Daily Graphic*, 10 July 1963, 22 July 1963, 18 October 1963, 5 November 1963, 3 December 1963, 13 March 1964, 30 April 1964, 21 May 1964, 12 June 1964, 15 November 1964, 23 November 1965, 3 December 1964, 25 June 1965, and 2 October 1965; *Evening News*, 2 December 1965, 3 December 1965, and 22 March 1965; *Ghanaian Times*, 17 May 1963, 20 May 1963, 13 June 1963, 17 August 1963, 12 October 1963, 9 December 1963, 18 February 1964, 24 April 1964, 13 May 1964, 21 May 1964, 23 May 1964, 3 September 1964, 28 September 1964, 13 October 1964, 26 October 1964, 10 February 1965, 23 February 1965, 22 March 1965, 26 March 1965, 10 May 1965, 25 May 1965, 25 October 1965, and 3 December 1965.

11. See also *Daily Graphic*, 21 May 1964.

12. *Ghanaian Times*, 21 May 1964. See also *Daily Graphic*, 21 May 1964 and Reitsch (1968. 113).

13. *Ghanaian Times*, 23 May 1964. The story sits right above another miracle of modernization tale—that of "The Man-Made Volta Lake and Its Benefits."

14. The remnants of those instruments still sit within a fenced enclosure at the Afienya site.

15. *Ghanaian Times*, 23 February 1963; see Reitsch (1968, 136–41).

16. *Ghanaian Times*, 22 March 1965.

17. See *Air Force Day*, printed program, Public Records and Archives Administration Department, RG 17/2/947, Accra, Ghana. See also Reitsch (1968, 151) and *Ghanaian Times*, 26 October 1964.

18. On that occasion, her glider nearly crashed. She was able to land safely, but "I myself was paralyzed by pain, the audience by fear" (Reitsch 1968, 157).

19. *Evening News*, 22 March 1965.

20. The president of Gambia was the first to make an official state visit.

21. Reitsch (1968, 163–64). I have not been able to trace the source of the quote or to check its accuracy. Multiple drafts of her planned speech to the OAU representatives are on deposit in Reitsch Papers, NL 130/32.

22. *Daily Graphic*, 25 October 1965; and *Ghanaian Times*, 25 October 1965. See Reitsch (1968, 161, 65).

23. *Ghanaian Times*, 25 October 1965.

24. *Daily Graphic*, 23 November 1965.

25. *Daily Graphic*, 4 December 1965.

26. Correspondence with various schools regarding model-making can be found in Reitsch Papers, 130/32.

27. See *Ghanaian Times*, 8 March 1966; and *Evening News*, 7 March 1966. For her description of the coup and the events immediately after, see Reitsch (1968, 205–16).

28. As Rieger (2008, 402n113) points out, this "interpretation of Africa enjoyed considerable popularity among Germans. Leni Riefenstahl, who resurrected her career with glossy books on the indigenous population in the Sudan in the early 1960s, expressed similar sentiments." See also Riefenstahl (1973) and Susan Sontag's (1980) critical essay on Riefenstahl.

29. Reitsch is portrayed in several films about the Second World War: *Operation Crossbow* (1965), *Hitler: The Last Ten Days* (1973), and *Downfall* (*Der Untergang*) (2004).

30. Rieger is citing Ambassador Lüders, report to Auswärtiges Amt, 25 March 1963, Auswärtiges Amt, Berlin, Politisches Archiv, B94/1081.

31. Nkrumah (1957, 1) explains that the priest who baptized him recorded his birth year as 1909, but his mother had always calculated his birth year as 1912.

32. For a comparison of airmindedness in the United States and Germany, see Fritzsche (1992, 134). For related sources on airmindedness and the spectacle of flight, see Corn (1983); Edgerton (1991); Palmer (2006); Vance (2002).

33. For a discussion of the way in which flight has functioned as a metaphor for visual perception and the logistics of political power, see Virilio (1989).

34. Indeed, in a document from Reitsch's papers (n.d., NL 130//114) released in 2009, "Youth Organisation in Ghana," apparently written after her first visit to Ghana in 1962, she remarks on what to her are striking parallels: "I am certain of one fact: from the viewpoint of origin and initial stages, there is hardly any difference in constitution between the Young Pioneers and former Hitlerjugend. Both groups spring from the basic human desire for freedom and independence and from the almost revolutionary élan inspired by an epoch of struggle." This is one of the only documents in Reitsch's papers in which she tries to draw explicit connections between Hitler and Nkrumah. It is likely that she very quickly learned not to make such comparisons in official correspondence.

35. Interestingly, Tetteh (1999, 80–81) completely excludes Reitsch from his account and provides a very different chronology for gliding in Ghana. He considers gliding central to the training of the Young Pioneers, but argues that Pioneer gliding began in Takoradi, before it moved to Afienya. In addition to the "Code of Discipline," the Young Pioneers pledged to "live by the ideals of Osagyefo Dr. Kwame Nkrumah, Founder of the State of Ghana, and Initiator of the African Personality. To safeguard by all means possible, the independence, sovereignty and territorial integrity of the State of Ghana from internal and external aggression. To be always in the vanguard for the social and economic reconstruction of Ghana and Africa. To be in the first ranks of men fighting for the total liberation of and unity of Africa, for these are the noble aims guiding the Ghana Young Pioneers. As a Young Pioneer, I will be a guard of workers, farmers, co-operatives and all other sections of our community. I believe that our dynamic Convention People's Party is always supreme and I promise to be worthy of its ideals." The pledge is quoted in Owusu (2005, 133–34).

36. *Ghanaian Times*, 20 May 1963.

37. *Ghanaian Times*, 23 February 1965.

38. Rieger (2008, 384) notes that Reitsch was only one of thousands of "German luminaries . . . who went on to flourish in both ideological blocks during the Cold War. Around 3,000 German scientists and engineers worked in the Soviet Union in the late 1940s . . . [and] over 500 German aeronautical researchers were transferred to the United States" in the late 1940s.

References

Cooper, Frederick. 2005. *Colonialism in Question: Theory, Knowledge, History.* Berkeley: University of California Press.

Corn, Joseph J. 1983. *Winged Gospel: America's Romance with Aviation, 1900–1950.* New York: Oxford University Press.

Edgerton, David. 1991. *England and the Aeroplane: An Essay on a Militant and Technological Nation.* Basingstoke: Macmillan Academic and Professional.

Fritzsche, Peter. 1992. *A Nation of Fliers: German Aviation and the Popular Imagination.* Cambridge, MA: Harvard University Press.

Lomax, Judy. 1988. *Hanna Reitsch: Flying for the Fatherland.* London: John Murray.

Nkrumah, Kwame. 1957. *Ghana: The Autobiography of Kwame Nkrumah.* Edinburgh: Thomas Nelson.

Owusu, Robert Yaw. 2005. *Kwame Nkrumah's Liberation Thought: A Paradigm for Religious Advocacy in Contemporary Ghana.* New York: Africa World Press.

Palmer, Scott W. 2006. *Dictatorship of the Air: Aviation Culture and the Fate of Modern Russia.* Cambridge: Cambridge University Press.

Piszkiewicz, Dennis. 1997. *From Nazi Test Pilot to Hitler's Bunker: The Fantastic Flights of Hanna Reitsch.* Westport, CT: Praeger.

Reitsch, Hanna. 1958. *The Sky My Kingdom: Memoirs of the Famous German World War II Test-Pilot.* London: Greenhill Books.

———. 1968. *Ich flog für Kwame Nkrumah.* Munich: J. F. Lehmanns Verlag.

Riefenstahl, Leni. 1973. *Die Nuba.* Munich: Paul List Verlag.

Rieger, Bernhard. 2008. "Hanna Reitsch (1912–1979): The Global Career of a Nazi Celebrity." *German History* 26, no. 3: 383–405.

Sontag, Susan. 1980. "Fascinating Fascism." In *Under the Sign of Saturn,* 73–105. New York: Farrar, Straus and Giroux. Originally published in the *New York Review of Books,* 6 February 1975.

Tetteh, M. N. 1999. *The Ghana Young Pioneer Movement: A Youth Organisation in the Kwame Nkrumah Era.* Accra: Optimum Design and Publishing.

Vance, Jonathan. 2002. *High Flight: Aviation and the Canadian Imagination.* Toronto: Penguin.

Virilio, Paul. 1989. *War and Cinema: The Logistics of Perception.* London: Verso Books.

11 The African Personality Dances Highlife

Popular Music, Urban Youth, and Cultural Modernization in Nkrumah's Ghana, 1957–1965

Nate Plageman

> From now on, today, we must change our attitudes, our minds. We must realize that from now on, we are no more a colonial but a free and independent people! But also, as I pointed out, that entails hard work. . . . As I said in the Assembly just minutes ago, I made a point that we are going to see that we create our own African Personality and identity; it is the only way in which we can show the world that we are masters of our own destiny.
>
> —Kwame Nkrumah, Independence Day Address, 6 March 1957

> When dancing rock 'n' roll [as a young man in the early 1960s] I felt joy. I felt joy because it was a new life. I wore trousers at that time, my first time wearing trousers, and a good shirt and went out. And we used to behave like Yankees you know? . . . I felt proud, that wisdom was taking place, that I was different than others.
>
> —Bob Biney, 1 April 2005

On any given weekend evening in the late 1950s and early 1960s, thousands of Ghanaian men and women left their homes, set out for a nearby nightclub, and enjoyed an evening of popular musical recreation. Shortly after dusk, they put on a fashionable set of clothes, met up with their dancing partner or a group of friends, purchased admission tickets and rounds of refreshments, and found a table where they could relax and converse. Around eight o'clock, a set of bandsmen took the stage and began to play long and varied musical sets designed to pull the gathered crowd out of their seats and onto the nightclub dance floor. Most dance bands solicited audience participation by playing selections from the local highlife, a combination of local and international musical elements that prompted individuals to move in a simple side-to-side pattern accentuated by any number of additional steps or improvisations (Hanna 1973, 144–51). In Accra, the nation's largest city, administrative capital, and popular musical center, prominent dance bands such as E. T. Mensah's Tempos, King Bruce's Black Beats, and Jerry Hansen's Ramblers Dance Band also played a range of international styles, including ballroom forms, calypso, jazz, swing, and rock 'n' roll, that had their own accompanying forms of dancing. Since the city's vibrant popular music scene was varied and eclectic, many nightclub enthusiasts patronized the venue and ensemble that featured their favorite styles so that they could congregate with others of similar tastes, display their well-practiced dance moves, and have a great deal of fun (Plageman 2013, 100–46).

While popular musical recreation gained status as a "household word" in many towns in the years surrounding Ghana's independence,[1] it was also a target of the Convention People's Party (CPP) government's ambitious program of state-directed modernization. In a speech to Parliament on 4 March 1959, the party's leader and nation's prime minister, Kwame Nkrumah, unveiled his five-year development plan, an elaborate £G350 scheme of industrialization, hydroelectric works, communications, and health programs designed to allow Ghana to "advance confidently as a nation" (Government of Ghana, iii). Sixteen months later, with his development plan fully successfully launched, Nkrumah announced how Ghana's diverse popular musical scene might be reformulated to complement his elaborate vision of the future. First, he declared that highlife was Ghana's "national" dance music and that it, as well as other local musical forms, deserved priority both in nightclubs and on radio airwaves. Announcing that the country's popular music scene needed to become more "Ghanaian" in composition and character, he asked popular musicians to limit (and over time eliminate) the performance of foreign numbers, play highlife songs at a uniform tempo, and employ a standardized set of dance steps that nightclub crowds could emulate while on the dance floor. Finally, Nkrumah noted that since the term "highlife" did not befit a medium that was essentially "African in content," it needed a different name. He ultimately charged the National Association of Teachers of Dancing with the task of selecting a new moniker, but suggested that it might be rechristened *osibi*, a title that made explicit reference to *osibisaaba*, a popular musical style that had flourished in the early twentieth century.[2]

Although these proclamations had little immediate impact, they reflect how popular music, and the broader realm of arts and culture, was an important component of the CPP's program of state-sponsored modernization in the years following Ghana's independence. Under Nkrumah, modernization was much more than a top-down process designed to secure Ghana's economic future: it was a means of facilitating the incomplete task of nation-building, extending the government's power, and encouraging Ghanaians to develop a collective identity based around local rather than foreign cultural elements. The centerpiece of this project of cultural modernization was the "African Personality," a package of shared principles and practices selected to cleanse all Ghanaians of their past colonial subjugation and facilitate their creation of a new prosperous society based upon equality, pride, and other intrinsic "African" values (Botwe-Asamoah 2005, 75–87; Biney 2011, 110–33). From 1957 to 1965, Nkrumah also promoted the African Personality as a means of providing guidance to the nation's youth, the demographic he envisioned to be the key agents of Ghana's future. If his government could convince young people to adopt the African Personality, embrace an invented national culture, and participate instate-directed plans, he was confident that it would successfully secure Ghana's place in a newly liberated Africa and postcolonial world (Biney 2011,101–10).

One important way in which Nkrumah's government attempted to decipher the African Personality into a readily identifiable set of practices and behaviors that young people could adopt and emulate was by restructuring the country's popular music scene. Throughout the late 1950s and early 1960s, the CPP attempted to transform Ghana's eclectic popular musical realm into one that mirrored official directives and prioritized particular "Ghanaian" elements, values, and cultural practices.[3] It did so largely under the auspices of the Arts Council of Ghana, a government body that used both persuasive and coercive tactics to encourage popular musicians and musical patrons to adopt particular styles of dress and forms of dance; enjoy local, rather than foreign, musical styles; and take part in musical concerts and competitions in a uniform and orderly fashion. By revamping Ghana's popular musical scene into a regulated domain, the council hoped to facilitate the CPP's more ambitious task of inciting cultural pride, civic responsibility, and a commitment to national development amongst all of the country's residents.[4]

While such efforts forced many of the country's musicians and musical patrons to alter their approach to a once-open recreational realm, they did not convince all Ghanaians to abandon their established musical tastes or practices. In fact, instead of bringing people together to enjoy a uniform cultural product, the state's efforts placed great strain on several musicians and prompted numbers of young musical enthusiasts to patronize private, and more autonomous, realms of music and dance. Although a few musicians found that upholding the Arts Council's wishes greatly improved their professional prospects, many others found that the regulations threatened their individual creativity, asked them to ignore audience demands, and diminished their ability to earn a reliable income. Urban youth who favored rock 'n' roll, such as Bob Biney, viewed the state's program of modernization as an attempt to silence their political voice and further marginalize their social and cultural influence. Instead of willingly adhering to CPP demands, young people turned to rock 'n' roll clubs, private organizations that enabled them to flaunt their music of choice and reclaim levels of agency within their urban environment. As a result of their efforts, Ghana's popular musical scene never became a readily exploitable avatar of the CPP government's program of modernization, instead remaining a domain that mediated between the wishes of those who managed the political realm and those increasingly excluded from its purview (White 2008, 15–16).

The African Personality and the "Problem" of Urban Youth

When he announced Ghana's independence from Great Britain, Kwame Nkrumah insisted that colonialism's end was a cultural, as much as a political and economic, phenomenon. True liberation, he declared, was not a mere transfer of power; it was an act of self-realization that required Ghanaians to cultivate a shared identity oriented around the conventions of the traditional "African" culture colonialism had sought to displace. The best way for Ghanaians to resuscitate these common values and core principles was to adopt the African Personality, a persona that embraced both an age-old "cluster of African humanist principles" and the current need to "to liberate and unify the continent and to build a just society." As a source of cultural pride and self-empowerment, the African Personality would enable Ghanaians to fully transcend the "artificial barriers erected between them by the colonists," relocate lost modes of self-expression, and initiate a wider "African rebirth" (Biney 2011, 101–10; Botwe-Asamoah 2005, 47–87; Hagan 1991, 1–26). As a communal ethos that underpinned everyday life, it would encourage men and women to embrace hard work, accumulate an array of skills and knowledge, and contribute to Ghana's ambitious program of industrialization and economic development. If adopted by all Ghanaians, the African Personality would not only enable them to demonstrate that they had "never really surrendered to the British" or lost an appreciation of their own self-worth; it would allow them to secure their country's emergence as a leading force in a newly liberated continent.[5]

At the same time, the African Personality, as well as Nkrumah's wider program of cultural modernization, was also a way for the CPP government to ensure that the nation's populace willingly cooperated with its demands. Although it had been immensely popular in the years leading up to Ghana's 1957 independence, the CPP did not have the wholehearted support of all Ghanaians. It faced staunch opposition from a variety of organizations, such as the National Liberation Movement and Ga Shifimo Kpee (Ga Steadfast Organization), which attracted residents of particular geographical regions or members of specific ethnic groups (Austin 1964, 44, 267–76; Allman 1993, 186–92). Additional unrest came at the hands of urban youth, a cohort that had championed the CPP's rise only to quickly accuse it of overlooking their welfare and continuing "colonial" abuses of power (Austin 1964, 371–81). What made such protests particularly disconcerting was that their participants not only highlighted the fundamental weaknesses of state development plans, such as rising rates of urban unemployment and homelessness, but that they did so by employing a number of local cultural elements, including libation, prayer, and forms of music and dance (Austin 1964, 371–81; Salm 2003, 109–23). To ensure that it, rather than its opponents, retained strict control over the deployment of culture for political purposes, the CPP government instructed individual citizens on how to adopt the African Personality, embrace an invented "Ghanaian" culture, and profitably contribute to the nation's future.

Over the course of the late 1950s and early 1960s, Nkrumah outlined the tenets of Ghana's "new" men and women: idealized citizens who embodied the specific gendered qualities needed to sustain the nation's full liberation (Lindsay and Miescher 2003, 1–29). In a series of public speeches, he encouraged all men to aspire to the standard of the "new man": an adult male dedicated to the country's prosperity, moral standards, and women and children. For Nkrumah, Ghana's new man was a loyal and reliable guardian of national values. He shunned adultery, violence, and social vice, pursued literacy and education, and was committed to upholding longstanding cultural principles. He despised laziness, was infused with "the spirit to work hard and learn fast," and provided for all members of his family. In short, Ghana's new man aligned his individual aspirations with the needs of a nation recently emerged from the oppressive conditions of colonial rule.[6]

Concurrently, the state promoted its own vision of the nation's "new woman." To a wide degree, such efforts focused on regulating women's public appearance and dress. In the late 1950s and early 1960s, various state-owned newspapers, including the *Daily Graphic* and the *Sunday Mirror*, published pictures and articles that depicted the dress, hair, and accoutrements emblematic of "true Ghanaian womanhood."[7] Such pieces encouraged women to reject foreign fashion, transform *ntama* and *kente* into new forms of dress, and to wear such outfits to work, recreational events, and social gatherings.[8] To further encourage such practices, the state sponsored national beauty pageants, whose winners earned grand titles such as "Miss Cedi" or "Miss Ghana" and promotion as feminine idols.[9] Though beautiful and image-conscious, Ghana's "new woman" was also committed to the CPP's multifaceted program of modernization. She contributed to Ghana's economic growth by working in its fields, factories, and offices, as well as by fulfilling her role as a dedicated wife and mother.[10] By managing her home, tending to her family, and encouraging her children to adopt the African Personality at a young age, she improved "her country and Africa as a whole."[11]

Nkrumah's government further reinforced these gendered ideals by encouraging local authorities to identify and punish those who openly defied them. In Accra, prostitutes were a common target for official angst, as their brazen dress, embrace of ostentatious behaviors such as drinking alcohol and smoking cigarettes, and immoral sexual practices clearly violated official guidelines.[12] Although many Ghanaians disparaged such women as *ashawo* (a Yoruba term for "moneychanger"), the Accra police force aggressively confirmed that they were un-Ghanaian persons who grossly violated the African Personality. Throughout the late 1950s and early 1960s, city officers regularly arrested prostitutes, tried them in city courts, and fined them two to twenty-five Ghanaian pounds for an array of charges, including loitering and "obstructing the public way."[13] Overtime, similar actions targeted young women whose appearance defied the African Personality in less striking ways. In the early 1960s, Accra police often arrested young women who wore short skirts, makeup, and wigs on the basis that these foreign items symbolized their immorality and promiscuity.[14] In 1963, Ghana's education minister, A. J. Dowouna-Hammond, declared that the imported short skirts favored by many female secondary students constituted a crude disfiguration of "Ghanaian Womanhood." A month later, the *oguaahene,* the paramount chief of the Cape Coast Municipality, upheld the African Personality by declaring that all skirts that cutoff above the knee were "alien to our pattern of behavior and incompatible with our cultural background" and should be criminalized as illegal forms of dress.[15]

While the CPP government applauded such actions as means of promoting reforms central to its modernization plans, it also upheld them as effective means of addressing the "youth problem" plaguing Accra and other towns. In the years following independence, many CPP officials, including Nkrumah and Kojo Botsio, considered city youth to be a cohort that embraced foreign behaviors and practices adversative to Ghana's future. In part such concerns were extensions of long-standing worries about juvenile delinquents, young men and women who moved to town, lost contact with family members, and made a living through theft, gambling, and other illicit means.[16] While the Department of Social Welfare expended great energy identifying and reforming these "wayward" youth, it also reported that the nation's number of "potential delinquents," young people who "roamed [city] streets," used foul language, and embraced a "cowboy lifestyle," was rapidly on the rise (Clarkson 1955, 1–4; Gold Coast 1955, 1–7). Some of the most "dangerous" youth, department officials insisted, were those enamored with foreign films, Americanized mannerisms and styles of speech, and flamboyant popular musical styles such as rock 'n' roll. Overtime, the young people regularly exposed to these mediums gained feelings of "being important, experienced, and adult," sentiments that encouraged them to openly defy authority and fall into patterns of social vice (Clarkson 1955, 4).

The embrace of foreign cultural mediums by youth culture became a source of concern to the authorities because it was perceived to coincide with the rising criticism leveled against Nkrumah's government. Shortly after independence, cohorts of young men and women in Accra, many of whom had supported the CPP's rise to power, expressed frustration with the party's failures and betrayal of "the common man." One vocal source of opposition was the "Tokyo Joes," a group of unemployed youth who openly denounced the city's widespread shortage of housing, jobs, and basic necessities, particularly in the dilapidated quarters omitted from the government's program of infrastructure improvement. Before long the Tokyo Joes—a name also adopted by self-proclaimed rock 'n' rollers—joined forces with the Ga Shifimo Kpee and other discontented persons to hold rallies that questioned the government's concern about the hardships they endured (Austin 1964, 374–76; Salm 2003, 100–103). The CPP responded by publicly disparaging the Tokyo Joes as idlers and delinquents who had embraced "social vices as a substitute for productive pursuits" and developed an unhealthy obsession with foreign cultural forms.[17] To put a stop to such acts of youthful insubordination, the government not only enacted the Preventative Detention Act of 1958, which allowed for the imprisonment of those whose disobedience jeopardized "state security," but also directed the National Board of Film Censors and state-owned press outlets to launch a vigilant campaign aimed at removing rock 'n' roll and other "corrupting" cultural influences from the nation's venues of public recreation.[18] Importantly, it also began to sponsor an array of new organizations designed to refashion misguided young people into self-respecting advocates of an invented national culture.

One of the CPP government's most ambitious efforts was the Workers Brigade (later renamed the Builders Brigade), a collective of work camps designed to increase employment and public order by providing young men and women with occupational training, an ethic of hard work, and a sense of patriotic service. The brigade got off to a slow start, but by 1960 it had enlisted over eleven thousand young men and women, who received a "healthy respect for the dignity of manual labour and national service" (Ahlman 2011, 79–80). Though technically open to Ghanaians between the ages of fifteen and forty-five, the brigade's primary target was individuals under the age of twenty-four who completed a regular program of strict discipline, physical training, lectures, and training in literacy and general sanitation.[19] Female members received additional lessons on topics such as cooking, sewing, child care, and catering designed to lay the groundwork for their future roles as wives, mothers, and guardians of the domestic sphere. Young men, meanwhile, had instruction in technical trades such as electrical engineering, vehicle mechanics, and tractor operations, and received hands-on training in the construction of new roads, waterworks, schools, drainage systems, and low-cost housing.[20]

As young brigadiers obtained the education and skills needed to participate in Nkrumah's economic development program, they also received extensive lessons on how to adopt the African Personality in their leisure time and recreational pursuits. All brigadiers received meals, housing, and uniforms—provisions that fulfilled their basic needs and prevented them from developing tastes for "unhealthy" foreign items. They also participated in a variety of handpicked recreational activities designed to cultivate uniformity, cooperation, and an appreciation for Ghana's cultural heritage.[21] Shortly after creating the brigade, its administrators formed the Builders Brigade Band, a ten-piece dance band that unabashedly promoted the local highlife and other "Ghanaian" musical styles. The band, which performed at parades, marches, and other public events, quickly became a visible symbol of government-sponsored modernization. Its young male members sported brand-new instruments, wore matching outfits, and performed behind bandstands painted with the black star, Ghana's distinctive national emblem. The group also received first-class instruction from Spike Anyankor, a professional saxophone player who had been a member of two of Ghana's most beloved dance bands, the Rhythm Aces and the Tempos, and served as the band's director.[22] In 1959, the ensemble was a finalist in the National Dance Band Competition, miraculously (and rather suspiciously) advancing further than many well-established groups, including the Tempos, the Black Beats, and Joe Kelly's Band. Over the next few years, the Brigade Band featured prominently on state radio airwaves, provided entertainment at government functions, and became a regular feature of Accra's nightlife scene. The Brigade Band was so successful that officials created regional offshoots of the ensemble so that large numbers of youth had regular access to their carefully screened repertoires of highlife and pro-government tunes.[23] By the end of the 1950s, the band's success also prompted the government to direct another recently created body, the Arts Council of Ghana, to initiate a large-scale effort to transform the nation's diverse popular musical scene into one that was wholly "Ghanaian" in character.

The Arts Council's Efforts to Modernize Popular Musical Recreation

The CPP government's most ardent effort to reform the confines of popular musical recreation came at the hands of the Arts Council, a national body the Legislative Assembly created in 1958 to organize, encourage, and supervise the nation's arts.[24] The council, headquartered at the Arts Centre in Accra, was comprised of highly educated and distinguished men and women, including Nana Kwabena Nketsia (chair), Dr. Seth Cudjoe (deputy chair), Philip Gbeho, Professor J. H. Kwabena Nketia, Kofi Antubam, Efua Sutherland, J. C. de Graft, and W. P. Carpenter. Nkrumah served as the council's acting president and many other political figures, including Dr. J. B. Danquah, Sir Arku Korsah, Sir C. W. Techie-Mensah, and all six regional presidents of the House of Chiefs were honorary members.

Shortly after the council's creation, this group of prestigious individuals set out to "foster, preserve, and improve" Ghana's cultural realm, establish a national theater movement, and awaken public interest in and appreciation of local forms through state-sponsored exhibitions and events. To facilitate these tasks, the council organized its members into subcommittees responsible for overseeing particular artistic mediums. The section on music, drumming, and dancing, for example, worked to annotate and record traditional music, train local musical ensembles, and prepare musical "propaganda" that could be distributed to the Ministry of Education, Department of Social Welfare, and the nation's schools. Each subcommittee was based at the council's Accra headquarters, but many also established committees in each of the country's regional capitals so as to expand the scope and quality of their efforts.[25]

Over the next several years the Arts Council endeavored to modernize the arts into a top-down version of "Ghanaian" culture through three interrelated processes. First, it attempted to identify and directly observe the work of the country's artists, theatrical groups, and musical ensembles. In the late 1950s and early 1960s, most subcommittees deployed scouts to identify particularly talented persons whom the government could employ and promote.[26] Second, the council evaluated how the "objectives, quality, and integrity" of individual artists matched the tenets of Nkrumah's program of cultural modernization. As one council member's evaluation of the Black Star Troupe, an Accra ensemble of drummers and dancers, reveals, the African Personality was central to their assessments:

> The dances being produced by the Black Star Troupe in projecting African Personality . . . have a different meaning to what I understand. . . . The sort and the type of drumming and dancing produced by the Black Star Troupe is in fact very appalling. I am not in a position to condemn the dances they produced, but as far as my twelve years research to Ghanaian customs, drumming, and dancing is concerned, I feel their production is not the Ghanaian type. The Leader should be invited with his troupe to put up a show at the Art Centre in the near future . . . to verify my findings.[27]

Lastly, the council implemented changes that would better align artists' practices with an invented version of national culture. While it usually imposed small-scale changes, such as altering a band's name, costumes, or song titles, the council also censored particular aspects of a band's performance, added or removed group members, or completely revised its existing repertoire so as to privilege local, rather than foreign, styles and aesthetics.[28]

One of the council's most urgent priorities was standardizing popular bands' eclectic repertoires and modes of self-presentation.[29] After observing dance bands in Accra and other towns, the council concluded that most were far too reliant upon foreign influences and imported musical styles. One of its greatest concerns, reflected in Nkrumah's announcements that opened this chapter, was Ghanaian bands' continued embrace of ballroom and rock 'n' roll in their repertoires, genres that remained popular amongst urban audiences but clearly conflicted with the African Personality mandate. To begin the difficult task of removing foreign music from the nation's nightclubs, the council asked dance bands to adopt Gha-

Figure 11.1. Kwame Nkrumah announces Ghana's independence, 6 March 1957. During his speech, amidst a variety of state symbols including the black star and the *fugu*, which later he endorsed as national dress, Nkrumah charged Ghanaians to develop an "African Personality." Photo courtesy of Ghana Information Services Department Photograph Library.

naian, rather than Western, forms of dress. In 1960, nearly all Ghanaian popular musicians, who were overwhelmingly men, took the stage wearing imported collared shirts, suits, and ties, a mode of dress that bandsmen had favored, with slight modification, for roughly forty years (Plageman 2013, 67–99). The council quickly discouraged this practice and insisted instead that musicians appear before audiences adorned in either *kente* or the *fugu*, clothing that Nkrumah had promoted as "national" since Ghana's 1957 independence (see figures 11.1 and 11.2) (Hagan 1991, 14–16).

While the council promoted local forms of dress as an important step in reforming the country's popular music scene, it spent much more time attempting to prevent dance bands from playing anything other than "Ghanaian" musical styles. In 1961, it directed such groups to replace their liberal embrace of jazz and Afro-Caribbean elements with a focused infusion of traditional rhythms and forms of dance.[30] To facilitate this change, the council unveiled a six-month training course designed to teach bandsmen how to play rhythms from various parts of the country and incorporate local dances, dancers, and elements into their staged performances.[31] Enrolled bands received this training free of charge, but had to at-

Figure 11.2. The members of the Professional Uhuru Dance Band wear *fugu* in order to reflect Nkrumah's African Personality during a 1963 performance. Photo courtesy of Ghana Information Services Department Photograph Library.

tend daily rehearsals at council headquarters and willingly accept all revisions to their repertoire, organization, and self-presentation. Most council-trained bands obtained new songs, had portions of their regular repertoire eliminated, and received new personnel handpicked by council staff. All band members were also expected to conform to the expectations central to Ghana's "new" men and women. Male bandsmen had to demonstrate that they were disciplined, punctual, and willing to refrain from smoking or drinking while onstage. Recruited female dancers, meanwhile, were selected for their talent and beauty as well as their ability to read, write, and present themselves in a respectable fashion.[32]

The council's first pupil was the Messengers Dance Band, a prolific ensemble that had already acquired the CPP's favor. The Messengers, led by George Lee, were the resident band at one of Accra's most prominent nightspots, the state-owned Star Hotel, until the summer of 1961, when they enrolled in a council training program designed to improve members' familiarity with Ghana's "traditional and folk music." Over the course of the next six months, council officials regularly gave their CPP counterparts glowing updates on the Messengers' progress.

Within three short months the band, which had long relied on imported musical styles such as jazz, calypsos, and ballroom forms, had "acquired an almost uncanny prowess in interpreting a wide variety of authentic Ghanaian dances and rhythms." A few months later, when the band performed a set of highlife and traditional numbers for a group of government officials, the council concluded that the band had become an ideal instrument for promoting the merits of the African Personality.[33] In 1962 and 1963, other dance bands, including Takoradi's Broadway Band (later renamed the Professional Uhuru Dance Band), the Globemasters Dance Band, the Builders Brigade Band, and the Ghana Farmers Dance Band completed similar council training courses, where they learned how to play traditional numbers, acquired female dancers, and procured a repertoire that reflected official tastes and desires.[34]

While band members recalled these programs as rigorous and somewhat onerous, they agreed that completing them allowed them to procure a new set of professional opportunities. In the early 1960s, council-trained ensembles often secured lucrative government engagements that offered attractive pay and the chance to perform in front of distinguished audiences.[35] Trained bands also received enhanced press coverage in state-owned newspapers, extended play on the national airwaves, and preference in government-sponsored band competitions.[36] Few dance bands benefited more from their council training than the Professional Uhuru Dance Band, a group owned and managed by two CPP ministers, Krobo Edusei and E. K. Dadson. As Stan Plange, the guitarist and eventual band leader, recalled, the group's council training, adoption of traditional elements, and government connections secured it a prosperous position in an otherwise competitive popular musical marketplace:

> [In the 1960s] we came for a special traditional course at the Arts Centre because Nkrumah's government decided that all the dance bands should add cultural [i.e., traditional] components to their music. . . . They trained us in *fontonfrom* drumming, *agbadza,* and others so [that] we would incorporate them into our performances. . . . You know, Nkrumah was interested in getting his African Personality into the mainstream of everything. Occasionally we would go to him to perform, especially when foreign ministers were in town. I remember playing for the president of the World Bank. Another time, we performed for the [assistant] secretary of state in charge of African affairs from the United States.[37]

Over time, the Professional Uhuru Dance Band's ability to perform traditional rhythms, such as *fontonfrom* (an Akan royal music) and *agbadza* (an Ewe recreational music), and showcase dancers who modeled fixed dance moves made it the government's popular band of choice, a distinction that gave it an enviable reputation, financial security, and state-sponsored bookings in international cities such as Moscow, London, Beirut, Khartoum, Nairobi, and Kampala. After ob-

Figure 11.3. The signboard outside the Professional Uhuru Dance Band's head office in Accra, ca. 1963. Its inclusion of "Cabaret Troupe" indicates that the band could perform traditional music and dancing styles. Photo courtesy of Ghana Information Services Department Photograph Library.

taining government favor, the band also established a head office near the Accra post office, so that nightclub owners and other interested persons could inquire about hiring it for future engagements (see figure 11.3).[38]

Although the council rarely matched the favor it lavished on the Professional Uhuru Dance Band, it ensured that other ensembles followed its directives through a mixture of reprimand and reward. Bands with "problematic members"—those who were frequently truant, lazy, or disobedient—faced a range of punishments aimed at the offending musician, such as fines or suspension, as well as the entire group, such as the loss of official bookings or prohibition from future events. Cooperative ensembles, meanwhile, received letters of official recommendation, invitations to play at state-sponsored events, and opportunities for international travel. In the early 1960s, the council decided that only those bands trained as "musical envoys" capable of accurately projecting the African Personality should be allowed to perform abroad. In addition to rejecting a proposal to send E. T. Mensah, a popular musician whom Ghanaians widely upheld as the "King of Highlife," as a delegate to a conference sponsored by the Société Africaine de Culture in Paris because he was not "qualified in traditional African culture," the council provided the government passport office with firm instructions about which bands should be issued visas to travel outside of the nation's boundaries.[39] Bands approved for international performances faced additional scrutiny, as the council handpicked those who would conduct interviews with members of the foreign press and best "protect the reputation of the country and people of Ghana."[40]

To achieve its aim of reforming dance bands into outfits that could extol the virtues of the African Personality on- and offstage, the council also employed the help of Ghana's state-owned newspapers. Throughout the early 1960s, two of Ghana's most prominent newspapers, the *Daily Graphic* and the *Sunday Mirror*, ran features on those musicians who had proven themselves to be talented artists as well as dedicated professionals who attended daily rehearsals, followed strict rules, and obeyed figures of authority. Others framed musicians as role models for Ghana's "new man" and extolled their commitment to fulfilling their duties as husbands, fathers, and household heads.[41] The press awarded additional acclaim to musical ensembles that wrote songs promoting the state's modernization program. The *Sunday Mirror* ran several pieces lauding the Ramblers Dance Band for their 1964 song "Work and Happiness," which, like the Nkrumah speech of the same title, encouraged Ghana's young men and women to work hard on behalf of their nation's future:

> Work, and happiness, yes I must confess
> All must give their best
> For beautiful Ghana
> United Farmers and Workers of Africa
> God will bless you wherever you are
> Work and happiness, yes I must confess
> We must give our best
> For beautiful Ghana[42]

Other bands such as the Stargazers and Professional Uhuru Dance Band performed like-minded tunes, such as "*Gyae Nsanomna Kuro Wo Dan*" ("Stop drinking and put a roof on your house"), "*Akpeteshi*" (a type of locally distilled gin), and "*Krakye Brokeman*" ("impoverished gentleman"), which lampooned young men who wasted their time and money on alcohol and idleness instead of providing for themselves, their families, and their nation.[43]

The council's final means of altering Ghana's popular music scene came through its provision of state-sponsored concerts and band contests. Throughout the early 1960s, the government held regional and national highlife competitions, events designed to commemorate state holidays, attract heavy crowds, and showcase the merits of "Ghanaian" culture. While bands approached these competitions as vital moments in which they could unveil their talents, enhance their prestige, and possibly land new bookings or recording contracts (Plageman 2013, 207–209), most found that they were actually vehicles for promoting state aims. Council members went to great lengths to supervise these contests, determining which bands were eligible to perform, the length of their set, and even which songs they were allowed to play onstage.[44] In addition, they asked judges to rank participating groups according to how their "appearance, showmanship, and general behavior and discipline" matched the dictates of the African Personality.[45] Government-sponsored dance competitions, which frequently took place alongside band contests, ranked participants according to their dress, posture, and quality of steps—criteria that were also emphasized in council-sponsored courses on how to "correctly" dance to highlife music in a way that emphasized not "exotic [i.e., foreign] innovations" but movements, gestures, and other "characteristics derived from folk dances [such] as *askosuatuntum, ashewa, kolomashi,* and *adabaa.*"[46]

Although the Arts Council ambitiously pursued these efforts throughout the late 1950s and early 1960s, it never fully transformed Ghana's popular music scene into an avatar of the CPP government's program of cultural modernization. Many residents of Accra recalled weekend evenings in the mid-1960s not as spectacles of an invented national culture, but as occasions when they could continue to put on their favorite clothes, meet up with their friends, and dance to an array of musical styles. Numerous people, particularly those who favored the local highlife, avidly supported the CPP, or simply turned to popular music as a means of occasional fun, found little reason to question or challenge official interventions.[47] For many others, however, government reforms became a source of tension, hardship, and anxiety. A number of musicians, particularly those who did not enroll in a council training program or have alternative forums for instruction in "traditional" musical styles, found that council efforts made it increasingly difficult to procure regular performances, accumulate a steady income, or obtain consistent play on the state-run radio airwaves. When struggling bandsmen contrasted their plight with the prosperity enjoyed by government-favored bands with celebrity status and exorbitant contracts—the Ramblers earned six hundred to eight hundred Ghanaian pounds per night as the resident band at the Star Hotel—several concluded that they needed to either overhaul their onstage practices or abandon music as a viable means of earning an income.[48] Nana Ampadu recalled that he and his fellow bandsmen selected the name African Brothers Band with the hope that they might attract the attention and favor of nightclub owners, producers, or Kwame Nkrumah's government.[49]

Other musicians found that the government's promotion of local rather than foreign musical styles made it difficult for them to both uphold official directives and meet the demands of their loyal audiences. Very few dance bands could simply eliminate international numbers from their repertoires because such songs continued to garner great enthusiasm on the nightclub dance floor. Dance bands that catered primarily to older, well-to-do, and "respectable" crowds of nightclub patrons addressed this problem by continuing to infuse their highlife-centered sets with occasional calypso or upbeat ballroom numbers, an act that rarely attracted official attention, upset nightclub owners, or jeopardized established favor.[50] For bands that catered primarily to urban youth who continued to favor rock 'n' roll and the twist over highlife or other "Ghanaian" forms, such balances were much more difficult, if not impossible, to strike. Because the government deemed rock 'n' roll to be an "alien" music that corrupted its listeners, some nightclub owners instructed bands to refrain from playing such numbers or from consciously seeking the favor of "raucous youth."[51] As a result, many young musicians such as Francis Laryea, who played trumpet with the Red Spots, a well-known dance band that had an eclectic repertoire, began to find it increasingly difficult to maintain their popularity with their "pet crowd" of rock 'n' roll enthusiasts. Since Laryea felt a loyalty to his young peers, he began to perform at private parties or gatherings on the beach—locales where he could retain his creative license, perform rock 'n' roll songs, and freely delight those in attendance (see figure 11.4). While Laryea recalled that these opportunities allowed him to skirt government directives, he confessed that they rarely accorded him any monetary income, secured him fame in state-owned media outlets, or connected him to powerful government officials.[52]

Those most infuriated with the government's attempts to modernize urban Ghana's popular music scene were the large numbers of urban youth who placed rock 'n' roll at the center of their recreational ventures. Although many young people realized that they were the prime targets of Nkrumah's modernization efforts, many confessed that they failed to understand how they could reconcile its directives with their established tastes and practices. Alex Moffatt remembered the African Personality as "big words" that constituted a nebulous call for cultural change, but confessed that he saw no compelling reason to abide by its tenets. Others understood that Nkrumah wanted to use culture to motivate Ghanaians "to come together," but failed to appreciate why they needed to abandon foreign styles of music or dance in order to make this happen.[53] Rather than finding inspiration in official edicts, many young people maintained that they, not government authorities, were best positioned to outline a national culture capable of commemorating Ghana's independence and ensuring its future prosperity. Rock 'n' roll, they insisted, was not an "unhealthy" music antithetical to "Ghanaian" culture; it was a powerful medium that linked its participants to an international cohort of youth who promoted liberation, celebrated consumption, and publicly combated the depersonalization that generations of Ghanaians had experienced under colonial rule. Numerous youth were convinced that the music's vibrant beat,

Figure 11.4. A young Francis Laryea plays trumpet at a rock 'n' roll dance sponsored by the Black Eagle Club, ca. 1960. Photo courtesy of Francis Laryea.

flashy style of dance, and corresponding aesthetics were the perfect mediums to announce the end of an oppressive era and celebrate the new freedoms they had claimed since its demise (Salm 2003, 183–87; Diawara 2005, 242–65).

Since many youth valued rock 'n' roll as a symbol of their personal and national liberation, they viewed the CPP government's suppression of it as a deliberate attempt to dismiss their expanding knowledge and sociopolitical importance. Bob Biney recalled rock 'n' roll not simply as his music of choice, but as a cultural form that helped him "open his eyes" and enabled him and his young peers to behave "like Yankees" rather than disempowered persons.[54] Frankie Laine and his friends approached rock 'n' roll with similar aspirations, adopting American nicknames, modeling their dress after actors in American films, and encouraging their peers to dance to rock 'n' roll "all night long" so that they could claim their rightful place as enfranchised city residents.[55] If they allowed the government to remove rock 'n' roll from Ghana's musical scene, many young people argued, they would lose both a valued mode of enjoyment and their future ability to voice their concerns and shape national affairs.

In Accra, many youth elected to counter the CPP's program of cultural modernization by joining rock 'n' roll clubs, private organizations that promoted the music, offered instruction in its corresponding forms of dance and dress, and prioritized an open environment of self-expression and collegial exchange. Although Accra's first rock 'n' roll clubs emerged in the late 1950s, such organizations grew considerably throughout the early 1960s, when many city neighborhoods had several clubs comprised of hundreds of young members (Salm 2003, 192). Most of these clubs attempted to deflect accusations about their "rebellious" nature by instituting a strict culture of organization, electing officials, establishing rules, instituting membership fees, and issuing identity cards—actions that provided members with a collective identity and communal framework (195–200). Despite their embrace of such structured components, most clubs went to great lengths to ensure that they offered their members a safe haven of encouragement, experimentation, and camaraderie. As Nii Agden Tettey explained, clubs did not ask their members to dance to rock 'n' roll in a uniform fashion, but implored them to move in a way that corresponded to their abilities and sentiments:

> We the young ones went to the beach to practice rock 'n' roll. We would learn the dances there, but we wouldn't accuse each other. We didn't talk about who knew what; you did what you liked. Highlife and rock 'n' roll, they were open dances based on how you felt. There wasn't right or wrong! In the Ga language we have a proverb, "However I dance, it's a dance." . . . Whether you dance rough or you dance smooth, the ground will not die. It doesn't kill the land. . . . We would use that phrase to encourage everybody.[56]

In addition to offering rock 'n' rollers autonomous arenas in which they could listen to the latest American hits, experiment with new dance steps, and express notions of self, most clubs accorded their members means of fulfilling nonrecreational needs. Many rock 'n' roll clubs operated as voluntary associations that assisted their members in their efforts to create a successful personal and professional life. They offered members access to financial resources, help finding employment or temporary housing, and training in particular trades, enabling them to gain new skills without joining the Builders Brigade or another government program.[57] By allowing city youth to improve their personal futures without relying on a government determined to dictate Ghana's political, economic, and cultural domains, such clubs endeavored to preserve the optimism, energy, and sense of personal freedom that national independence had unleashed amongst them (Diawara 2005, 246).

Conclusion

In a 1964 newspaper article entitled "Nkrumahism and Africa's Youth," Abbey Okai expressed concern about the growing number of Ghanaian youth embracing foreign, rather than local, cultural forms. Although they were unquestionably "aware that twist and rock 'n' roll have no place in our culture," these wayward young people continued to engage the "ugly monster" of "cultural imperialism" and, in the process, adopt the very "colonial mentality" that Nkrumah and the CPP had fought so hard to defeat. In his estimation, young people were perpetuating Ghana's move backward rather than forward, thereby countering Nkrumah's central maxim—forward ever, backward never—as well as his government's larger efforts to dismantle the lingering impacts of Ghana's oppressive past. Their efforts, moreover, unveiled why it was so important that the CPP, rather than Ghanaian citizens, retain control over the nation's cultural realm. Without having the ability to correct its citizen's mistakes, Okai noted, the government could never fully guide the nation toward a prosperous future.[58]

In a sense, Okai's piece offered readers an efficient summation of Nkrumah's approach toward cultural modernization in the years following Ghana's independence. The best path forward, his government insisted, was for Ghanaians to resurrect their lost heritage and self-worth through the "African Personality," a set of collective practices and shared values that had flourished prior to colonial rule. If revived, these tenets would not only bring Ghanaians together under a cemented nationalist ethos; they would facilitate the daunting task of transforming Ghana from an ex-British colony into a fully functional nation-state. At a broad level, Nkrumah saw culture, especially local elements that he and Arts Council officials handpicked for their invented national culture, as essential to his efforts to create an industrial society predicated on hard work, education, and patriotic service. More narrowly, it approached urban Ghana's popular music scene as an ideal realm in which to promote those ideals over those favored by its various constituents. From 1957 to 1965, the CPP government and the Ghana Arts Council worked to transform popular musical recreation into something that was indisputably "Ghanaian," that could promote the merits of local, rather than foreign, cultural forms, and that could help convince the country's "problematic" populations, particularly urban youth, to adopt the African Personality.

At the same time, however, Okai's 1964 article demonstrates the limited impact that this ambitious program of modernization had, particularly in regard to altering the tastes and practices of the young residents deemed central to the nation's future. While Nkrumah's CPP pursued its agenda of modernization with the hopes of solidifying its power and facilitating its wider development plans, many of those who took part in popular music considered state interventions to be unjust impositions that had recreational and nonrecreational impacts. Many musicians, particularly those who were unable to participate in a council training program, found it difficult to learn local musical styles, remove foreign songs from their repertoires, and secure the bookings, radio airplay, or contracts needed to ensure that they earned an adequate income. Musical audiences, particularly young people who favored rock 'n' roll, saw the council's efforts as attempts to silence their voice, limit their freedom, and suppress their contributions to Ghana's cultural fabric. They continued to embrace rock 'n' roll because it amply demonstrated that they ignored the CPP's cultural agenda. Like the state, they approached popular music as a place of power that they could use to fulfill their own aims.

Notes

1. "Night Life in Christiansborg," *Sunday Mirror,* 1 November 1953.

2. "'Highlife' Takes on a New Name," *Sunday Mirror,* 1 July 1960; "'Osibi' is New Name," *Sunday Mirror,* 4 September 1960. For more on *osibisaaba,* see Plageman (2013, 48–55).

3. For more on the diverse character of popular musical recreation in Ghana's urban areas, see Plageman (2013); Collins (1994, 1996); Darkwa (1971); Akyeampong (1996).

4. Nkrumah's government was not alone in its efforts to co-opt popular music for "national" aims: Askew (2002, 171–91); Turino (2000, 177–84); White (2008, 69–79).

5. "Osagyefo's Speech at the Drama Studio, Saturday 21st October 1961," Public Records and Archives Administration Department [PRAAD]-Accra, RG 3/7/33.

6. "Ghana Republic Is Born," "To the Students of Ghana College, Tamale," "On Home Affairs," "The Noble Task of Teaching," and "Visit to Sunyani," in Nkrumah (1979, 1:93, 203–204, 206–11, 226–30, 251–54).

7. Both the *Daily Graphic* and the *Sunday Mirror* were purchased by Nkrumah's government in 1962. An exhaustive listing of all newspaper articles addressing the appearance of the "new woman" is not possible here, but see the following issues of the 1965 *Sunday Mirror:* 3, 24, and 31 January; 7 and 14 February; 28 March; 11, 18, and 25 April; 2, 9, and 16 May; 13, 20, and 27 June; 4 and 18 July; 15 and 22 August; 5, 12, 19, and 26 September; 3, 10, and 31 October; 7, 14, and 21 November.

8. Interviews with Isaac Amuah, Cape Coast, 30 March 2005; and Diana Oboshilay, Accra New Town, 24 May 2005; "Three Ways to Elegance," *Sunday Mirror,* 20 October 1963. For more on the debates surrounding women's dress, see Allman (2004, 144–65).

9. See the following issues of the *Sunday Mirror:* 13 March 1960; 17 April 1960; 3 July 1960; 17 March 1963; 5 May 1963; 26 December 1963; and 28 March 1965.

10. "Ghana's Republic Is Born," and "To Ghana Women and Women of African Descent," in Nkrumah, *Selected Speeches,* 1:94, 116–21; "Wanted: Ghana's New Girl," *Sunday Mirror,* 1 March 1964.

11. "My Ideal Girl," *Sunday Mirror,* 29 March 1964; "Keep Those Looks But . . . ," *Sunday Mirror,* 3 January 1965; "Serve Country with Love and Courage," *Sunday Mirror,* 2 May 1965.

12. Interviews with Charity Agbenyega, Accra New Town, 27 April 2005; Harry Amenumey, Chokor, Accra, 3 May 2005; J. O. Mills, La Paz, Accra, 6 May 2005.

13. Interviews with J. J. Sarpong, James Town, Accra, 7 June 2005; and Aeshitu Zinabo, Comfort Kwame, and Victoria Quainoo, Accra New Town, 12 June 2009; "Stop This Menace in Ghana," *Daily Graphic,* 22 December 1959.

14. Interview with J. O. Mills, 6 May 2005.

15. Interview with James Allotey, Accra New Town, 27 April 2005; "Cape Coast Takes the Lead . . . 'Fish' Skirts Now Banned," *Sunday Mirror,* 19 June 1963; "Must We Ban Such Dresses," *Sunday Mirror,* 30 June 1963.

16. For more on such concerns, see "Juvenile Delinquency and Welfare," PRAAD-Accra, CSO 15/3/340/88; "Department of Social Welfare and Housing," PRAAD-Sekondi, WRG 24/1/232/47; "Case No. 2898, James Town Police," PRAAD-Sekondi, WRG 47/1/15/221.

17. Ahlman (2011, 78–79); "War on Anti-Social Practices," *The Ghanaian*, 7 October 1964.

18. Austin (1964, 380–84). In 1961, the Censorship Board banned two films, *Love Me Tender* and *Rock Pretty Baby*, for their musical contents; "Censored Films," PRAAD-Sekondi, WRG 34/1/12; "Ghana Today," *The Ghanaian*, January 1961.

19. Hodge (1964, 114–21); "Builders' Brigade Is to Curb Love for White-Collar Jobs," *Ghana Times*, 3 October 1958; "Work and Workers Page: Nothing Is More Hopeful in Ghana Than the Builder's Brigade Camps," *The Ghanaian*, June 1960.

20. Hodge (1964, 115 and 124); "The Achievements of the Workers Brigade," *Ghana Pictorial*, September 1962, 14.

21. Interview with Margaret Esi Andrews, Accra New Town, 12 June 2009; Hodge (1964, 119–22); "New Sporting Era in West Africa" and "Sports and African Unity," in Nkrumah (1979, 1:26–29).

22. "Builders' Brigade Band," *Ghana Times*, 11 April 1959; "No. 1 Builders' Brigade Band," *Sunday Mirror*, 5 July 1959; "Tops of the Pops: Harvest of Discs" *Sunday Mirror*, 11 October, 1959.

23. "Spike and Tommy the Winners," *Daily Graphic*, 10 July 1959; "9 Will Play in Accra August 1," *Sunday Mirror*, 26 July 1959. Many Brigade songs, such as "*Hedzole* [Freedom] *aha Brigades*," espoused pro-government messages (Collins 2003, 7).

24. The council originated as an interim committee in 1955, but was formally instituted as a permanent government body by the Arts Council of Ghana Law in December 1958. For more on its early operation, see "Interim Committee for an Arts Council," PRAAD-Accra, RG 3/7/212.

25. "Arts Council, General Matters: 1959–60," PRAAD-Accra, RG 3/7/31; "Arts Council General Matters and Policies," PRAAD-Accra, RG 3/7/33.

26. "Brong-Ahafo Region Arts Committee Monthly Report for May, 1961," and "Monthly Report Eastern Region Arts Committee, August 1961," PRAAD-Accra, RG 3/7/243.

27. "Report on the Black Star Troupe—'Un-Ghanaian Dancing,'" PRAAD-Accra, RG 3/7/57/1.

28. "Monthly Report Eastern Regional Arts Committee, April 1961," PRAAD-Accra, RG 3/7/243/3; "Minutes of the First Meeting of the Dance Panel," PRAAD-Accra, RG 3/7/156/5.

29. "Minutes of the First Meeting of the Dance Panel," PRAAD-Accra, RG 3/7/156/5; "Arts Council General Matters and Policies," PRAAD-Accra, RG 3/7/33.

30. Interview with Stan Plange, Osu, Accra, 5 October 2005; "The Ghana Institute of Art and Culture: Drumming and Dancing," PRAAD-Accra, RG 3/7/57/121.

31. "Local Government Dance Band," PRAAD-Accra, RG 3/7/57; "Messengers Dance Band Activities," PRAAD-Accra, RG 3/7/68; "Globemasters Dance Band, General Correspondence," PRAAD-Accra, RG 3/7/193.

32. "Dance Band General Matters," PRAAD-Accra, RG 3/7/197.

33. "Messengers Dance Band Activities," PRAAD-Accra, RG 3/7/68.

34. "Messengers Dance Band Activities," PRAAD-Accra, RG 3/7/68; "Globemasters Dance Band, General Correspondence," PRAAD-Accra, RG 3/7/193. In his second quarterly report of 1963, Opoku Ware reported that he taught the Workers Brigade Dance Band a pro-government highlife entitled "*Nkrumah Wo Ho Yɛhu*" ("Report: From April-July, 1963," PRAAD-Accra, RG 3/7/57).

35. Interviews with Henry Ayawovie, Accra New Town, 30 May 2005; and Ebo Taylor, Legon, Accra, 1 September 2005.

36. "Dance Band General Matters," PRAAD-Accra, RG 3/7/197/13, 18, 21, 46; "Messengers Dance Band Activities," PRAAD-Accra, RG 3/7/68/92; "Globemasters Dance Band, General Correspondence," PRAAD-Accra, RG 3/7/193.

37. Interview with Plange, 5 October 2005.

38. Interviews with Stan Plange, Airport Residential Area, Accra, 29 June 2005 and 5 October 2005.

39. "National Drama Company," PRAAD-Accra, RG 3/7/171/165, 177, 211, 317; "Messengers Dance Band Activities," PRAAD-Accra, RG 3/7/68/92; "Report on My Staff—Drumming and Dancing Section," PRAAD-Accra, RG 3/7/57.

40. "Dance Band General Matters," PRAAD-Accra, RG 3/7/197/13, 18, 21, 46.

41. "Modernaires Dance Band Is Reborn," *Ghana Pictorial,* September 1962; "Aikens—the First Picture," *Sunday Mirror* 2 June 1963; "Joe Mensah—A Singer with a Vibrant Voice," *Sunday Mirror,* 8 September 1963; "Who Earns More Fame for Ghana: Sportsmen or Musicians?" *Sunday Mirror,* 9 February 1964.

42. Interviews with Jerry Hansen, North Kaneshie, Accra, 3 October 2005 and 13 October 2005; "Encore Ramblers!" *Sunday Mirror,* 2 February 1964; "Work and Happiness," *Sunday Mirror,* 16 February 1964. The song's title corresponds to that of a speech given by Kwame Nkrumah on 5 May 1962: "Work and Happiness: Ghana's Seven-Year Development Plan," in Nkrumah (1979, 3:65–70).

43. Interviews with Ebo Taylor, Legon, Accra, 24 August 2005 and 1 September 2005; Stan Plange, 5 October 2005.

44. "Outline Program for the Fourth Republic Anniversary Celebrations in 1964," PRAAD-Accra, RG3/7/9/31, 43, 44, and 45.

45. "The National Dance Bands Competition," PRAAD-Accra, RG 3/7/197/84; "Minutes of Meeting Held between the Arts Council Members and the Bandsmen," PRAAD-Accra, RG 3/7/197/100–104; "The National Dance Bands Competition—Round 3, Western Region," PRAAD-Accra, RG 3/7/197/158.

46. "Regional Music Activities," PRAAD-Accra, RG 3/7/154; "Arts Council of Ghana," PRAAD-Sekondi, WRG 34/1/11; "Drumming and Dancing," PRAAD-Accra, RG 3/7/145; Salm (2003, 202).

47. Interviews with Grershon Gaba, Lartebiokorshie, Accra, 29 April 2005; Justina and Edna Fugar, Accra New Town, 29 April 2005; Margaret Akosua Acolatse, Accra New Town, 19 May 2005.

48. Interviews with Ebo Taylor, La Paz, Accra, 26 July 2005; Saka Acquaye, Korle Gonno, Accra, 24 August 2005; Jerry Hansen, 3 October 2005.

49. Interview with Nana Ampadu, La Paz, Accra, 24 September 2005.

50. Interviews with Kofi Lindsay, Cape Coast, 22 June 2005; Saka Acquaye, 24 August 2005; Jerry Hansen, 3 October 2005.

51. Interviews with Bob Biney, Cape Coast, 1 April 2005; and J. J. Sarpong, James Town, Accra, 24 August 2005.

52. Interviews with Francis Laryea, Mamprobi, Accra, 6 June 2009; and Peter Manuh, Legon, Accra, 23 July 2005.

53. Interviews with James Allotey and Alex Bakpa Moffatt, Abose Okai, Accra, 19 July 2009; Felicia Kudiah, Accra New Town, 19 July 2009; Elizabeth Amonoo, La Paz, Accra, 20 June 2009.

54. Interviews with Bob Biney, 1 April 2005; and Frankie Laine, James Town, Accra, 3 June 2009.

55. Interview with Frankie Laine, 3 June 2009; Salm (2003, 208–12).

56. Interview with Nii Adgin Tettey, Alajo, Accra, 11 September 2005.

57. Interview with Nii Adgin Tettey, 11 September 2005; Salm (2003, 235).

58. Abbey Okai, "Nkrumahism and Africa's Youth," *The Ghanaian,* 7 July 1964; also cited in Salm (2003, 224).

References

Newspapers and Periodicals

Daily Graphic, 1957–1965
Ghana Pictorial, 1962
Ghana Times, 1958–1959
Ghana Today, 1957–1959, 1968
The Ghanaian, 1960–1961, 1964–1965
Sunday Mirror, 1957–1965

Secondary Works

Ahlman, Jeffrey S. 2011. "Living with Nkrumahism: Nation, State, and Pan-Africanism in Ghana." PhD diss., University of Illinois, Urbana-Champaign.

Akyeampong, Emmanuel. 1996. *Drink, Power and Cultural Change: A Social History of Alcohol in Ghana, c. 1800 to Recent Times.* Portsmouth, NH: Heinemann.

Allman, Jean. 2004. "'Let Your Fashion Be in Line with Our Ghanaian Costume': Nation, Gender, and the Politics of Cloth-ing in Nkrumah's Ghana." In *Fashioning Africa: Power and the Politics of Dress,* edited by Jean Allman, 144–65. Bloomington: Indiana University Press.

———. 1993. *The Quills of the Porcupine: Asante Nationalism in an Emergent Ghana.* Madison: University of Wisconsin Press.

Askew, Kelly. 2002. *Performing the Nation: Swahili Music and Cultural Politics in Tanzania.* Chicago: University of Chicago Press.

Austin, Dennis. 1964. *Politics in Ghana: 1946–1960.* London: Oxford University Press.

Biney, Ama. 2011. *The Political and Social Thought of Kwame Nkrumah.* New York: Palgrave Macmillan.

Botwe-Asamoah, Kwame. 2005. *Kwame Nkrumah's Politico-Cultural Thought and Policies: An African-Centered Paradigm for the Second Phase of the African Revolution.* New York: Routledge.

Clarkson, M. L. 1955. *Juveniles in Drinking Bars and Nightclubs: A Report on Conditions Observed in Accra, Kumasi, and Takoradi.* Accra: Department of Social Welfare.

Collins, John. 1994. "The Ghanaian Concert Party: African Popular Entertainment at the Cross Roads." PhD diss., State University of New York at Buffalo.

———. 1996. *Highlife Time.* Accra: Anansesem.

———. 2003. "The Importance of African Popular Music Studies For Ghanaian/African Students." Paper presented at CODESRIA's 30th Anniversary Humanities Conference, Accra, 17–19 September.

Darkwa, K. Ampom. 1971. "Migrant Music and Musicians: The Effect of Migration on Music; Pt. 1; Nima Opinion Survey." PhD diss., University of Ghana, Institute of African Studies.

Diawara, Manthia. 2005. "The Sixties in Bamako: Malick Sidibé and James Brown." In *Black Cultural Traffic: Crossroads in Global Performance and Popular Culture,* edited by Harry J. Elam Jr. and Kennell Jackson, 242–65. Ann Arbor: University of Michigan Press.

Gold Coast. 1955. *Problem Children of the Gold Coast.* Accra: Government Printer.

Government of Ghana. 1959. *Second Development Plan, 1959–64.* Accra: Government Printer.

Hagan, George P. 1991. "Nkrumah's Cultural Policy." In *The Life and Work of Kwame Nkrumah: Papers of a Symposium Organized by the Institute of African Studies,* edited by Kwame Arhin, 1–26. Accra: Sedco.

Hanna, Judith Lynne. 1973. "The Highlife: A West African Urban Dance." In *Dance Research Monograph One: 1971–1972*, edited by Patricia A. Rowe, 139–52. New York: Committee on Research in Dance.

Hodge, Peter. 1964. "The Ghana Workers Brigade: A Project for Unemployed Youth." *British Journal of Sociology* 15, no. 2: 113–28.

Lindsay, Lisa A., and Stephan F. Miescher, eds. 2003. *Men and Masculinities in Modern Africa*. Portsmouth, NH: Heinemann.

Nkrumah, Kwame. 1997. *Selected Speeches of Kwame Nkrumah*. 5 vols. Compiled by Samuel Obeng. Accra: Afram Publications.

Plageman, Nate. 2013. *Highlife Saturday Night: Popular Music and Social Change in Urban Ghana*. Bloomington: Indiana University Press.

Quarcoopome, Samuel S. 1992. "Urbanisation, Land Alienation, and Politics in Accra." *University of Ghana Research Review* 8, nos. 1–2: 40–54.

Salm, Steven J. 2003. "The Bukom Boys: Subcultures and Identity Transformation in Accra, Ghana." PhD diss., University of Texas.

Turino, Thomas. 2000. *Nationalists, Cosmopolitans, and Popular Music in Zimbabwe*. Chicago: University of Chicago Press.

White, Bob W. 2008. *Rumba Rules: The Politics of Dance Music in Mobutu's Zaire*. Durham, NC: Duke University Press.

12 Building Institutions for the New Africa

The Institute of African Studies at the University of Ghana

Takyiwaa Manuh

In the volume *African Intellectuals,* Thandika Mkandawire (2005) and his coauthors contend that Pan-Africanism has been an enduring framework that has shaped several generations of African intellectuals and nationalists in their imaginings of the nation. This embrace of Pan-Africanism formed an intrinsic component of the struggle against foreign domination and underdevelopment on the one hand, and the desire, on the other, to put Africa on par with other modern nations, expressed by the nationalists' dual track of nation-building and economic development. Crucially, African nationalists and intellectuals linked Africa's domination to its technoeconomic backwardness (see Rodney 1972). The demand for independence was therefore to bring material progress to African people and to end the deprivations and extortions that had characterized colonial rule. Presaging later demands for a "New International Economic Order" by the global South (United Nations 1974; Bagwati 1977), nationalists viewed "the *right* to industrialization" as part of the self-assertion and freedom that was to accompany independence, famously expressed by the noted Pan-Africanist Edward Wilmot Blyden, as the *imperative* of "modernization," in order for Africa to escape the domination and humiliation it had suffered at the hands of the West and attain "self-reliance and independence."[1]

But the "catch-up" that Africa was embarking upon was not to be seen as imposed from outside, but as arising from an objective analysis of African realities and needs, if Africans were to emerge as self-respecting and responsible citizens claiming their rightful place in the world to escape the unholy trinity of ignorance, poverty and disease.[2] Indeed as Blyden stated in his 1872 campaign for a West African university, which he insisted must be "native-controlled," this would be a means of "unfettering the negro mind in expiation of past wrongs to the African race" (cited in Agbodeka 1998, 2). Francis Agbodeka glosses Blyden's phrase "unfettering the negro mind" as "among other things, the creation and building of an indigenous literature." Moreover, he attributes these demands to what he terms the "growing national consciousness" among Africans. Agbodeka cites J. E. Casely Hayford, whose *Ethiopia Unbound* set out his ideal university whose characteristics would include the promotion of "love for one's own language, customs and institutions . . . a university thoroughly conscientious of, and adapted to its environment, but simultaneously maintaining an international standard."[3] But the few universities established by colonial authorities across Africa, often under pressure from nationalists, were conceptualized and molded in a different tradition, and aimed only at attaining "international standards" rather than being rooted in specifically African intellectual traditions and bodies of knowledge.[4]

Undergirding African economic development was the process of nation-building, which was concerned not only with establishing institutions, competencies, and brick-and-mortar structures, but also with reversing the centuries-old psychological conditioning and mental slavery and the denial of Africa's humanity and capacity that imperialism and colonialism had unleashed. Nationalist politicians and intellectuals viewed the task of African self-recovery and the resuscitation of its histories, cultures, and values not only as setting straight the colonial record and righting old wrongs, but also as claiming an African modernity adapted to its own history and culture, distinct from European and imperialist claims of universalism. Thus, as Mkandawire (2005, 6–7) asserts, Léopold Senghor's "Negritude," Julius Nyerere's "African Socialism," and Kwame Nkrumah's "African Personality" should be seen as part of attempts by prominent African political actors to give "the project of modernization an African soul, in the attempt to rescue African memories from colonial clutches, and to embed them within African cultures," in an attempt to turn African cultures into pillars of a self-confident Africa. To do this successfully required the development of new historiographies, as well as the use and propagation of the hitherto denigrated and marginalized African languages to ground scientific knowledge in African realities. This, in turn, would be the appropriate vehicle to convey African literary, philosophical, and sociological thought and productions to the majority of African populations who often did not speak any imperial or trade language (Chumbow 2005).

It is within this project of recovery and self-assertion that this chapter addresses the establishment of the Institute of African Studies (IAS) at the University of Ghana, Legon. With the direct encouragement and support of President Nkrumah in the newly independent Ghana, the IAS, alongside other institutions such as the Ghana Academy of Learning (later the Ghana Academy of Sciences) and the Bureau of African Affairs, was to form the bedrock for the emergence of the African Personality and African renaissance. The latter two institutions are briefly presented before turning to an examination of the institute and its fortunes, particularly after the overthrow of President Nkrumah. Much of the information on the establishment of the institute was obtained from the institute's own recently organized archives.[5]

Ghana's Independence and the Pan-Africanist Project

In 1957, Ghana attained independence as the first colonized sub-Saharan country to free itself from colonial rule. Kwame Nkrumah, who galvanized the struggle, conceived of Ghana's independence as only a part of the struggle for a continental union of Africa. In his speech to an assembled gathering of Ghanaians on the eve of independence, he proclaimed that Ghana's independence was "meaningless unless it [was] linked up with the total liberation of the African continent" (Nkrumah 1961, 107). For Nkrumah, total African liberation, unity, integration, and Pan-Africanism were seen as necessary to deal with the legacies of colonialism and underdevelopment and to transform African societies.

To assist in this effort, several regional and continental organizations were to be set up, and Ghana soon became a beehive of activity and home to several intellectuals of radical persuasion, including W. E. B. Du Bois, George Padmore, Richard Wright, and Basil Davidson, alongside many Diasporic Africans who directly assisted in this effort (Gaines 2006). In December 1957, Nkrumah appointed Padmore, a Trinidadian, as special advisor on African affairs, as a parallel organization in Ghana's Ministry of Foreign Affairs; this office was renamed the Bureau of African Affairs after Padmore's death in 1959.[6] It was from this office in Accra that Padmore assisted Nkrumah in organizing the Conference of the Independent States of Africa (Ghana, Liberia, and Ethiopia) in April 1958, followed by the All-Africa Peoples' Conference in December 1958. Both of these conferences were seen as precursors to the union government of Africa (a United States of Africa or an African Commonwealth), and these led, in 1963, to the establishment of the Organization of African Unity, now the African Union, albeit not in the form desired by the progressive group led by Nkrumah.[7] In both conferences, issues of culture and of continental self-discovery were raised as paramount, to restore the dignity, will, and personality of the African so trampled upon under colonialism.

In 1959, the Ghana Academy of Learning (later the Ghana Academy of Sciences) was established on the initiative of Prime Minister Nkrumah, who became a founding member and keen supporter, to promote the study, extension, and dissemination of knowledge of the arts and sciences in Ghana. And in 1961, the *Encyclopaedia Africana* project, described as a "scientific and authentically African Compendium of the known facts concerning African Life, History and Culture"[8] that would "reveal the genius of her people, their history, culture and institutions; their achievements as well as shortcomings,"[9] was launched under the editorship of the venerable Pan-Africanist W. E. B. Du Bois, who had relocated to Ghana from the United States at the invitation of President Nkrumah. The establishment of the Institute of African Studies at the University of Ghana in 1961 can therefore be placed as part of the institutional arsenal in the process of intellectual recovery aimed at rewriting history and ending the erasure of Africans and Africanist knowledge from dominant interpretive frameworks, to buttress the intellectual work of the African revolution and the Pan-Africanist project. In the modernist project that the newly independent Ghanaian state was engaged in, new institutions needed to be created to both recall the African past and project it into the future.

These direct actions by the state complemented the efforts made by the first generation of post-independent African historians and social scientists to create alternative, sometimes radical narratives of African history and development at universities in Ibadan, Dakar, Zaria, and Dar-es-Salam that dealt with questions of evidence, method, interpretation, and theory (Olukoshi 2007; Mkandawire 2005).[10] These efforts also connected to Africanization processes within the bureaucracy, the military, and educational institutions that the newly minted African states were to launch to signify their accessions to power and black control. As (Joseph Hanson) Kwabena Nketia, first African director of the institute, was later to state, emancipation from slavery and the attainment of independence from colonial rule saw the restoration of

> the freedom to drum, sing and dance in the traditional way in contemporary contexts . . . a symbolic affirmation of the declaration of independence while the re-conceptualization of the arts as national arts enabled them to be used in fostering national consciousness. (Nketia 1996)

Mkandawire (2005) has called attention to the many intellectuals who committed themselves to the nation-building and developmentalist projects set out by the new nationalist political leaders, in much the same way that Nketia asserted for the arts. But this meeting of minds was short-lived for many of the intellectuals, since the homogenizing tendencies and growing authoritarianism of the nation-building project soon created irreparable barriers between them and the political leaders.[11]

The Establishment of the Institute of African Studies

The beginnings of the Institute of African Studies go back to the immediate postwar years. During the 1948–1949 session, K. A. Busia started a School of African Studies under the Faculty of Arts at the University College of the Gold Coast, then located at Achimota College. As Agbodeka recounts, the initiative for setting up the school seemed to have come from the Inter University Council (IUC) that had been formed following the Asquith Commission on Higher Education in the Colonies, in response to "the age-long African pressure for inclusion of African Studies in the curricula of proposed African universities" (Agbodeka 1998, 60). The IUC proposed the establishment of a department of African studies to be concerned with the study of African languages, traditions, and culture. The department was to be wholly devoted to research in its early stages, and the person to be appointed as head, who would be of professorial status, was to possess qualifications in either social anthropology or the study of languages, with experience in the study of African languages (Agbodeka 1998, 61). Busia, a sociologist, was appointed as lecturer to launch the school in 1949, and it was proposed that the school should consist of three divisions, namely, sociology, archaeology, and African languages. But there were problems with staffing and the school was closed in 1950 and replaced by the Department of Sociology, while a separate Department of Archaeology was also set up. However, a remnant of the African Studies section continued to be attached to the Department of Sociology, and it was to this that Kwabena Nketia was appointed in 1952 as research fellow in traditional music, folklore, and festivals in West Africa, beginning a flourishing program of research.

In 1959, an interim committee recommended the setting up of an Institute of African Studies. The committee considered the establishment of a research institute or a teaching department of African languages and/or studies where research and teaching could proceed. The view was that the new institute should not at that stage concern itself with subjects in which research was already being carried out in other departments. Essentially, the interim committee endorsed the proposal of J. D. Fage of the History Department to create an Institute of Ethnology concerned mainly with "collecting, studying, and publishing material relating to the cultures of Africa not otherwise catered for in the College and in particular (i) to record, analyze, and map the distribution of African languages; and (ii) to collect, record, translate, and publish chronicles, folk-tales, music, dance and, other cultural material." The committee also considered the proposal that an Institute of Islamic Studies should be set up, but did not think it appropriate at the time, on the grounds of cost, and also because several such facilities were being set up in other places around the world.[12] As Ivor Wilks (2008) recalls, in 1960 foundations for the institute began to be laid under acting director Peter L. Shinnie, professor of archaeology, and appointments were made for music and arts, as well as historical and social studies, while two linguists were recruited to build up materials on the study of Ghanaian languages. Subsequently a small committee was formed to coordinate African studies in departments that wanted their students to study African material (Agbodeka 1998, 168).[13]

But the shape of the institute that was to emerge changed with the appointment of Thomas Hodgkin, formerly of Balliol College, University of Oxford, as

IAS director in 1961. This appointment also coincided with the decision of the government to have the university college take on full university status and cease its special relation with the University of London. As Agbodeka (1998, 123) records, the other matter which the nationalist government considered a problem was that the Oxbridge (Oxford and Cambridge) tradition had been implanted in the embryo universities of the colonial territories, which were "adorned with the outward trappings of the older British universities."[14] To remedy this, an international Commission on University Education in Ghana was set up, to reorientate higher education in Ghana (Government of Ghana 1961).

In his proposals for the institute, Hodgkin rejected the narrow frame that the original movers of the institute had cast for it. Instead Hodgkin opted for an institute that addressed issues of history, identity, culture, and continental self-recovery as part of the process of rewriting Africa back into the history that it had been denied. This new approach was to focus on the human agency of Africans as makers of their history. As Frederick Cooper (1999) and others have noted, Africa had been the domain of anthropology, while history was the domain of European expansion.

The proposed institute had unique objectives. Unlike African studies centers in Europe and North America, the institute was envisaged neither as a mere coordinating "program" for scholars working in existing departments nor as an organization for promoting teaching and research in African studies across the disciplines. Although all these were to be a part of its functions, the institute was conceived as a separate organization with its own director and research fellows.[15] The institute was to provide a base for "research workers from overseas engaged in fieldwork" including postgraduate students from other universities, and it was also envisioned that a number of temporary appointments, particularly visiting professorships and lectureships, would be made as the need arose. Finally, the institute was to establish links with "Ghanaians in every walk of life who were making a contribution to African Studies in such fields as local history, ethnology, linguistic studies, literature and the arts."[16]

On staffing, Hodgkin proposed that in addition to a director and associate director, there would be eight permanent or semipermanent members and four visiting professors or visiting research fellows; four to five research assistants; a publications officer/editor; a full-time specialist librarian; an Arabist; a linguist, specializing in Hausa; a specialist in Amharic and Ethiopian history who could be short-term or a visiting professor; and a French-speaking African, who would be a specialist in either the history of the Western Sudan or the institutions of French West Africa. Hodgkin also saw the institute as producing "Chatham House" papers, to influence policy and thinking on African affairs.[17] The commission's report supported Hodgkin's position. It recommended the establishment at Legon of an institute "concerned with the study of African societies in all aspects which would work in close association with appropriate teaching departments at both (Legon and Kumasi) universities" (cited in Agbodeka 1998, 126).

The government's statement on the report noted that the main focus for research and postgraduate teaching in the University of Ghana should be in the Institute of African Studies, which was to take an active interest in the *whole range* (emphasis original) of African studies. But the report conceded that there would be practical limitations on research and teaching in particular sectors. According to the report, the range of African studies was defined as history (including geographical background to African history) and archaeology; sociology and social anthropology, with related studies of African government, law, economics, religion, and philosophy; and African languages, literature, and arts (including music).[18]

The institute was also charged with organizing lecture courses in African studies for students in Legon and at the other public universities in Kumasi and Cape Coast.[19] This was to be a special course, or cycle of courses, in which all the departments working in the field of African studies were expected to cooperate and deliver. This course was initially envisaged as a three-year degree course and the general approach was to be historical, emphasizing the region of West Africa. But the university's academic board decided that the course should be limited to the first year because it would fit better into the new degree structure. A School of Music and Drama was also added, and outstanding faculty were recruited from what was then the Kumasi College of Technology. Further, a National Dance Company, later called the Ghana Dance Ensemble, was set up within the institute as an experimental dance company (Nketia 1965, 1996). The Institute of African Studies was established in 1961 and commenced operation two years later. In October 1963, President Nkrumah formally opened the institute with his seminal speech "The African Genius," which set out strategic directions for the institute (Nkrumah 1963). Nearly fifty years later, the speech, key elements of which are set out below, is still regarded as the founding charter of the institute by successive directors and staff members.[20] The speech is also instructive for rethinking modernization in Nkrumah's Ghana and what the institute's role was envisioned to be.

As understood by Nkrumah, the African Genius was different from the *Négritude* philosophy of Senghor.[21] It was not apologetic, but dynamic, based on African values, conceptions, and agency, as well as on an African sense of hospitality. The institute was to give expression to this genius and, in the process, fertilize the university, as it also made its own specific contribution to the advancement of knowledge about the peoples and cultures of Africa through the study of their past history and contemporary challenges. Nkrumah (1963) called on the institute to reinterpret and make a new assessment of the factors which make up the African past, in place of the "colonial studies" of Africa in many institutions in

Europe. The institute was charged with studying the history, culture and institutions, and languages and arts of Ghana and of Africa in new *African-centered* ways, away from the then-dominant interpretative frameworks. But Africa was defined as more than the continental space, and close relations were to be fostered with scholars of African descent in the Americas and the Caribbean.

The second guiding principle emphasized by Nkrumah in his speech was the urgent need for the institute to search for, edit, publish, and make available sources of all kinds, to create an extensive and diversified Library of African Classics (see also Jeppie and Diagne 2008). Such a library was to include editions with translations and commentaries on works—whether in African, Asian, or European languages—that were of special value for the student of African history, philosophy, literature, and law. This included the collection of a substantial body of Arabic and Hausa documents that revealed an indigenous scholarly tradition in Ghana about which little had been previously known.[22] It was Nkrumah's hope that the collection would shed new light on Ghanaian history as part of a larger exploration of the African past, in addition to the collection of "stool histories" and other oral traditions, including poetry and African literature in various forms.[23] Nkrumah suggested that teaching in the university faculties and departments, such as law, economics, politics, history, geography, philosophy, and sociology, ought to be substantially based on African material as soon as possible. Hence he charged the institute to assist in the production of textbooks for secondary schools, training colleges, workers' colleges, and other educational institutions.

The arts of Africa were to have a prominent place in the institute and their study was expected to enhance the understanding of African institutions and values, while comparative studies of, for example, musical systems might illuminate historical problems or provide data for the study of African ethical and philosophical ideas. Similarly, in place of a view of culture as frozen, Nkrumah proffered it as experimental, creative, and adaptive. The institute was to assist in developing new forms of dance, drama, music, and creative writing that were at the same time closely related to Ghanaian traditions and expressed the ideas and aspirations of Ghanaian people at this critical stage in history.

Finally, Nkrumah viewed the institute as essentially an Institute of *African* Studies, not of Ghanaian or West African Studies, although it was bound to take a special interest in exploring the history, institutions, languages, and arts of the Ghanaian people, and in establishing these studies on a sound basis. For Nkrumah, Ghana could only be understood within the total African context. This call for conceptualizing the task ahead in continental terms also applied to the study of modern Africa, which had to be understood from the "standpoint of [Africans'] common characteristics and objectives, as well as from the standpoint of the special kinds of colonial situation within which they have had to operate and the special problems, which they have had to face" (Nkrumah 1963, 12).

From Nkrumah's perspective, the institute was established to study Africa in the widest possible sense, in all its complexity and diversity, while also noting its essential unity. For example, studies conducted by the institute on musical forms, dances, literature, plastic arts, philosophical and religious beliefs, systems of government, patterns of trade, and economic organization that had been developed in Ghana were expected to lead outward and enable explorations of the interconnections, as well as differences, between Ghana and the cultures of other African peoples and regions. While Nkrumah acknowledged that no single institution could possibly attempt to cover the whole range of African studies, he hoped the institute would nurture a cohort of scholars with as many-sided and diversified interests as resources would allow. This approach was to provide opportunities for the institute's students to explore the history, major languages and literatures, music and arts, and economic, social, and political institutions of the entire African continent. This was to ensure that no major sector of African studies would be unrepresented. Moreover, the institute was to assist in breaking down the artificial divisions between so-called "English-speaking," "French-speaking," and "Portuguese-speaking" Africans.

In its first years, the IAS enjoyed the active support of President Nkrumah and received its budget directly from the National Council of Higher Education to "free it from a seemingly unfriendly university."[24] As its students received bursaries, the institute was able to attract top scholars, such as Ivor Wilks and John Hunwick, and students from around Africa and the world, such as Paulo F. de Moraes Farias (later of the Centre for West African Studies, University of Birmingham) and John Schram (who became Canadian high commissioner to Ghana) as well as Ray Kea (later of the Department of History at the University of California, Riverside). During this early period, the institute's work progressed rapidly. Agbodeka (1998), however, hints at coming problems when he notes that the institute's relations with the rest of the university and with other academic institutions in Ghana threatened to block its further development. Matters came to a head with the military overthrow of Nkrumah's government in 1966.

Contests over the Institute of African Studies

Following the coup d'état of 1966, the question of the place and role of the Institute of African Studies was reopened. The institute had to defend itself against charges that it had been an outpost for Nkrumahism and socialist ideologies. Then-director Kwabena Nketia stated that initially the IAS had not been expected to work actively in any way for the political achievement of African unity or subscribe to any political program, though it was reminded of the need to keep the continental African context in view in its work. According to him, Nkrumahism and other socialist ideologies were taught within the framework of specific courses in African philosophies and theories of the state. Nketia noted that some of heads of other departments "turned out to be the most bitter critics of the Institute" and that they would have liked it "demolished." This was because they wanted the opportunity to start their own graduate programs, instead of having to do so from within the IAS, as the Commission for Higher Education had recommended. While he conceded the right of those departments to start their own graduate courses instead of teaching them within the institute, he decried proposals that sought to integrate the IAS into existing departments to appease certain persons, and threatened to resign if such a recommendation was carried out. He did not see himself working in "the kind of 'Oxbridge Institute of African Studies' which the University might set up, on the advice of Dr. Jack Goody."[25]

The vice-chancellor, Professor Alexander Kwapong, set up a committee chaired by Dr. Busia to determine inter alia the proper concept of the Institute of African Studies and, in particular, to examine and clarify what the relationship between the institute and other university departments should be.[26] Interestingly, Busia had also served as chairman of a special committee appointed by the National Liberation Council, the regime that ousted Nkrumah's government, on the "Delimitation of Functions of University Institutions, which took a look at the Institute of African Studies."[27] Busia reproduced for Professor Kwapong the recommendations that the committee had made to the National Liberation Council.

In his report, Busia reiterated the fundamental aim of the institute: to be the main focus of research and postgraduate teaching in African studies, based at the University of Ghana.[28] He recommended that the institute should continue to be based at Legon, but should be a semiautonomous institute, primarily concerned with research but also providing courses at appropriate levels, either in its own right (provided they did not duplicate existing courses), or in conjunction with other university institutions, and to strengthen its relations with cognate departments. And in place of the established positions proposed by Thomas Hodgkin, Busia stressed the need to strengthen the work of the institute through the appointment of visiting professors, which he saw as an expensive but necessary option. Busia was of the view that courses in African studies provided a useful background to education at an African university, and recommended that the institute should initiate action toward arranging similar courses at both Kumasi and Cape Coast, in consultation with the authorities there, and that the award of degrees at Kumasi and Cape Coast should be made dependent on passing an examination in African studies, as was the case at Legon. He suggested that it might be appropriate to integrate African studies into the education course at the University of Cape Coast. However, he also recommended the separation of the School of Music and Drama from the institute as demanded by the lecturers in charge, who noted that music and drama "transcended the boundaries of Africa," and the school's inclusion in the Institute of African Studies was said to have "limited its scope and orientation."[29]

Since the Busia report, there has also been the Boateng Committee Report (1990) on Institutes and Centers at the University, which examined their functioning and challenges. While no further reconstitution of the IAS has been proposed, the institute has been subject to recurrent questioning over its functions, and misgivings exist in some quarters about the continued relevance of African studies in an African university. In particular, the compulsory course in African studies, which has undergone massive reorganization over the years to cater to rising student numbers, continues to attract misgivings from within the university. Those who oppose the continued existence of the institute argue that the compulsory course in African studies must be eliminated in favor of courses in computing or entrepreneurship training, for example, to enable students to acquire more "marketable" skills. Others claim that university courses have been sufficiently "Africanized" and students therefore do not need the "extra" dose administered through the compulsory course in African studies. But this claim is belied by a cursory perusal of some course outlines where there is not a single reference to African material or sources, as well as by the continuing inability to produce textbooks locally in several disciplines and courses and the continued reliance on foreign textbooks and materials for the majority of courses. Still other opponents charge that class sizes in the African studies courses are "large and unwieldy," but this is a general problem in the public universities which is beginning to be addressed administratively.[30]

In regard to the institute's graduate programs, naive comments have sometimes been made about what should constitute the focus of a program in African studies. In the view of some faculty members outside the institute, graduate students of the institute should concern themselves with work on "rituals, music, and dance"[31] (the stuff of old ethnology and ethnography), instead of investigating poverty, population issues, or broad developmental concerns which are key to Africa's regeneration and development.

Internally, the institute has faced dwindling budgets, low student numbers in some graduate programs as a consequence of policy changes in the Ghana Education Service itself, aging faculty in some sections of the institute, and the relative inability to attract new staff to some of the sections.[32] But as Agbodeka attested, the institute also recorded several achievements, including its research and publications portfolio, its engagements with existing departments, and, one may also add, new additions such as gender studies, environmental studies, and performance studies within the existing sections. It has also acquired a status as a "useful international study centre" (Agbodeka 1998, 171), no doubt aimed at international students from North American and European universities, interpreting Africa for non-Africans. But it is doubtful whether this addresses the mission envisaged for the institute as a tool for African and African-descended persons to engage with endogenous knowledge systems and local social players and emergent challenges. Neither does such a status assist in building local epistemic communities that engage actively and directly with scholars in other parts of the world, including from Asia and Latin America, in addition to the regular engagements with scholars from Europe and North America.

Conclusion

The establishment of the Institute of African Studies in 1961 was seen as a critical component in the building of the new nation of Ghana, which was itself only a part of a larger continental effort. Ghana as forerunner of African independence aimed to blaze a new path that would modernize the country and its institutions, to address the neglect and underdevelopment that colonialism had wrought. As Philip Foster and Aristide Zolberg (1971) among others have argued, Ghana's chosen path was firmly within the modernization paradigm. The institute, endowed with financial resources and much political capital, formed part of the new institutions such as the Ghana Academy of Arts and Sciences, the *Encyclopaedia Africana,* and the Bureau of African Affairs, as well as new infrastructural projects such as the Akosombo Dam (see Miescher, this volume), which the newly minted modernizing state showcased as part of the rupture from colonial rule. An important component of the intellectual cadre for the modernization project was expected to come from within the institute, which was to serve to restore Ghana and Africans to history while also producing the resources, whether in the performing and creative arts or in law and politics, to orient the new nation.[33]

Conceived as a firm support in the struggle against the vestiges of colonialism for the emergence of the African personality, it engendered much hostility and suspicion within the conservative environment of the University of Ghana from staff and students intent on acquiring a universal and international education. While the study of African languages, arts, and cultures were conceded to have a place in the university, this was to be for those who desired it, rather than for all. Even in its modified form proposed by Busia in 1967, African studies needed to be reined in so that schools such as that of music and drama (now the School of Performing Arts) could "transcend" their African boundaries and shine in the world.

As this discussion of the history of the institute and relevant portions of the "African Genius" speech demonstrate, the institute was conceived to go beyond the pigeonholing that the Interim Committee for African Studies designed for it, and to have a broad mandate, even beyond Ghana. Hodgkin's provision in the establishment for an Arabist, a linguist specialized in Hausa, a specialist in Amharic and Ethiopian history, and a French-speaking African specialist in either the history of the Western Sudan or the institutions of French West Africa, was to find no place in the Ghana that emerged after 1966. Rather, Ghana had little appetite for a continental union government, and inveighed against what it saw as Nkrumah's "wasteful" expenditure in pursuit of that dream. Henceforth, Ghana was to mind its own business while its institutions and government aspired to international standards, and the institute narrowed its gaze to become largely an Institute of Ghanaian Studies, instead of one on Africa and its Diasporas, or even on West Africa. Effectively, this meant that over time, the institute did not develop substantial expertise relative to other West African societies, and even less on Eastern and Southern Africa, resulting in little comparative perspective.

In the decades of crises that Ghana and a majority of African countries have experienced since the mid-1970s, funding to universities and for research was severely curtailed. The Africa Travel Grant that facilitated academic exchanges within Africa dried up in the 1980s. The many micro studies that students and staff have undertaken in such conditions have produced minutiae of data that are useful but often lack any comparative focus or the ability to generalize or theorize (Olukoshi 2007), forcing the institute back into the ethnological mode. The Afro-pessimism that the period engendered, and the race to find new epithets to describe African venality, failure, and hopelessness by Africans and Africanists, did not create a greater sense of confidence. This was especially the case in institutions invested in developing African-centered ways of doing or scholarship, as the reach toward the global and its proffered bounties took hold, following the neoliberal turn from the mid-1980s.

But within the means open to it, it can be argued that the institute has continued, sometimes haltingly, to keep the dream alive. The (re)assessments of the institute that have occurred have often been based on criteria of relevance and efficacy derived from different starting points, and this has usually provoked suspicion from the institute. While Nkrumah's "African Genius" speech continues to be regularly invoked by staff as the charter for the institute, the institute itself has not conducted a critical self-assessment of what is usable within the speech, to guide it as it maneuvers a vastly changed African universe where the market, investment, macroeconomic growth, and poverty reduction are what frame governmental and policy action. Unfortunately, even universities have adopted these corporatist frames and use them to assess what is considered relevant. Thus the challenge for the institute is in defining its own relevance and producing knowledge that assists Ghana and Africa out of its current morass, even within existing institutional constraints, including funding. What is needed is the self-confidence, the critical analysis, and the generation of new ideas, tools, and practices necessary to move Africa forward in this current phase, on par with what many of the leading Pan-Africanists and intellectuals, referred to at the beginning of the chapter, had demonstrated. Instead of the extraversion and wholesale adoption of frameworks and theories from everywhere else but Africa that generally characterizes knowledge production in the university, the institute needs to build critical intra- and cross-national knowledge of Africa through the exchange of ideas and practices, as it engages with other Africanists, in ongoing conversations with other scholars and researchers investigating similar issues in non-African contexts.

Notes

1. Blyden, cited in Mkandawire (2005, 13); emphasis added.

2. The noted Ghanaian composer Ephraim Amu expressed these same sentiments in his composition "*Yaanom Abibriman,*" which urged black people to rise up and make their mark in the world in order to avoid disgrace.

3. Agbodeka (1998, 2); he also cites Nnamdi Azikiwe's *Renascent Africa* (1937), which expressed similar sentiments on indigenous African universities to be sustained through African initiative.

4. Thus while the West African Governors' Conference of August 1939 agreed on one university for West Africa, to be located at Ibadan in Nigeria, the Gold Coast intelligentsia mobilized for the establishment of a university in the Gold Coast (Ghana), to be funded initially by voluntary donations from cocoa farmers. £897,000 was donated by the farmers and people of the Gold Coast as a contribution toward the establishment of the university college (Agbodeka 1998, 13).

5. Mr. T. K. Aning, retired principal archivist at the Manhyia Archives in Kumasi, created the IAS archives in 2006–2008 from old files of the institute, which were in danger of being destroyed. I am indebted to him.

6. Padmore's role was described by A. L. Adu, then permanent secretary in Ghana's Foreign Affairs Ministry, as "to carry through (Nkrumah's) policy for the emancipation of those parts of Africa still under foreign rule and therefore to work with nationalist movements and political parties, an area of activity which it would be inappropriate for civil servants to engage in at the time" (cited in Afari-Gyan 1991, 4). See Ahlman's (2011) dissertation on Pan-Africanism and nation-building in Nkrumah's Ghana.

7. Founded in 1961, this group, known as the Casablanca bloc and comprising Algeria, Guinea, Morocco, Egypt, Mali, and Libya, wanted a federation of all African countries. Opposing it was the Monrovia bloc, led by Senghor of Senegal, which felt that unity should be achieved gradually, through economic cooperation, and did not support the notion of a political federation. Its other members were Nigeria, Liberia, Ethiopia, and most of the former French colonies.

8. David Graham Du Bois and Gamal Gorkeh Nkrumah, "Concerning the Status of the Encyclopaedia Africana," statement, 19 August 1998, EAP History Archive, http://www.endarkenment.com/eap/legacy/980819duboisnkrumah.htm. While Du Bois had conceived the idea for the encyclopedia as early as 1909, he had had to drop it for lack of financial support (Afari-Gyan 1991).

9. Kenneth Kaunda, president of Zambia, in a prefatory note to volume 1 of the *Enyclopaedia*, the *Dictionary of African Biography*, 11 (cited in Afari-Gyan 1991, 10).

10. It is significant that no such radical schools emerged at the University of Ghana, Legon, where the university establishment constituted itself as a major focus of opposition to Nkrumah.

11. Mkandawire (2005, 25) quotes the Burkinabe historian and intellectual Joseph Ki-Zerbo, who captured the rupture in the phrase "Silence: Development in Progress." Intellectuals were either to join in, to build the nation without raising critical questions, or to keep quiet, so development could proceed.

12. "Report of a Discussion of the Interim Committee for African Studies," 10 November 1959, IAS Archives, Legon

13. Members of the committee were Peter Shinnie from Archaeology, Ivor Wilks from Philosophy, and Kwabena Nketia from Sociology.

14. As far as the government was concerned, the Oxbridge tradition extended beyond Oxford and Cambridge to engulf the older British universities such as the University of London, with which the University of Ghana was affiliated.

15. Cf. Peter Shinnie and Thomas Hodgkin, correspondence, 9 January 1961, IAS Archives, Legon. According to Shinnie, there were a large number of existing departments in which research problems of Africa were being explored, so "compromises must be made. . . . Go ahead with a scheme which is broadly acceptable to the College as a whole."

16. T. L. Hodgkin, note, 31 October 1961, IAS Archives, Legon.

17. Ibid. Chatham House, also known as the Royal Society of International Affairs, is the leading think-tank in the United Kingdom, producing influential papers and agenda-setting initiatives on foreign affairs

18. Government of Ghana (1961), Appendix 1.

19. Agbodeka (1998, 126) refers to government emphases on the need for universities to foster African unity and on wiping out the colonial mentality through the courses in African studies.

20. This position is evident in an unpublished interview I conducted with Professor Kwabena Nketia on the *The African Genius* in November 2010.

21. For a discussion of *Négritude* see McMahon (this volume).

22. This was a reference to the *Ajami* manuscripts, or manuscripts in non-Arabic languages written with Arabic scripts.

23. Stools are the symbol of office of traditional chiefs in southern Ghana, especially among the Akan.

24. Agbodeka (1998, 168) notes that the institute's role, assigned by Nkrumah, of wiping out the "colonial mentality" among African intellectuals could not have been received well by the "dons" (senior professors) at Legon. They particularly disliked this role and not the institute itself, although Agbodeka (1998, 190) concedes that it was difficult to distinguish between the two.

25. Nketia to Alexander Kwapong, vice-chancellor, 8 November 1966, IAS Archives, Legon. "The advice of Dr. Jack Goody" was a reference to a memorandum on the future status of the IAS submitted by the British anthropologist Jack Goody, who was then on the staff of the University of Ghana, to the vice-chancellor.

26. It was perhaps lucky for the institute that it was Busia, later prime minister of Ghana's Second Republic (1969–1971), who chaired this committee. As a scholar who could not be tarred with Nkrumahism and who was an important member of the transition to parliamentary democracy after Nkrumah, his recommendations could be relied upon. As the originator of the School of African Studies at Legon, albeit in its much-altered form, he was sufficiently knowledgeable about and invested in a program of African studies.

27. The National Liberation Council and its civilian advisors and backers appeared determined to root out Nkrumahism and the several initiatives that had been embarked upon often in pursuit of African unity, and to restore Ghana and its institutions to the international register. The period 1966–1969 witnessed the reversal of several policies, the closure of institutions, and the arrest and detention of persons associated with Nkrumah. The Institute of African Studies was clearly seen as an anomaly.

28. K. A. Busia, "Report on the Re-organization of the Institute of African Studies, 1967," paras. 18–22, IAS Archives, Legon.

29. Ibid.

30. The report of the University of Ghana Visitation Panel (2007) recommended that no classes in the university could enroll more than five hundred students. http://ghanahero.com/Documents/UNIV_of_Ghana_REPORT_OF_VISITATION_PANEL_2007.pdf.

31. I heard this comment made at a meeting of the Board of Graduate Studies, of which I was a member.

32. For example, music is no longer taught as a separate subject in several public schools, leading to few students' offering it as an examinable subject at the West African Senior Secondary Schools' examinations. As a result, the pool of students majoring in music at the undergraduate level is negligible, except for students at training colleges.

33. A notable example of this was in the attempts of the institute's Ghana Dance Ensemble to modernize traditional dances. According to Nii-Yartey (2013), the Ghanaian choreographer Mawere Opoku, who was the first director of the Ghana Dance Ensemble, used his artistic creations to challenge the sensibilities of traditionalists in Africa.

References

Afari-Gyan, Kwadwo. 1991. "Kwame Nkrumah, George Padmore and W.E.B. Du Bois." *Research Review* NS 7, nos. 1–2: 1–10.

Agbodeka, Francis. 1998. *A History of the University of Ghana*. Accra: Woeli.

Ahlman, Jeffrey S. 2011. "Living with Nkrumahism: Nation, State, and Pan-Africanism in Ghana." PhD diss., University of Illinois, Urbana-Champaign.

Bhagwati, Jagdish, ed. 1977. *The NIEO: The North-South Debate*. Cambridge, MA: MIT Press.

Chumbow, Sammy Beban. 2005. "The Language Question and National Development in Africa." In *African Intellectuals: Rethinking Politics, Language, Gender and Development*, edited by Thandika Mkandawire, 165–92. Dakar: CODESRIA; London: Zed Books.

Cooper, Frederick. 1999. "Africa's Pasts and Africa's Historians." *African Sociological Review* 3, no. 2: 1–29.

Foster, Philip, and Aristide R. Zolberg, eds. 1971. *Ghana and the Ivory Coast: Perspectives on Modernization*. Chicago: University of Chicago Press.

Gaines, Kevin. 2006. *American Africans in Ghana: Black Expatriates and the Civil Rights Era*. Chapel Hill, NC: University of North Carolina Press.

Government of Ghana. 1961. *Report of the Commission on University Education*. Accra: Government Printer.

Jeppie, Shamil, and Souleymane Bachir Diagne, eds. 2008. *The Meanings of Timbuktu*. Cape Town: HSRC Press.

Mkandawire, Thandika, ed. 2005. *African Intellectuals: Rethinking Politics, Language, Gender and Development*. Dakar: CODESRIA; London: Zed Books.

Nii-Yartey, Francis. 2013. "Dance Symbolism in Africa." In *Africa in Contemporary Perspective*, edited by Takyiwaa Manuh and Esi Sutherland-Addy, 412–28. Accra: Sub-Saharan Publishers.

Nketia, J. H. K. 1965. *Ghana, Music, Dance and Drama: A Review of the Performing Arts of Ghana*. Accra: Ghana Publishing Corporation.

———. 1996. "National Development and the Performing Arts of Africa." In *The Muse of Modernity: Essays on Culture as Development in Africa*, edited by Philip G. Altbach and Salah M. Hassan. Trenton, NJ: Africa World Press.

Nkrumah, Kwame. 1961. *I Speak of Freedom: A Statement of African Ideology*. New York: Praeger.

———. 1963. *"The African Genius": Speech at the Opening of the Institute of African Studies. University of Ghana, Legon, October 25th, 1963*. Accra: Ministry of Information and Broadcasting.

Olukoshi, Adebayo. 2007. "African Scholars and African Studies." In *On Africa: Scholars and African Studies,* edited by Henning Melber, 7–22. Discussion Paper 35. Uppsala: Nordic Africa Institute.

Rodney, Walter. 1972. *How Europe Underdeveloped Africa.* London: Bogle-L'Ouverture; Dar es Salaam: Tanzania Publishing House.

United Nations. 1974. "Declaration for the Establishment of a New International Economic Order." United Nations General Assembly document A/RES/S-6/3201. 1 May.

Wilks, Ivor. 2008. "Nehemiah Levtzion and Islam in Ghana: Reminiscences." *Canadian Journal of African Studies* 42, no. 2–3: 250–64.

PART FIVE

Modernization and the Literary Imagination

13 Theater and the Politics of Display

The Tragedy of King Christophe *at Senegal's First World Festival of Negro Arts*

Christina S. McMahon

Stone, that's what I want!
Cement, give me cement!
All this, oh! to set it upright!
Upright in the face of the world, and solid!
—Césaire (1969, 32)

In Aimé Césaire's 1963 play, Henri Christophe dreams of constructing a grandiose Citadel that would broadcast to the world Haiti's glory in becoming the first free Black republic after a hard-fought revolution against France in the early nineteenth century. Casting the Citadel as a symbol of the labor of nation-building, Christophe likens himself to an engineer, the "builder" of the Haitian people (Césaire 1969, 44). As John Conteh-Morgan notes, this is a strange metaphor for Césaire to employ, given that he is one of the architects of Négritude philosophy. Césaire's earliest writing on the subject, his epic poem *Notebook of a Return to My Native Land* (1939), privileged "agrarian, non-industrial" cultures—the domain of Négritude—over the "scientific rationalism" and "civil engineering" mentality he associated with the West (Conteh-Morgan 1994, 95).

Indeed, Christophe's zeal to showcase Haiti's competence at construction and technology, as well as its strong centralized government in the shape of Christophe's European-style court, appears to play right into the modernization agendas so in vogue at the time Césaire wrote the play. In other passages, however, Haiti's self-anointed king seems to personify Négritude. He views the Citadel as a source of pride and self-esteem for a demoralized people, envisioning it as "canceling out the slave ship" that forcibly transported their ancestors from Africa to Haiti's shores (Césaire 1969, 45). Restoring cultural pride to the Black world was also the thrust of the Négritude literary movement, as a young Aimé Césaire and Léopold Sédar Senghor conceived of it in Paris in the 1930s and 1940s. Moreover, Christophe's wisdom is grounded in his intuition and his senses: "He may not *know*, but what's more important, he *feels*, he *smells* the sinuous line of the future, in a word, the form" (Césaire 1969, 22; emphasis added). Haiti's first Black king thus embodies Senghor's controversial associations of reason with classical Greek thinking and emotion with Blackness that came to define the Négritude movement for its critics.

In short, Césaire's postcolonial rendering of Christophe offers us a seemingly paradoxical blend of post–World War II modernization ideology and Négritude philosophy. Yet Christophe's rhetoric is not strikingly different from the shape Négritude was taking in Senghor's speeches of the same era, when the Senegalese poet had assumed the presidency of his newly independent nation. By the mid-1960s, Senghor's writings on Négritude, which he filtered into his political agenda of African Socialism, became more pragmatic, addressing issues such as economic development and production with an emphasis on science and technology (Markovitz 1969, 70–71).

Among scholars of Africa and the Diaspora today, it has become almost as fashionable to reappraise Négritude as it was for artists and intellectuals to disparage it in an earlier era,[1] when Senghor was maligned as essentialist, race-obsessed, and an easy prey to the primitivist views of Africa espoused by Eurocentric philosophers and ethnologists.[2] Yet if we attend to the contours of Senghor's writings in the 1960s, then exhuming Négritude also means revisiting African modernization, as the editors of this volume have invited us to do. Césaire's *Tragedy of King Christophe* provides an intriguing entrée into this question, not only due to the uncanny parallels between its protagonist and Senghor, but because the play made its much-applauded African debut in 1966 at the First World Festival of Negro Arts, which Senghor hosted in Dakar.

How did Césaire's play resonate, on a cultural and symbolic level, within the echo chamber that was the Dakar festival? In Senghor's (1966, 7–8) view, the gala event would operate as a cultural call to arms for Black artists from "Africa, America, and the very heart of Europe" to defend their humanity and indispensability to world history as a whole. Yet the image of Christophe that Césaire projects to the world is ambiguous at best. Indeed, Haiti's king incarnates the "Pitfalls of National Consciousness" that Frantz Fanon (1961) elaborated in his essay. Purportedly representing the Haitian people in his quest to construct the Citadel, Christophe ultimately fails to incorporate their actual voices and everyday needs into his governance agenda, even conscripting them into the same slave labor that the former French colonizers enforced. The play thus sounds a warning bell to the Africa of the 1960s (Harney 2004, 118; Conteh-Morgan 1994, 89), when a host of newly independent countries were facing uncertain futures with former revolutionary leaders at the helm of new governments. Indeed, Césaire took pride in the fact that many African audiences who viewed the play could strongly identify with Haiti's predicament under King Christophe; the Senegalese actor who played Christophe at the Dakar festival, Douta Seck, even mentioned that Christophe could have been any African ruler, either ancient king or contemporary head of state (Ojo-Ade 2010, 146–47).

Certainly, Christophe could be interpreted as an allegory for any African leader taking the reins in the 1960s. Yet as I have previously argued, the meaning of global allegories, when incorporated into theater, shifts as a play moves to a new location and takes on a new production context (McMahon 2005). In this chapter, I argue that *The Tragedy of King Christophe*'s African debut at the First World Festival of Negro Arts was portentous not merely for African leaders in general, but for Senghor and the new Senegalese nation in particular. Just as Christophe dominates Césaire's play, Senghor's aura prevailed at the festival: he delivered multiple speeches, quotes from his poetry were splashed across promotional materials, and a rendering of his face adorns the album cover of recorded African music produced in the festival's wake.[3] If spectators at *The Tragedy of King Christophe* needed the image of an African leader to fill in the blanks of Césaire's dramatic allegory, Senghor's was abundantly available to them. Further, there are overt connections between the spirit of Négritude that the play conveys and Senghor's pronouncement about the overall mission for the Dakar fête, "the defense and celebration of Negritude" (quoted in Deliss 1995, 224), which he directly stated to festival attendees.

Performed in Senegal at the critical moment when Senghor was transforming Négritude into a pragmatic, nation-building ideology, the festival production offered, I argue, a very specific warning about the perils of mixing Négritude with notions of modernization and development. By the end of the play, King Christophe is on his deathbed, disillusioned with leadership and rejected by the very people he sought to inspire. In a parallel sense, just one year after the Dakar festival Senghor was the object of an assassination attempt in Senegal, and in 1968, students, trade unionists, and rural workers manifested their discontent with the Senegalese government's labor and economic policies (Gellar 1982, 25). If we listen carefully to what the Dakar production tells us, we can hear whispers of the overt criticism of Négritude later expressed at Algiers' First Pan-African Cultural Festival in 1969. There, Dahomey's Stanislas Adotevi and Haiti's René Depestre pointed out Négritude's shortcomings as an economic strategy and political call to action (Jules-Rosette 1998, 71). Adotevi (1969, 71) pointedly called Négritude "hostile to the development of Africa," as it associated Black labor with the "slow rhythm of the fields" at a time when Africans needed incentive to industrialize.

In this chapter, I argue that Césaire and other Diasporan artists attending the Dakar festival were able to offer subtle commentaries on the particular economic and political circumstances of Senegal in that era and, potentially, Senghor's own policies, which included development and modernization schemes. These critiques emerged through the theatrical texture of the various performance events at the festival and were epitomized by the much-applauded production of *The Tragedy of King Christophe*. Significantly, these commentaries arose at a festival that occurred at the crux of the modernization era and that was itself envisioned as a way of attracting tourism to Senegal and boosting foreign aid and industrialization efforts. Thus, the First World Festival of Negro Arts in Senegal was more than a mere "'cultural' project" (Edwards 2001, 70), since it potentially carried political resonance through the performances' execution and reception. It should thus be viewed as an important forerunner to later, more radical expressions of African culture, such as the Algiers Pan-African Festival in 1969 and Nigeria's FESTAC 1977, the Second World Black and African Festival of Arts and Culture.[4] Therefore, I suggest that we view Césaire's and other artists' cultural expressions at the festival in Senegal as a staging ground for the ideological critique of both Négritude and modernization that became more pronounced in the years to follow.

To this end, I examine crucial themes raised in *The Tragedy of King Christophe*—construction and technology, dependency and foreign intervention, and class and elitism—and illustrate how these same issues were ripe for critique within the First World Festival of Negro Arts and Senegal at large. By studying how Caribbean and Black American attendees addressed these issues at Senegal's festival, we can glimpse how the Diaspora responded to the mix of Négritude and development ideologies that Senghor proposed in the 1960s. In short, if we attend to the nuances performance took on within the First World Festival of Negro Arts, we can better understand how political expressions may be embedded in what appeared to be merely aesthetic gestures. First, a word on Senghor's changing stance on Négritude is in order.

Négritude, Development, and Modernization: Intertwining Discourses

By the time Senghor hosted Dakar's festival in 1966, his thinking on Négritude had already transformed considerably since his early years as a student in Paris. One blind spot of Négritude critics has been linking Senghor solely to the essentialist bent of his early writing, rather than looking at the Paris years as a notch on an evolving philosophical spectrum (Thompson 2002, 144). The notion of a shared race, as well as a resulting black aesthetic practiced by Africans and African-descended people, was indeed Senghor's starting point for Négritude (Wilder 2005, 188). In a 1935 essay that appeared in the student journal *L'Étudiant Noir*, Senghor discussed a "black sensibility" that would contribute to an emerging universal humanism (4), a sensibility that he linked four years later with rhythm, emotion, and spirituality.[5] Yet we must take into account that the French-speaking authors who ignited the Négritude movement, including Senghor and Martinican poet Aimé Césaire, wrote in response to their specific predicament as Black intellectuals inheriting a legacy of French colonialism (Irele 1990, 68), with its checkered history of using French language and literature as the yardstick for successful assimilation into so-called universal culture. Senghor's vocation, then, contributed to a demonstration of the Black world's complementarity to European cultural and literary traditions.

Senghor's intellectual development was deeply rooted in elite French educational institutions including Lycée Louis-Le-Grand, École Normale Supérieure, and Université de Paris. Therefore, it is no surprise that as late as 1958, just two short years before Senegal's independence from France, Senghor was still declaring himself to be a "Frenchman culturally" (quoted in Hymans 1971, 17). Even after Senghor was elected Senegalese deputy to the French Parliament in the mid-1940s, he resisted the idea of independence from France. As Jacques Hymans (1971, 155) points out, Senghor was "not a nationalist" like Sékou Touré, who boldly opposed Charles de Gaulle's overtures toward a partial union with France after Guinea Conakry's independence. Senghor maintained that a connection with France was desirable even after Senegal's independence, earning him robust criticism from his more radical counterparts in Africa. Yet as Hymans notes, Senghor's partiality toward French culture was complicated by the fact that while studying in France, he also learned to criticize it from within. Therefore, throughout Senghor's political career, "France was simultaneously venerated and disparaged" (Hymans 1971, 18). He began to argue for a kind of cultural independence for Senegal and Africa at large based on the concept of Négritude, while still maintaining political connections to France.

This is not unlike Césaire's own positionality as a Martinican poet and politician. At the end of Césaire's life, after having served many years as mayor of Fort de France and deputy to the French National Assembly, he still maintained that Martinique was better off as a French-administered territory rather than advocate for independence from France (Ojo-Ade 2010, 342–44). Yet it is important to remember that these sentiments come from the same author who wrote the vitriolic attack on European colonialism in the form of the 1955 tract "Discourse on Colonialism." Thus, for both Césaire and Senghor, a deferential attitude toward France and European culture at large was always balanced by a hefty dose of criticism toward Western imperialism.

Nevertheless, Senghor's early writings on the Black world's contribution to a European-defined universalist aesthetic did garner him scathing critique for capitulating to racist Eurocentric binaries. His 1939 essay, "What the Black Man Contributes,"[6] bore the brunt of this backlash for its notorious assertion that emotion was Black while reason was Hellenic. The Paris-based journal *Présence Africaine* hosted many heated responses to Senghor's positions over the years, including articles by René Depestre and Albert Franklin. The gist of the critique is that Senghor buttressed notions of racial inequality and the mental inferiority of Blacks generated by colonialist French theorists such as Joseph-Arthur de Gobineau. Yet as scholars of Senghor have recently reminded us, he was working within a different European school of thought—emblematized by the philosophies of Henri Bergson, Arthur Rimbaud, and Pierre Teilhard de Chardin—that rejected rationalist frameworks and valued intuition and emotion as credible generators of knowledge (Diagne 2002, 2011; Irele 1990, 81).

As Souleymane Bachir Diagne (2011) argues, Senghor did not adopt ideas of these European thinkers wholesale or indiscriminately. For example, his correlation of emotion with Blackness and reason with Hellenic modes of thought came from his reading of Guillaume and Munro's 1926 book *Primitive Negro Sculpture,* in which the two authors compared the aesthetics of Greek and African statues. Senghor adopted that comparative framework but added the notion that embedded in African aesthetics was an African ontology founded in rhythm, a theme found throughout Senghor's large corpus of writings. While Senghor never fully defined this metaphysics of rhythm, he consistently linked it with vitality and in the co-presence of seemingly contradictory themes in one unified whole. He was particularly inspired by French philosopher Henri Bergson's theory that intellect and intuition were two separate yet complementary epistemological modes. Like Bergson, Senghor believed that humanity was ultimately destined to merge these two modes into one perfect ontology, but Senghor specified that Blacks would contribute the intuitive knowledge to this evolution. Yet as Diagne (2011, 96) notes, for Senghor, rhythm was more than an essentialist expression of race; it was "an approach to reality and a means of knowing it." Senghor (1964, 73–75) clarified this idea of a Black epistemology in *On African Socialism,* where he linked "black reason" to feeling and dancing.[7] Thus, even while Senghor was derivatively using Western ideas to prove African equality, he was also carving out a space for the body and intuition as viable transmitters of knowledge.

For the purposes of this chapter, most significant is the way in which Senghor's definition of Black "contributions" began to solidify into strategic ways that France's African colonies could collaborate with the metropole on industrialization. In 1939, Senghor described his vision of a "two-way" movement in which France sent to the colonies "machines and engineers" as well as "professors and teachers," while the colonies reciprocated by sending back "raw materials" and "new modes of feeling and living and also of expressing themselves" (quoted in Wilder 2005, 243). Here, Black African cultural expression becomes the humanist hope for a future dominated by the cold severities of Western modernism. Senghor vividly expressed this notion in his later poem "Prayer to Masks," printed in his 1945 anthology, *Chants d'Ombre:*

> Let us report present at the rebirth of the World
> Like the yeast which white flour needs.
> For who would teach rhythm to a dead world of machines and guns?[8]

Significantly, variations of these three lines from Senghor's poem were sprinkled liberally throughout the promotional materials for Senegal's First World Festival of Negro Arts, held nearly twenty years later.[9] Framing the festival, then, was a newfound emphasis on industry, machines, and development in Senghor's pronouncements on Négritude. Conceivably, motivating this shift in rhetoric was a critique of Négritude as cultural mystification far removed from the concrete realities of the contemporary world. This critique had come across loud and clear at the First Congress of Black Writers and Artists, organized by Alioune Diop, founder of *Présence Africaine,* in Paris in 1956. There, several Black participants from Africa and the Diaspora took issue with the approach Senghor adopted in his paper, which advocated the collective articulation of "a universal black culture" rooted in African cultural expressions (Jules-Rosette 1998, 53). African American author Richard Wright urged the African elite to turn their attention to issues of production, politics, economics, and technology, while Senegalese economist Mamadou Dia (who later became Senghor's ousted prime minister) recommended that Négritude take on a more economic perspective (Jules-Rosette 1998, 58–63). Evidently, by 1966, Senghor had taken their earlier criticisms to heart, and responded to the changing signs of the times in the nationalist era in Africa.

Senghor's position at the First World Festival of Negro Arts thus represented a kind of middle ground. Weaving his cherished philosophy into the very fabric of development and modernization rhetoric, he maintained the stance that Négritude was the humanist solution to a rapidly changing world. In an address to the Senegalese people in 1963, he claimed the forthcoming festival would illustrate that Négritude could prevent the "development of techniques and machines," and the forces of production themselves, from creating a "new type of slavery" in Africa.[10] Here, Négritude appears guarded, the last line of defense against a bellicose Western modernity. Yet the philosophy took on a more conciliatory tone as Senghor began to address the mix of outsiders and Senegalese nationalists who populated the festival crowds, which encompassed 2,500 Black artists from Africa and the Diaspora, as well as nearly 25,000 guests (Snipe 1998, 48), including a host of foreign emissaries from Europe, Africa, and North America. In his opening address, "The Function and Meaning of the First World Festival of Negro Arts," Senegal's president proudly proclaimed that "Negro art sustains us in our effort toward economic and social development," and, further, that Senegalese artists, "whether they dance the Development Plan or sing the diversification of crops, . . . help us to live . . . a better, more abundant life" (Senghor 1966, 8). In that scenario, Négritude became a soothing corporeal and vocal performance capable of facilitating the economic turnaround that the United States, France, and other European governments sought in their mid-twentieth-century development drive.

Science also featured prominently in Senghor's festival addresses. In "Négritude: A Humanism of the Twentieth Century," notions of African rhythm as "wave particles" displaced his earlier emphases on Black essences and spiritual properties. Specifically, Senghor rehearsed French philosopher Pierre Teilhard de Chardin's assertion that matter consists of two forms of energy, of which "radial energy" is explained as "internal . . . , psychic and qualitative" (Senghor 1994 [1970], 29). This gave the Négritude theorist a scientific basis for the creative spirit and intuitive rhythm he had long attributed to Black peoples. Thus, his speech revised his earlier stance on Négritude, even while it uncritically mimicked the science-centered bias of modernization theories. Overall, Senghor's focus on science and the economy played into the post–World War II zeal for modernization, which called for African nations dominated by "traditional" structures like chiefs and kinship systems to move ineluctably toward national models exemplified by "civilized" Western countries boasting industrialization, new technology, scientific advances, robust capitalist economies, and strong centralized governments (Geschiere, Meyer, and Pels 2008, 3).

Concretely, Senghor sought to showcase the starring roles the Senegalese nation and his presidency would assume in African development. True to his government agenda in the 1960s, which highlighted the role of culture in national economic development (Snipe 1998, 59), Senghor envisioned the festival as the spectacular debut on the world stage of the "École de Dakar," the Négritude-inspired aesthetic his government was cultivating among young Senegalese visual artists at the time (Harney 2004, 70), as well as a nurturing ground for Black arts, literature, and performance on a global scale. He thus cast Senegal as a "modern, stable, and cultured society," and a "forward-looking nation" ready to dazzle on the global economic and cultural scene (Harney 2004, 73). His diplomatic performance aimed at attracting the foreign aid and tourism to Senegal that would bolster his development scheme for the nation. Indeed, all of Senghor's actions at the festival echoed what the master of ceremonies proclaims at King Christophe's august coronation scene in Césaire's play: "It is a ceremony of the utmost importance, gentlemen. The whole world has its eyes upon us" (Césaire 1969, 20).

The sheer range of Black art and performance certainly did not disappoint. *The Tragedy of King Christophe* was produced at Dakar's newly built, state-of-the-art Daniel Sorano Theatre along with other African plays, while Duke Ellington and the Alvin Ailey Dance Company staged rollicking concerts at the gigantic Amitié Stadium. Dance troupes from Sierra Leone, Mali, the Ivory Coast, and Chad performed to great acclaim. Gospel performances rang out from the intimate space of Dakar's cathedral, while poetry recitals peppered the festival venues.

The freshly constructed Musée Dynamique, modeled after a Greek temple, exhibited over six hundred paintings and sculptures from all over Africa and Europe. On nearby Gorée Island, an erstwhile stop on the transatlantic slave trade, spectators could attend a nightly sound and light theatrical spectacle in which Senegalese and French actors rehearsed the historical trauma of slavery.

The magnitude of the festival necessitated outside economic assistance. Indeed, UNESCO and the Paris-based Society of African Culture, an offshoot of *Présence Africaine,* cosponsored the festival along with the Senegalese government. France also poured money into the endeavor, particularly the art exposition and the Gorée pageant. The United States contributed nearly $400,000 in support of its participants and in transportation of art pieces to Dakar.[11] Interestingly, Senghor's intimations that Négritude was integral to modernization on a global front facilitated his quest for foreign aid to the festival. In a press release generated by the U.S. committee to kick off a fundraising campaign among private donors in the United States, Senegal is described as "by far the most industrialized state of what was formerly French West Africa." Mining and fishing are mentioned, as well as the Senegalese government's ambitions for constructing a "Cité des Arts in Dakar for the permanent preservation and study of African culture" on the festival's grounds.[12] Prospective U.S. patrons were thereby assured that their financial contributions to the United States' participation in the festival simultaneously secured a successful development campaign in Africa. Senghor's Négritude rhetoric thus worked in conjunction with foreign aid mechanisms to frame Senegal—and, by extension, the festival itself—as a pulsing epicenter for West African development and modernization.

King Christophe, Part I: Construction, Technology, and National Culture

In *The Tragedy of King Christophe,* a young European engineer visits Christophe's court in the midst of the Haitian king's frenzy to build the Citadel. Declaring his intent to "engineer" the new Haitian nation, Christophe calls the Citadel an "extravagant venture" whose majesty will restore the people's self-worth because it was built by their own hands: "This people, forced to its knees, needed a monument to make it stand up" (Césaire 1969, 44–45). Christophe's vision of the Citadel as generating cultural self-esteem leads Seth Wolitz (1969, 201) to characterize the fortress as "a teleological symbol of the aims of Negritude," and the Haitian monarch himself as a "Hero of Negritude." Yet true to the Brechtian style in which Césaire wrote (Bradby 1984, 146), Christophe's character is replete with contradictions that complicate any hero narrative and compel us to think critically about what exactly Christophe's brand of Négritude represents.

Christophe's mania for a Négritude-inspired cultural agenda for Haiti is balanced by his obsession with building, technology, and science. He proudly announces to the court his enrollment in European "scientific societies," and his national plan for agricultural development involved new technological methods, such as raising "the water levels in the canals ten notches" (Césaire 1969, 40, 86). Indeed, Christophe sees no real separation between construction, technology, and culture. The Citadel is his answer to the engineer's assertion that what the people really need is "a patrimony" (44); for Christophe, brick-and-mortar construction constitutes national patrimony and, by extension, Négritude.

How, then, are we to understand a key line from Césaire's 1939 epic poem, *Notebook of a Return to My Native Land*? Embedded in that lyrical musing on a young Césaire's re-entrance into Martinique after study in Paris is the defiant claim, "My negritude is neither a tower nor a cathedral." The speaker's Blackness is instead rooted in the "red flesh of the soil" of his native land (Césaire 1995 [1956], 115). By situating the Citadel at the heart of *The Tragedy of King Christophe* nearly thirty years later, is Césaire suggesting that Christophe's vision of Négritude is *false*? Conteh-Morgan (1994, 95) suggests that Césaire the playwright is in fact critiquing the essentialism of Césaire the poet, since the *Notebook* seems to associate building and science with whiteness, and blackness with roots and intuition. Roxanna Curto (2011, 160), however, sees no inherent contradiction in the portrayal of Christophe, explaining that Césaire's thinking about Négritude within those thirty years had transformed along lines similar to what I outlined above in Senghor's writing, particularly regarding the relationship between race and technology.

My alternative reading is that the Citadel is not Césaire's Négritude; it is Senghor's. The two men, after all, articulated different visions of Négritude, with Senghor's rooted in reveries of his childhood in Senegal and Césaire's anchored in history (Berktay 2010, 206).[13] If history is Césaire's pathway to Négritude, it is not surprising that he chose the post-revolution era in Haiti as an allegorical warning to African leaders assuming governance in the 1960s, since in the *Notebook,* he calls Haiti the place "where Négritude stood up for the first time and said it believed in its humanity" (Césaire 1995 [1956], 91). There are indications in the play that Haiti symbolically stands in for Africa. On the battlefield against his rival Pétion, Christophe cries, "Poor Africa! Poor Haiti, I mean. Anyway, it's the same thing" (Césaire 1969, 36). Yet we must also bear in mind that Senghor was Césaire's pathway to *Africa*. He describes his first encounter with Senghor in Paris two days after his arrival from Martinique thus: "I literally drink from his lips whatever he can tell me about Africa" (Césaire 1989, 51). In a 1994 documentary, Césaire was still calling Senghor "Africa as eternity sees it."[14] By uniting all of this evidence, we can draw a line in the play from Haiti to Négritude to Africa to, potentially, Senghor. Without staking a direct claim for authorial intent, I suggest that an interpretive possibility of *King Christophe* is that it is Césaire's commentary on the pro-development posture Négritude was assuming in Senghor's thinking in the 1960s, an epistle delivered to Senghor in the shape of a production at Dakar's First World Festival of Negro Arts.

By the time of the festival, Senghor had already laid out his plans for an African Socialism that melded culture with modernization. While Africa would supply the communal values he perceived to be inherent to African civilizations, Europe—and in particular, France—would supply the economic, scientific, and technological means for development (Berktay 2010, 209–10). Senegal in fact built up its trade network via France's partnership with the European Economic Community, and the government worked with the Club du Sahel, a French economics and humanitarian organization, to bolster agriculture and mining in the early 1960s. Christophe's obsession with building the Citadel was mirrored in Senghor's vast road-building endeavors meant to expand farming and peanut production in rural areas (Gellar 1982, 51, 59). In Christophe's court, the King's architectural projects, undertaken with European advisors, are balanced by ornate ceremonies and the playful singing of his jester, Hugonin. Similarly, in a speech to the National Assembly in 1963, Senghor declared that they must train engineers and economists to meet the nation's development goals, but they would need "philosophers to explain this development, and some poets to praise it" (quoted in Markovitz 1969, 73). As in Césaire's play, culture went hand in hand with scientific and industrial advancement.

Yet we may also draw parallels between what went *wrong* for the two leaders in both of those realms. In the play, Christophe's fascination with culture quickly becomes a desire to institutionalize it. When the official court poet declaims verses on rum, Haiti's "national beverage," Christophe's ears prick up: "It sounds very patriotic. We'll have it taught in the schools. . . . Don't we need our own national poetry?" (Césaire 1969, 40). Similarly, Senghor's zeal for Négritude drove him to institutionalize everything from the National Ballet Company, founded a year after Senegalese independence, the Traditional Instrument Ensemble, and the National Theatre,[15] to the École des Arts, whose visual arts department cultivated an aesthetic called the École de Dakar, an imagistic exploration of Négritude that captured Senghor's ardor for rhythm and symbolism via bold colors, swirling lines, and the majestic depiction of African masks, mythical heroes, market scenes, and nature.[16] For both Christophe and Senghor, the codification of national culture generates mistrust among their people. After Christophe mandates that royal court ladies visit the Citadel building sites to wave flags and sing in order to bolster workers' spirits, a buzz begins that he is conscripting his people into an unofficial slavery (Césaire 1969, 52–53). Similarly, artists and intellectuals in 1960s Senegal, including prominent filmmaker Ousmane Sembène, began to regard the Négritude aesthetic as ideological imposition, with the result that in the next decade, visual artists began to rebel against the strict restrictions they experienced at the École des Arts (Harney 2004, 51, 79).

In the domain of construction and industry, the backlash that Christophe experiences in Césaire's play for treating his Citadel builders like "slaves at the mill" (1969, 68) is mirrored in the unrest of the *malaise paysanne* period in Senegal during 1967 and 1968, defined by worker and union strikes and student demonstrations (Gellar 1982, 25). At issue were a frozen minimum wage, sparse employment opportunities for the labor force, a decline in living standards in the city, and the fact that Senegal's "capital-intensive technologies" and "modernizing industries" were primarily benefiting elite bureaucrats and foreign technicians (63). Thus, Conteh-Morgan's (1994, 96) astute pronouncement on Césaire's protagonist rings eerily true for Senghor himself: "Like most revolutionaries, Christophe forgets the actual individuals whom he set out to defend."

The First World Festival of Negro Arts was a microcosm for the larger industrial and technological failures occurring in Senegal in the 1960s. Just as Christophe's Citadel is suspended incomplete by the end of Césaire's play, the Senegalese government's plans to build upscale hotels for foreign visitors to the festival fell through. Thus, Senghor had to accept the Soviet Union's offer of an opulent cruise ship and floating hotel docked near Dakar, a move that hurled him into the eye of the Cold War tornado.[17] Performances laid bare problematic economic and technological issues. The Gorée Island pageant relied on an "Aid and Co-operation agreement" with the French government, who provided the audiovisual equipment and projectors (*Spectacle Féerique de Gorée*, 31). Using a multicircuit electronic device the French patented as "Lumitone," which brought the open-air show to life with prerecorded light and sound cues,[18] the pageant illustrated Senghor's rhetorical turn toward science and technology in his speeches on Négritude at the time, even while it revealed France's dominance in the "cultural dialogue" Senghor sought within the festival itself. France also supplied the technical equipment for the Daniel Sorano Theatre, which hosted the production of Césaire's play. Yet African American festival attendee Fred O'Neal comically relayed that several of the performances at the Sorano were interrupted because the Senegalese running the theater had not yet learned how to operate the complex lighting and sound systems.[19]

If the Citadel represents Christophe's vision of Négritude as enveloping national culture, construction, and technological innovation, then the Dakar festival, broadly regarded as the "crowning achievement of Senegalese cultural policy" (Snipe 1998, 47), was perhaps Senghor's Citadel. However, the technical breakdowns at the Sorano Theatre, coupled with the construction failures that plagued Senghor's plans for accommodating festival visitors, pointed to a larger pattern of failures within the very development and modernization ideologies employed by Senghor's government in the 1960s.

King Christophe, Part II: Dependency and Foreign Intervention

> Whom did Europe send us when we applied to the International Technical Aid Organization for assistance? Not an engineer. Not a soldier. Not a professor. A master of ceremonies. Form is what counts, my friend. That's what civilization is . . . the forming of man.
>
> —Césaire (1969, 21)

There is surely more than a touch of irony in Césaire's penning of this speech by Vastey, Christophe's baron and secretary, about the French emcee who instructs the Haitian courtiers in the art of bowing and procession. Eric Livingston (1995, 186) calls the passage a "satirical dig at Western aid programs" and their colonialist tendencies to provide what they *think* a country needs. Indeed, it seems almost an ironic retort to Senghor's own vision of France sending "engineers" and "professors" to Senegal, while Senegal reciprocates by sending back Négritude and humanism, as I discussed earlier. Curto (2011, 160), however, reminds us that Césaire's vision of development valued the role of theater directors as highly as that of technicians, and asserts that the play actually *advocates* European assistance in the development process, whether that means cultural experts or new technologies. After all, Christophe ultimately welcomes at his court not just the French emcee but also the European engineer.

How might this particular scenario read against the broader background of Senegal in the 1960s? Like Christophe, Senghor was indeed embracing French assistance with open arms in that decade; external aid to the country constituted 70 percent of capital expenditure (Le Brun 1979, 192). While agriculture comprised the highest percentage of Senegal's GDP, its weak earning power led the state to seek help first from France and then, in later years, from the World Bank (O'Brien 1979, 20–21). At the time of the festival, 1966, Senegal's government was in the midst of a four-year plan that placed far less emphasis on African Socialism and overtly courted foreign intervention. This Second Plan (1965–1969) foregrounded production and cash crops, but disempowered rural Senegalese cooperatives by granting French technical support agencies near-exclusive domain over the burgeoning peanut industry. Further, the plan rearranged the country's tariff laws in order to bolster foreign investment in industry (Gellar 1982, 59).

French hegemony in Senegal was hard to miss at the First World Festival of Negro Arts. American visitors noted the prominence of French imports in markets, as well as the seemingly ubiquitous French management and clientele at cafés and hotels in Dakar.[20] Journalists also recognized the festival as integral to Senghor's development plan for the nation. In their eyes, it was the Senegalese government's fraught attempt to "stave off economic collapse" and a "gamble at stimulating tourism" from Europe and the States, especially among African Americans wishing to reconnect with Africa spiritually (Fuller 1966, 102). Thus, the festival's tourism drive was presumably undertaken to diversify international investment in Senegal beyond French aid.

In contrast to Curto's reading of *King Christophe,* I suggest that certain moments warn definitively against the kind of foreign encroachment Senghor and other African leaders were courting in the 1960s. In the coronation scene, Christophe grows impatient with the French archbishop's ceremonial grandeur and snatches the coronet out of the clergyman's hands in order to crown himself. This revealing gesture shows Christophe's pride in being a "self-made" leader and in keeping Haiti autonomous, since his first vow is to "preserve the . . . independence of the kingdom" (Césaire 1969, 27). At other times, Christophe is outright resistant to European assistance, as when he scoffs at his British friend Wilberforce's suggestion to slow down the pace of industrialization in Haiti, or when he overrides the European engineer's idea to forestall the building of the Citadel.

Reporting on the play's production in Dakar, Thomas Cassirer (1967, 181), an American visitor to the festival, explained that the French emcee cut a ridiculous figure since the "stilted" dances he taught the Haitian court were already outdated in France, which proved a stark contrast to the majesty of the native Haitian dancing at Christophe's court. Since the French director of *King Christophe,* Jean-Marie Serreau, played the role of the emcee (Curto 2011, 158), the critique of French aid was, conceivably, doubly visible in the production. Through the late 1950s and 1960s, Serreau worked closely with playwrights from Africa and the Diaspora on productions targeting various facets of decolonization (Livingston 1995, 183–84). Thus, the notion of a self-assigned French theater "aid" transcended the world of the play and directly applied to Césaire's work at the festival. Taken together, the play and the production potentially served as a caution to African leaders: if Europe is supplying cultural, technical, and economic "experts" to Africa, make sure that the collaboration takes place on equal footing.

King Christophe, Part III: Class and Elitism

> We were going to build a country
> All of us together!
> Not just to stake out this island!
> A country open to all the islands!
> To black men everywhere. The blacks of the whole world.
>
> —Césaire (1969, 30)

The rebel leader's anguished cry in act 1 of *The Tragedy of King Christophe* resonates beyond Haiti. It echoes the dashed hopes of an entire continent when, after decades of Pan-Africanism and the euphoria of Négritude, the first hints of neocolonial African governments appeared in the 1960s. Visitors attending the First World Festival of Negro Arts no doubt felt this sentiment when they watched Wole Soyinka's ominous play *Kongi's Harvest* performed in the Sorano Theatre and recognized Ghana's Kwame Nkrumah as the inspiration for the despotic African leader at the heart of the play's critique (Cassirer 1967, 180–81). Could the "blacks of the whole world" still unite when the continent's best-known independence leader was going the way of King Christophe?

Yet in Césaire's play the rebel cries out against both Christophe, "the brute," and Pétion, his rival for power in Haiti and a member of the elite Creole class. Pétion's pompous, inflated speech marks him as a "cheap orator" with no real sense of democracy (Conteh-Morgan 1994, 101), so that the subjects of his self-declared republic in the south of the island are seemingly no better off than the exploited subjects of Christophe's kingdom in the north. Both betray the ideals of Négritude: Christophe for his antihumanist behavior toward his people, and Pétion for his failure to include the lowly in his highbrow version of civilization. By the play's end, Christophe's refusal to rout both Pétion and the elitism he embodies proves to be his downfall. Pétion's successor, Boyer, handily defeats a weakened Christophe and his precarious kingdom.

We might imagine that Christophe's error is in seeing the Citadel, a symbol of pride and Négritude, as obviating the need to reconcile class differences in Haiti. Although a former slave and cook himself, Christophe quickly becomes seduced by courtly manners and distances himself from the laboring class he exploits. The parallels to Senghor are clear. As the son of a successful merchant and product of an elite Catholic education, Senghor did not share Christophe's humble upbringing. Yet his fascination with Négritude and the European curriculum he studied in Paris led him to impose an abstruse political philosophy on a Senegalese public that lacked the tools to decipher it. As Asli Berktay (2010, 212) notes, Senghor's rhetoric of African Socialism and Négritude increasingly obscured the real social inequalities plaguing his nation. Senghor's elitism was also present in the persisting French-centered educational system in Senegal, which students in Dakar vehemently protested in 1968 amidst a "de facto single-party" rule that brooked little political opposition (Castaldi 2006, 198–99). In his increasingly iron-fisted control of Senegal, Senghor was both Christophe and Pétion, both autocrat and pedant.

Césaire was well aware of the pitfalls into which decolonized nations could fall in the postcolonial era (Walker 2002, 190). In *The Tragedy of King Christophe,* it is the monarch himself who menacingly warns the Pétions of the world that revolution does not mean "taking the place of white men and behaving in the same way" (Césaire 1969, 56). In Dakar, acclaimed Senegalese actor Douta Seck portrayed Christophe with great intensity. Fellow actor Ivan Labéhof, also present at the Dakar festival, remembers that director Serreau instructed Seck to deliver those lines from the front of the stage, gazing directly out into the audience before retreating back. Labéhof then recalls a moment of silence as the audience registered the broader implications of the passage, followed by thunderous applause. Yet Labéhof also highlights how a number of African dignitaries sitting in the front row of the theater stood up and walked out.[21] This telling anecdote underscores how Césaire's political critique was recognizable in the elite Dakar audience, and perhaps even to Senghor himself.

Within the larger context of the festival, Senghor behaved like the Pétion of Christophe's critique by crafting it as an elitist venue whose average ticket price, in U.S. currency, of roughly one dollar and fifty cents per show far exceeded what the typical Senegalese worker could pay.[22] In Césaire's play, a ruthless Christophe shoots a peasant to indicate how he was undermining the kingdom's work ethic (1969, 61); at Dakar's festival, Senghor "sacrificed" the lower class, sanitizing the city to create the illusion of global wealth and abundance. Street beggars had either been locked up or forcibly removed from the city limits (Harney 2004, 76),[23] while a government-erected aluminum screen encircled the slum dwellings in the poor neighborhood of Médina so that foreigners could not peer in (Garrison 1966b).

Cognizant of class disparity at the festival, African and Diasporan artists took the initiative to stage impromptu outdoor performances. A Nigerian highlife band took over a former French outpost, Camp Mangin, entertaining crowds for free. Local musicians dressed in "outrageous costumes" spilled into Dakar's streets and invaded Médina—the same run-down neighborhood that Senghor's government tried to hide away from festival attendees—with "spontaneous explosions of song and dance" (Fuller 1966, 100). U.S. gospel singer Marion Williams followed up her hit concert at the cathedral with an impromptu performance on the ferry back from Gorée Island the next day, as Senegalese passengers chimed in eagerly with their own instruments (1966, 12).[24] Performing for free, these artists rejected the elitist bent of the festival. Read alongside the critique of class oppression and strong-handed government embedded in Césaire's play, this cluster of impromptu performances perhaps constituted an embodied response to Senghor. If the festival foregrounded modernization in the new Senegalese nation, attendees were made aware of the class-based exclusionism that the government's brand of development entailed.

The Tragedy of King Christophe was the "hit of the festival" in Dakar in 1966 (Cassirer 1967, 181). Its wide exposure suggests that festival attendees received the message of a leader who, as Césaire (1989, 61) put it, "gets lost" in the process of nation-building. As I have argued, the shape of that message related to the dangers of using Négritude rhetoric to prop up state ideologies of modernization. One might suggest that the performance venue at the festival potentially obstructed critical thinking about the play and its larger implications for African leaders, including Senghor. While Césaire's brand of theater was akin to Bertolt Brecht's in its demand for an active, questioning spectator (Walker 2002, 181), the Daniel Sorano Theatre was a straightforward proscenium stage that kept the imaginary wall between actors and audience in place. Senegalese multimedia artist Issa Lamb lamented the neocolonial design adopted for the theater, because it made "the African audience sit with their hands in their laps like Europeans" (quoted in Harney 2004, 107). Yet Senghor's dominance at the festival, as well as the arch of his speeches on Négritude, made his image as a "modernizing" leader ripe for critique. At the play's end, Christophe lies on his deathbed, disillusioned with the science and medicine that is powerless to heal him, literally leaving him paralyzed. What might that have portended for Senghor? Festival attendees, I suggest, were encouraged to fill in the blanks.

Notes

1. See Castaldi (2006); Diagne (2007, 2011); Ekpo (2010); Harney (2004); Irele (2002); Wilder (2005).

2. For thorough reviews of the strains of criticisms against Négritude, see Irele (1990 [1981], 67–88); Thompson (2002).

3. See *Premier Festival Mondial des Arts Nègres: Contributions musicales des nations Africaines*, Schomburg Center for Research Culture, the New York Public Library (hereafter Schomburg). Many thanks to Brian Granger, my research assistant, who gathered all of the documents cited here from the Schomburg.

4. See Apter (2005, 65–66); Castaldi (2006, 56); Harney (2004, 76–77); Jules-Rosette (1998, 67–78); Snipe (1998, 47–50).

5. I am quoting from Wilder's English translation of selections from the 1935 essay (2005, 188–89). See Souleymane Bachir Diagne's discussion of the 1939 article (2007, 95–96), which appears in Senghor's 1964 publication, *Liberté I.*

6. See Wilder's discussion of this essay, whose French title is "Ce que l'homme noir apporte" (2005, 245–50).

7. See the discussion of this idea in Castaldi (2006, 52).

8. I am quoting the English translation by Reed and Wake (Senghor 1965, 107).

9. See, for example, the cover of the opening report in "First World Festival of Negro Arts," box 1, folder "Pre-Festival Packet," Schomburg.

10. "Message from President Senghor to the Senegalese People," 4 February 1963, in "First World Festival of Negro Arts," box 1, folder "Pre-Festival Packet," Schomburg.

11. See "Budget for United States Representation in the First World Festival of Negro Arts," in "First World Festival of Negro Arts," box 1, folder "Post-Festival Reports," Schomburg.

12. See "For Your Information," box 1, folder "Press releases," Schomburg.

13. In an interview segment of Palcy's (2006 [1994]) *Aimé Césaire: Une voix pour l'histoire*, vol. 2, Césaire himself upholds this distinction between his version of Négritude and Senghor's, explaining that as a Diasporic subject whose ancestors were uprooted from Africa, he had no African values to which to cling.

14. Ibid.

15. See Snipe (1998, 45).

16. For a full description of the École de Dakar, see Harney (2004, chap. 2).

17. Onboard the ship, an exhibit reminded African American visitors that the Soviet Union, as opposed to their own home country, had not participated in the transatlantic slave

trade, using that historical detail as a rationale for "Russian-Negro brotherhood" (Garrison 1966a). See Wofford's discussion of the Russian cruise ship in relationship to William Majors's etching, *Ecclesiastes V*, a prize winner at Dakar's festival (2009, 185). Mention of the Russian cruise ship also abounds in the documents produced by the U.S. committee for the festival. See "Recorded Remarks by Fred O'Neal," box 1, folder "Post-Festival Reports," Schomburg.

18. See "First World Festival of Negro Arts," box 1, folder "Pre-Festival Packet," Schomburg.

19. See "Recorded Remarks by Fred O'Neal," box 1, folder "Post-Festival Reports," Schomburg.

20. Ibid.; Farrell (1966, 88B).

21. See the segment on *The Tragedy of King Christophe* in Euzhan Palcy's documentary, *Aimé Césaire: Une voix pour l'histoire*, vol. 2 (2006 [1994]).

22. See Leslie Rivers, "The World Festival of Negro Arts," *World Outlook* (September 1966): 30–32. Available in the vertical file on the First World Festival of Negro Arts, General Research and Reference Division, Schomburg.

23. Ibid.

24. See "Recorded Remarks by Fred O'Neal," box 1, folder "Post-Festival Reports," Schomburg.

References

Adotevi, Stanislas. 1969. "Negritude is Dead: The Burial." *Journal of the New African Literature and the Arts* 7–8: 70–81.

Apter, Andrew. 2005. *The Pan-African Nation: Oil and the Spectacle of Culture in Nigeria*. Chicago: University of Chicago Press.

Berktay, Asli. 2010. "Negritude and African Socialism: Rhetorical Devices for Overcoming Social Divides." *Third Text* 24, no. 2: 205–14.

Bradby, David. 1984. *Modern French Drama: 1940–1980*. Cambridge: Cambridge University Press.

Cassirer, Thomas. 1967. "Africa's Olympiad of the Arts: Some Reflections on the Dakar Festival." *Massachusetts Review* 8, no. 1: 177–84.

Castaldi, Francesca. 2006. *Choreographies of African Identities: Négritude, Dance, and the National Ballet of Senegal*. Chicago: University of Illinois Press.

Césaire, Aimé. 1969. *The Tragedy of King Christophe*. Translated by Ralph Mannheim. New York: Grove Press.

———. 1989. "It is through Poetry that One Copes with Solitude." Interview with Charles H. Rowell. *Callaloo* 38: 49–67.

———. 1995 [1956]. *Notebook of a Return to My Native Land*. Translated by Mireille Rosello. Newcastle upon Tyne: Bloodaxe.

Conteh-Morgan, John. 1994. *Theatre and Drama in Francophone Africa: A Critical Introduction*. New York: Cambridge University Press.

Curto, Roxanna. 2011. "The Science of Illusion-Making in Aimé Césaire's *La tragédie du roi Christophe* and *Une tempête*." *Research in African Literatures* 42, no. 1: 154–71.

Deliss, Clementine, ed. 1995. *Seven Stories about Modern Art in Africa: An Exhibition*. New York: Flammarion.

Diagne, Souleymane Bachir. 2002. "Now is the Time to Read Senghor Afresh." *Northwestern University Program of African Studies News and Events* 13, no. 2: 2.

———. 2007. "Rhythms: L.S. Senghor's Negritude as a Philosophy of African Art." *Critical Interventions* 1, no. 1: 88–105.

——. 2011. *African Art as Philosophy: Senghor, Bergson and the Idea of Negritude*. Translated by Chike Jeffers. New York: Seagull.

Edwards, Brent Hayes. 2001. "The Uses of Diaspora." *Social Text* 19, no.1: 45–73.

Ekpo, Denis, ed. 2010. "Beyond Negritude; Senghor's Vision for Africa." Special issue, Social Text 24, no. 2.

Fanon, Frantz. 1961 [1963]. "The Pitfalls of National Consciousness." In *The Wretched of the Earth*, 148–205. Translated by Constance Farrington. New York: Grove Weidenfeld.

Farrell, Barry. 1966. "Within the Show's Excitement, the Deeper Issue of Negritude." *Life*, 22 April.

Fuller, Hoyt. 1966. "World Festival of Negro Arts." *Ebony*, July: 95–106.

Garrison, Lloyd. 1966a. "A Gentle Cold-War Wind Wafts Through Senegal's Festival of Negro Arts." *New York Times*, 19 April.

——. 1966b. "Real Bursts Through the Unreal at Dakar Festival." *New York Times*, 26 April.

Gellar, Sheldon. 1982. *Senegal: An African Nation Between Islam and the West*. Boulder, CO: Westview.

Geschiere, Peter, Birgit Meyer, and Peter Pels. 2008. Introduction to *Readings in Modernity in Africa*, edited by Peter Geschiere, Brigit Meyer, and Peter Pels, 1–7. Bloomington: Indiana University Press.

Harney, Elizabeth. 2004. *In Senghor's Shadow: Art, Politics, and the Avant-Garde in Senegal, 1960–1995*. Durham, NC: Duke University Press.

Hymans, Jacques Louis. 1971. *Léopold Sédar Senghor: An Intellectual Biography*. Edinburgh: Edinburgh University Press.

Irele, Abiola. 1990 [1981]. *The African Experience in Literature and Ideology*. Bloomington: Indiana University Press.

——, ed. 2002. "Leopold Sedar Senghor." Special issue, *Research in African Literatures* 33, no. 4.

Jules-Rosette, Benetta. 1998. *Black Paris: The African Writers' Landscape*. Chicago: University of Illinois Press.

Le Brun, Olivier. 1979. "Education and Class Conflict." In *The Political Economy of Underdevelopment: Dependence in Senegal*, edited by Rita Cruise O'Brien, 175–208. Beverly Hills, CA: Sage.

Livingston, Eric. 1995. "Decolonizing the Theatre: Césaire, Serreau and the Drama of Negritude." In *Imperialism and Theatre: Essays on World Theatre, Drama, and Performance*, edited by J. Ellen Gainor, 182–98. New York: Routledge.

Markovitz, Irving Leonard. 1969. *Léopold Sédar Senghor and the Politics of Negritude*. New York: Atheneum.

McMahon, Christina S. 2005. "Globalizing Allegory: Augusto Boal's *A Lua Pequena e a Caminhada Perigosa* in Brazil and Cape Verde." *Latin American Theatre Review* 39, no. 1: 71–93.

O'Brien, Rita Cruise. 1979. Introduction to *The Political Economy of Underdevelopment: Dependence in Senegal*, edited by Rita Cruise O'Brien, 13–37. Beverly Hills, CA: Sage.

Ojo-Ade, Femi. 2010. *Aimé Césaire's African Theatre: Of Poets, Prophets, and Politicians*. Trenton, NJ: Africa World Press.

Palcy, Euzhan. 2006 [1994]. *Aimé Césaire: Une voix pour l'histoire*. Vol. 2, *Au rendez-vous de la conquête*. DVD. France: JMJ Productions.

Senghor, Léopold Sédar. 1935. "L'humanisme et nous: René Maran." *Étudiant Noir* 1, no.1: 4.

——. 1964. *On African Socialism*. New York: Praeger.

——. 1965. *Prose and Poetry*. Edited and translated by John Reed and Clive Wake. London: Heinemann.

——. 1966. "The Function and Meaning of the First World Festival of Negro Arts." *Africa Forum* 1, no. 4: 5–10.

——. 1994 [1970]. "Négritude: A Humanism of the Twentieth Century." In *Colonial Discourse and Post-Colonial Theory: A Reader*, edited by Patrick Williams and Laura Chrisman, 27–53. New York: Columbia University Press.

Snipe, Tracy D. 1998. *Arts and Politics in Senegal: 1960–1996*. Trenton, NJ: Africa World Press.

Spectacle féerique de Gorée: Opéra populaire en huit tableaux créé à l'occasion du Premier Festival mondial des arts nègres, 1/24 avril 1966, Dakar. 1966. Paris: Impressions André Rousseau.

Thompson, Peter S. 2002. "Negritude and a New Africa: An Update." *Research in African Literatures* 33, no. 4: 143–53.

Walker, Keith L. 2002. "Art for Life's Sake: Rituals and Rights of Self and Other in the Theatre of Aimé Césaire." In *Black Theatre: Ritual Performances in the African Diaspora*, edited by Paul Carter Harrison, Victor Leo Walker II, and Gus Edwards, 181–208. Philadelphia: Temple University Press.

Wilder, Gary. 2005. *The French Imperial Nation-State: Negritude and Colonial Humanism between the Two World Wars*. Chicago: University of Chicago Press.

Wolitz, Seth L. 1969. "The Hero of Negritude in the Theatre of Aimé Césaire." *Kentucky Romance Quarterly* 16, no. 3: 195–208.

Wofford, Tobias. 2009. "Exhibiting a Global Blackness: The First World Festival of Negro Arts." In *New World Coming: The Sixties and the Shaping of Global Consciousness*, edited by Karen Dubinsky, Catherine Krull, Susan Lord, Sean Mills, and Scott Rutherford, 179–86. Toronto: Between the Lines.

14 Reengaging Narratives of Modernization in Contemporary African Literature

Nana Wilson-Tagoe

The challenge in revisiting modernization in Africa is to pluralize its contexts and conditions in order to understand its formations in non-Western and ex-colonial regions of the world. We ought to be able to engage with modernization in ways that can unravel the agency of modern African societies in shaping a place beyond the paradigms of center and margin. How, for instance, can we characterize modernizing processes in societies that were incorporated in global systems of modernity? To what extent have Western institutions reshaped these dynamics in unique ways? Are these societies modern? This chapter focuses on narratives of modernization in African literature that acknowledge a fundamental difference in the epistemologies of the social sciences and the humanities, particularly in relation to the use of language. It historicizes African literature's preoccupation with modernization by demonstrating how the politics of cultural nationalism and a postcolonial focus on otherness stalled a fuller engagement with modernization in the critical assessment of African literature. In rereading key texts in African literature, the chapter focuses more fully on discourses of modernization which have been unrecognized in critical analyses of African literature. In the process it poses and addresses a number of key questions: What does it mean to be modern in Africa? How have African cultures become modern, and how have processes of modernization in Africa been understood, conceptualized, and explored in literature?

I suggest that these broad historical and cultural questions establish a credible framework for understanding and theorizing modernizing processes in Africa as they encompass the entire thrust of precolonial African history with its centuries of movement, change, and innovation, as well as with its more dramatic and traumatic encounter with modern Europe. I argue that we cannot conceptualize African agency in modernization outside this broader background because in spite of the developmental thrust and the ethnocentrism of early modernization theory, the agents of modernization in Africa have been Africans themselves. It was Africans who experienced and defined their modern status in political, cultural, and intellectual terms as they sought to engage and rethink their cultures in new ways. We should see modernizing processes in Africa, then, in terms of collisions, struggles, conflicts, and negotiations that open up spaces for creating new knowledge about contemporary Africa.

Imaginative literature opens several exploratory doors for creating this knowledge. Its capacity to capture both objective reality and its utopian possibilities, its ability (through its various genres) to accommodate competing discourses, and its strategies for uncovering the deeper psychological impact of everyday culture, make it a dynamic tool for illuminating the complex ramifications of modernization in modern Africa.

In modern African literature these possibilities have not always been vigorously utilized in exploring the project of modernization on the continent even though the modern experiences of Africans continue to be a hidden and recurring theme in the literature. This is because the ramifications of modernization are frequently suppressed and marginalized in African literature and its schools of criticism. Indeed, one of the major paradoxes of this literature is that whereas it came into being as a product of modernization, and its narratives focus on change and transformation, its major themes are ironically themes of history, tradition, and culture that affirm the validity and continuity of African cultures. It is this paradox, perpetuated by both writers and critics, that continues to obscure confrontations with modernity in the literature. Thus the often glaring contrasts between the rhetoric of modernization and the reality of modern colonial and postcolonial experiences remain only as gaps in the narratives of African literature. Reengaging this literature from the framework of modernization should uncover hidden discourses on modernity that produce more relevant knowledge about Africa's contemporary predicament than narratives of tradition that merely consolidate assumed traditions and affirm their continuity in the present.

My reengagement with narratives of modernization in African literature takes a historical approach both in its conception and in the selection of texts. It contextualizes the discussion of modernization within existing ideas in Africa by engaging with nonfictional works by Kenyatta (1938) and Nkrumah (1957). It traces the movement of ideas by considering early texts of literature such as J. E. Casely Hayford's *Ethiopia Unbound* (1911), Chinua Achebe's *Things Fall Apart* (1958) and *No Longer at Ease* (1960), and Wole Soyinka's *The Lion and the Jewel* (1963), exploring connections between colonial and transitional worlds and perspectives on modernization. The focus on Dangarembga's *Nervous Conditions* (2004 [1988]) and Ama Ata Aidoo's *Changes* (1991) foregrounds a later phase of African literature marked by political and economic crisis as well as a rethinking of ideas and representations in literature. Perspectives on modernization have for years circulated within these contexts, and a literary exploration of these representative texts should generate a body of knowledge from a specifically literary perspective.

The early texts of African literature heavily influenced by the nationalist discourses of Black Atlantic thinkers like Edward Blyden (1887) set a nationalist agenda that distanced the story of modernization in explorations of African identities. This kind of distancing is nowhere more glaring than in Casely Hayford's *Ethiopia Unbound* (1969 [1911]). In this semiautobiographical novel, Casely Hayford emphasizes his crucial ideological thrust when he subtitles his fictional work *A Study in Race Emancipation*. *Ethiopia Unbound* is really the self-conscious story of the African's emergence as a distinctive figure in the modern world at the dawn of the twentieth century. Though it focuses on the Gold Coast (present-day Ghana) and shifts settings between this location and England, it speaks to all "Ethiopians"[1] and is, as such, an amalgam of Casely Hayford's thoughts on black nationalism, colonial politics, and race relations. Casely Hayford's protagonist is the new African who is "modern," educated, intelligent, confident, and conscious of his race's contribution to world knowledge, seeking to make Western knowledge native to African institutions rather than unthinkingly assimilating into it.

For Casely Hayford, the story of modernization in Africa is inextricable from the construction of racial identity. This is because economic, political, and social transformations of modernization are also part of the history and ideology of colonialism. *Ethiopia Unbound* is structured around this proposition, and the protagonist's task is to direct the argument by exploring cultures, institutions, and communities while also reframing existing dichotomies like Christian/pagan, civilized/uncivilized, superior/inferior. Thus in spite of its distinct social settings and the interactions of individual characters within these social worlds, the novel is in part nonfictional, discursive, allegorical, and often surreal in its construction of racial and spiritual symbolism. The emphasis on race and spirituality is crucial, for it is through his conception of an African spirituality that Casely Hayford builds a case for African racial distinctiveness as a counterdiscourse to modernization as intertwined with colonial ideology. In a pivotal scene in which the novelist constructs a Fanti afterworld of ancestors as the repository of Akan cosmogony, the protagonist, Kwamankra, becomes the earthly emissary to the spirit world of his ancestors. Schooled, tested, and purified, he earns his status as both a race leader and the novel's philosophical consciousness. This consciousness is a distinctive ethical worldview that reverberates throughout the novel. As Kwamankra himself declares, reflecting on the African's place in the world and on individual and collective encounters with the modernist project, "The African's way to proper recognition lies not at present so much in the exhibition of material force and power, as in the gentle art of persuasion by the logic of facts and achievements before which all reasonable men must bow" (1969 [1911], 168).

Contemporary commentators on *Ethiopia Unbound* generally operate within the novel's ideological framework. They accept its mixture of genres and allegorical characterizations as part of a visionary quest for an African essence as an empowering principle in the challenging contexts of global modernity (Ugonna 1969, xxvi–vii; Newell 2002, 140–41; Korang 2004, 13). But the interplay between this larger quest and the marginalized modern themes of the novel reveal an important tension in Casely Hayford's work. The philosophical quest sits rather uneasily with the evocation of a modern context characterized by new socioeconomic spaces, new forms of social and economic power, and new modern dilemmas for Africans.

In spite of the novel's multiple fictional and nonfictional genres, it manages to convey an imagined community impacted by the political economy of modernization and its institutions of social and cultural domination. These are the specific contexts from which we can unravel challenges and competing visions that may suggest African struggles for agency in modernization. We recognize how particular characters either succumb to or stand up against cultural impositions. On many occasions, however, the competing visions are framed or conceptualized by the protagonist himself. For instance, his ironic evocation of the "metropolis" of Sekondi as a symbol of the failures of modernization does not just present a derelict colonial outpost in the Gold Coast; it projects an alternative vision of modernization as what Frederick Cooper would describe as "an aspiration for a life that could be understood and changed for the better" (2005, 118), a world where water systems, harbors, and railway tracks work, and where change does not necessarily "sap the foundations of native authority and institutions" (Casely Hayford (1969 [1911], 69). The protagonist's alternative vision is, however, predicated on a colonial condition that makes the vision itself impossible to achieve since modernization and colonialism are intertwined in this context. For Kwamankra, then, the ultimate insight is the resolution to save his people from national and racial death. "If my people are to be saved from national and racial death, they must be proved as if by fire—by the practice of a virile religion" (75). Is Kwamankra the subject of irony in the novel, the mouthpiece of Casely Hayford's racial ideology, or does his predicament serve as a symbol of the tension at the heart of *Ethiopia Unbound*? Ironically, he is himself a "modern" subject who grapples with his multiple situations as an African, who is both a colonial and a modern man. His ability to negotiate these different claims is what makes him modern and engaging. Yet this potential is also precisely what he subsumes in his overarching discourse of race emancipation.

In *Writing Ghana, Imagining Africa,* Larbi Korang characterizes Casely Hayford's perspective in *Ethiopia Unbound* as an "untranscendable contradiction between a modernist self-fashioning and the need to kill the modernist self within" (Korang 2004, 13). While this is an apt characterization, the significant point is that the paradox also stalls a vigorous grappling with modernization and the role of Africans in shaping and defining it. It confines themes of modernization within the unhelpful categories of tradition and modernity that have shaped decolonizing movements and the agenda of modern African literature. The paradox remains in the text, however, as evidence of gaps that may be uncovered and examined with each reading.

Casely Hayford published *Ethiopia Unbound* in 1911. A little over two decades later, Jomo Kenyatta's *Facing Mount Kenya* (1938) presented another perspective on modernization in Kenya as part of his ethnographic study of his Gikuyu tribe. Bruce Berman's (1996) research into the background of the book's production opens doors for exploring connections between Kenyatta's politics, his ethnographic text, and his understanding of modernization processes in Africa. A functionalist approach to ethnography helped Kenyatta not only to speak as a representative Gikuyu but also to present an integrated and unified view of Gikuyu culture as a competing vision to colonialism and its modernizing changes. But the narrative and analytical tools of functional ethnography work against an understanding of the internal and external struggles involved in modernization processes. In *Facing Mount Kenya,* Kenyatta has no framework for analyzing these processes since the thrust of his narrative is toward integration and conservation. His grasp of modernization's impact on the organic Gikuyu culture he constructs amounts generally to what Europeans might offer (material prosperity, medicine, hygiene, literacy) and what Gikuyus might choose to take. For instance, when he writes that "[Europeans] would have to offer [Africans] the benefits of white civilization in real earnest before they could obtain the African labor they want so much," he writes only tentatively about the presumed benefits of modernization (Kenyatta 1938, 305). He envisages the modernist project not as a remaking of Gikuyu traditional society but almost as something separate from their tribal institutions. This is because he assumes erroneously that science and modernization would exist side by side with an unmediated traditional system in which women would remain in their traditional roles at the margins of power. This is an important irony to note because unraveling such ambivalence in the making of modernized communities is also a way of understanding why the project generated enormous crises in postcolonial societies.

In the mid-twentieth century, African nationalist politicians such as Jomo Kenyatta and Kwame Nkrumah actually sought to link notions of liberation to the right of Africans to benefit from modernization. Indeed, James Ferguson (quoted in Cooper 2005, 131) has persuasively argued that modernization had concrete meaning as the promise of material well being (health facilities, education, commerce) for most Africans of the 1950s and 1960s. Nonetheless, as a theory, it also pointed to what Cooper calls "the depth of global hierarchy and promise that eventually material standards would converge upwards" (131). The point to consider, then, is not whose modernity this was, but how it was used to reshape African communities, while making Africans modern in the process.

In the 1950s, Kwame Nkrumah's political writing explored other visions of modernization beyond material prosperity and progress. By the time he published his autobiographical work, he was already thinking beyond Casely Hayford's brand of racial uniqueness to the creation of new political systems within which the meaning of modernity could be explored and possibly rethought. "Only a free and independent people—a people with a government of their own—," he writes in his autobiography, "can claim equality, racial or otherwise, with another people" (Nkrumah 1957, 14). Interestingly, however, the political push for the fruits of modernization also coexisted with a cultural nationalism that privileged African traditions and cultures even though modernization itself posed challenges for traditions, beliefs, and cultures. Simon Gikandi identifies the paradoxical nature of this dual quest when he observes that the "craving for the pre-modern was calibrated by the anxiety of modernity and modernization, and it is for this reason, among others, that the notion of a traditional African culture . . . came to be shadowed by the very forces it sought to exorcise" (Gikandi 2008, 11).

Our challenge in reengaging texts of African literature, then, is to bring out the paradoxes and at the same time unravel the discourses of modernity that invariably lurk behind the texts. As argued earlier, what distinguishes imaginative literature from the anthropological, historical, and political narratives we have looked at is literature's ability to transcend the merely empirical. The language of imaginative literature does not only function as a descriptive sign; it is a tool for uncovering the hidden, the puzzling, and the enigmatic as crucial aspects of human experience. For even in an apparently straightforward comic text like Wole Soyinka's *The Lion and the Jewel,* where the opposition between tradition and modernity seems obvious and clear-cut, there is an implied discourse on modernization that is much more subtle and sophisticated than a simple rejection of it. In spite of its comic framework and communal celebratory mood, *The Lion and the Jewel* is a serious and contemporary exploration of how African cultures may become modern. While the comedy revolves around the two main opposing perspectives of the small Yoruba village, the traditional chief and the educated village teacher, the question posed by the drama is not just who will win and marry the village beauty, but what the community's future will be, and all are invested in the outcome. The contrast drawn between Lakunle (the village teacher, an iconic figure of the modern elite) and Baroka (the arch-traditionalist of the same period) may suggest a binary opposition between two different perspectives. But Soyinka's interrogative play of 1963 raises questions that suggest a more complex wrestling with the meaning of modernization in the colonial contexts of the 1920s.

The contest between the two male figures for the hand of Sidi, the village belle, is metaphorically also a contest of ideas on how best to live in the new time of colonial modernity. But the two male contestants do not maintain wholly entrenched positions on modernization and tradition. Lakunle's half-baked modern ideas are ridiculed and rejected as slavish imitation but he is never placed outside the community, and the seemingly intransigent Baroka is given a perspective on modernization that is more in tune with the needs of his community even though he is a notorious conservative known to have opposed the modernizing impact of a colonial railway line through his village. Baroka is in this sense not the categorical opposite of Lakunle or even the play's alternative to him. The drama's struggle is not a choice of modernization over tradition and vice versa, but a struggle over the definition of a modernized community and a modernist subject. Indeed, Soyinka's own vision of a modernized scenario foisted onto an unmediated traditional community is problematic and betrays the anxiety that Gikandi has identified. For while his protagonist, Baroka, is not the play's alternative to the ridiculous Lakunle, his perspective on modernization is indirectly validated in the communal victory dance that marks the play's comic resolution of conflicts. Yet Baroka's vision of his community's agency makes no room for the personal transformation of marginal characters. Woman is still a sign of tradition even though major sections of the play focus on women's self-awareness and change in consciousness as possible aspects of the modernizing project. The oppositions are therefore more like constructs for probing intersecting issues involving the entire community.

We can unravel similar hidden debates on modernity and paradoxical representations of tradition even in a text like Achebe's *Things Fall Apart* (1958), which has an established reputation as an ethnographic text. Because a greater portion of the novel's action dramatizes the tropes of tradition and the rituals that explore their rationale and meanings, we may be tempted to read it as a novel about a community and its traditions. Change in *Things Fall Apart* comes slowly and takes a dramatic turn only toward the end of the novel, when the white man's power becomes palpable and dangerous. The other reason why the modern theme may be missed in a reading is that the novel's focus is overwhelmingly historical. It begins in the present but moves in between past and present to create a wide stretch of historical time within which the modern story can be viewed. Thus by the time the community meets the white men we have a credible sense of their history even if the white people do not.

It is in these intersections that *Things Fall Apart* explores the nature, dynamics, and crises of modernization. Modernity and modernization need not be seen solely in terms of the violent conquests and political impositions of colonialism. The collisions, struggles, countermovements, and negotiations they inspire open up fissures and possibilities that help to rethink colonized societies and identities in new ways. As Albert Paolini argues in his work on modernity, postcolonialism, and identity, "Modernity is not simply a systemic phenomenon, it provides a theatre of action and reaction for a whole series of agents and groups it encounters along the way. Not only does it force people to engage with otherness, it requires them to examine their own circumstances and world view in its march forward" (Paolini 1999, 9–10). In *Things Fall Apart*, we recognize the new context of modernity in the collision between an Umuofian world that has repeatedly seen itself as unified and sufficient, and a competing new cosmology with a different interpretation of nature, religion, and social relations. The encounter is laden with both crisis and paradox because it generates fundamental changes in the traditional world by introducing a new concept of time, new systems of economic exchange, and a new concept of religious brotherhood that undermines the unity of the clan.

More crucially, the modernizing project in this contested space becomes problematic since it is mediated through the power and ideologies of colonialism. Gikandi has argued that "the process of rationalization on the continent was never wholly conceived by the colonized themselves as the conduit for positive and revisionary ideas about society" (2008, 10). Ironically, however, narratives of modernization in African literature that imagine colonial encounters from the perspective of the colonized often work against the grain of Gikandi's assertion. The power to narrativize is, after all, a liberty that fiction takes with history and what makes historical fiction fundamentally an interpretation of the past from the perspective of the present. How Achebe represents modernity in narrative, then, has a lot to do with his location in the postcolonial present and with the fact that as a modern subject he has the tools and resources to rethink his past and culture in new ways.

In *The Lion and the Jewel* Soyinka virtually distances the story of modernization by locating it in a comic drama and suggesting the perils of uncritically appropriating its tenets. Achebe, on the contrary, makes modernity his central theme in *Things Fall Apart* and presents it in tragic terms. The African's encounter with European modernity culminates in a metaphysical rupture when the logic behind an old system appears to collapse, giving way to a new dispensation with a radically different understanding of nature and society. Achebe's narrative focuses on the encounter between white colonials and an Eastern Nigerian community in the late nineteenth century. The colonials enter the village initially as harmless missionaries seeking converts. The village offers them space in the evil forest, a place replete with sinister forces that could annihilate them in no time. But the missionaries thrive, and in time become a political establishment backed by a military force that takes over the community and institutes a new "modern" government. Though Achebe narrates the encounter as part of the rise, fall, and death of one of the village's prominent men, his focus throughout is on the village, its people, and their value systems. Okonkwo, the novel's central character, sees himself as the embodiment of his people's values and bitterly opposes the incursion of the white colonials and the divisions they create within the community. On an occasion when arrogant messengers of the colonials disrespect the community and the elders, Okonkwo's anger and bitterness overwhelm him. He guns down the chief messenger (who is a member of the clan), believing he is following the warrior traditions of the clan. But no one follows his call for battle because the colonials have penetrated too deeply into the clan and have brought a religious ideology that has earned them converts. Okonkwo knows he has lost. He has killed a clansman and he knows the clan's penalties. He hangs himself.

Though the story revolves round Okonkwo, the village, and the gods of the community, the crucial conflict is played out as a clash of cosmologies between the community and the white colonials. For Achebe's communities in *Things Fall Apart* the question is whether or not the power of their gods to regulate and intervene in their affairs (the very principle behind the fabric of their universe) is maintained. Therefore, when against all odds the Christian community survives and thrives in the evil forest instead of being annihilated by its sinister forces (as was expected), the people's confidence in their own system is severely tested. More than that, they become aware of the power and efficacy of other gods. The new system of the white man is not only an assault on the community's belief systems; it also brings a proliferation of alternatives, and for a people who have consistently seen their society as an organic whole, this vision of alternatives constitutes remarkable newness.

It would be inadequate, however, to read this encounter and rupture in strictly binary terms. The defeat of traditional metaphysics by European rationality, as Achebe's narrative asserts, also dramatizes the complex ways in which the Nigerian Igbo community understands and relates to the modernizing project. For instance, the community interprets the Christians' triumph in the evil forest in metaphysical terms, but we know that the Christians survive and thrive not because of their powerful fetish but because they conceive of space (in scientific terms) as a place to live in and cultivate. It is their secular rationality that defeats the sinister forces of the evil forest. Yet as Olakunle George argues persuasively, it is through the channels of Christianity that the Igbo converts experience and relate to modernity: "[In] the matter of what to worship, the indigenes of Umuofia are asked to trade in the pagan fetish for the Holy Trinity" (George 2003, 178). One significant consequence of the community's relation to the new system is that African converts make their own calculation about how best the new power would serve their needs and aspirations, and it is their calculation and input that makes the Christian community not only a viable one but a major threat to the traditional system. Such exercises of choice, however minute, give the converts a measure of agency that makes them participants rather than objects in shaping the new religion.

The duality apparent in European modernity has another consequence for the Igbo community. The new religion is also embedded in a colonial ideology that negates the very basis of Umuofia's system. And it comes with secular extensions: a military force that terrorizes the community and generates its own peculiar corruptions; a governing apparatus that works according to its own ethics; a new system of economic exchange that has new determinants of wealth, status, and power. These ground-shifting changes (most of which are merely summarized in the final sections of the novel) portend major conflicts and struggles in the new modernized space. But *Things Fall Apart* gives surprisingly little space to the actual processes of the modernizing project, since its relentless focus is on the tragic impact of the rupture on Okonkwo, the character who believes he embodies the community's core values. The bigger struggles around modernity, we are made to think, would be in the future and in another context of the trilogy Achebe had envisaged. For this reason, the thematic link between *Things Fall Apart* and *No Longer at Ease* is crucial for the interpretation of both novels, and the framework of modernity offers the most productive analytical perspective for interpretation.

There is a major sense, then, in which the entire action of *No Longer at Ease* (Achebe 1960) can be seen as a drama of modernization that evokes the contexts within which the modern nation comes to birth. Because the novel is set on the eve of Nigeria's independence, most commentators see it as a projection of the new nation's uncertain character and future. The narrative links the new nation and its contexts strategically to the career and downfall of Obi, the young protagonist whose promise and contradiction mirror those of the young nation. The spaces and contexts of modernity generate a different problematic whose source can be traced back to the encounter with modernity in *Things Fall Apart.* By the 1950s (the fictional time of the novel) we have moved several years and two generations beyond the encounter that splintered the clan and led to Okonkwo's suicide. The initial rupture has given way to wider structural and social transformations that are partially generated and mediated by colonial action and ideology. The notion of community and communal space has also shifted to a larger entity called Nigeria, a conglomerate of disparate cultural communities linked together by the colonial city of Lagos. It is this entity that is poised for independence and nationhood at the beginning of the novel. The idea of nationhood, itself a modern concept, becomes part of a wider debate on modernization that may be examined in relation to the initial encounter with modernity in *Things Fall Apart.* How is this context represented in the narrative? What can we grasp about the nature of the modern space, and how does the society in *No Longer at Ease* make its transition to nationhood in its modern context?

Achebe's narrative opens up the complex relationships between culture, modernization, and nationhood and appears to ask how a nation can be constructed from a modern context that is mediated by colonialism, tradition, and patriarchy. We know from the initial encounter with modernity in *Things Fall Apart* that Umuofia's experience of modernity has not been a process of "one dimensional secularization away from illiberal tradition" (George 2003, 182), and we can understand why Achebe's delineations point to a confusing mixture of modern and traditional elements in the experience of the modern. Throughout the novel there is a recurring incongruence between the spaces, institutions, and rhetoric of modernization and the reality of people's experience and articulation of it. For instance, the elders of Umuofia know they live in a world whose center has shifted to the city and its institutions. They recognize that the ethical codes that once defined social standing and greatness have changed. Yet they perceive and articulate these changes in the vocabulary of the old world. Similarly, Umuofians in Lagos know that the old notion of work has been complicated by a new concept of money associated with a modern system of exchange. Yet they do not connect this phenomenon to their self-conceptions as city dwellers but continue to see themselves as sojourners and strangers in an alien city. For instance, Isaac Okonkwo (the protagonist's father) assumes the guttural laughter of a masked spirit in defense of an old tradition of caste even though he is a "modern" subject living in a new modern time.

How should we read such disconnections between language and the reality it describes, between reality and its perception? Should we see these merely as evidence of the persistence of tradition in modernity or should we probe them for other meanings? The narrative itself points a way to interpretation by opening up spaces and modalities of the colonial city that demand definition and critique from all characters in the novel. The city of Lagos, long crystallized in the young protagonist's memory as a city of lights, reveals its tensions as the narrative evokes it in several sections of the novel. We recognize its dynamism and stasis, its false glamour and rottenness, its apparent freedom and colonial constriction, its corruptions, exclusions, and gendered spaces. How should this world be defined in the restructuring of society in a modern nation? What are the new codes and languages that may describe this new way of being?

These are the questions raised and explored in *No Longer at Ease*. Their answers are not clear-cut but are embedded in the very tenor of the narrative's exploration. Achebe's strategy is to allow the characters themselves to articulate how they understand their new modern experience. Commentators on *No Longer at Ease* have not always stressed this strategy. But there are, for instance, important differences in the interpretations characters give to the word "pioneer" that ultimately determine their ability to understand or interpret their new context. Most Umuofians in the city describe themselves as pioneers not in the sense of forging new paths and identities in response to their "modern" experience, but as a people suspended in the unstable zone between the old world and the new, yet committed firmly to the old. Obi's friend, Joseph, speaks for most Umuofians when he remarks that "[in the] future when we are all civilized, anybody may marry anybody. But that time has not come. We of this generation are only *pioneers*" (Achebe 1960, 63; emphasis added). For these city men, to be a pioneer is to stand within the advantage of the modern city while consolidating the values and traditions of the old world.

To these interpretations, the narrative opposes Obi's more appropriate definition of "pioneer" as "someone who shows the way," even though he himself fails like most characters in the novel, to uphold and live his pioneering vision. To be a pioneer in the fluid conditions of Obi's world is not merely to "show the way" by envisioning an autonomous modern nation, but also to negotiate several competing claims in the making of a modern nation: the claims of Umuofians still groping for a language to define the new society, the attitudes of colonials still powerful in entrenched institutional structures, and the paradoxes of hybrids like Obi himself, shaped by their colonial education, seeking a new nation yet unable to transcend established norms of gender and caste that work against the concept of nationhood. To all these complex responses and claims, Obi offers not analysis and vision but incoherence and a personal philosophy of individual choice. For instance, at a climactic moment in the novel when he has the chance to defend a new way of being in opposition to his father's defense of an ancient system of caste, Obi is unable to challenge his father honestly.

His vision of himself as a pioneer, Achebe reveals, is not backed by any understanding or conviction of what it means to be a modern subject in a world caught between old traditions and ongoing transformations. Alienated from the traditions of his people, he has not yet acquired the core tenets and perspectives of a modern subject. Gikandi explains the confusion and incongruity of vision in *No Longer at Ease* in terms of the impact of colonial structures and ideologies: "If the ideology of colonialism determines the values by which people live and define the new modernity, how can young men like Obi hope to escape from the prison house of the colonizing structures? How do you organize a world in which the old dispensation has collapsed?" (Gikandi 2008, 16). But while this is a valid explanation of the colonial mentality at the heart of the incongruity in Obi's vision and action, it does not fully account for the totality of the narrative's presentation of him. For it is in its critique of Obi that Achebe's narrative indirectly rethinks the meaning of modernity and modernization in the context of colonialism. Unlike Obi, who views the modern Nigerian nation through the corruption of its institutions and his own individual perspectives and choices, Achebe suggests that modernity yields its true meaning through its translation within specific locations. It is through such translations, Homi Bhabha has argued, shedding some light on postcolonial modernity, that we can rewrite the universalism of modernity. "The postcolonial translation of modernity," he writes in *The Location of Culture*, "makes possible another time, within whose pauses a certain interrogation is rewriting the universalism of modernity and man" (Bhabha 1994, 5).

What Bhabha means by "another time" is not the linear and chronological time within which Obi envisages the overhaul of pagan traditions. It is rather the in-between space of struggle and interrogation in which new meanings of tradition and culture would be produced. It is within this larger context of translation that questions of tradition, caste, gender, and modern subjectivity may be framed and productively explored. In such a context Obi would not be speaking from the periphery, rehashing colonial clichés. He would be thinking in larger terms and in new ways about tradition and modernization and may find the need for both, however contradictory their coexistence may seem. Indeed, Obi does come close to such a translation at rare moments in the narrative when he attempts to counter the colonial perspectives of characters like Mr. Green, and when his modern mind engages the logic and insights in indigenous songs and narratives. But his grasp and understanding of the modern context is so filtered through his own perspectives and choices that in the end an ethic of individualism overwhelms all other considerations, and he gives up even the naive idealism of his youthful days. Obi's dualities, contradictions, and evasions are crucial for grasping how Achebe's narrative works to destabilize apparently entrenched concepts like tradition, caste, and gender within the new modern experience. The contradictory ways in which characters interpret these concepts work to unhinge them from received usage and force new interpretation. This kind of representation, where language works to suggest dualities and oppositions in meaning and characterization, is deepened further when Achebe takes on the modern theme again in *Anthills of the Savannah* (Achebe 1987). Here, he appears to question the old fictional framework in which a handful of male elites assume the right to define the modern nation and act on its behalf. He structures *Anthills* not as a narrative with a single implied narrator and a lone protagonist, but as an interrogative text that brings several points of view into an unresolved collision in which dialogue and debate produce several possible scenarios and answers.

A new crop of African women writers were, however, already creating such textual dialogues, changing the male-defined paradigms of modernization and exploring new ways of defining modern contexts that they saw as mediated and limited by the dominant ideologies of colonialism and patriarchy. For these writers, modernity is not only mediated by a colonial past, but impacted by norms of gender. Because "woman" is often a sign of tradition even in modernizing societies, most of these writers work with a variety of fictional forms to explore new relationships to tradition. The crucial question that frames their revisionary narratives is how modernization would be understood if its spaces and processes were seen from the marginal worlds of women. In most of these texts the story of modernization is told from female perspectives with the underlying assumption that marginal spaces provide the most revisionary insights about the symbolic order.

This is the case, for instance, in Tsitsi Dangarembga's *Nervous Conditions* (2004 [1988]), where the experience of modernization in colonial Rhodesia is narrated from the perspective of the novel's woman protagonist. Set in Rhodesia in the 1950s and encompassing periods in the 1890s, *Nervous Conditions,* like *Things Fall Apart,* centers the narrative of modernization in the traumatic confrontation between white colonists and an indigenous Zimbabwean community. Marked by conquest, seizure of indigenous lands, and the exploitation of indigenous labor, the encounter is presented in the narrative as a series of struggles to understand a new modern context and the modern identities it creates. Though the new world is reshaped according to the plans and dreams of the white colonial elite it bears the scars of a brutal past that defines its character and creates a range of nervous conditions in all the characters. The new world is also complicated by the oppressions of an indigenous patriarchy. Cultural life, norms of gender, and notions of womanhood and masculinity are defined by an indigenous male elite that is itself weakened by its marginalization in the new order. What challenges does such a scenario of colliding worlds present for Tambu, the young female protagonist, as she navigates this new world? How would she make sense of her modern world?

Dangarembga's strategy of placing Tambu both in her parents' village and in the town where her uncle heads the colonial school achieves a double and paradoxical effect: it grounds Tambu in the two worlds and gives her the critical distance to examine her interactions in both worlds. Indeed, *Nervous Conditions* is structured to ensure that Tambu's early conceptualizations of her traditional world—her perception of colonial and patriarchal control, her understanding of the limits placed on women's aspirations and self-expression, her rootedness in the physical and cultural landscape of her world, and her awareness of the risks of alienation—all become points of reference as she moves from her family's village into the new colonial town and its modern ways. What is striking in *Nervous Conditions* is that Tambu's entry into her uncle's modern world is a choice based on her rejection of the model of womanhood offered her by the traditions of her home and community. Yet her move is not a simple transition from a strictly traditional world to an entirely new modern world, even though Tambu believes naively that this is the case. Her view of her new "modern" life at her uncle's great house is a radical transformation into another self, "a clean, well-groomed, genteel self who could not have been bred, could not have survived in the homestead" (Dangarembga 2004 [1988], 59), is of course illusory, and must be seen against the gaps and inconsistencies in her own reading of this world.

In spite of Tambu's ability to see through and evaluate her father and brother, her cognitive grasp of her world is often weakened because it works by separating thoughts "she can ponder safely" from "complex dangerous thoughts" she suppresses because they might force her to confront her compromises. It is because of such gaps and inconsistencies in Tambu's judgment that she reassesses her uncle, Babamukuru, and his enviable place in the modern world of the colonial establishment, as the condition for a new discourse on modernity. But her assumption that her uncle shares her modernist view of education as the cultivation of the spirit and the "creation of consciousness" is soon dispelled. It becomes clear that for Babamukuru education and modernity mean nothing more than a chance to elevate his family and give it social and "proper" status—that in his view, as in the view of the entire community, Tambu's education "was an investment but in terms of cattle so was [her] conformity" (Dangarembga 2004 [1988], 34). Modernity and tradition are inseparable in this new world, and "woman" (educated or illiterate) functions as a sign of tradition. How can Tambu navigate this male-defined and colonial "modern" world as an agent and a subject when she is unable (or unwilling) to confront "complex" and "dangerous" issues about her experience as a female and as an African? What new words can reframe and interpret the meaning of the modern in this world? Dangarembga's narrative addresses these questions by structuring Tambu's modernist quest as a process in which other characters' lives and struggles are implicated. It is through such composite representations that the narrative establishes the path to modernity as a complex drama of desire and crisis that must be continually negotiated.

As part of this strategy, Tambu's narrative intersects with the narrative of her uncle's educated wife, Maiguru. It opens up the anglicized spaces of Maiguru's big house and reveals the ironic incongruities between the antiseptic cleanliness she strives for and the reality of a house located on a dusty road in colonial Rhodesia. Maiguru's own life—from the joy of her anglicized children to the baby talk that conceals anger, frustration, and anxiety over her double colonization—constitutes a reassessment of Tambu's naive assumption that education and modernity are conduits for self-transformation in her world. By connecting the struggles of all the women characters in Tambu's narrative, the novel not only allows commonly silenced women access to the understanding and interpretation of their modern condition, but also complicates women's subjectivity by revealing their multiple and contradictory locations in modernity.

I would contend, though, that in *Nervous Conditions* the dialectic that illuminates all the various crises of the modern experience is contained in the narrative's doubling of the characters of Tambu and her cousin, Nyasha. The strategy is an effective one for exploring the possibility of a feminine agency in modernity. For instance, Nyasha finds security and solace in Tambu's grounded understanding of her traditional world, and Tambu recognizes an aspect of her hidden self in Nyasha's adventurous, exploratory personality but resists this trait by quickly defining herself as different from her cousin. Yet it is precisely this aspect of Nyasha's core personality (hidden within Tambu herself) that enables Tambu to defy Babamukuru's oppressive impositions and his attempts to limit the possibilities of her modern experience. But Tambu not only ignores but sometimes actually resists the implications of this doubling. Indeed, by distancing Nyasha's struggles and psychological turmoil, she suppresses and therefore undermines the salient insights of her own *bildung* as they are manifested powerfully and tragically in Nyasha's illness. For while Nyasha's illness is a form of resistance, it is not the price she pays in her "search for bodily perfection" (Appiah 2004, ix), nor is it the result of the Englishness that will "kill them if they aren't careful" (Dangarembga 2004 [1988], 207). Rather, it marks the complex intersections of modernization, colonialism, gender, and oppressions in the unique conditions of colonial Rhodesia during the 1960s. In resisting the wider possibilities of her identification with Nyasha, Tambu loses a radical critique of colonialism and therefore achieves only a limited subjectivity. The paradigm, however, remains in the novel as a possibility for confronting intersecting oppressions within the modern context of the novel.

The questions *Nervous Conditions* raises about women's subjectivity and agency in colonial modernity reappear within a different problematic in *Changes: A Love Story,* Ama Ata Aidoo's 1991 novel set in postcolonial Ghana. These correspondences and differences are important indications of the extent to which African women writers are raising similar issues yet experimenting with different forms and strategies of exploration. Though *Changes* is often inadequately interpreted as a narrative about the dilemmas and choices of professional women in Africa, it is a much more ambitious engagement with the larger crisis of modernity and modernization in postcolonial Africa of the 1980s. Its central question is predicated on the very crisis that theories of modernization failed to predict. The collapse of modern institutions in postcolonial Africa during the 1970s and 1980s raised questions about conceptions of modernization that demanded new thinking, and Aidoo's novel should be seen as part of this debate. How, it seems to ask, may questions of modernity and modernization be reframed in the "dangerous confusions" of postcolonial Africa? If Aidoo addresses this question from the perspective of women's lives and relationships, it is because such relationships also structure economic and social relations and can provide a channel for reading a community's political and social terrain. It is in this sense that the domestic theme of *Changes* also explores inextricable links between gender and larger questions of modernization and politics.

The novel focuses primarily on three contrasting modern marriages that are linked to other marriages in the past, so that intersections between them reveal the nature of the new modern terrain and the various ways in which change is managed or negotiated. *Changes* names its world as a confused neocolonial African city, only nominally independent, barely able to feed itself, and lacking any consensus on values or truth. This is a world that struggles more visibly with its paradoxes and contradictions than the colonial world of *Nervous Conditions.* For on the one hand, its institutions and other structures give it the appearance of a modernizing world, while on the other hand, these same institutions prove ineffectual, and old notions of gender and sexuality remain entrenched. Linked to these modern institutions, the major characters in the new buzz and mobility of their city lives seem separate from the virtually unseen poor, living at the margins of the city and the narrative.

In a context where modernist ideals of nationhood, democracy, rights, and progress have collapsed, what should be the role of art? Should it, as Gikandi observes, "embrace what Adorno called dissonance in order to account for and transcend an alienated reality? Or must literature adopt its utopian possibility and restore the place of art as the site in which new identities can be forged or imagined?" (Gikandi 2008, 17–18). Aidoo's novel adopts the second option, and imagines the possibility of change not just in the power relations between men and women, but also in the individual consciousness, thereby investing in the other idea of modernity as subject formation, as a new way of being. Yet we may be tempted to ask how *Changes* works to suggest these possibilities when almost all the women in the narrative end up compromising on the exploitative connotations of "wifehood" in the face of their personal suffering, frustrations, and yearnings.

My view is that the different narratives of marriage in *Changes* intersect with each other for a particular dialectical effect that holds possibilities for rethinking the meaning of modernization from the perspectives of women's lives within cultures. While they range across different time periods (traditional, colonial, modern) and geographical spaces in West Africa, the fundamental issues of gender and power, of female desire and aspiration and their constant collision with male power and prerogative, link the narratives to suggest how little things have changed in the area of gender relations. Equally, the internal struggles and psychological turmoil of all the wives—old and young, educated and illiterate—intersect, not only because "each manifests a different feminist consciousness" (Elia 1999, 140), but because they are all implicated in the woman protagonist's modernist quest. Esi's "adventure" in *Changes* may appear to be an individual and selfish quest, but it is in reality an attempt at exploring other ways women can relate to men, an attempt to redefine wifehood, marriage, sexuality, and the female body in a changing world. Aidoo casts her protagonist, Esi, in opposition to the "good woman," Opokuya, but only to suggest that unlike her, Esi interrogates her new modern world and would put her emotions, desires, yearnings, and anxieties out in the open as she seeks answers to questions about life, love, marriage, and modernity.

In this quest, Esi seems united with her author. For the narrative itself points to the necessity for such questions when it presents a postcolonial modernity riddled with "dangerous confusions." Neither Esi nor any of the modern characters can ever meaningfully reenter the world of their mothers and grandmothers. Yet none has a theoretical grasp on the character of the modern as it shapes up in the new postcolonial time. The male figures attempting to name and define this world manipulate and recycle old conceptualizations of modernization based on dichotomies between public male spaces and private domestic spaces. Thus Musa

Musa knows that nothing has changed with independence, but when he envisages the possibility of change he can only think of the masculine arenas of commerce, trade, and governance, and never of his domestic life and the cultural conditions that permit him to indulge his appetite for teenage wives regardless of the dangers they may face in childbirth. Ali decries the combined traditional, religious, and colonial values that conspire to make modern African women timid about themselves and their bodies, but he fails to see his own proprietary attitude toward women, which contributes another layer to their diminishment. For Oko, a woman's devotion to advancement in her career, even in a modern world of opportunities, is "un-African," and the only way he can think of giving his marriage a chance is to prove his manhood through the most masculine assertion of power: sexual assault.

All the conflicting assumptions about women's relationships with men and their obligations in marriage surface in the marriages of Opokuya, Fusena, and Esi. Yet only Esi is willing to ask questions and imagine alternative possibilities. The questions she asks probe accepted notions about women's bodies, needs, aspirations, and sexuality and are posed on behalf of all the women. How else would sexuality itself be defined, she seems to ask, if sex were more than what a man claimed from his wife as a right? What if a wife were a partner in marriage and not just the "occupied territory" of any man who could afford to put a ring on her finger? And what would society itself look like if its survival and prosperity did not depend on the sacrifice of wives to the egos of their husbands? These are all urgent questions inspired by the new modern context and its paradoxical blend of opportunity and stasis, of mobility and constriction. Yet neither Opokuya nor Fusena can face the penetrating self-scrutiny that can translate into alternative visions. Their reticence betrays not just an accommodation with inequalities as they exist but also a fatalism that legitimizes assumptions and clichés that Aidoo thinks should be posed as theoretical problems.

The strategy of giving the novel's main insight and resolution to the old grandmother (and not to the protagonist, Esi) raises important questions about how fully the younger characters understand the historical roots of women's place in Ghanaian society. For, in the final analysis, it is the grandmother who clarifies the fundamental principle behind relationships between men and women in the society. Only the grandmother can see the bigger picture and connect gender inequities to other forms of social inequity.

Unlike Opokuya and Fusena, who merely state or live seemingly normative truths, Nana identifies a fundamental problem of domination and diminishment that defines all forms of unequal relations even in a modernizing context. In this way she retrieves and illuminates the political issues that hover on the margins of the narrative to remind us that everything, including love, is political, and we must take in the larger picture of this modernizing world and see the neocolonial structure that has only replaced the colonial elite with a black bourgeoisie. It is Nana's analogies that force us to connect women's subordination with colonial domination, to look beyond the blazing lights of the modern city for continuing inequities that separate the modern lives of the middle-class protagonists from the lives of the struggling poor. Beyond posing the problem, the old grandmother also imagines the solution in a complete rethinking of the assumptions that structure male-defined ideas of modernization. Giving an old "traditional" woman such a central role in articulating fundamental questions about modernization and change is Aidoo's way of complicating simplistic dichotomies between tradition and modernity and suggesting that political, economic, and structural changes in modernization do not simultaneously overhaul the ethos of traditional society.

Aidoo's strategy of balancing the immediate world of her narrative with an imagined reality of new possibilities reflects the utopian striving that distinguishes imaginative literature from the empirical disciplines. Imaginative writers strive not only to represent and account for their fictional worlds, but also to mediate them through strategies of narrative and language. For it is through such mediation that they reflect on the worlds they create. This quality of the literary imagination is what I have harnessed in my rereading of narratives of modernization in African literature.

The major advantage that these imaginative texts reveal is a capacity to hold multiple representations simultaneously. Their narratives do not just mirror concrete reality; they suggest its possibilities and illuminate several different ways in which communities and individuals relate to a phenomenon like modernization. Such multiple representations are often the site of insights that even the characters do not grasp. For instance, as this chapter illustrates, Casely Hayford's protagonist in *Ethiopia Unbound* assumes he can hold both his racial and modernist identities without mediation, but the narrative's tensions and gaps reveal the extent to which deep anxieties about modernization mask his privileging of racial identity and how both identities are ultimately limited and confining.

In *Things Fall Apart* multiple representations and gaps in narrative are Achebe's tools for suggesting the various ways in which Africans became both the agents and the interpreters of their modern experience. I see these strategies as part of a larger attempt to explore a notion of agency in a narrative that celebrates a people's culture but ultimately mourns its rupture. The gap between the long narrative of Igbo history and culture and the relatively shorter story of colonial modernity suggests that the modernizing impact of white colonists can only be properly understood within the community's own trajectory of history and culture, and in this context the choices African converts make in relation to the new modern order are made in self-interest. The suggestion of agency in a colonial context that denies agency represents a contrasting modernist theme in a narrative that has focused incessantly on history and culture. This kind of double-voicedness disperses dissonant and competing voices in narrative and conveys the varied ways in which African characters internalize social and spiritual issues generated by a modernizing colonialism. A similar strategy works effectively to complicate the modernist theme even in *The Lion and the Jewel,* where oppositions between the forces of tradition and the agents of modernization seem clear-cut and fixed.

In later African novels where there are more sustained explorations of modernization, double-voicing operates on a much larger scale to suggest two parallel universes within the novels: the concrete reality and the imagined possibility which can be gleaned through strategies of narrative and language. Exploring how this strategy works in three novels set during different periods in African history is itself a way of mapping changes in the meaning and impact of modernization in Africa. My reading of *No Longer at Ease, Nervous Conditions,* and *Changes* explores these fluctuations in theme by examining interactions between the immediate and imagined worlds of the novels. It presents contrasting perspectives on how the novelists confront, interrogate, and rethink categories such as woman, ethnicity, caste, and gender from their different locations. In *Nervous Conditions* and *Changes* it is the notion of tradition itself that is deconstructed when the two novelists choose to explore the modern context from the perspective of women's lives. The approach is both revisionary and transformative. The construction of women's history as components of a coherent tradition was part of Kenyatta's anthropological approach to Gikuyu culture and the basis for his contradictory understanding of modernization. In *Nervous Conditions* and *Changes,* modernizing processes and their contexts defy such confinements as they open up flexible spaces for disentangling women from tradition and exploring new relationships to the collective. As in all the other narratives, modernization, with its contexts of change, struggle, and negotiation, provides a fruitful paradigm for rethinking African cultures in new ways.

Note

1. For comments on the religious and political connotations of the term, see Ugonna (1969).

References

Achebe, Chinua. 1958. *Things Fall Apart.* London: Heinemann Educational.
———. 1960. *No Longer at Ease.* London: Heinemann Educational.
———. 1987. *Anthills of the Savannah.* New York: Doubleday.

Aidoo, Ama Ata. 1991. *Changes: A Love Story*. London: Women's Press.
Appiah, Kwame Anthony. 2004. Introduction to *Nervous Conditions*, by Tsitsi Dangarembga, vii–xi. Bambury: Ayebea Clarke.
Bhabha, Homi K. 1994. *The Location of Culture*. London: Routledge.
Berman, Bruce. 1996. "Ethnography as Politics, Politics as Ethnography: Kenyatta, Malinowski and the Making of *Facing Mount Kenya*." *Canadian Journal of African Studies* 30, no. 2: 313–44.
Blyden, E. W. 1887. *Christianity, Islam and the Negro Race*. London: Whittingham.
Casely Hayford, J. E. 1969 [1911]. *Ethiopia Unbound: Studies in Race Emancipation*. London: Frank Cass.
Cooper, Frederick. 2005. *Colonialism in Question: Theory, Knowledge, History*. Berkeley: University of California Press.
Dangarembga, Tsitsi. 2004 [1988]. *Nervous Conditions*. Bambury: Ayebea Clarke.
Elia, Nada. 1999. "'To Be an African Working Woman': Levels of Feminist Consciousness in Ama Ata Aidoo's *Changes*." *Research in African Literatures* 30, no. 2: 136–47.
George, Olakunle. 2003. *Relocating Agency: Modernity and African Letters*. Albany: State University of New York Press.
Gikandi, Simon. 2008. "African Literature and Modernity." *Matatu: Journal for African Culture and Society* 35, no. 1: 1–18.
Kenyatta, Jomo. 1938. *Facing Mount Kenya: Traditional Life of the Gikuyu*. London: Secker and Warburg.
Korang, Kwaku Larbi. 2003. *Writing Ghana, Imagining Africa: Nation and Modernity*. New York: University of Rochester Press.
Newell, Stephanie. 2002. *Literary Culture in Colonial Ghana: "How to Play the Game of Life."* Bloomington: Indiana University Press.
Nkrumah, Kwame. 1957. *Ghana: The Autobiography of Kwame Nkrumah*. Edinburgh: Thomas Nelson.
Paolini, Albert J. 1999. *Navigating Modernity: Postcolonialism, Identity, and International Relations*. London: Lynne Rienner.
Soyinka, Wole. 1963. *The Lion and the Jewel*. London: Oxford University Press.
Ugonna, F. Nnabuenyi. 1969. Introduction to *Ethiopia Unbound*, by J. E. Casely Hayford, v–xxxvi. London: Frank Cass.

15 Between Nationalism and Pan-Africanism

Ngũgĩ wa Thiong'o's Theater and the Art and Politics of Modernizing African Culture

Aida Mbowa

> None of these cultures can be conceived as anthropologically independent or autonomous, rather, they are all in various distinct ways locked in a life-and-death struggle with first-world cultural imperialism—a cultural struggle that is itself a reflection of the economic situation of such areas in their penetration by various stages of capital, or as it is sometimes euphemistically termed, of modernization.
>
> —Frederic Jameson (1986)

Modernization was an important and guiding philosophy on how best to build the newly formed nation-state in post-independence Africa. Modernization encapsulated more than the matter of industrialization and infrastructure. It also incorporated cultural efforts to bolster the psychology of the formerly colonized. Significant objectives for cultural politicians to achieve under the rubric of modernization included how to empower citizens, how to facilitate pride and allegiance to the nation-state, and how to overcome divisions or in some instances maintain ethnic specificity while facilitating national unity. The arts in general, and performance arts in particular, were a key method through which to disseminate the ideologies geared toward engendering modern subjects. The arts disseminated modernist ideologies through the artistic productions they offered their spectators who were engaging in the consumption of cultural products.

For the East African intellectual-cum-artist, the 1960s and 1970s represented a dynamic period filled with the possibility to redefine their history and determine post-independence alternatives to the British cultural imperialist legacy. Key movers and shakers were individuals who through both their art and politics actively engaged in the effort to determine what constituted African and black aesthetics. The question *du jour* for these figures was: in the wake of sociopolitical liberation, what could be considered a modern African style that both embraced the promise of a postliberation future and simultaneously unshackled black people from a legacy of derided aesthetics, negated histories, and undermined selfhoods? This chapter considers the way new black aesthetics were constructed by the celebrated Kenyan playwright Ngũgĩ wa Thiong'o, in light of the prevailing discourse on cultural politics not only in East Africa, but also in the context of global black identity discourses of the 1960s and 1970s. I shall dually contextualize Ngũgĩ's theater to understand, on the one hand, how his work understood and represented modernization in light of colonialism, and, on the other, how his work might be situated in a Diasporic discourse on black interconnection (whether through the notions of Pan-Africanism, Diaspora, seriality, or Black Nationalism).[1] While I start with an investigation of the *Black Hermit* (1961), I also examine *The Trial of Dedan Kimathi*, which Ngũgĩ co-authored with Micere Mugo, who quite possibly influenced Ngũgĩ's embrace of gendered politics.

For Africans in newly liberated nations, like Ngũgĩ wa Thiong'o, modernization involved negotiating technologies, ideas, and aesthetics brought to East Africa by way of engaging in a discourse with many other parts of the world. And yet simultaneously, modernization for figures like Ngũgĩ meant naming, lauding, and embracing Kenyan/African values, ideas, and aesthetics that the British lambasted under colonialism. These postcolonial modernisms—enactments of tension between encapsulating the past and forging new futures—took on different iterations for playwrights who were wrestling with tradition versus innovation. This African modernization was not a case of blindly privileging a Western notion of "development," usually packaged as part and parcel of capitalism. This modernization lay in the tensions between these ideas and aesthetics. Writers in particular played out these tensions in the various ways they chose to retell African and black history, as well as in the ways they chose to construct both their present and future realities. Modernization meant de-provincializing their African tribes or villages and placing their realities inside of a larger discourse on black subjectivity, ergo universalizing their realities.

This chapter tackles questions of modern African subjectivity through a consideration of politics on- and offstage, together with the politics within and of productions. I examine how the question of modernization was treated in the convergence of discourses on liberation, development, socialism, and black aesthetics. Furthermore, following Marxist political theorist and literary critic Frederic Jameson's contention, I look at Ngũgĩ's struggle against "first-world cultural imperialism," as explicated by Jameson, through the aesthetics of his plays, as well as at his representation of this struggle through the narratives of his plays (Jameson 1986, 68).

Scholars have considered East Africa's cultural and philosophical position and activity in relation to provincial debates or continent-wide conversations (Mazrui 2007; p'Bitek 1973; East African Institute of Social and Cultural Affairs 1966). But not enough attention has been paid to the relationship between African American social and cultural revolutions and East Africa's concurrent transformation during the 1960s. When scholars consider cross-cultural conversations between African America and the black Diaspora, they have focused on West Africa as their major interlocutor for genealogical reasons. However, my analysis of Ngũgĩ wa Thiong'o's work and philosophy during the 1960s and 1970s shall reveal the ways in which East African artists were also engaged in what was ultimately a global debate on cultural liberation, aesthetics, and blackness/Africanness. The following discussion will elucidate and recontextualize a significant East African voice in the discursive construction of black aesthetics. It reveals the way in which modernization was also conceptualized as the newly liberated African states' ability to be seen and valued within an international framework.

Artists and political figures convened and debated the state and future of the psyches and cultures of the newly liberated nations with the same urgency as the precipitous political activity that navigated transitions of government and legislative amendments in the 1960s. Figures engaged in the discourse on cultural liberation were not only artists, and not artists alone. They were a category of people not easily defined by their craft, their art, or their vocation, one which I term "cultural politicians." These men and women wrote treatises, books, and manifestos on what constituted black art and a black performance of the self and actively engaged in conversations about blackness and black art in multiple mediums, from magazines, conferences, and festivals, to political rallies and the theatrical stage.

Similar concerns, questions, and proposals arose at conferences and in literary debates that convened cultural politicians. In 1965, speaking about East Africa's cultural heritage at a seminar on African Culture held in Nairobi, Mbiyu Koinange, minister of state in the Kenyan president's office, inaugurated the conference by highlighting African imitation of British culture as the primary example of the need for African cultural independence (East African Institute of Social and Cultural Affairs 1966). And writing about the relics of British cultural imperialism, Ugandan poet and cultural politician Okot p'Bitek (1973, 4) asked the question, "What have the nations of post-Uhuru Africa to do with British culture and history?" Four years earlier, in a provocative and transformative endorsement of p'Bitek's rhetorical question, Ngũgĩ wa Thiong'o interrogated "the basic assumption that the English tradition and the emergence of the modern west is the central root of our [Kenyan, African, and black] consciousness and cultural heritage . . . [whereby] Africa becomes an extension of the west." His words culminated in a bold proposal for the University of East Africa—which had colleges in Nairobi, Dar es Salam, and Kampala—captured in the title of his treatise: "On the Abolition of the English Department" (Ngũgĩ 1972, 146). While simultaneously promoting Pan-Africanism and individual African nationalisms, Ngũgĩ sought to establish departments of African literature, whose curricula would focus on African writers. This move would unseat English cultural dominance and bolster new African literary projects.

Technology, architecture, and other physical artifacts can be easily read as visual cues signifying modernization. However, in the realm of aesthetics, decolonization diversifies and delimits how we understand the concept of modernization. European imperial powers no longer need to serve as the index for what constitutes "modern" or "culture." Having previously been the clear sign for what was new in an African setting, during the 1960s and 1970s cultural politicians were charged with elucidating what was not only non-Western and clearly African, but also what was new.

Modernization saw a tension between proving retentions and embracing inventions; in the first instance, the cultural politician imagined an uninterrupted genealogy and situated cultural practices and beliefs in terms of memory, history, continuation, originality, and authenticity; in the latter instance he or she embraced the constructed nature of traditions, culture, fantasy, performance, and the legitimacy of contemporary creation. During the 1960s, cultural politicians and artists such as Ngũgĩ wa Thiong'o traveled, borrowed, and devised styles of performance that were in conversation with a real and imagined past, as well as with new and evolving aesthetics in nations throughout the African Diaspora.

An East African Cultural Politician

Ngũgĩ wa Thiong'o was born James Ngũgĩ in rural Kenya in 1938. He excelled at the subject most lauded and rewarded at the time, English, which earned him scholarships to Uganda's Makerere University, then to Leeds University in the United Kingdom. While he has gone on to become perhaps the most renowned Kenyan playwright and writer, publishing seminal theoretical texts, most notably the treatise *Decolonizing the Mind* (1986), Ngũgĩ began boldly. As an undergraduate student at Makerere University from 1959 to 1964, Ngũgĩ published in literary journals as well as prominent newspapers, and, most significantly, in 1962 he wrote and produced the play *The Black Hermit* at the National Theater in honor of Uganda's independence from British rule. During the 1960s and 1970s, Ngũgĩ's style, oeuvre, and influence grew as he lectured, debated, and traveled not only to universities in Tanzania and Kenya but also to the United States. By the end of the 1970s, Ngũgĩ was producing plays that saw him arrested, detained for a year without trial, adopted as a prisoner of conscience by Amnesty International, released, and forced into exile. *The Black Hermit* and *The Trial of Dedan Kimathi* serve as two poignant pieces to bookend Ngũgĩ's intellectual trajectory during a time ripe for an analysis of a cultural politician's shifting politics and aesthetics in relation to East African modernization.

Theater texts are not only blueprints for embodied performance on the stage, but also, specifically in the case of many political theater practitioners, they offer ideological models for their readers and audiences to emulate. While literary debates excluded the majority of illiterate populations, theater, especially when performed in rural areas and alternative arenas, allowed a more socioeconomically diverse audience to participate in the dialogue on black liberation and Africa's cultural heritage. For this reason, the Kenyan government would eventually arrest Ngũgĩ for his role in the Kamĩrĩĩthũ theater project, which advocated the same ideas that had been published in his novels years earlier.

Black Hermeticism

With the two plays, *The Black Hermit* and *The Trial of Dedan Kimathi*, we can consider the nature of the ideologies Ngũgĩ espoused and the ways in which both plays appealed to a particular sense of Kenyan history while significantly engaging transnational black cultural discourses. The modern nation's relation and revision of history, as well as its position within a global context, are the fundamental arenas through which Ngũgĩ partook in the discourse on modernization.

In the wake of East Africa's independence from British colonial rule, Ngũgĩ staged the conflicts of the modern East African man. *The Black Hermit* tells the story of a young man's return to his rural province after studying in Europe and then living in an African city. The play dramatizes classic postcolonial ideological dissonance. Set several years after independence, *The Black Hermit* offered Ngũgĩ's East African audience a Fanonian caution about cosmopolitan nationalism, the rhetoric of Pan-Africanism, and tribalism, as well as the subsequent unrealized ideals of independence. In this play, the modern African subject is constituted by his very inability to reconcile the seemingly contradictory societal pulls and dissimilar communities he must navigate.

The first act establishes a tribe, a village, and a people four years after independence (*Uhuru*). They all lament the state of things post-*Uhuru* and express strong desires for Remi (the yet-unseen protagonist, the black hermit) to return and transform the people and the village. Remi's wife (Thoni) mourns the absence of her husband and the meaninglessness of her life without a man and child to tend to. The village elders inform Remi's mother (Nyobi) that in consultation with a medicine man they plan to send a delegation to the city to find and return her son. Nyobi is a Christian; she visits her priest who, frustrated with Remi's unholy journey, sees the potential for Remi's return to inspire villagers to return to the Christian faith (not unlike a prodigal son).

These different groups invest Remi, as the village's most educated man, with the responsibility to help realize their aspirations. For the pastor, "God wanted [Remi] for a sower of Christ's seeds / Why else did god give him that education?" (Ngũgĩ 1968, 21). The leader of the elders expresses the disappointments of post-independence, with an emphasis on the unrealized promises (land, schools, and tribal representation in the government). The elders of the tribe list trappings of the modern world and conventional markers of modern success. Within the first few moments of the play, Ngũgĩ establishes the local tensions between tribal elders and the Christian church. He further reveals that the power of both these institutions remain tenuous in the wake of African political growth.

Encouraging Remi's wife to seek a new husband, initially Nyobi wants her son to return out of love and a feeling of neglect, not a particular promise, for she reflects, "The lot of women will never change. . . . Independence has no meaning" (Ngũgĩ 1968, 3). With this statement, the mother provides stark commentary on the displacement of women inside liberation movements. The subjugation of women is something that Ngũgĩ took for granted in 1962. In a poignant and provocative critique, Evan Maina Mwangi (2009, 93) contends, "At the center of Ngũgĩ's early drama is the betrayal of masculinity that symbolizes imminent failure of the emergent East African nations." However, by the end of the 1960s, Ngũgĩ's treatment of gender changed. When engaging with African history, part of his objective became to portray a society and an old world whose treatment of women supersedes a sexism he might contend was taught to Africans by the British during colonization.

The second act introduces a conflicted Remi enjoying a life of endless parties with his white girlfriend and working as a clerk for a multinational oil company. Speaking to his friend, Remi explains that the true reason why he left the village came out of a suspicion of unrequited love and confusion for the woman he loved and married (Thoni). Earlier Thoni had married his brother while he was studying overseas, but was then forced to marry Remi—as per traditional practice—after his brother was killed in a car accident. Remi expresses mild remorse for pushing his tribe to support the Africanist party and overthrow white rule, and then abandoning them when the change in government offered no change to their lives. The elders visit Remi, asking him to return and save their tribe. Frustrated, he refuses as he exclaims, "Has our nationalist fervor that gave us faith and hope in days of suffering and colonial slavery been torn to shreds by such tribal loyalties? All my life I believed in the creation of a nation. Where are we now?" (Ngũgĩ 1968, 41) With this question, Remi unearths the fallacy that nationalism is a prerequisite and means to modernization, political progress, and a better life. After a visit from the pastor, Remi, at his wits' end, decides to cease his reclusion from the village and pursue a mission to serve his people and "save them from traditions and bad customs / Free them from tribal manacle" (45). The notion of an empowered individual saving the masses is one that Ngũgĩ later abandons as he adopts a more socialist standpoint, wherein the masses can be empowered to bring about the changes they wish to see.

Following a heated exchange with his girlfriend in the city at the end of act 2, act 3 finds Remi in the village. Villagers narrate Remi's verbal abuse of the elders as he derides tribalism and leads people to sing "Africa's anthem."[2] While he remains proud of his work to combat tribalism, the play ends tragically, because after refusing to see his wife, he learns from his mother and other village women that she has always loved him but has killed herself. Remi learns the error of his ways when it is too late, and a woman has paid the price for his self-discovery. By having a woman pay the price of Remi's inefficient learning curve, Ngũgĩ highlights the way in which history has sacrificed its women for the anagnorisis (critical discovery and growth) of its protagonists. But is this a case of repeating and revealing certain realities without adequate critique? By the time Ngũgĩ goes on to write *The Trial of Dedan Kimathi,* he is far more critical of history's abuse of women for the aggrandizement of male hero figures.

The Black Hermit charts a young, educated African man's quest for the meaning and function of his life, bound in his social responsibilities. Ngũgĩ does not fault or critique the different categories of people who rely upon Remi to access their liberty. In the world of this play, and the world of the 1960s, African villages invested finances and resources in select individuals with the hope of seeing an economic, social, and even physical return (Shachtman 2009). An individual is the hope of the masses.

Remi's journey overseas gives him a new perspective whereby he comes to see the "real" needs of the village as psychological. He wants to heal what he understands as their epistemological shortcomings, to alter their *weltanschauung.* But the play calls into question the nature of Remi's foreign education, suggesting that his true education may unfold through life experiences, through a return to his village, and through heeding his wise mother's words. From this perspective, Ngũgĩ resists the notion that modern African subjectivity necessarily comes about as result of the prescribed British formula of a university education. Remi's character serves as the key aspect of analysis in this play, which might otherwise be considered a rehearsal for more complex styles and narratives at the beginning of a legendary writer's career.

Though telling a story that imagines Kenya, Ngũgĩ wrote the play for Uganda's independence and so for a primarily Ugandan, albeit international and diverse, audience. Additionally, the original cast hailed from all three East African nations and included a Malawian, an Indian, and a British woman. Ngũgĩ, de-provincializing the story, provides a context of an African country that is interchangeable with others on the brink of attaining independence among British colonies in Africa and beyond. Suzie Oomen, an Indian woman, played the role of Nyobi, giving the character and the play a transcontinental appearance. Importantly, it was the Malawian actor Goody Godo who played the role of Remi's friend from another tribe, Onange, with whom Remi demonstrates the pitfalls of tribalism and how it can be overcome. Whether or not Godo's nationality was visible on stage, Ngũgĩ considered it significant enough to include this information in the play's first edition, published in 1968. The fact that Onange is played by another African widens the debate and message of interethnic unity from the level of tribes to that of nations. It speaks to a Pan-African philosophy that was prevalent and popular at Makerere University, which, during the 1960s, served as the center for intellectual exchange on the eastern side of sub-Saharan Africa.

The format of Ngũgĩ's play mirrors that of a well-made Western play. Gikandi highlights the problem of form (novels and plays) and their relation to Ngũgĩ's politics as he articulates "an aesthetic dilemma, a crisis of representation." The question of form and its relation to ideologies is a pertinent and poignant way to compare the manifestations of anti-imperialism during the 1960s and 1970s. One of the contradictions and elements of form that Ngũgĩ engaged with and partook in is the issue of "disenchantment . . . performed in a theater of colonialism in a grammar and context that colonial rule had created" (Gikandi 2000, 20).[3] Ngũgĩ did not yet employ Kenyan styles and aesthetic techniques to the same degree as he would in his late-1970s plays.

Frantz Fanon's *The Wretched of the Earth* can be read as a key interlocutory text for Ngũgĩ's *Black Hermit*. In Fanon's seminal text (1963), he speaks of the way the "Manichaeism of the colonist produces a Manichaeism of the colonized." The theory of the "absolute evil of the colonist" is in response to the theory of the "absolute evil of the native." The binary critique is something Ngũgĩ attempts to avoid as he portrays Remi's white girlfriend as a woman disassociated from the former structures of colonialism. Yet Remi cannot reconcile their genuine interest in each other and cannot create space for her history and place in his life. Upon leaving her, Remi declares, "You are different from me, from us, from the tribe. . . . To you African nationalism and what it means to us who suffered under colonial rule for sixty years can only be an intellectual abstraction" (Ngũgĩ 1968, 47). With this position, Remi reconciles that his erotic life cannot contain a white woman, and he begins to question his love for her. By constructing a character whose truth involves the inability to love a white woman and the rejection of a relationship with her, Ngũgĩ's text aligns with playwrights and artists of the Black Arts Movement in the United States during the 1960s, whose project focused on interrogating and negating the place of white women in the black man's world (Neal 1989; Baraka 1965; Gayle 1971; Benston 1976). Propositions in Black Arts Movement manifestos align with that of the black power movement. Two key cultural politicians, Amiri Baraka (formerly LeRoi Jones) and Larry Neal, best espouse them. Instead of focusing on integration and gaining the acceptance of the larger white community in the United States, these advocates of black power and black art called for the simultaneous rejection of the quest to attain white approval, and a turn inward to improve their black communities (Baraka 1965).

Fanon (1963) was highly critical of leaders, particularly nationalist leaders and their relationship to the rural masses. He believed nationalism functioned as a term without a cohesive program attached to it and thus the term risked being manipulated by national leaders. As part of his psychosocial critique, he speaks of the colonized's vulnerability toward any humanizing gestures. We can see this echoed in the plot of *The Black Hermit,* in the way the people from Remi's village are happy to support a party that they think will treat them as valid entities and attend to their wants. Fanon details the role that the national bourgeoisie was expected to play—betraying their destiny—and he is critical of the vague notion of "African unity" and the way the national bourgeoisie essentially capitalizes on the unity galvanized against the colonizer while manipulating ethnic divisions and endorsing tribalism. These are themes taken up by Ngũgĩ in *The Black Hermit,* as well as problems that are quintessentially tethered to the modern African subject. In his city life, Remi is on the path of becoming a prototypical member of the national bourgeoisie. Changing course, he is ill-fitted for a move to his rural village and learns too little too late. Ngũgĩ wrote *The Black Hermit* prior to his exposure to Fanon's text; he only read *The Wretched of the Earth* when he was a graduate student at Leeds University in 1964. Ngũgĩ's embrace of Fanon's theses became more pronounced in his later plays and novels. Toward the end of the 1970s, as his personal situation had dramatically altered, so did his drama productions.

The Trial of Dedan Kimathi

In 1976, Ngũgĩ wa Thiong'o, along with Micere Githae Mugo, co-authored the play text *The Trial of Dedan Kimathi.* Though they met and studied together at Makerere University in the 1960s, it was not until the mid-1970s that the pair was able to reconnect and pen a play recovering "neglected heroes and heroines of the Kenyan masses" (Ngũgĩ and Mugo 1977, vi). Michael Etherton contends that Mugo and Ngũgĩ's shared hatred of capitalism, colonialism, and class inspired their collaboration (1982, 167). The play was first produced at the National Theater of Kenya in October 1976 and was performed at the Festival of Black Arts and Culture (FESTAC '77) in Nigeria a few months later. Fourteen years after *The Black Hermit,* Ngũgĩ, in collaboration with Mugo, offered the larger black Diasporic audiences a different take on the meaning of liberated subjectivity with *The Trial of Dedan Kimathi,* a play set a decade prior to Kenyan independence. With the early productions of his plays, Ngũgĩ's theater participated in its own nationalistic work, legitimating the nation and writing modern African subjectivity as less culturally ambivalent. These early plays were anchored within a narrative of a messianic founding father who led his flock to freedom, while contradictorily bolstering the role of the people as agents in their own quest for liberation.

Between *The Black Hermit* in 1962 and the first production of *The Trial of Dedan Kimathi* in 1976, Ngũgĩ's life had radically altered. During the production of the former, he was an undergraduate student in Uganda, albeit still a published and recognized author in multiple genres. When staging *The Trial of Dedan Kimathi,* Ngũgĩ had become an associate professor at the University of Nairobi. Not only had he matured as a writer but, significantly, he had traveled extensively and gained exposure by partaking in debates within a global context. This had impacted his work, not necessarily in terms of an aesthetics celebrating a rootedness in Africa, but rather in terms of the ideas, seemingly universal, and arguably easily aligned with "Third World Marxism." This ideological perspective contextualized political and economic struggles in Africa, parts of Asia, and Latin America within a global challenge against imperialism.

In the 1970s, Third World Marxism gained popularity among literary artists from former European colonies. In the preface to the published version of *The Trial of Didan Kimathi,* Ngũgĩ and Mugo recall discussing their impressions of the United States before planning to write Mau Mau stories. They saw technological advancement coupled with the poverty and oppression of workers living in black and Puerto Rican urban ghettos.

As was the case when they attained the National Theater in Uganda for *The Black Hermit,* Ngũgĩ and Mugo encountered cultural and political issues trying to claim performance space at the Kenyan National Theater (Ngũgĩ 1997), which staged plays by Europeans but rarely African playwrights. In his essay "Enactments of Power: The Politics of Performance Space" (1998), Ngũgĩ considers the spatial politics that surrounded theatrical productions before, during, and after colonialism in Kenya. East African leaders, such as Uganda's Idi Amin and Kenya's Jomo Kenyatta, used censorship to restrict and delimitate theatrical spaces.

By the time of his second international production, Ngũgĩ had been arrested and detained without trial for another play that he produced in rural Kenya, *I Will Marry When I Want* (1977). This reflects theater's potential as a subversive force, especially if a play is widely accessible, as *I Will Marry* was written and performed in Kikuyu. In either case, Ngũgĩ's arrest spoke to the political implications of his re-visioning of Kenya's liberation narrative, history, and political realities. As a fearless author, Ngũgĩ did not shy away from addressing the outright failures of Kenya's black government and the neocolonial nature of the country's statehood.

If we describe modernization as a project to reconcile the colonial past and the postcolonial present, temporality reveals itself to be a significant factor. In the 1960s and 1970s, the projects of cultural politicians included altering people's understanding of their past in order to influence their present and future realities. This is precisely what Mugo and Ngũgĩ's *Trial of Dedan Kimathi* does. They revisit and fictionalize the story of a Mau Mau freedom fighter to reconstruct his image as a national hero. East African history, primarily written by those affiliated with the colonial past and with colonial education, was in dire need of rewriting.

Ngũgĩ and Mugo's work involves an imaginative reconstruction of past events, which they describe as "envisioning the world of the Mau Mau and Kimathi in terms of the peasants' and workers' struggle before and after constitutional independence" (Ngũgĩ and Mugo 1977, viii). Their play sought to counter colonial conceptions of Mau Mau freedom fighters and their struggle, using Marxist language and a reinterpretation of historic events. The play tells the story of the eponymous hero Dedan Kimathi (1920–1957), born Kimathi wa Wachiru. Kimathi, a famed Mau Mau leader, became a key organizer in the armed resistance against British colonial rule. The Mau Mau comprised Gikuyu peasants who, between 1952 and 1960, launched one of the most significant anticolonial struggles. Although the guerilla warfare of Mau Mau ceased with the capture, arrest, and execution of Dedan Kimathi, the British continued a brutal campaign against former freedom fighters. This challenge to colonial rule forced the British to initiate political and structural reforms, paving the way for Kenya's independence in 1963.[4]

Ngũgĩ and Mugo's plot unravels through the presentation of characters traveling along two distinct threads, spliced with reenactments of history and across three movements that are de facto acts. Though there are characters who do not deify the protagonist, they are depicted as weak and treacherous. Instead, the play's main figures reinforce the heroism of Kimathi, teasing the limits of didacticism in their endless restatement of his valor.

The play opens with a brief scene prior to the first movement, where a judge reads Dedan Kimathi's sentence and asks him for a plea. Kimathi remains defiantly silent. The judge repeats the charges and request for a plea, and yet again, Kimathi remains defiantly silent. This brief scene reappears three times over the course of the play, marking transitions and resituating the audience in the past but most recent "present" of the play, which is the time and date of the trial itself.

Two backstories that are related to this "present" unfold. The first involves a woman, who is simply named Woman—perhaps to despecify her actions and attribute her behavior to all women involved in Mau Mau. Woman is characterized as noble, fearless, motherly, world-wise, and heroic. In the first movement, she is harassed by a white soldier named Johnnie who lasciviously objectifies her and whom she outsmarts as she sneaks a gun hidden in a loaf of bread past his inspection. Her heroic act symbolizes a marriage of domesticity with armed struggle. Just as Woman's involvement in Mau Mau remains under the soldier's radar, the metaphor also reveals that historians had completely ignored women's participation in Mau Mau. Over a decade after the first production of *The Trial of Dedan Kimathi,* historian Cora Presely (1988) detailed the nature of noncombatant forces in the Mau Mau struggle and how women smuggled food and arms, as well as transferred information, for the combatants in the forests. Presley reveals how this service has been undervalued and the misnomer "passive combatants" does not capture the degree of women's participation in the war. *The Trial of Dedan Kimathi* reinserted women into the way Mau Mau has been imaged, painting their involvement in the movement as just as noble and just as necessary as that of the men.

Sexism and women's stories are more complicated in this play; Ngũgĩ and Mugo deal with them better than in *The Black Hermit.* Instead of a token acknowledgment of the lack of women's stories, the role of women is acknowledged not only by Kimathi in a speech to his followers in the forest but also, begrudgingly, by a white soldier. Johnnie remarks, "You look like a Mau Mau. Like one of them, Kimathi women. Wanjiru, they called her. She was lean, wiry and strong. Fought like a tiger in the battle of the beehive. No wonder the terrorists made her a Colonel" (Ngũgĩ and Mugo 1977, 10).

Women's fierce and brave presence in this revolutionary war also becomes evident through the figure of Woman, who risks her life and proselytizes the cause of the freedom fighters throughout the play. Theater scholar Sandra Richards (1996, 65) advocates that a writer of criticism ought to complicate a historical analysis by interjecting "informed accounts of the latent intertexts likely to be produced in performance." That is to say, where historiography reveals a silencing, an erasure, or a manipulation of particular voices, Richards deems it a valid enterprise for a critic to write-in the "speculative variables." Though Richards' project is directed toward potential scholars and critics of historical black performances, theater and performance studies are not the only fields braced with unknown and unknowable chasms that history writers and makers have neglected. Suzan-Lori Parks (2004) contends, "The History of Literature is in question. And the history of History is in question too." In popular and scholarly writings on Mau Mau until 1976, women's narratives in the insurgency constituted these unknown chasms or "speculative variables."

Who is Woman? In 2004, twenty-seven years after *The Trial of Dedan Kimathi,* Mugo published *Muthoni wa Kirima, Mau Mau Woman Field Marshal.* The subtitle reads, *Interrogation of Silencing, Erasure and Manipulation of Female Combatants' Texts.* Mugo (2004) cites the Western world's preference of literacy over orality as the primary condition perpetuating the absence of female histories. Committing Kirima's story to written language, her book begins the necessary and long overdue exposition of how a woman took over the Mau Mau leadership after Field Marshal Dedan Kimathi's arrest. But the publication remains an afterword to the powerful illustration of nameless Woman's smart and crucial manipulations of the systems and barriers that she encountered in a last bid to liberate Dedan Kimathi. In addition to her leadership, Woman's wisdom becomes apparent to the reader in her lectures to a boy and a girl, as well as in the advice we see her giving Kimathi in the forest during one of his flashbacks.

The discourse on gender in an African context was an important topic through which to argue about the nature of modern African subjectivity. While cultural politicians attributed "isms" such as sexism and racism to colonial powers, simultaneously colonial powers frequently criticized the position of women in African societies as backward. For Ngũgĩ and Mugo, part of reclaiming and rewriting African history involves making a case for the significant position of women in African societies in contrast to how the British conceptualized and wrote about them. Ngũgĩ and Mugo depict the sexism and the assault of black women by white men quite clearly—this is visible in the white man's crass objectification and fondling of the black woman. Similarly, racism is not just a given and a factual element of the backstory, but something that the audience witnesses and something articulated in language. Angry white settlers refer to Kimathi as "fucking black monkey" and describe Africans as "wild savages" (Ngũgĩ and Mugo 1977, 28–29). With such portrayals, these white characters appear backward-thinking and, implicitly, their society and culture appear to be the true embodiments of sexist ideology.

Once Woman escapes from the white soldier, she encounters a homeless boy chasing a homeless girl, over ten Kenyan shillings. The little amount is significant for Boy, but Woman chastises his villainy for the sake of money. Telling him about Kimathi, she enlists Boy's help in the quest to deliver a gun to the incarcerated Kimathi. From the politics of Boy, Girl, and Woman, we are introduced to the Field Marshal himself. In between scenes, we see him refuse to submit to the wishes of multiple parties. Big business, the church, politicians, nobody is spared—Kimathi vehemently chastises all as "neo-slaves." Kimathi's language strongly invokes Marxist ideology:

> KIMATHI: Rise, Rise workers and peasants of Kenya
> Our victory is the victory of the working people
> The victory of all those in the world
> Who to-day fight and struggle for total liberation.
> Long live Kenya People's Defense Council! . . .
>
> KIMATHI: Mightier than their best generals
> Is our unity and discipline in struggle
> With unity, discipline
> Along correct lines
> People's line
> With unity and discipline

Is our total commitment to
The liberation of us
Who sweat and labor (Ngũgĩ and Mugo 1977, 68–69)

Kimathi's call for workers to unite invokes the spirit of Karl Marx and his *Communist Manifesto:* "The proletarians of the world have nothing to lose but their chains. They have a world to win. Workers of all countries: Unite!" (Marx 2002 [1848], 19). In the play, when Kimathi utters these words that invoke Marx, it is as though he is a ventriloquized mouthpiece for Marxism. It is more likely that Kimathi spoke to his followers or fellow Mau Mau members in Kikuyu, and so these English and Marxist lines doubly alienate. Regardless of whether or not Dedan Kimathi himself espoused Marxism, the political projects of Ngũgĩ and Mugo overshadow their protagonist, and their art-as-politics, politics-as-art message becomes apparent.

Following Jameson (1986), if modernization had become synonymous with the progress of capitalism, allied with Western imperial power, then finding an alternative political and ideological framework was fundamental to constructing alternative modern identities. Mugo and Ngũgĩ's socialist critique highlights the societal impact of industrialization in Kenya. Peasants become workers and the plight of the workers remains lamentable. Homeless Boy tells Woman about his father, whose aspirations include looking after his motherless son, buying land in his home province, and leaving the city. Still, "the machine cut off his right hand . . . and . . . he died of bleeding. No medical care from his employers" (Ngũgĩ and Mugo 1977, 19). Although this play, written in the 1970s, looks back at the 1950s, Ngũgĩ and Mugo's use of a Marxist template serves as commentary on the definition of African modern subjectivity.

Africa expands to the Diaspora with the interjection of mimed history, a significant structural element of the play. The authors explicate action in stage directions that not only set the tone of those particular performances but also interpolate the entire African Diaspora, and they request drumbeats accompanied by mournful music as actors (re)enact what they call "the Black Man's History." The initial montage occurs in four phases, including:

Phase III: A labor force of blacks, toiling on a plantation under the supervision of a cruel, ruthless fellow black overseer. A white master comes around and inspects the work.

Phase IV: An angry procession of defiant black, chanting anti-imperialist songs and thunderous shouts. (Ngũgĩ and Mugo 1977, 5)

The phases invoke the historic intercontinental oppression of black people by white imperialists. What is the significance of miming black man's history in the context of Kenya but starting this history with slavery? What does it mean that the history goes to the plantation and the Americas and then lands in East Africa? Perhaps it suggests that all this history is the black person's legacy—a profoundly Pan-Africanist contention.

The meaning, function, and value of history continue to be in flux. By the late 1970s, Ngũgĩ and other East African cultural politicians adhered to Marx's (2002 [1848], 1) contention that "the history of all hitherto existing society is the history of class struggles." In 1962, *The Black Hermit* narrated a feared future reality and a vague treatment of the factuality of the past. By the late 1970s, the authors embraced the stage and the page as sites to disseminate class-based ideology, as well as sites upon which to literally make history.

Kimathi's story stands in for all black people's struggles, and Kimathi begins to signify all deified, murdered leaders of sociopolitical revolts, from Toussaint L'Ouverture to Malcolm X to Patrice Lumumba. In this moment when Ngũgĩ and Mugo draw the connections between Kimathi's plight and the plight of all black revolutionaries who challenged colonial control, the importance of an accurate depiction of Kimathi is subsumed under the importance of placing Mau Mau within a larger framework—the global dialogue on oppression and liberation. For Ngũgĩ and Mugo, writing in 1976, Marxist ideology was the format within which to analyze and portray Kenya, including Dedan Kimathi, during the 1950s.

Significantly, Black Arts Movement playwrights in the United States during the 1960s and 1970s utilized the stylistic device of miming the oppressive history of the black man while playing with the temporality of their plays. Amiri Baraka employed this technique in his 1967 experiential drama *Slave Ship*. Its detailed stage directions constitute the majority of the action that happens onstage, which provokes and often emotionally disturbs. Baraka's play and his work during the 1960s, like Ngũgĩ and Mugo's tableaux scenes, relied less upon language than upon visual pictures and bolstering other senses. Paul Carter Harrison has described this aesthetic as "kuntu drama." Discussing the significance of song, dance, and drum to black aesthetics, Harrison argues, "In the theatrical sense, Song has the power to transcend the static nature of literal word-meaning. Dance codifies and makes sensible the wide range of gestural signification in black life. And Drums makes evident the acoustic syntax of black speech with its varying tonal choices" (1989, 22). These aesthetic observations and analysis of black international theater aesthetics add nuance to a consideration of the relationships between East African and African American theater during this time period.

The phenomenon of racialized geography and the aesthetic considerations thereafter has myriad reverberations in multiple arenas. Historian Frederick Cooper (2002), raising the question about the space of Africa, highlights the racializing projects in African geography. Following philosopher Anthony Appiah (1992), Cooper arrives at history as the prime definition of Africa, given the failure to define an African identity. Mugo and Ngũgĩ open the play, and thus contextualize the drama and story of Kenyan revolutionary Dedan Kimathi, within the context of the violent history of the trans-Atlantic slave trade. In so doing, the authors claim this history for Kenyans, articulating a united, international, and transnational black and African identity.

How did inventions and reinventions of culture and tradition manifest themselves? Cooper (2002) discusses the British colonial invention of "tribe," false boundaries in the process of colonization, as well as the recurrence of savagery narratives (particularly with the Mau Mau in Kenya). The ideological standpoint that Ngũgĩ articulates in his theater pits itself against dominant Western, social, and political doctrines adopted by Kenya after independence. Although Ngũgĩ borrows from and works within the frameworks of nation and state, he also deploys the term "people" instead of "tribe," and redraws borders to critique the nation of Kenya as it was defined and delineated by British colonialism.

While one might be inclined to view the shift of colonial power to African leaders as a mere change of color, black skins in white masks (*pace* Fanon 1967), Cooper highlights that "the Africanization of personnel tied leadership into social networks with the African continent itself" (2002, 87). Thus, more than switching masks and skins, decolonization and independence brought more complex contexts and performances of black power. This is made visible in *The Trial of Dedan Kimathi,* wherein the enemy is nuanced, lying inside all the systems of power, which Ngũgĩ and Mugo reveal when they expose different tropes of powerful people and institutions. They include the church, big business, and even the seemingly revolutionary Mau Mau, who sell out or settle for less than total reform.

With this play, Ngũgĩ and Mugo rearticulate the need for Africans to question the role of religion and the notion of God, particularly as proselytized by Christianity. When Boy asks if the rumors about Kimathi's being able to speak to God are true, Woman retorts, "The fighting god within us." This is a bold assertion and contestation in a country where the Christian tradition reigns supreme. But Ngũgĩ and Mugo are sure to align Christianity with white settler power. At Kimathi's trial, one settler erupts, shouting, "That devil, Field Marshal . . . Milk Clerk, Oath clerk, Murderer! Poisoned simple minds led astray their God-fearing souls with his black mumbo jumbo" (Ngũgĩ and Mugo 1977, 29). It comes as no surprise that one of the play's major critics called it blasphemous, arguing that it presents Kimathi as Jesus in place of the Biblical God and Jesus (Dinwiddy 1979; Nichols 2010).

The play interrogates multiple divisions. One is not necessarily on the estimable side of Ngũgĩ and Dedan Kimathi's politics by virtue of skin color, tribe, or Mau Mau affiliation. Ngũgĩ and Mugo strongly highlight inter–black, African/Kenyan, and tribal divisions created by outsiders such as the British: "The way muzungu [whites] makes us thirst to kill one another!" (Ngũgĩ and Mugo 1977, 12). This "sellout" character is a trope borrowed by many honing in on a Black Arts aesthetic. During colonial rule, the "them" in the dichotomy of "us and them" was very clearly white/colonizers/masters/oppressor. Post-independence, the "them" incorporates black people who oppress their own, that is, black people still serving white imperial agendas. Race is irrelevant. By showing this in the late 1970s, Ngũgĩ not only draws attention to the nature of black armed resistance—more blacks were killed by Mau Mau freedom fighters than whites—but also shows a history that reverberates with the present.

Woman articulates a disdain for tribal prejudices and intimates the destructive nature of social constructs: "We are told you are Luo, you are Kalenjin, you are Kamba, you are Maasai, you are Kikuyu. You are a woman, you are a man, you are this, you are that, you are the other. . . . We are only ants trodden upon by heavy, merciless elephants" (Ngũgĩ and Mugo 1977, 14). This aligns with the fact that Ngũgĩ is very anti-"tribe," a term that tends to depict modern Africa as primitive. Ngũgĩ and Mugo use aesthetic components to support a portrayal of Kenya, even though this is very much a story about Kikuyu resistance to British imperialism, a story that united different groups in Kenya. During the second trial, a group of dancers provide an interlude and perform dances from different regions and peoples of Kenya. Kimathi narrates the history of a confidence in dance, which he states turned to timidity after the British arrived. This speaks to a larger message about a loss of faith in the beauty or value of African aesthetics and a succumbing to a British cultural imperative that relegates African performance traditions to the realm of the "other," the primitive, the fringe. For Ngũgĩ, in modern Africa, tribe ceases to exist. Ultimately, the modernization of post-independence necessitates the shift from tribal to national identity.

But the project of much of his and Mugo's play is to map socialist ideology onto a Kenyan national narrative, and the conclusion or overarching message after the Woman points out the different ways that others have divided Africans is that, ultimately, there is only one societal division that matters: "We are only ants trodden upon by merciless elephants." This message is overstated throughout the play: "The same old story. Our people . . . tearing one another . . . and all because of crumbs thrown at them by the exploiting foreigners" (Ngũgĩ and Mugo 1977, 18). This socialist message in the context of an English play performed first in the city of Nairobi at the National Theater and then in Nigeria for the Festival of Black Arts and Culture begins to answer the question: whom is this play for? Is it for Kenyans to see the socialism inherent in their history, or for others—blacks, the poor the world over—to also heed the message and unite? While it is possible for both these agendas to exist at once, the play definitely internationalizes a particular history, de-provincializing a Kikuyu/Kenyan, African/colonized story of resistance. Yet the authors intersperse a great deal of Swahili language that would be familiar to somebody living in Kenya, or that might be easily inferred by Kenyans, even if they were not native Swahili speakers. This supports the case for a Kenyan audience.

Conclusion

The political and social realities not only in East Africa but also for black people worldwide were one of the most significant changes that occurred between the first production of *The Black Hermit* and that of *The Trial of Dedan Kimathi.* The early 1960s had been a period characterized by a sense of urgency and a push toward political and social reform by black people seeking revolution not only in the courtrooms and senates but also in classrooms, theaters, and the streets. By the late 1970s, this momentum had dwindled; though some cultural politicians produced powerful work, the concept of a revolutionary moment had become a historic referent rather than a condition of the times. Yet even black theater in the 1960s in Africa and African America did not necessarily agree on a cohesive program or concede shared aesthetics or philosophies. Cultural politicians articulated new modes of presenting ideas and politics dialogically and dynamically.

The Trial of Dedan Kimathi calls into question the project of nation-building and what nation means in a period of nationalism and independence struggles. The perverse link between war, conquest, pride, and nation is something that both Kimathi and Shaw Henderson, the British law officer, highlight. Kimathi states, "Must you kill people? Wipe out nations for medals?" To which Henderson admits, "Between the two of us, we don't need to pretend. Nations live by strength and self-interest" (Ngũgĩ and Mugo 1977, 34). These statements are profound for in this moment of independence: the concern is not how nations are born, but rather how they live after that. If the nation-state is a newly historic, political, ideological, and most powerful arbitrary construct, what keeps people tethered to it to the point that they would die and kill in its name? This is something that Benedict Anderson (1983) asks in his book *Imagined Communities.* Ultimately, Ngũgĩ's theater actively engaged in the sinuous discourse on black national and transnational interconnectivity. Analyzing the man and his cultural productions during two significant periods in the wake of colonization uncovers the ideological terrain that cultural politicians navigated in their quest to construct new and modernized African aesthetics and ideas.

What changed between 1962 and 1976? Ngũgĩ's theater became more about articulating a particular story while universalizing and drawing connections to a larger demographic. In *The Trial of Dedan Kimathi,* poor white and Indian people are presented as allies of the cause: the plight of the oppressed and the worker. In *The Black Hermit,* they could not be on the same side as the protagonist and his plights. The stakes of Kenyans are embedded in the stakes of all the oppressed. This runs parallel to the important project of making historiographical interventions. Ngũgĩ and Mugo employ a mélange of temporalities in *The Trial of Dedan Kimathi* in order to disrupt and renarrate the history, the contemporaneous moment, and the future of the Kenyan underclass. By the latter half of the 1970s, black aesthetics and politics, as articulated by a significant East African cultural politician, no longer converged around questions of color, race, and freedom from white oppression. In order to express concerns about neocolonial power and oppression, Ngũgĩ's theater grappled with the boundaries of nation, the nature of power, the voice of women, and the restructuring of history, explicating the tenuous and complex nature of modernizing African culture.

This chapter has shown the significant way in which Ngũgĩ treated history writing as a project of modernization. In both his plays he attempts to promote and critique projects of modernization. Ngũgĩ is most critical of the effects of modern infrastructural and societal transformations upon those who straddle European and African worlds; in *The Black Hermit* this is represented as a city *weltanschauung* versus a village *weltanschauung*, and in *The Trial of Dedan Kimathi* we hear it in the narration of Boy's father's plight as an industrial worker.

Ultimately, on the project of modernization, Ngũgĩ's work attests that infrastructural and civil developments made in the name of modernization ought not to be ingested blindly. Furthermore, modern development must interrogate and incorporate an understanding of African history, which for Ngũgĩ, from 1962 to 1976, transforms from the history of irreconcilably isolated tragic figures to the history of the masses engaged in class struggles. These identities become integral to Ngũgĩ's perception and proposal of how best to mitigate or embrace the challenges of modernization.

Notes

1. Theorists have coined all these terms in attempts to codify and explicate the various political and social selves and superimpose identifications that occur between regions and across nations. All of these terms are contested and their definitions always in flux. When I use the term "Pan-Africanism," I refer to a school of thought that articulated African unity, if not politically, then ideologically and socially. It was bolstered by and received various renditions from notable thinkers and leaders such as W. E. B. Du Bois, Marcus Garvey, Kwame Nkrumah, Julius Nyerere, and Ahmed Sékou Touré, among many others. A commonplace understanding of the Africa Diaspora is that it includes those of African descent living outside of the continent. Benedict Anderson (1983) speaks of "unbound seriality" as a phenomenon exemplified by nationalists and workers that tends to be a self-identified categorization, unlike "bound seriality," which occurs by the hand of the state through census and other forms of categorization. Black Nationalism has been articulated through various sociopolitical institutions, most famously by Malcolm X through the Nation of Islam in the late 1950s and early 1960s, and by

Stokely Carmichael through the Black Panther Party in the 1960s. The range of the concept's definitions include a separate nation for black people within the United States and a call for black people around the globe to unite and fight for political, psychological, and social liberation from white supremacy and hegemony.

2. This is what Ngũgĩ terms the song that is now the Tanzanian national anthem, which was at one time the Zimbabwean national anthem. It is still the Zambian national anthem (with different words) and forms the first part of the South African national anthem (also with different words). For many, the song remains the unofficial African continental anthem: "Mungu Ibariki Africa," which translates into "God bless Africa."

3. Gikandi considers the contradictions inherent in Ngũgĩ's work, his theories, and their context, and highlights Ngũgĩ's purpose when relying upon fiction to deal with an opaque past. But Gikandi also highlights the use of nonfiction formats to bolster his art. He exposes the irony involved in Ngũgĩ's philosophy on colonial culture and Ngũgĩ's own relationship to Englishness and culture. The quest for Ngũgĩ to understand himself in relation to colonial culture informs the production of narratives that would collectivize individual experiences.

4. The scholarship on Mau Mau is vast, but see Alam (2007); Smith (2005); Anderson (2005); Elkins (2005).

References

Alam, S. M. Shamsul. 2007. *Rethinking the Mau Mau in Colonial Kenya*. New York: Palgrave Macmillan.

Anderson, Benedict. 1983. *Imagined Communities: Reflections on the Origins and Spread of Nationalism*. New York: Verso.

Anderson, David. 2005. *Histories of the Hanged: The Dirty War in Kenya and the End of Empire*. New York: W. W. Norton.

Appiah, Kwame Anthony. 1992. *In My Father's House: Africa in the Philosophy of Culture*. New York: Oxford University Press.

Baraka, Imamu Amiri (LeRoi Jones). 1965. *Raise Race Rays Raze: Essays Since 1965*. New York: Random House.

———. 1978. "Slave Ship: A Historical Pageant." In *The Motion of History and Other Plays*, 132–143. New York: William Morrow.

Benston, Kimberly. 1976. *W. Baraka: The Renegade and the Mask*. New Haven, CT: Yale University Press.

Cooper, Frederick. 2002. *Africa since 1940: The Past of the Present*. Cambridge: Cambridge University Press.

Dinwiddy, Hugh. 1989. "Biblical Usage and Abusage in Kenyan Writing." *Journal of Religion in Africa* 19, fasc. 1: 27–47.

East African Institute of Social and Cultural Affairs. 1966. *East Africa's Cultural Heritage*. Nairobi: East African Publishing House.

Elkins, Caroline. 2005. *Britain's Gulag: The Brutal End of Empire in Kenya*. London: Jonathan Cape.

Etherton, Michael. 1982. *The Development of African Drama*. London: Hutchison University Library for Africa.

Fanon, Frantz. 1963. *The Wretched of the Earth*. Translated by Constance Farrington. New York: Grove.

———. 1967. *Black Skin, White Masks*. Translated by Charles Lam Markmann. New York: Grove.

Gayle, Addison. 1971. *The Black Aesthetic*. New York: Doubleday.

Gikandi, Simon. 2000. *Ngũgĩ wa Thiong'o*. Cambridge: Cambridge University Press.

Harrison, Paul Carter. 1989. *Totem Voices: Plays from the Black World Repertory*. New York: Grove.

Jameson, Frederic. 1986. "Third World Literature in the Era of Multinational Capitalism." *Social Text* 15 (Autumn): 65–88.

Marx, Karl. 2002 [1848]. *The Communist Manifesto*. Translated by Gareth Stedman Jones. London: Penguin.

Mazrui, Alamin. 2007. *Swahili beyond the Boundaries: Literature, Language, and Identity*. Athens: Ohio University Press.

Mugo, Micere Githae. 2004. *Muthoni wa Kirima, Mau Mau Woman Field Marshal: Interrogation of Silencing, Erasure and Manipulation of Female Combatants' Texts*. Harare: Sapes Books.

Mwangi, Evan Maina. 2009. "Gender and the Erotics of Nationalism in Ngũgĩ wa Thiong'o's Drama." *Drama Review* 53, no. 2: 90–112.

Neal, Larry. 1989. "The Black Arts Movement." In *Visions of a Liberated Future*, edited by Michael Schwartz, 62–78. New York: Thunder's Mouth.

Ngũgĩ wa Thiong'o. 1968. *The Black Hermit*. London: Heinemann.

———. 1972. "Abolition of the English Department." In *Homecoming: Essays on African and Caribbean Literature, Culture and Politics*, 145–150. London: Heinemann.

———. 1977. *I Will Marry When I Want*. Nairobi: East African Educational Publishers.

———. 1986. *Decolonising the Mind: The Politics of Language in African Literature*. London: James Currey.

———. 1997. "Enactments of Power: The Politics of Performance Space." *Drama Review* 41, no. 3: 11–30.

———. 1998. *Penpoints, Gunpoints, and Dreams: Toward a Critical Theory of the Arts and the State in Africa*. Oxford: Clarendon Press.

Ngũgĩ wa Thiong'o, and Micere Githae Mugo. 1977. *The Trial of Dedan Kimathi*. London: Heinemann.

Nichols, Brendon. 2010. *Ngũgĩ, Gender and the Ethics of Postcolonial Reading*. Burlington, VT: Ashgate.

Parks, Suzan-Lori. 2004. "Possession." In *The America Play and Other Works*, 3–5. New York: Theatre Communications Group.

p'Bitek, Okot. 1973. *Africa's Cultural Revolution*. Nairobi: Macmillan Books for Africa.

Presley, Cora Ann. 1988. "The Mau Mau Rebellion, Kikuyu Women, and Social Change." *Canadian Journal of African Studies* 22, no. 3: 502–27.

Richards, Sandra. 1996. "Writing the Absent Potential: Drama, Performance, and the Canon of African-American Literature." In *Performance and Performativity*, edited by Andrew Parker and Eve Kosofsky Sedgwick, 64–88. New York: Routledge.

Shachtman, Tom. 2009. *Airlift to America: How Barack Obama, Sr., John F. Kennedy, Tom Mboya, and 800 East African Students Changed Their World and Ours*. New York: St. Martin's.

Smith, David Lovatt. 2005. *Kenya, The Kikuyu and Mau Mau*. East Sussex: Mawenzi.

Contributors

Jean Allman is the J. H. Hexter Professor in the Humanities at Washington University. Her recent books include *Fashioning Africa: Power and the Politics of Dress* (IUP, 2004) and (with John Parker) *Tongnaab: The History of a West African God* (IUP, 2005).

Andrew Apter is Professor of History and Anthropology at UCLA, where he directed the James S. Coleman African Studies Center. His books include *Black Critics and Kings: The Hermeneutics of Power in Yoruba Society, The Pan-African Nation: Oil and the Spectacle of Culture in Nigeria*, and *Beyond Words: Discourse and Critical Agency in Africa.*

Peter J. Bloom is Associate Professor of Film and Media Studies at the University of California, Santa Barbara. He is author of *French Colonial Documentary: Mythologies of Humanitarianism*, which was awarded the Laurence Wylie Prize in French Cultural Studies for books published in English between 2008 and 2009, and co-editor of *Frenchness and the African Diaspora* (IUP, 2009), among other publications. He is currently preparing a monograph about British colonial film and radio in Ghana and Malaysia.

Mhoze Chikowero is Assistant Professor of African History at the University of California, Santa Barbara. His work has appeared in the *Journal of Southern African Studies, Musiki: Journal of Music Research in Africa,* and in two edited volumes: *Redemptive or Grotesque Nationalism? Rethinking Contemporary Politics in Zimbabwe* and *African Music, Performance and Identities.* He is completing an in-depth monograph on African music, power, and being in colonial Zimbabwe.

Gabrielle Hecht is Professor of History at the University of Michigan. She is editor of *Entangled Geographies: Empire and Technopolitics in the Global Cold War* and author of *Being Nuclear: Africans and the Global Uranium Trade,* which was co-winner of the American Historical Association's 2012 Martin Klein Prize in African History.

Percy C. Hintzen, Professor of Global and Sociocultural Studies at Florida International University, is Professor Emeritus of African Diaspora Studies at the University of California, Berkeley, and co-editor of *Global Circuits of Blackness: Interrogating the African Diaspora.*

Takyiwaa Manuh retired as Professor of African Studies from the University of Ghana in 2011. She is the author, co-author, editor, or co-editor of nine books and more than forty published papers. Her publications reflect her research interests in women's rights and empowerment issues in Ghana and Africa; African development issues; the state, gender, and women in Ghana; contemporary African migrations; and higher education in Africa.

Aida Mbowa is a candidate for a dual PhD in Performance Studies and Humanities at Stanford University. Her dissertation, "Dialogic Constructions of New Black Aesthetics: East Africa and African America, 1952–1979," examines the transnational traffic of art, politics, and ideas. For this work, the Stanford Humanities Center has awarded her the Geballe Dissertation Prize fellowship.

Christina S. McMahon is Assistant Professor in the Department of Theater and Dance at the University of California, Santa Barbara. She is author of *Recasting Transnationalism through Performance: Theater Festivals in Cape Verde, Mozambique, and Brazil.*

Stephan F. Miescher, Associate Professor of History at the University of California, Santa Barbara, is author of *Making Men in Ghana* (IUP, 2005) and editor (with Catherine M. Cole and Takyiwaa Manuh) of *Africa After Gender?* (IUP, 2007), (with Lisa A. Lindsay) of *Men and Masculinities in Modern Africa*, and (with Luise White and David William Cohen) of *African Words, African Voices: Critical Practices in Oral History* (IUP, 2001). Currently, he is completing a monograph about the history of the Volta River Project in Ghana.

Nate Plageman is Assistant Professor of History at Wake Forest University and author of *Highlife Saturday Night!: Popular Music and Social Change in Urban Ghana* (IUP, 2013).

Rosaleen Smyth is a pioneering scholar in the area of cinema in British colonial Africa. She has lectured at universities in Africa, Australia, the Pacific Islands, Asia, and the Middle East, and is currently working at an education center for refugees on the Thai-Burma border.

Julia Tischler is a postdoctoral researcher in African history at the International Research Center "Work and Human Lifecycle in Global History," Humboldt University in Berlin, Germany. She is author of *Light and Power for a Multiracial Nation: The Kariba Dam Scheme in the Central African Federation.*

Nana Wilson-Tagoe is Visiting Professor of Black Studies at the University of Missouri-Kansas City. She is author of *Historical Thought and Literary Represen-*

tation in West Indian Literature and co-editor of *National Healths: Gender, Sexuality and Health in a Cross-Cultural Context.*

Aaron Windel is Assistant Professor of History at Simon Fraser University in British Columbia, Canada. He has published several recent essays, including "The Bantu Educational Kinema Experiment and the Political Economy of Community Development" in *Film and the End of Empire* (edited by Lee Grieveson and Colin MacCabe), and "Co-operatives and the Technocrats, or 'The Fabian Agony' Revisited" in *Brave New World: Imperial and Democratic Nation-Building between the Wars* (edited by Laura Beers and Geraint Thomas).

Index

Italicized page numbers refer to figures.

Printed and bound by CPI Group (UK) Ltd, Croydon, CR0 4YY
23/04/2025
14661003-0004